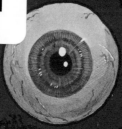

MEGUMI OSUGA

I LOVE CLEANING OUT MY EARS. SOMETIMES I GET A LITTLE TOO
ENTHUSIASTIC ABOUT IT, AND SOME STRANGE FLUIDS DRIP OUT...
I HATE THE FACT THAT DESPITE MY MANY MENTAL REMINDERS TO TAKE
IT EASY WITH THE CLEANING, I WIND UP LOSING MY EDGE AND GOING
OVERBOARD AGAIN.

MEGUMI OSUGA

BORN DECEMBER 21 IN CHIBA PREFECTURE, MEGUMI OSUGA MADE HER
DEBUT WITH *TONPACHI*, WHICH RAN IN *SHONEN SUNDAY R*, AND HAD A
SHORT SERIES IN *SHONEN SUNDAY SUPER* CALLED *HONOU NO ANA NO YOMI*.
IN 2007, HER SERIALIZATION OF *MAOH: JUVENILE REMIX* STARTED IN
SHONEN SUNDAY.

KOTARO ISAKA

BORN IN 1971 IN CHIBA PREFECTURE, KOTARO ISAKA IS ONE OF THE MOST
POPULAR JAPANESE NOVELISTS AND HAS RECEIVED NUMEROUS AWARDS.
HE HAS MANY TITLES UNDER HIS BELT, MOST OF WHICH HAVE BEEN
TURNED INTO LIVE-ACTION MOVIES.

MAOH
JUVENILE REMIX

MAOH: JUVENILE REMIX
Volume 02

Shonen Sunday Edition

Original Story by **KOTARO ISAKA**
Story and Art by **MEGUMI OSUGA**

Original Japanese edition "MAOH JUVENILE REMIX" published by SHOGAKUKAN Inc.

Logo and cover design created by Isao YOSHIMURA & Bay Bridge Studio.

Translation/Stephen Paul
Touch-up Art & Lettering/James Dashiell
Design/Sam Elzway
Editor/Alexis Kirsch

VP, Production/Alvin Lu
VP, Sales & Product Marketing/Gonzalo Ferreyra
VP, Creative/Linda Espinosa
Publisher/Hyoe Narita

The rights of the author(s) of the work(s) in this publication to be so identified have been asserted in accordance with Copyright, Designs and Patents Act 1988. A CIP catalogue record for this book is available from the British Library.

Printed in the U.S.A.

Published by VIZ Media, LLC
P.O. Box 77010
San Francisco, CA 94107

10 9 8 7 6 5 4 3 2 1
First printing, August 2010

MAOH
JUVENILE REMIX

ORIGINAL STORY BY
KOTARO ISAKA

STORY AND ART BY
MEGUMI OSUGA

ANDO

High school student. Lost his parents at a young age and now lives with his brother Junya. Has a mysterious ventriloquism ability that allows him to force other people to say what he is thinking.

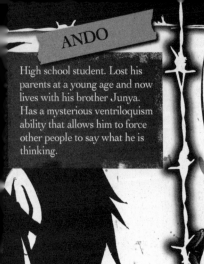

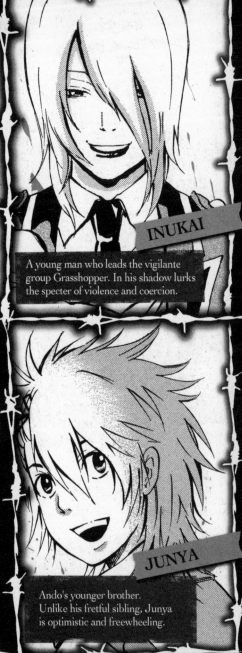

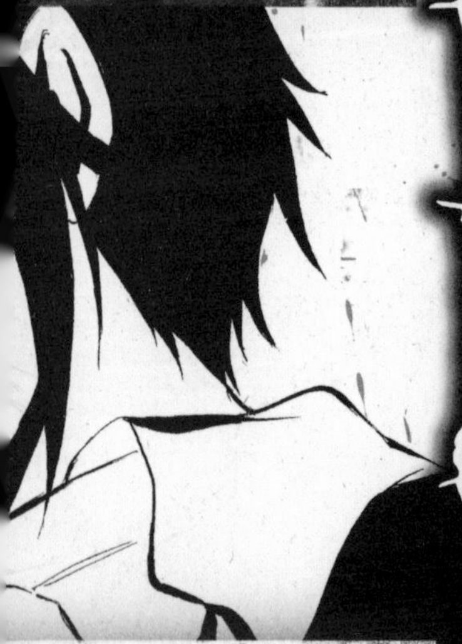

THE STORY UNTIL NOW

One day, Ando realizes that his strange ability to occasionally make other people speak his thoughts out loud is more than just a coincidence. At the same time, he becomes aware of the violent side of Inukai, a charismatic vigilante leader who looms large over the discussions of a civic plan to revitalize business in the city.

Inukai seizes the hearts of the citizens when he vows to rebuild the stagnant city in just five years.

INUKAI

A young man who leads the vigilante group Grasshopper. In his shadow lurks the specter of violence and coercion.

JUNYA

Ando's younger brother. Unlike his fretful sibling, Junya is optimistic and freewheeling.

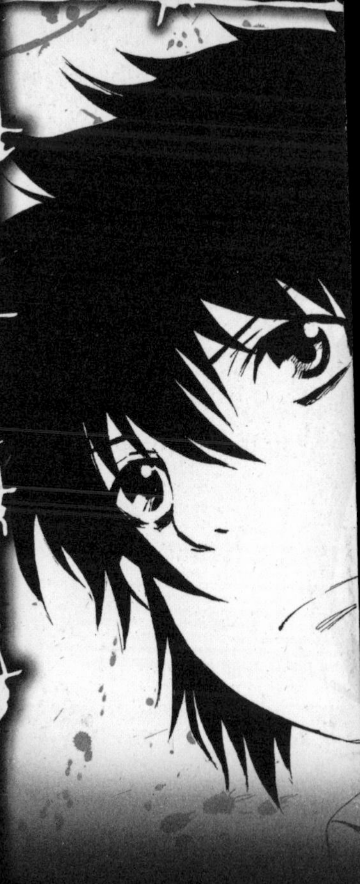

But Ando, who is skeptical of Inukai's plan, only grows more distrustful after hearing his classmate Kaname reverentially praise Inukai. Unlike Ando, with his lingering worries, Kaname believes that Inukai is a godlike hero who could change the world. But Ando's response to that is, "What if Inukai does change the world but it turns out to be the wrong choice? What if he is not a god at all...but a devil?"

But all Ando receives is a sharp, suspicious glare...

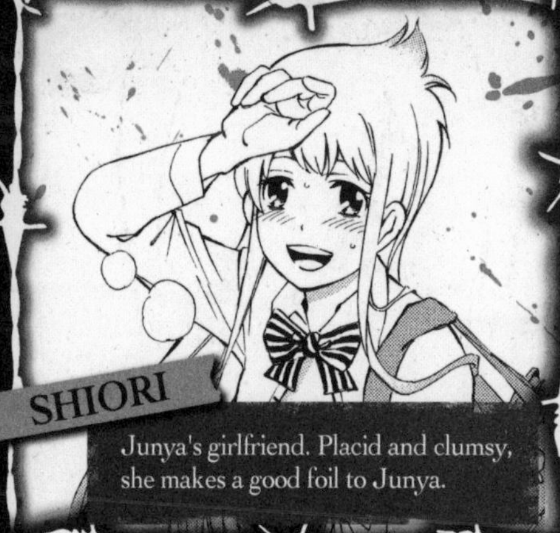
SHIORI
Junya's girlfriend. Placid and clumsy, she makes a good foil to Junya.

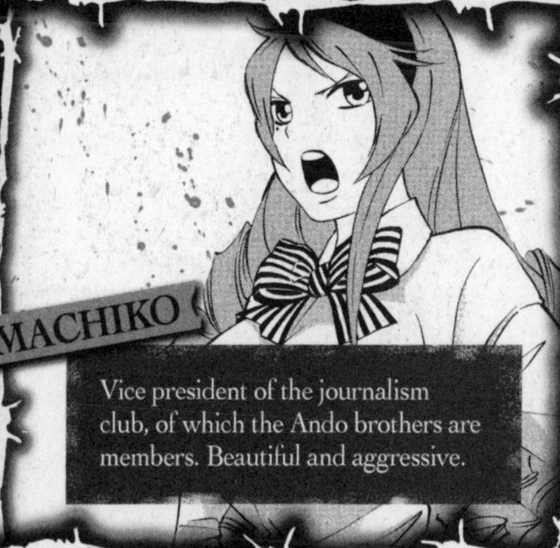
MACHIKO
Vice president of the journalism club, of which the Ando brothers are members. Beautiful and aggressive.

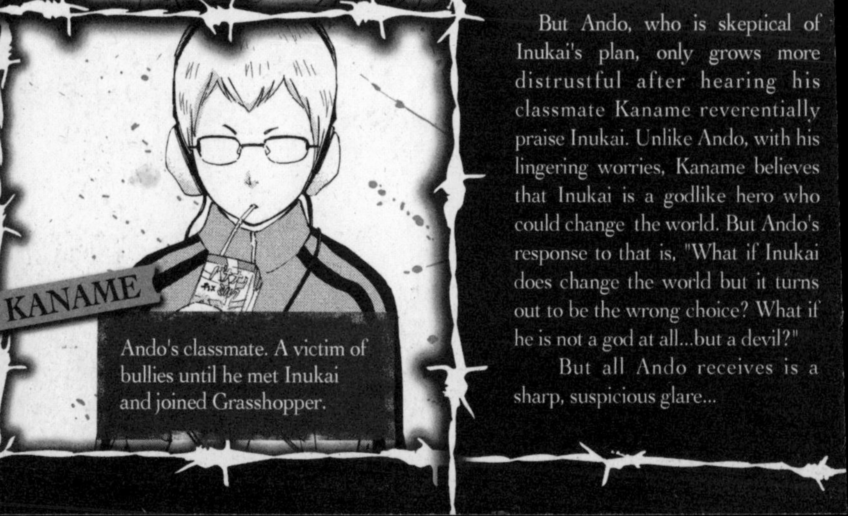
KANAME
Ando's classmate. A victim of bullies until he met Inukai and joined Grasshopper.

CONTENTS

Chapter 8 A Warning

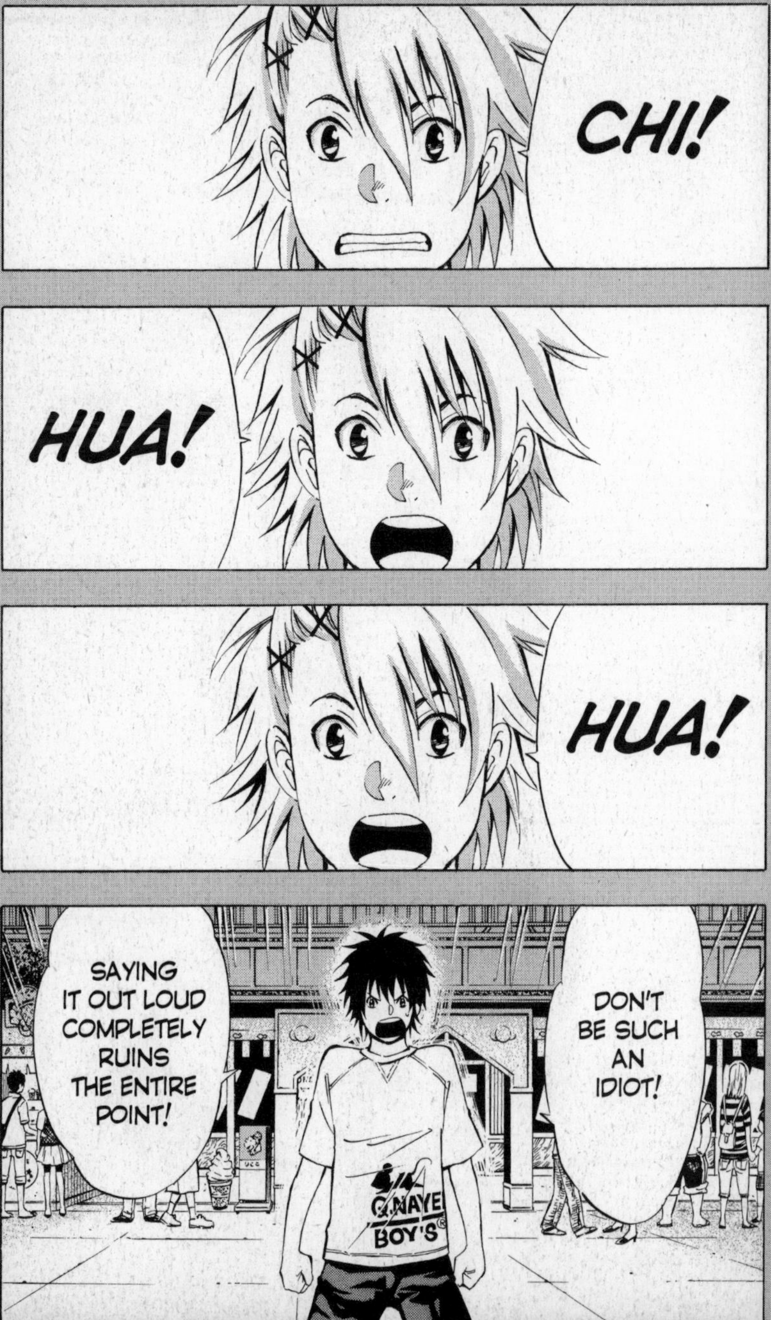
CHI!
HUA!
HUA!
DON'T BE SUCH AN IDIOT!
SAYING IT OUT LOUD COMPLETELY RUINS THE ENTIRE POINT!

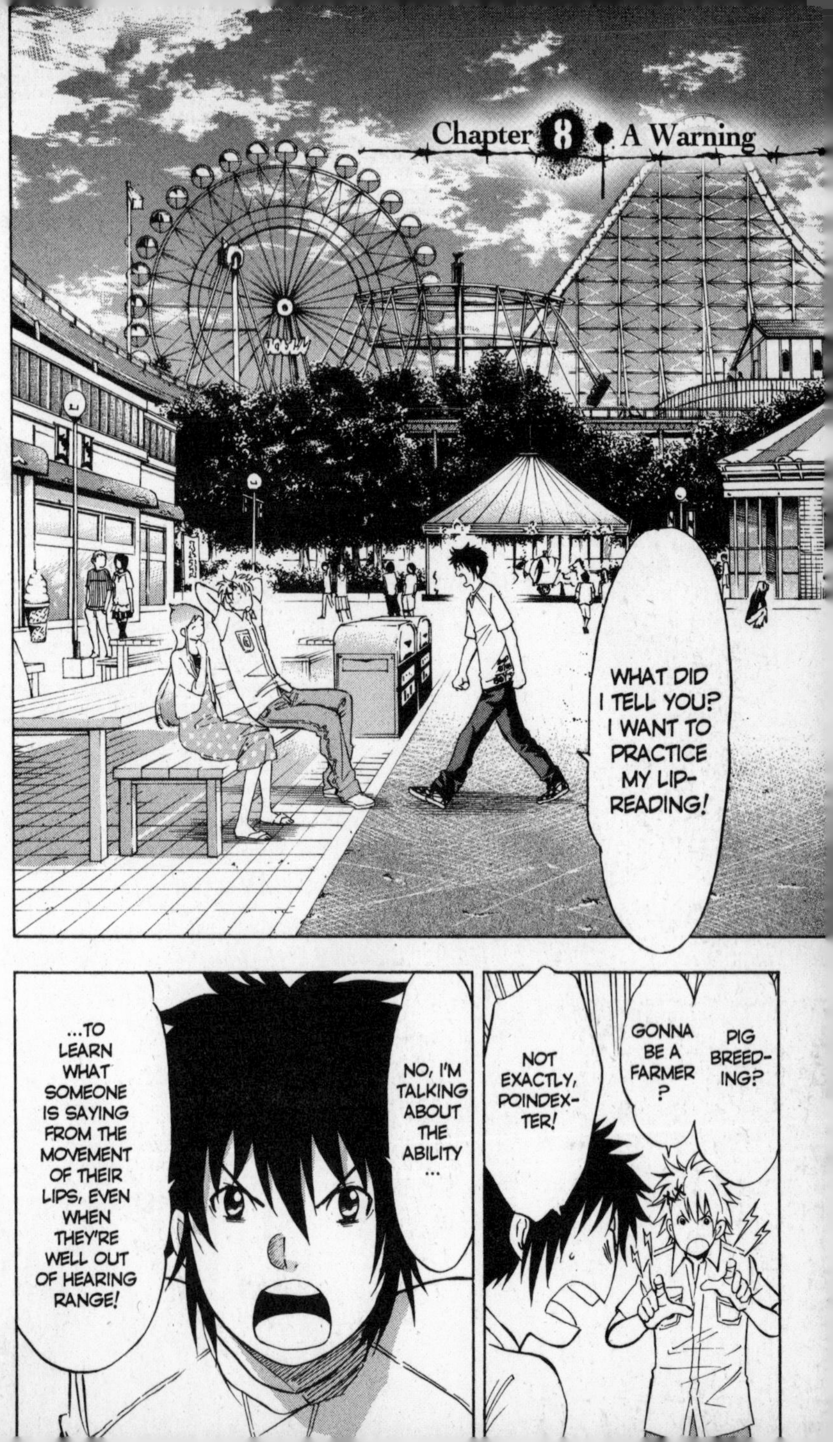
Chapter 8 A Warning
WHAT DID I TELL YOU? I WANT TO PRACTICE MY LIP-READING!
PIG BREEDING?
GONNA BE A FARMER?
NOT EXACTLY, POINDEXTER!
NO, I'M TALKING ABOUT THE ABILITY...
...TO LEARN WHAT SOMEONE IS SAYING FROM THE MOVEMENT OF THEIR LIPS, EVEN WHEN THEY'RE WELL OUT OF HEARING RANGE!

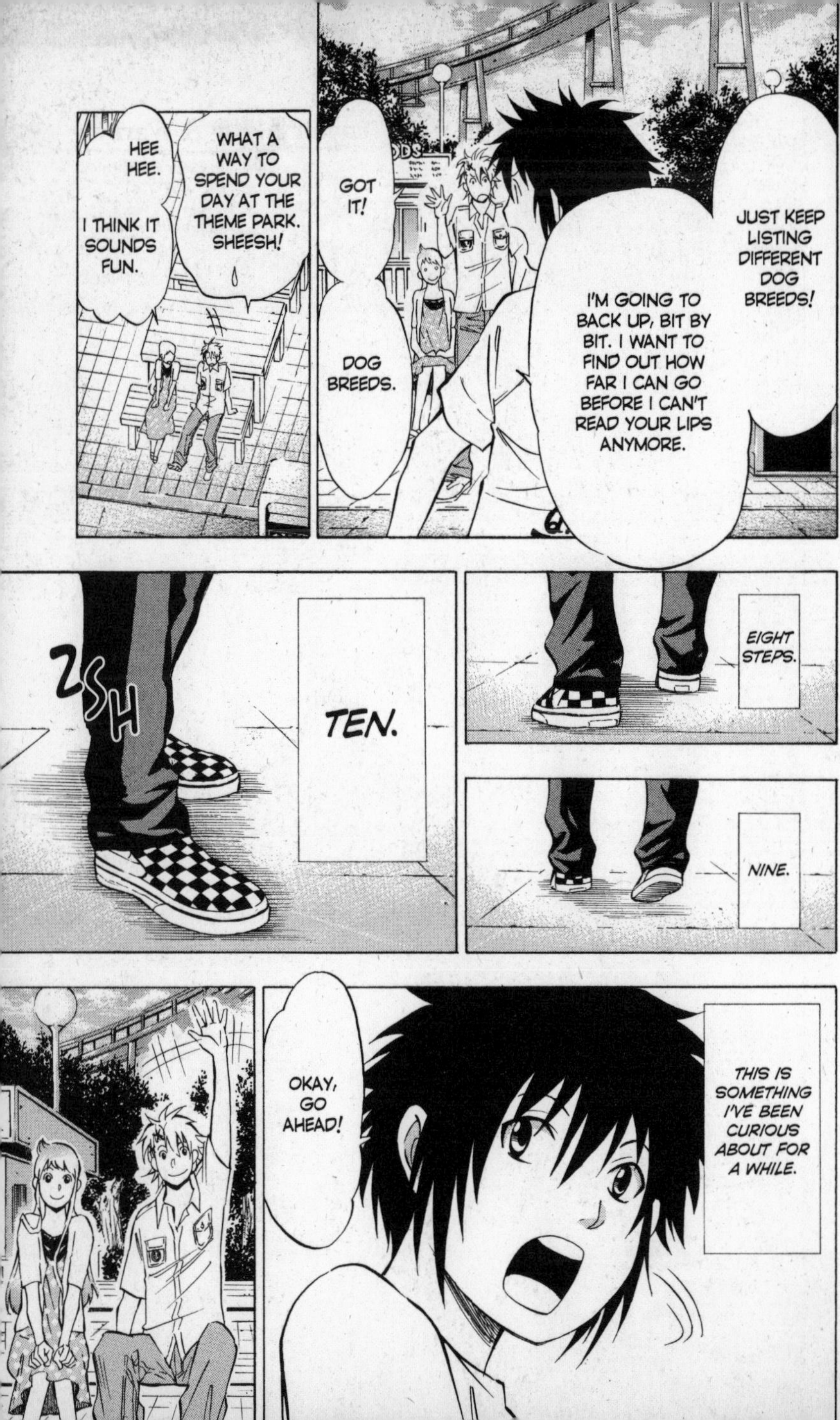
JUST KEEP LISTING DIFFERENT DOG BREEDS!
I'M GOING TO BACK UP, BIT BY BIT. I WANT TO FIND OUT HOW FAR I CAN GO BEFORE I CAN'T READ YOUR LIPS ANYMORE.
GOT IT!
DOG BREEDS.
WHAT A WAY TO SPEND YOUR DAY AT THE THEME PARK. SHEESH!
HEE HEE.
I THINK IT SOUNDS FUN.
EIGHT STEPS.
NINE.
TEN.
ZSH
THIS IS SOMETHING I'VE BEEN CURIOUS ABOUT FOR A WHILE.
OKAY, GO AHEAD!

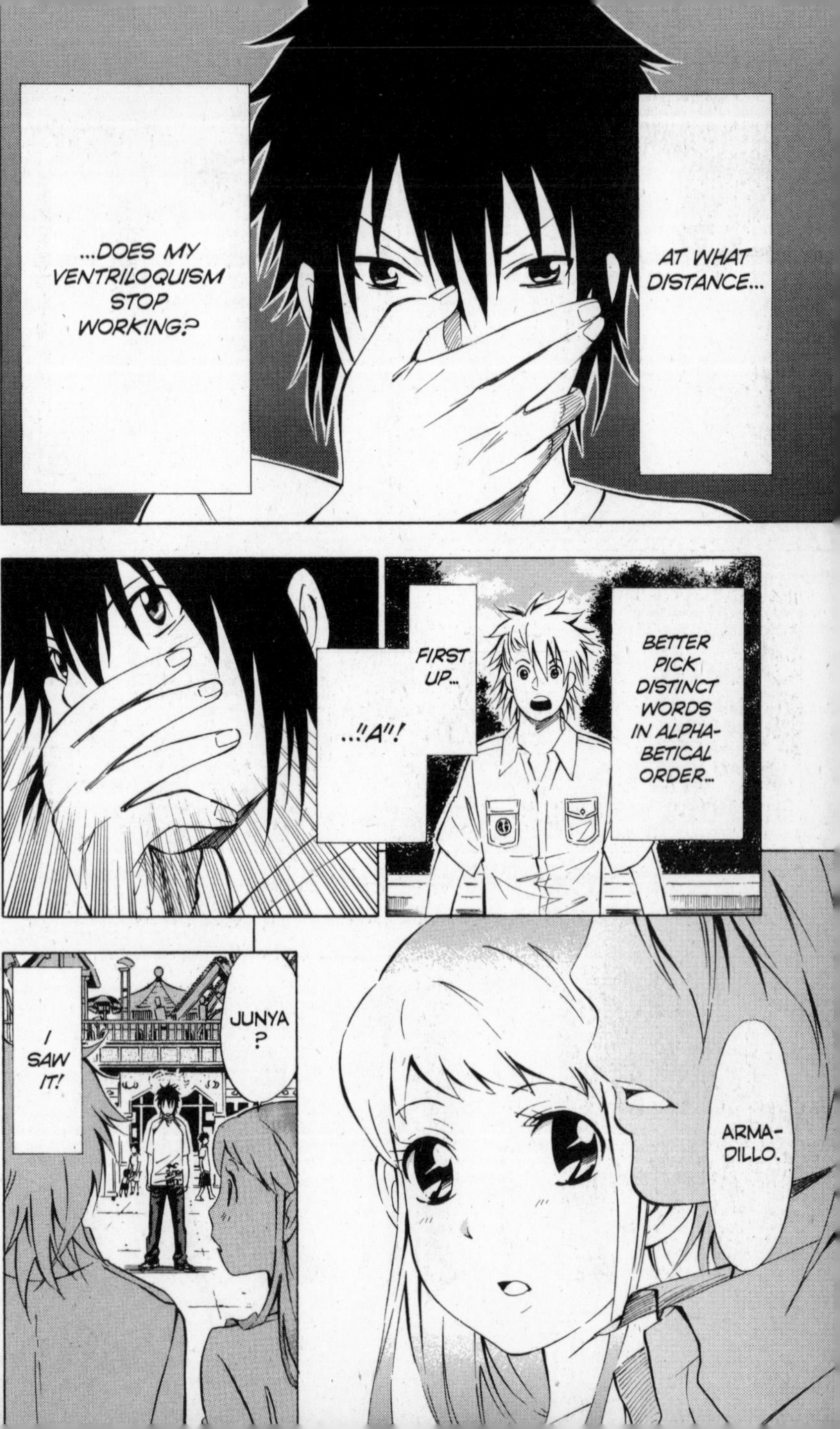
AT WHAT DISTANCE...
...DOES MY VENTRILOQUISM STOP WORKING?
BETTER PICK DISTINCT WORDS IN ALPHA-BETICAL ORDER...
FIRST UP...
...!"A"!
ARMA-DILLO.
JUNYA?
I SAW IT!

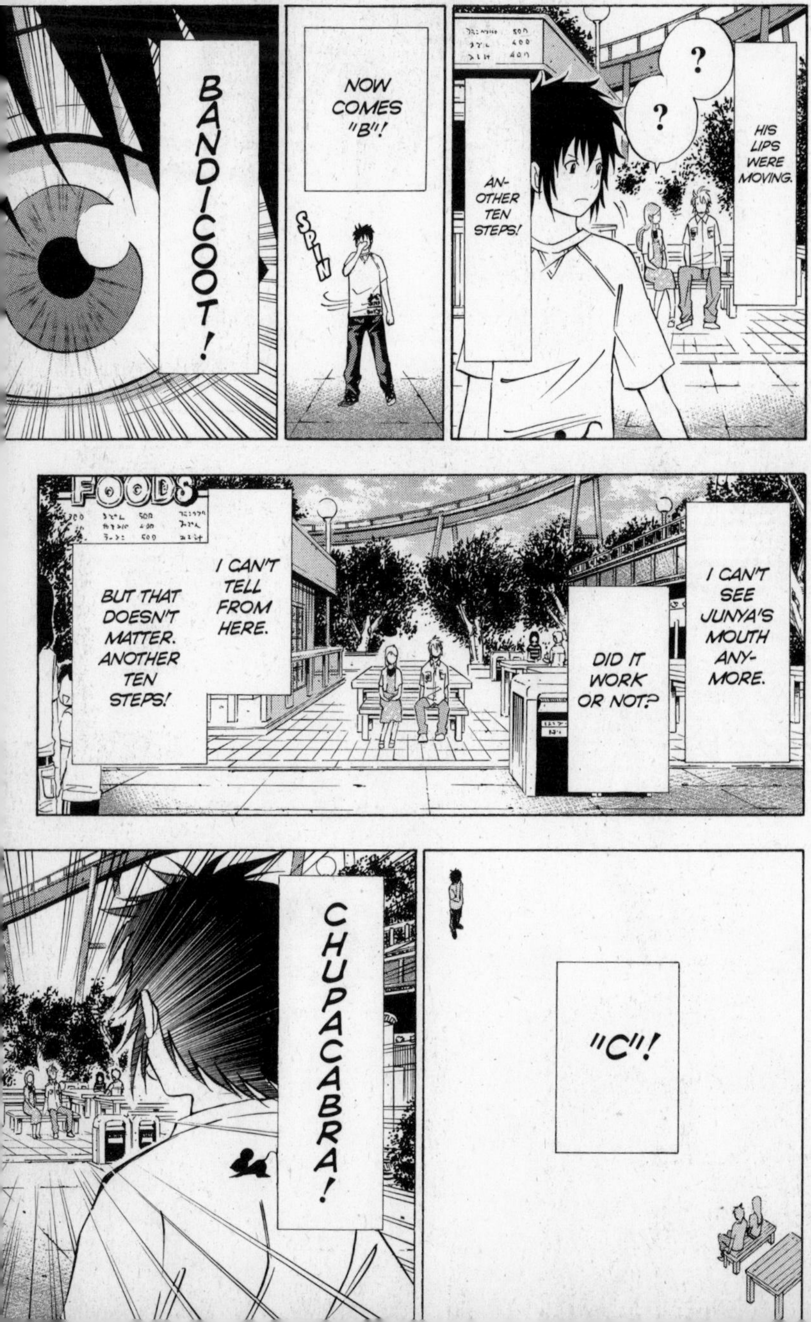
HIS LIPS WERE MOVING.
?
?
AN-OTHER TEN STEPS!
NOW COMES "B"!
SPIN
BANDICOOT!
I CAN'T SEE JUNYA'S MOUTH ANY-MORE.
DID IT WORK OR NOT?
FOODS
I CAN'T TELL FROM HERE.
BUT THAT DOESN'T MATTER. ANOTHER TEN STEPS!
"C"!
CHUPACABRA!

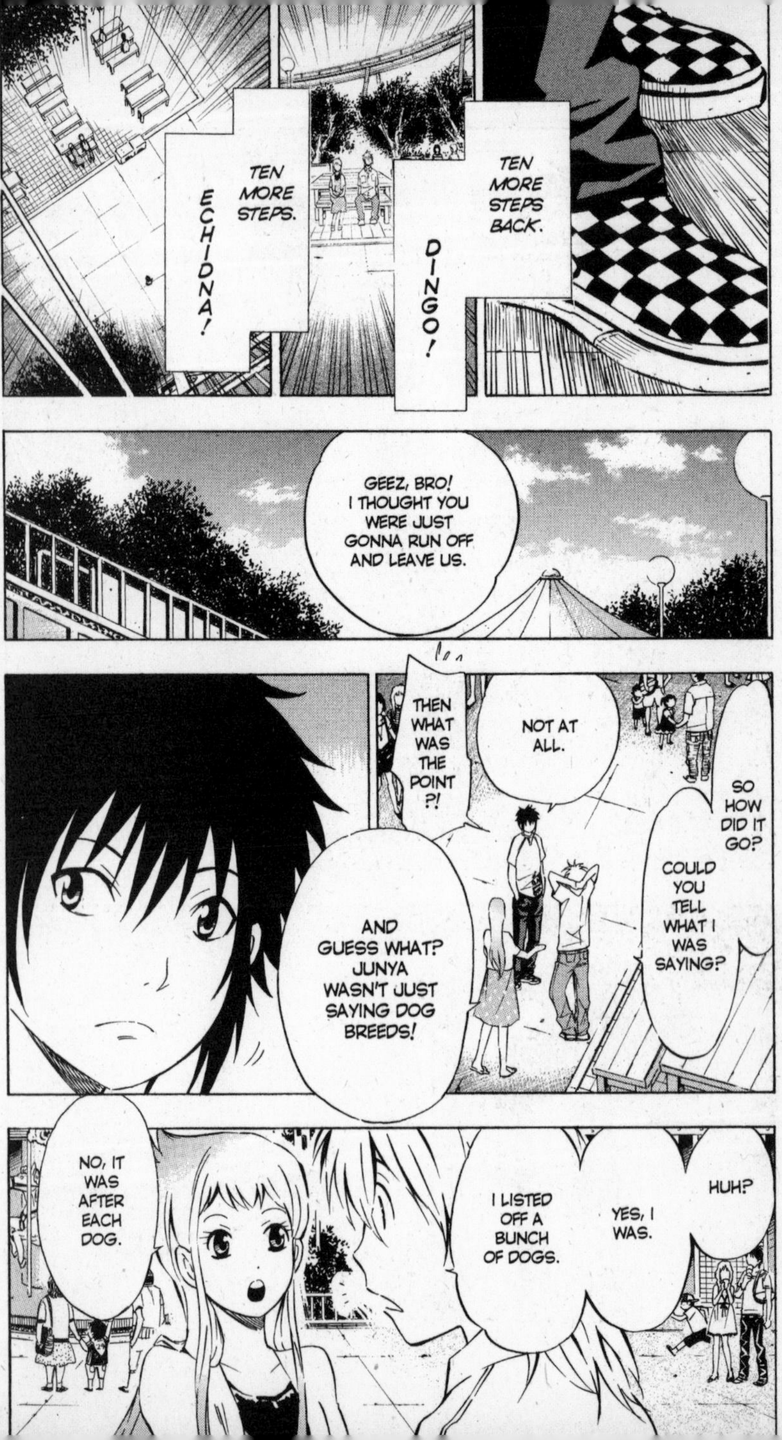
TEN MORE STEPS BACK.
DINGO!
TEN MORE STEPS.
ECHIDNA!
GEEZ, BRO! I THOUGHT YOU WERE JUST GONNA RUN OFF AND LEAVE US.
SO HOW DID IT GO?
COULD YOU TELL WHAT I WAS SAYING?
NOT AT ALL.
THEN WHAT WAS THE POINT ?!
AND GUESS WHAT? JUNYA WASN'T JUST SAYING DOG BREEDS!
HUH?
YES, I WAS.
I LISTED OFF A BUNCH OF DOGS.
NO, IT WAS AFTER EACH DOG.

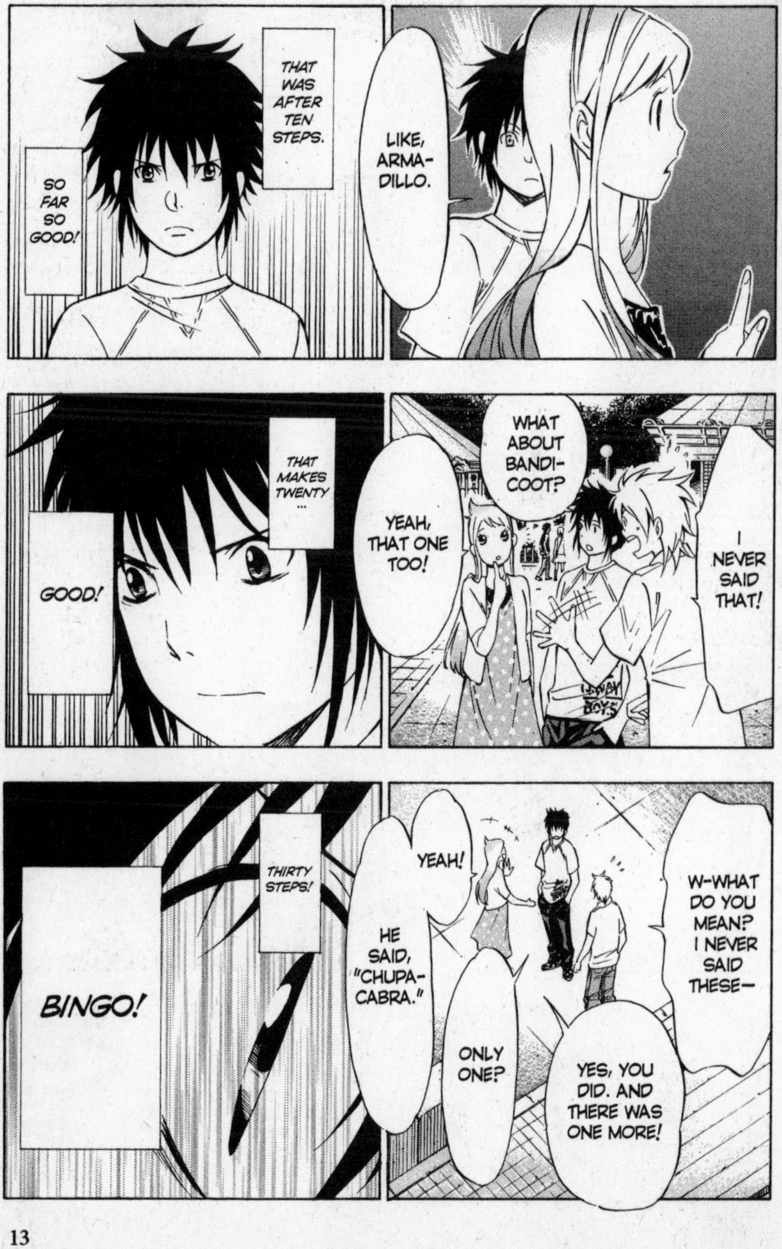
LIKE, ARMADILLO.
THAT WAS AFTER TEN STEPS.
SO FAR SO GOOD!
WHAT ABOUT BANDICOOT?
YEAH, THAT ONE TOO!
I NEVER SAID THAT!
THAT MAKES TWENTY...
GOOD!
W-WHAT DO YOU MEAN? I NEVER SAID THESE—
YEAH!
HE SAID, "CHUPACABRA."
YES, YOU DID. AND THERE WAS ONE MORE!
ONLY ONE?
THIRTY STEPS!
BINGO!

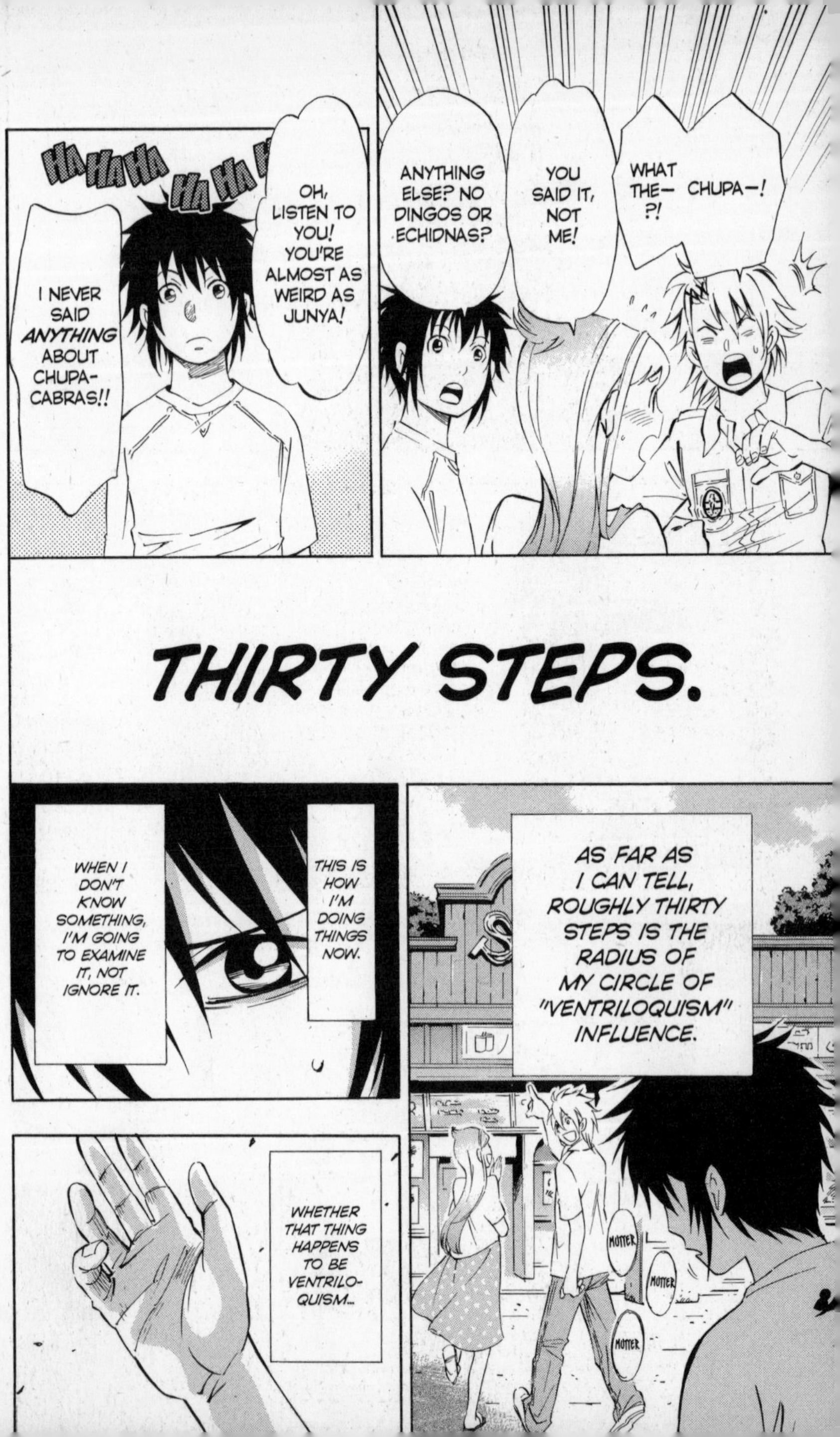
WHAT THE—?! CHUPA—!
YOU SAID IT, NOT ME!
ANYTHING ELSE? NO DINGOS OR ECHIDNAS?
OH, LISTEN TO YOU! YOU'RE ALMOST AS WEIRD AS JUNYA!
HAHAHA HA HA
I NEVER SAID *ANYTHING* ABOUT CHUPA-CABRAS!!
THIRTY STEPS.
AS FAR AS I CAN TELL, ROUGHLY THIRTY STEPS IS THE RADIUS OF MY CIRCLE OF "VENTRILOQUISM" INFLUENCE.
MUTTER
MUTTER
MUTTER
THIS IS HOW I'M DOING THINGS NOW.
WHEN I DON'T KNOW SOMETHING, I'M GOING TO EXAMINE IT, NOT IGNORE IT.
WHETHER THAT THING HAPPENS TO BE VENTRILO-QUISM...

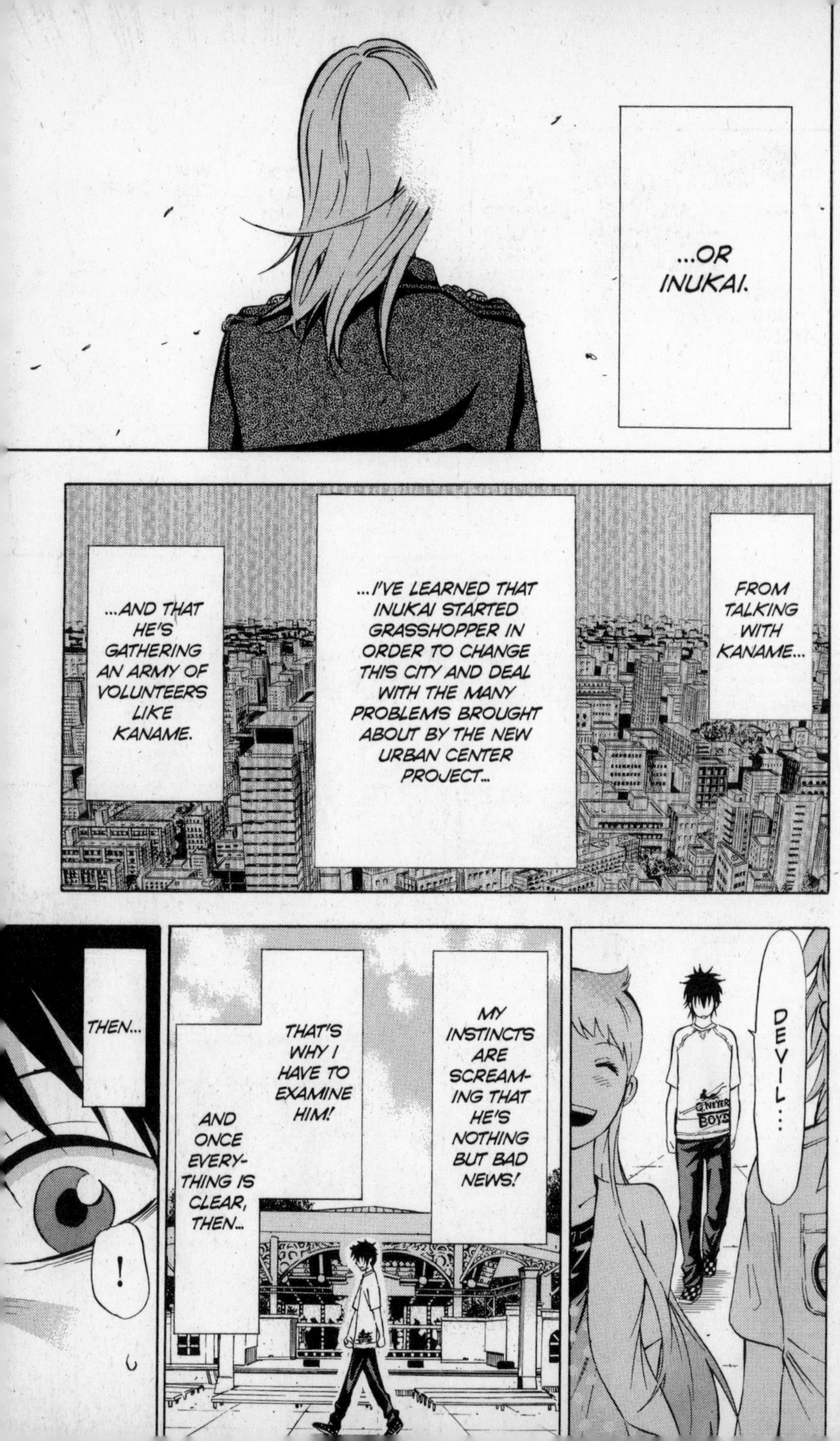
...OR INUKAI.
FROM TALKING WITH KANAME...
...I'VE LEARNED THAT INUKAI STARTED GRASSHOPPER IN ORDER TO CHANGE THIS CITY AND DEAL WITH THE MANY PROBLEMS BROUGHT ABOUT BY THE NEW URBAN CENTER PROJECT...
...AND THAT HE'S GATHERING AN ARMY OF VOLUNTEERS LIKE KANAME.
DEVIL...
MY INSTINCTS ARE SCREAMING THAT HE'S NOTHING BUT BAD NEWS!
THAT'S WHY I HAVE TO EXAMINE HIM!
AND ONCE EVERYTHING IS CLEAR, THEN...
THEN...
!

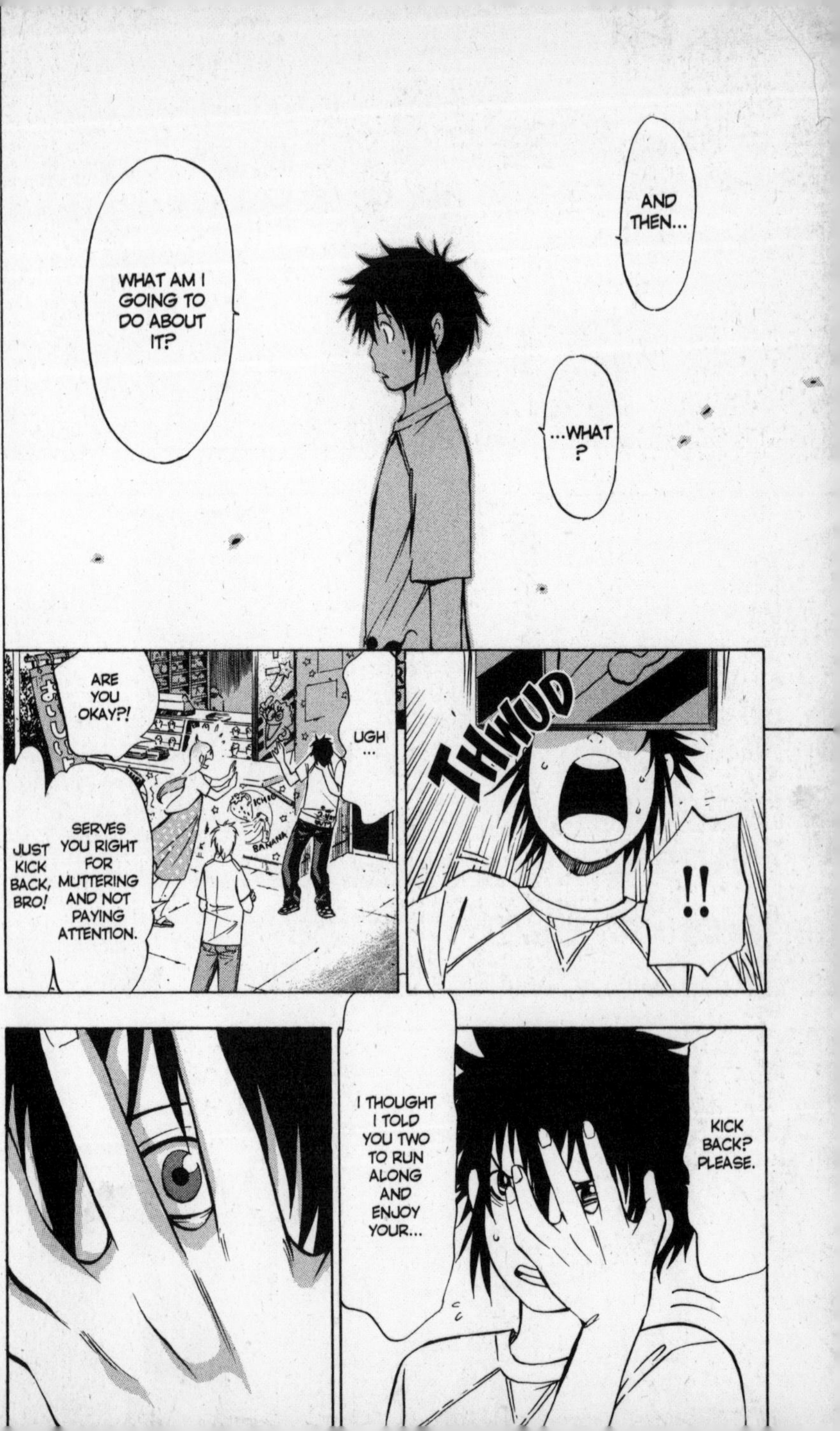
AND THEN...
...WHAT?
WHAT AM I GOING TO DO ABOUT IT?
THWUD
!!
UGH...
ARE YOU OKAY?!
SERVES YOU RIGHT FOR MUTTERING AND NOT PAYING ATTENTION.
JUST KICK BACK, BRO!
KICK BACK? PLEASE.
I THOUGHT I TOLD YOU TWO TO RUN ALONG AND ENJOY YOUR...

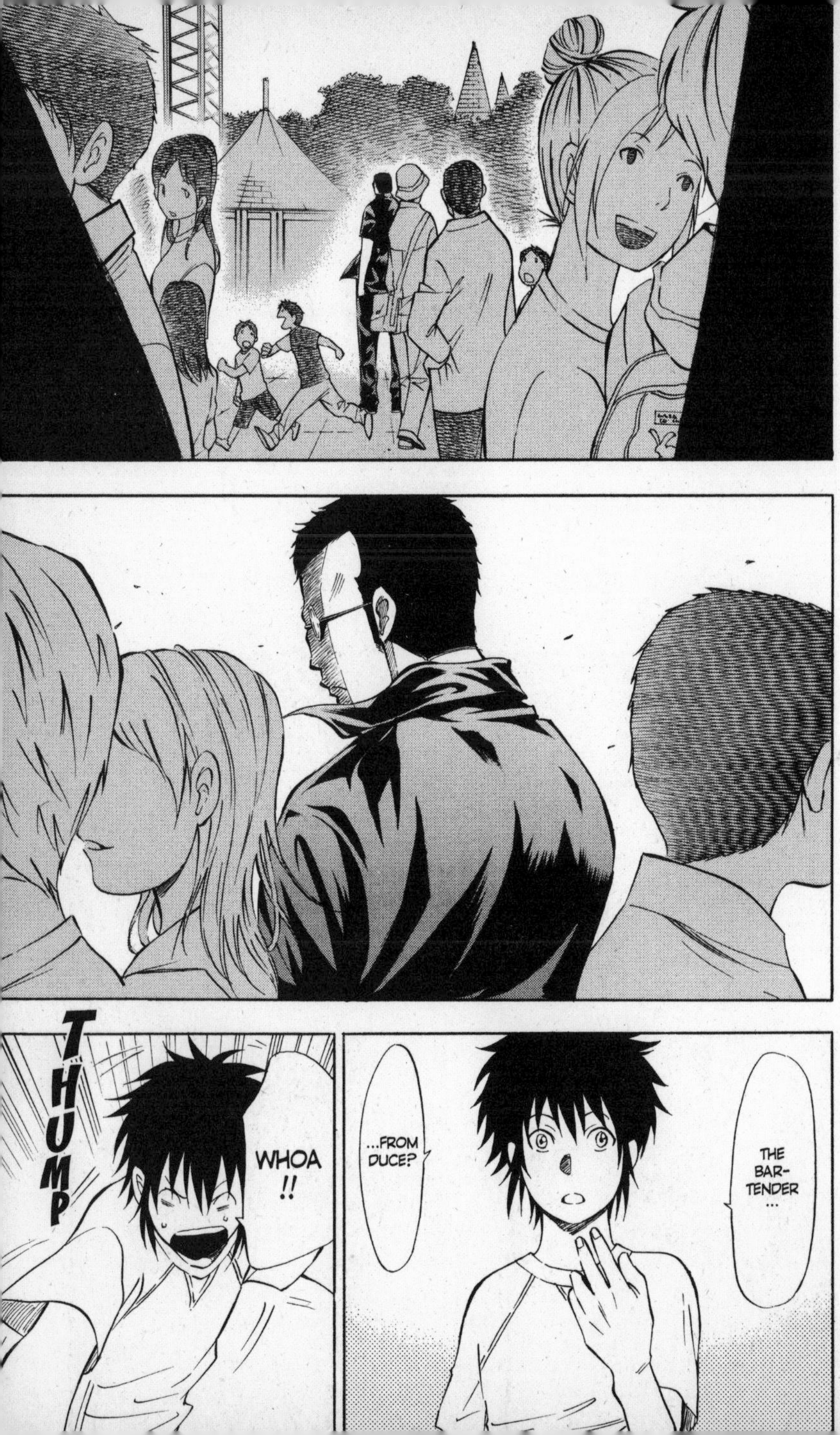
THE BAR-TENDER ...
...FROM DUCE?
THUMP
WHOA !!

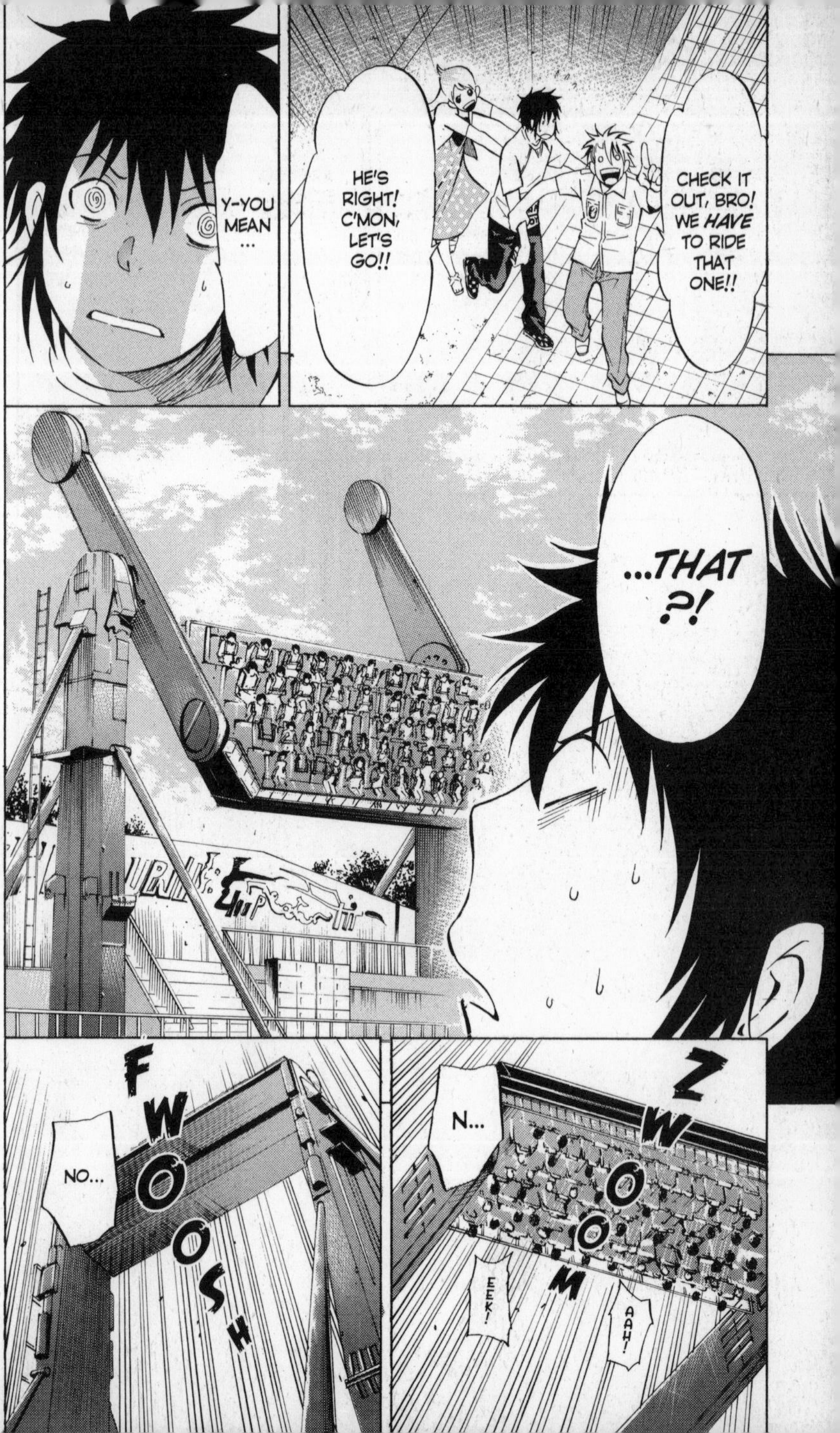
CHECK IT OUT, BRO! WE *HAVE* TO RIDE THAT ONE!!
HE'S RIGHT! C'MON, LET'S GO!!
Y-YOU MEAN ...
...THAT ?!
N...
ZWOOOM
EEK!
AAH!
NO...
FWOOSH

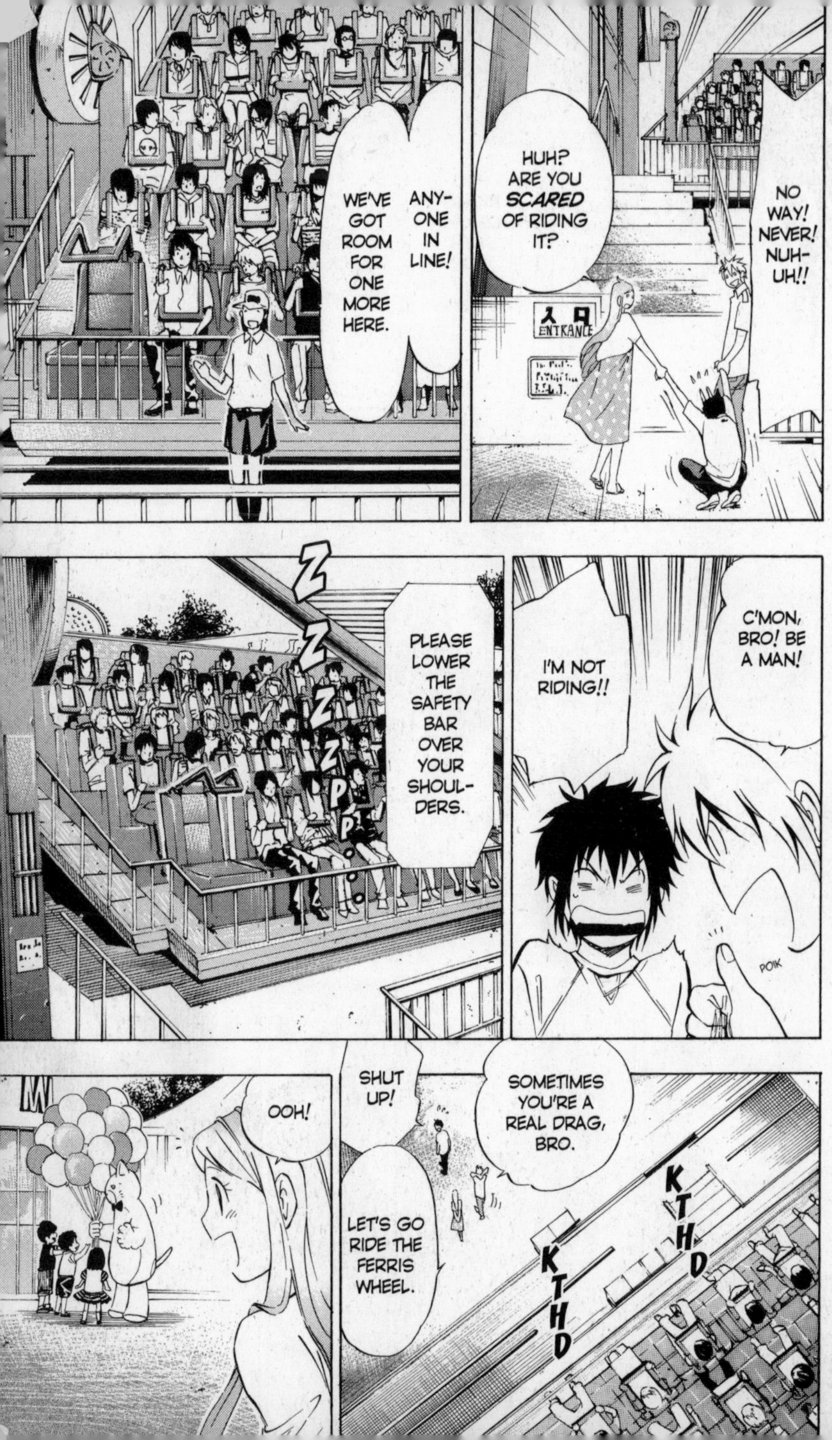
HUH? ARE YOU SCARED OF RIDING IT?
NO WAY! NEVER! NUH-UH!!
入口
ENTRANCE
ANY-ONE IN LINE!
WE'VE GOT ROOM FOR ONE MORE HERE.
C'MON, BRO! BE A MAN!
I'M NOT RIDING!!
POIK
PLEASE LOWER THE SAFETY BAR OVER YOUR SHOUL-DERS.
ZZZZP
SOMETIMES YOU'RE A REAL DRAG, BRO.
KTHD
KTHD
SHUT UP!
LET'S GO RIDE THE FERRIS WHEEL.
OOH!

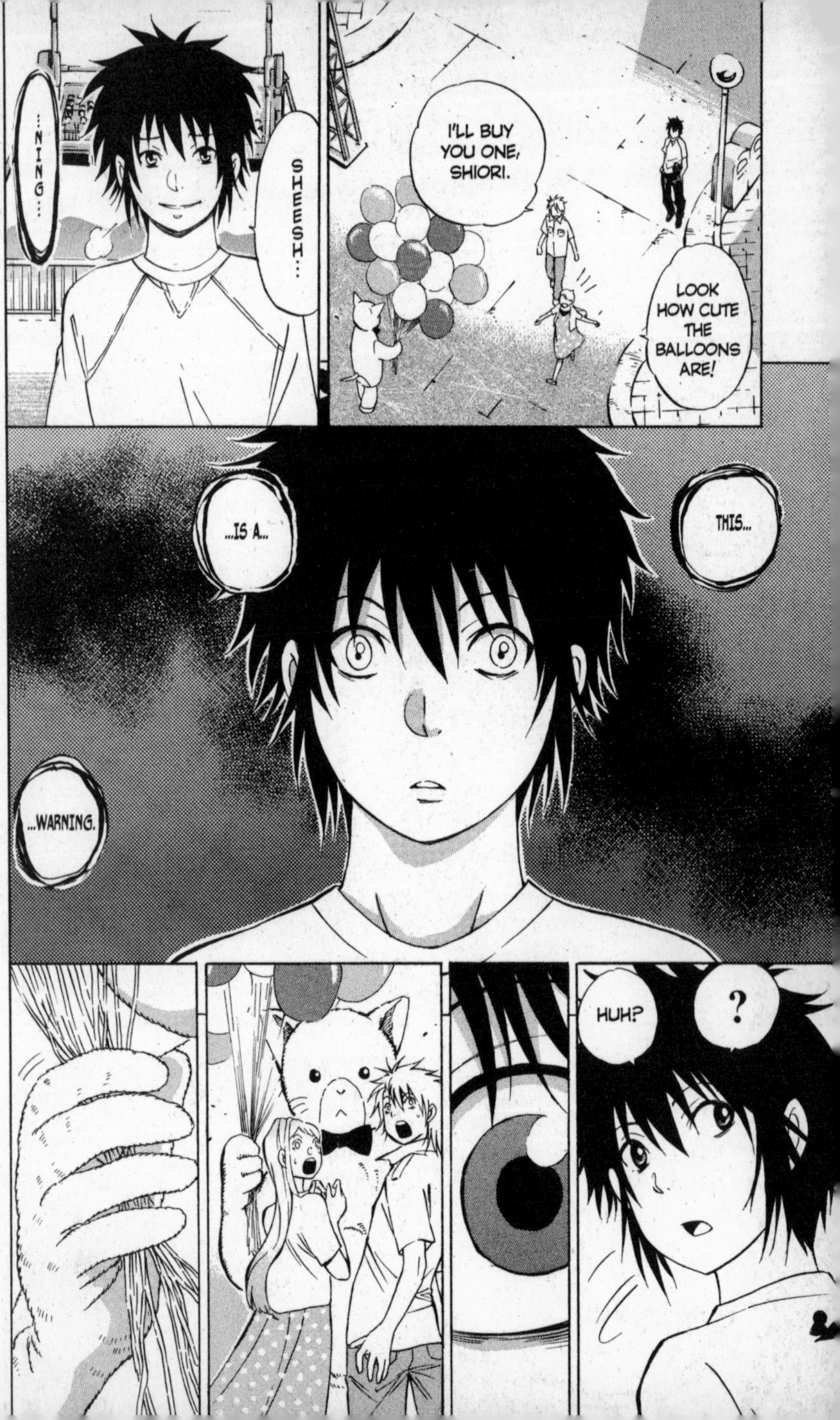
LOOK HOW CUTE THE BALLOONS ARE!
I'LL BUY YOU ONE, SHIORI.
SHEESH...
...NING...
THIS...
...IS A...
...WARNING.
?
HUH?

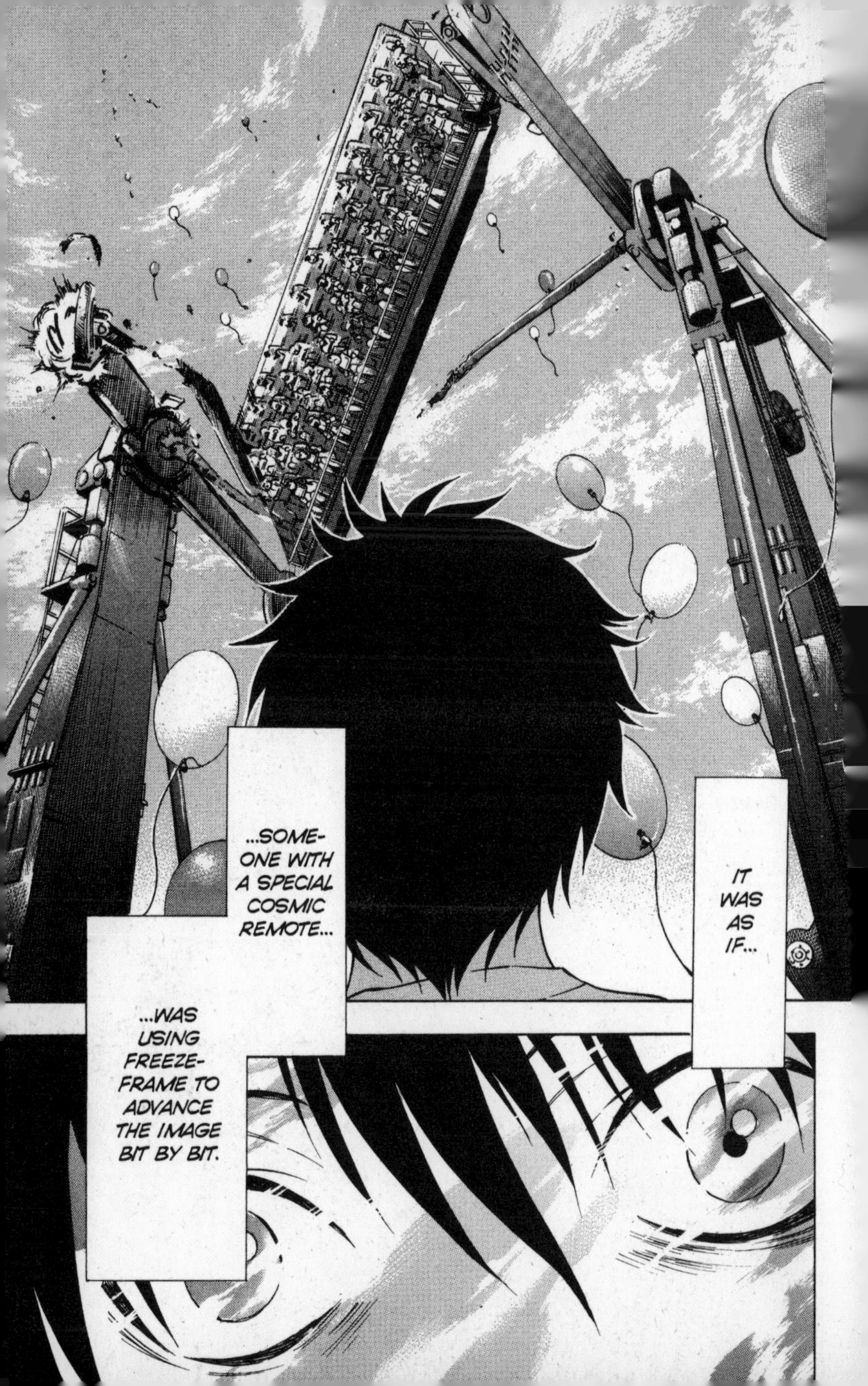
IT WAS AS IF...
...SOME-ONE WITH A SPECIAL COSMIC REMOTE...
...WAS USING FREEZE-FRAME TO ADVANCE THE IMAGE BIT BY BIT.

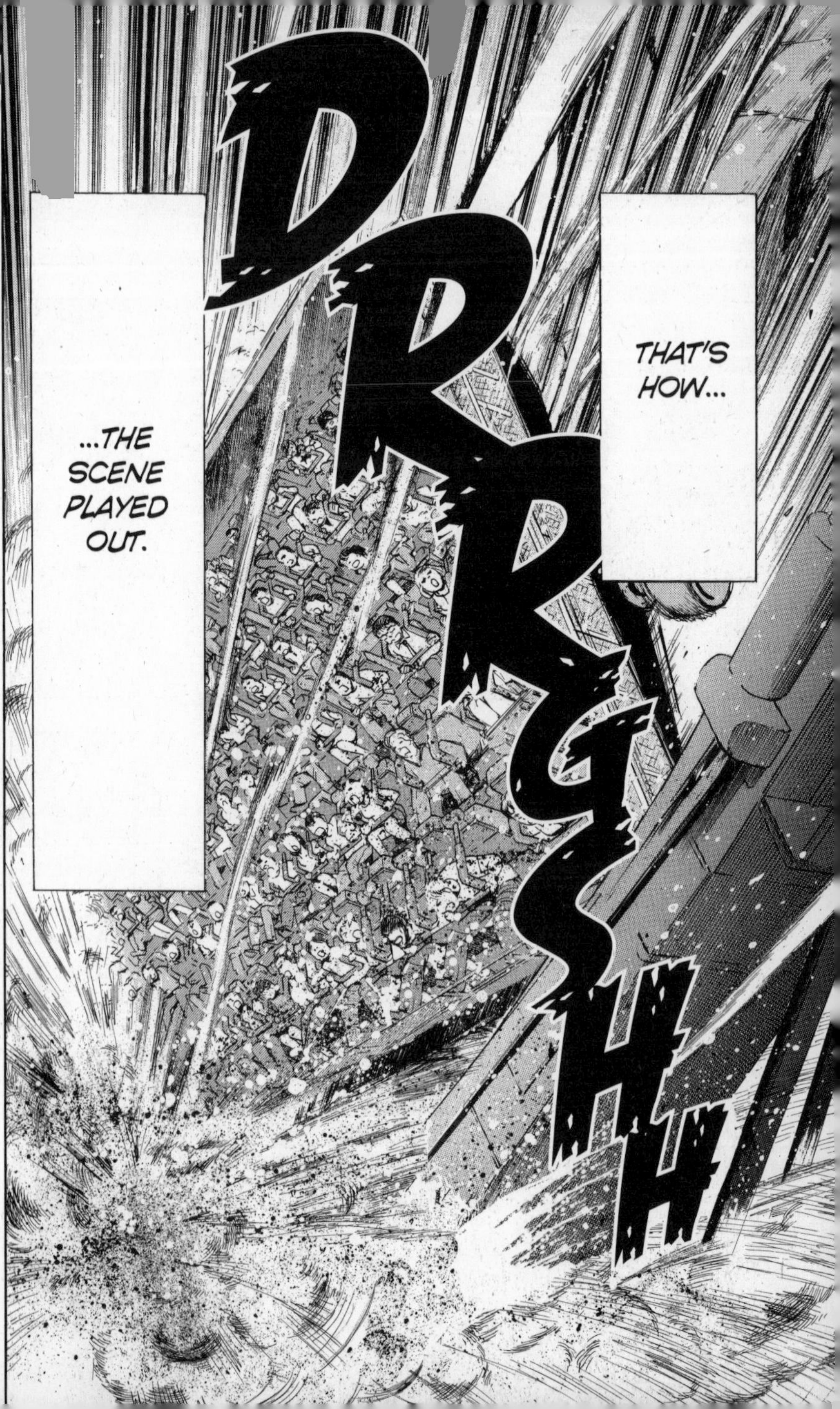
THAT'S HOW...
...THE SCENE PLAYED OUT.
DDRRGGSHHH

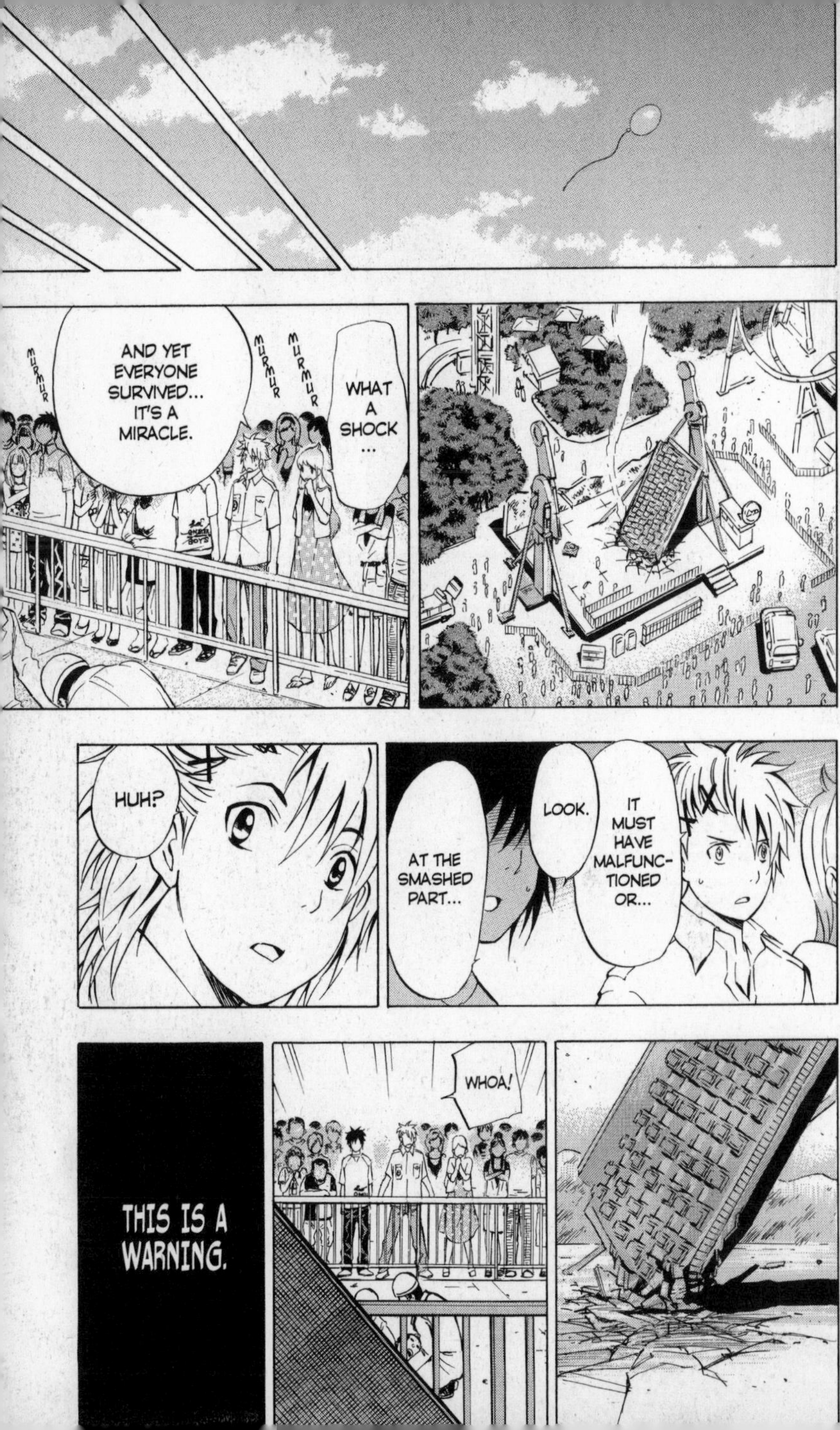
WHAT A SHOCK...
MURMUR
MURMUR
AND YET EVERYONE SURVIVED... IT'S A MIRACLE.
MURMUR
IT MUST HAVE MALFUNCTIONED OR...
LOOK.
AT THE SMASHED PART...
HUH?
WHOA!
THIS IS A WARNING.

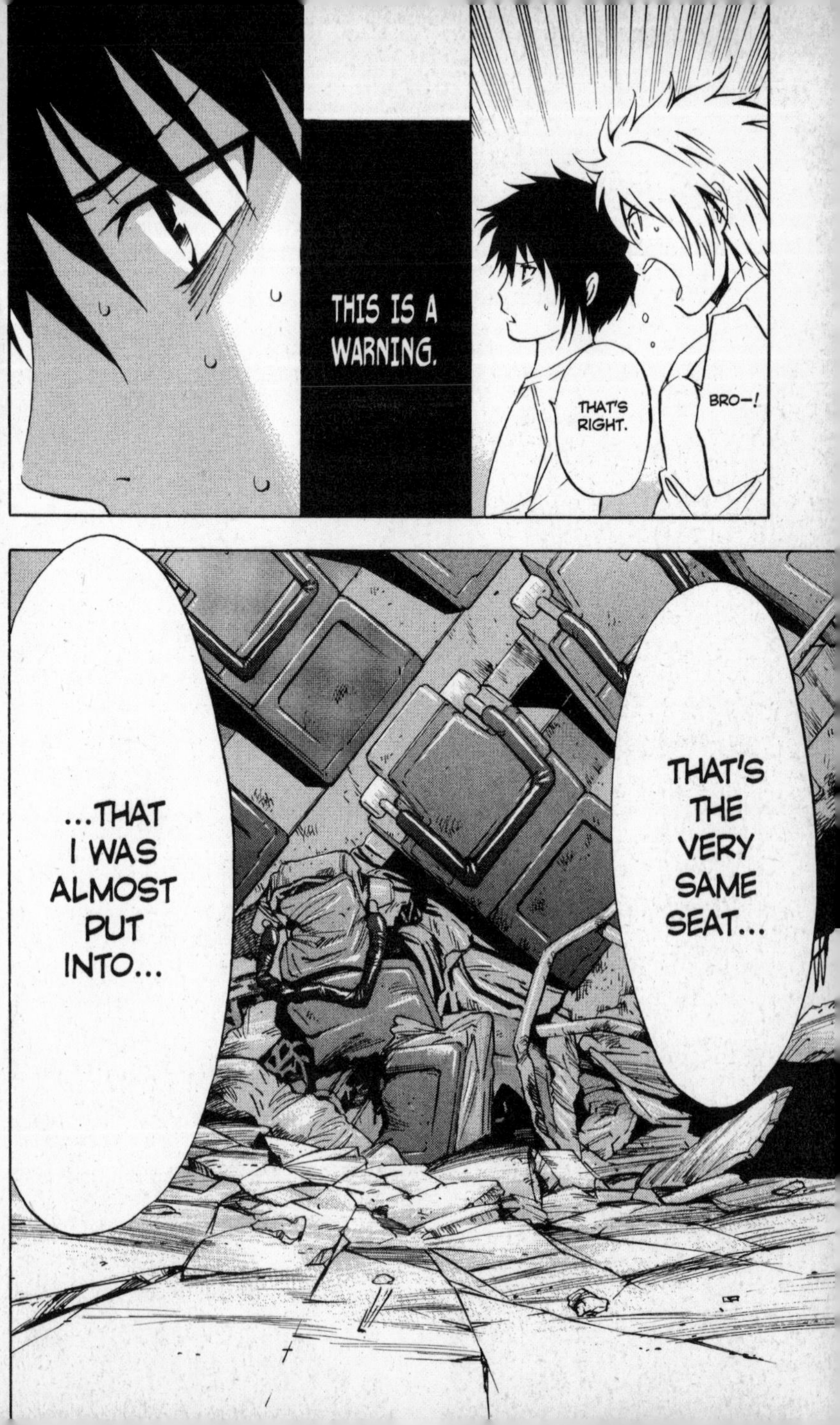
BRO—!
THAT'S RIGHT.
THIS IS A WARNING.
THAT'S THE VERY SAME SEAT...
...THAT I WAS ALMOST PUT INTO...

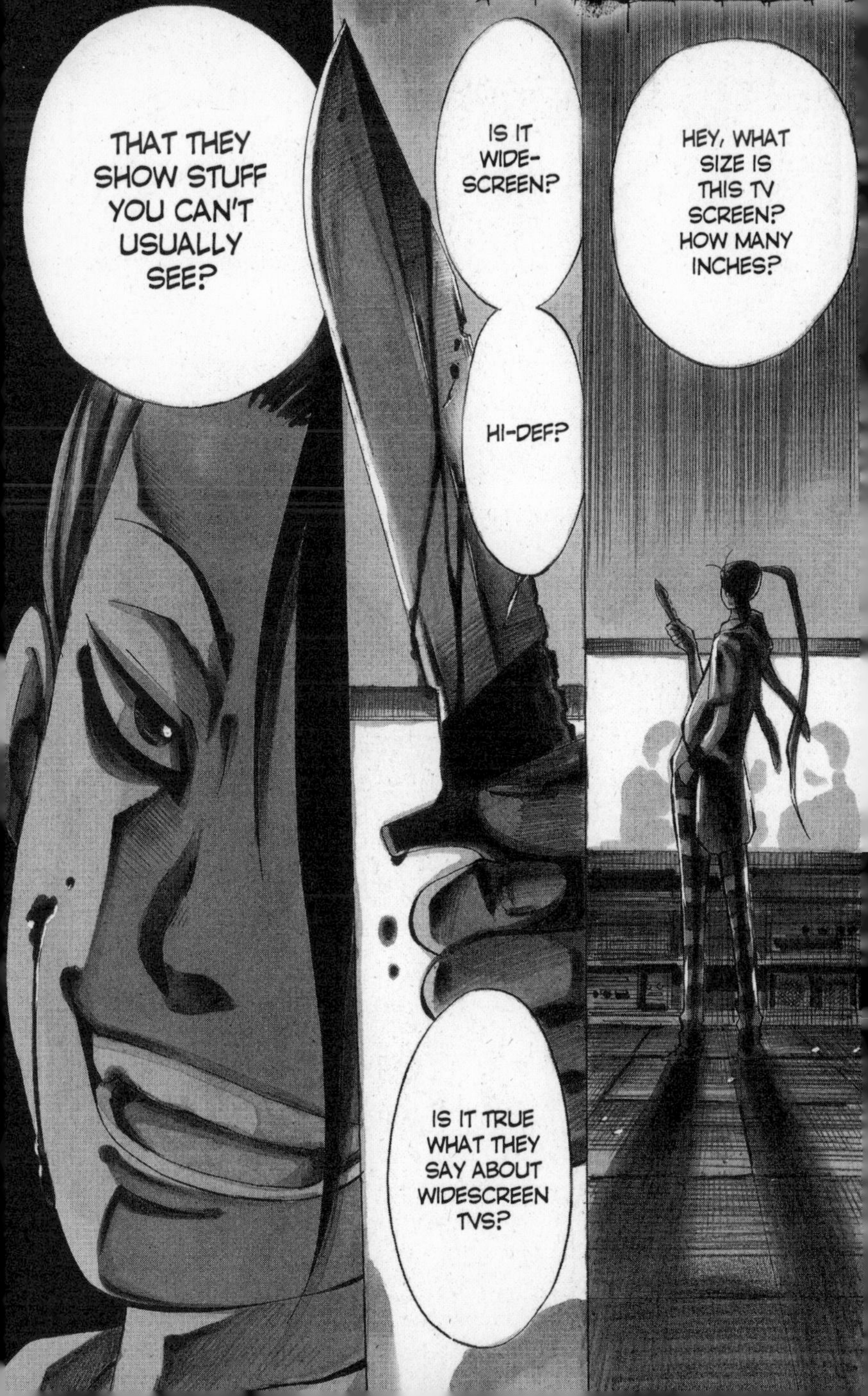
HEY, WHAT SIZE IS THIS TV SCREEN? HOW MANY INCHES?
IS IT WIDE-SCREEN?
HI-DEF?
IS IT TRUE WHAT THEY SAY ABOUT WIDESCREEN TVS?
THAT THEY SHOW STUFF YOU CAN'T USUALLY SEE?

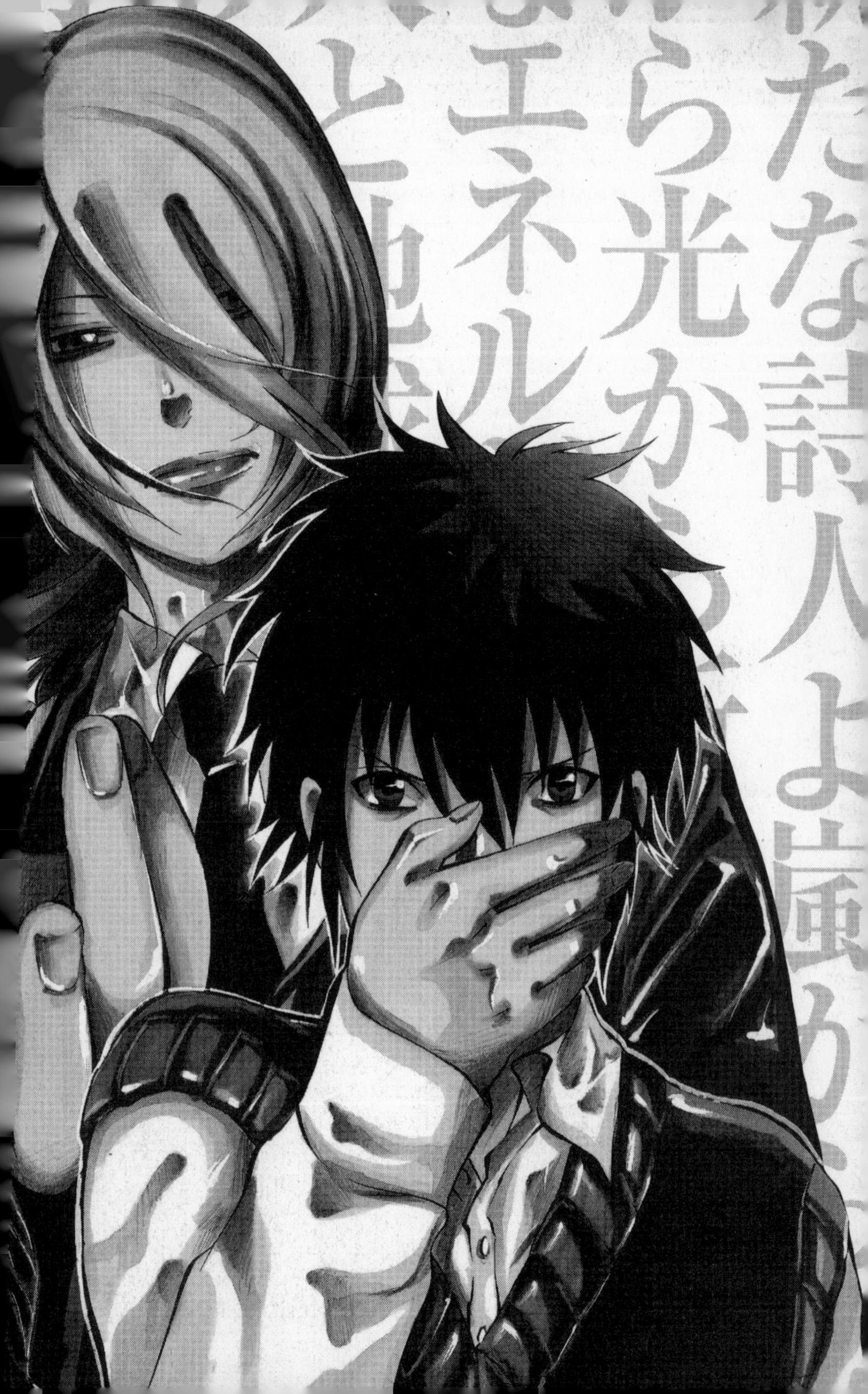
たな詩人よ届か
ら光か
エネル
と

Chapter 9 • A Cacophonous Night

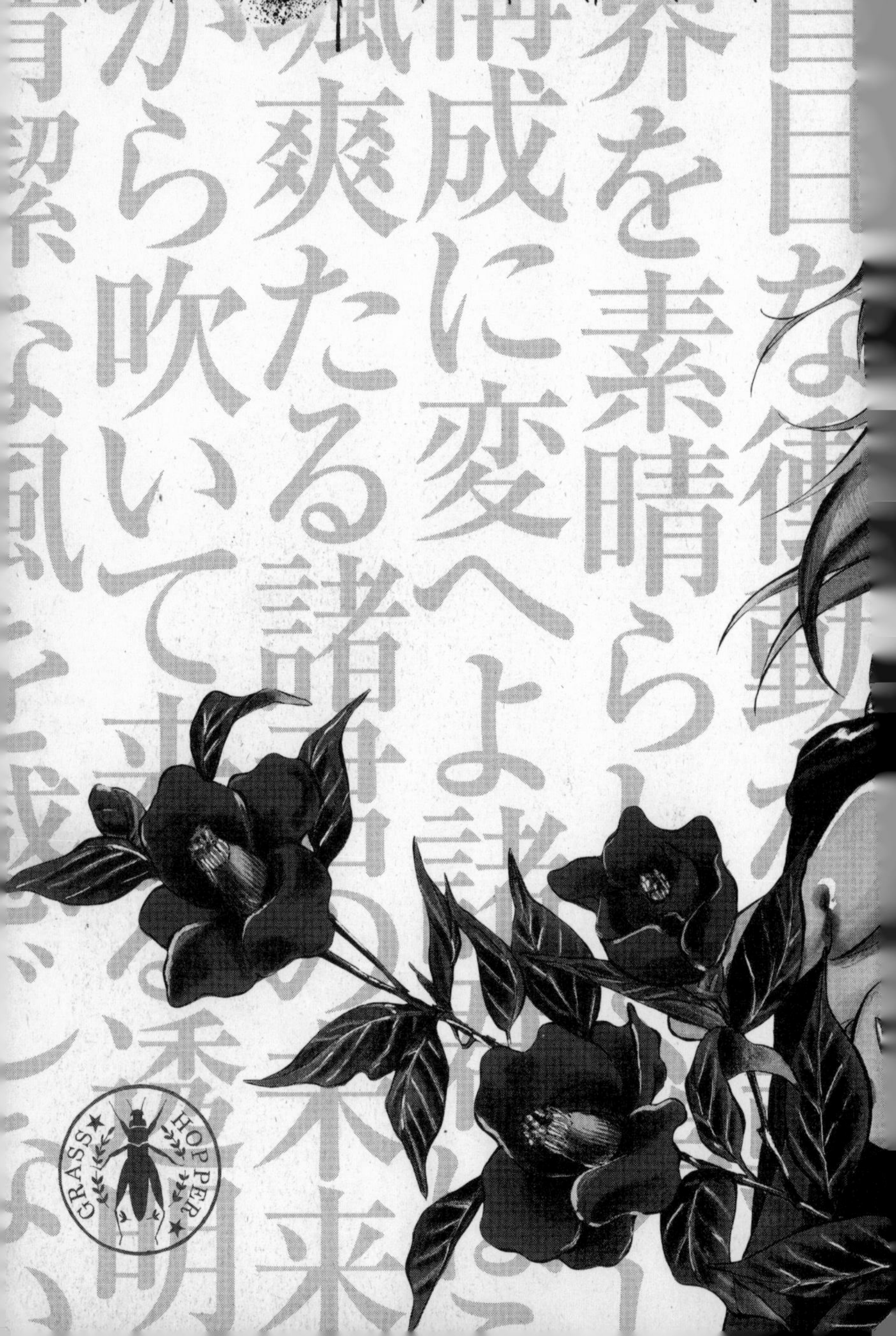
GRASS HOPPER

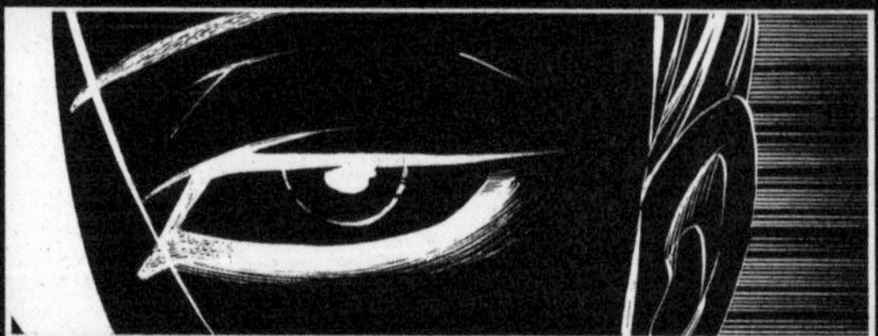

MAOH

JUVENILE REMIX

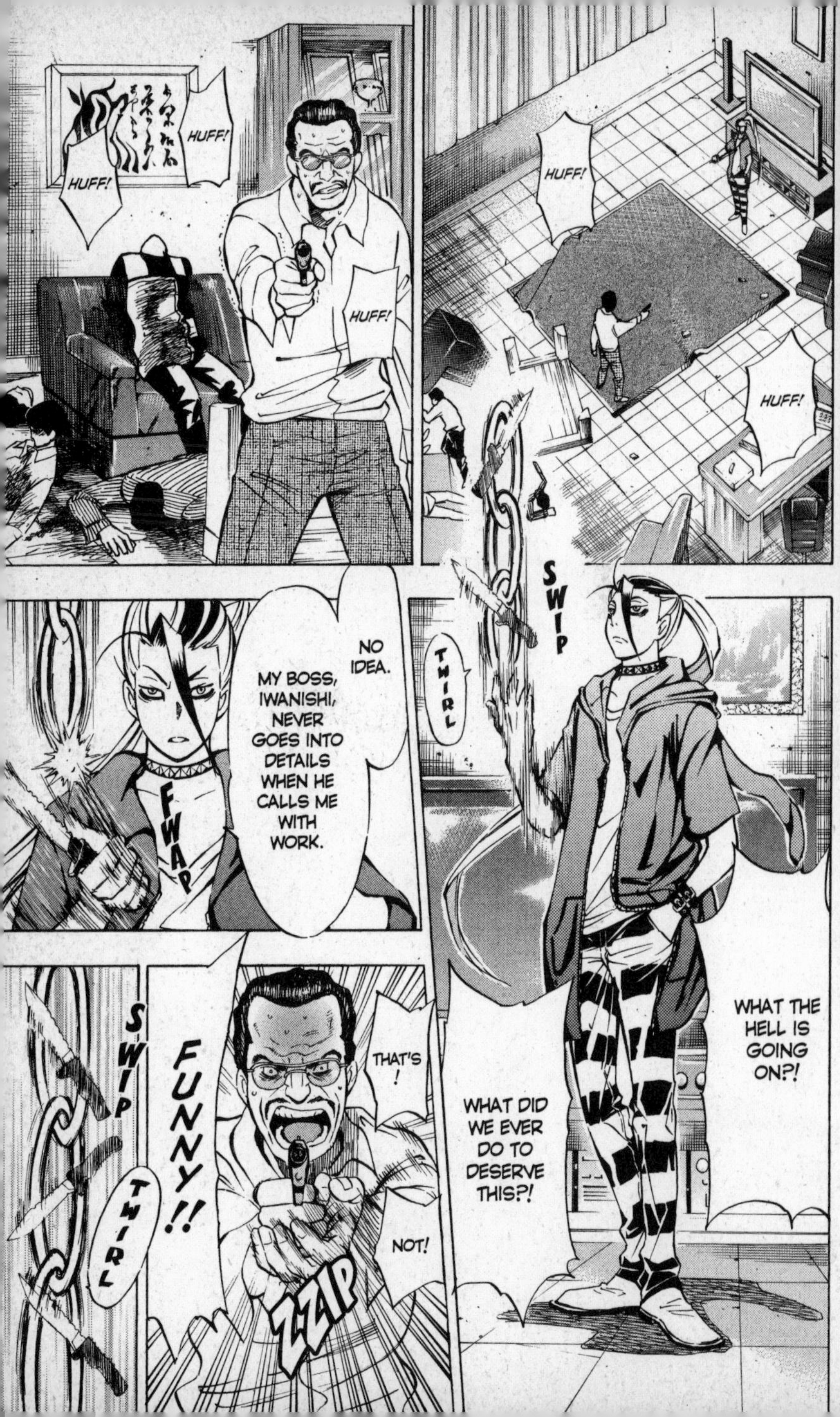
HUFF!
HUFF!
HUFF!
HUFF!
HUFF!
SWIP
THWIRL
WHAT THE HELL IS GOING ON?!
WHAT DID WE EVER DO TO DESERVE THIS?!
NO IDEA.
MY BOSS, IWANISHI, NEVER GOES INTO DETAILS WHEN HE CALLS ME WITH WORK.
FWAP
THAT'S
FUNNY!!
NOT!
SWIP
THWIRL
ZZIP

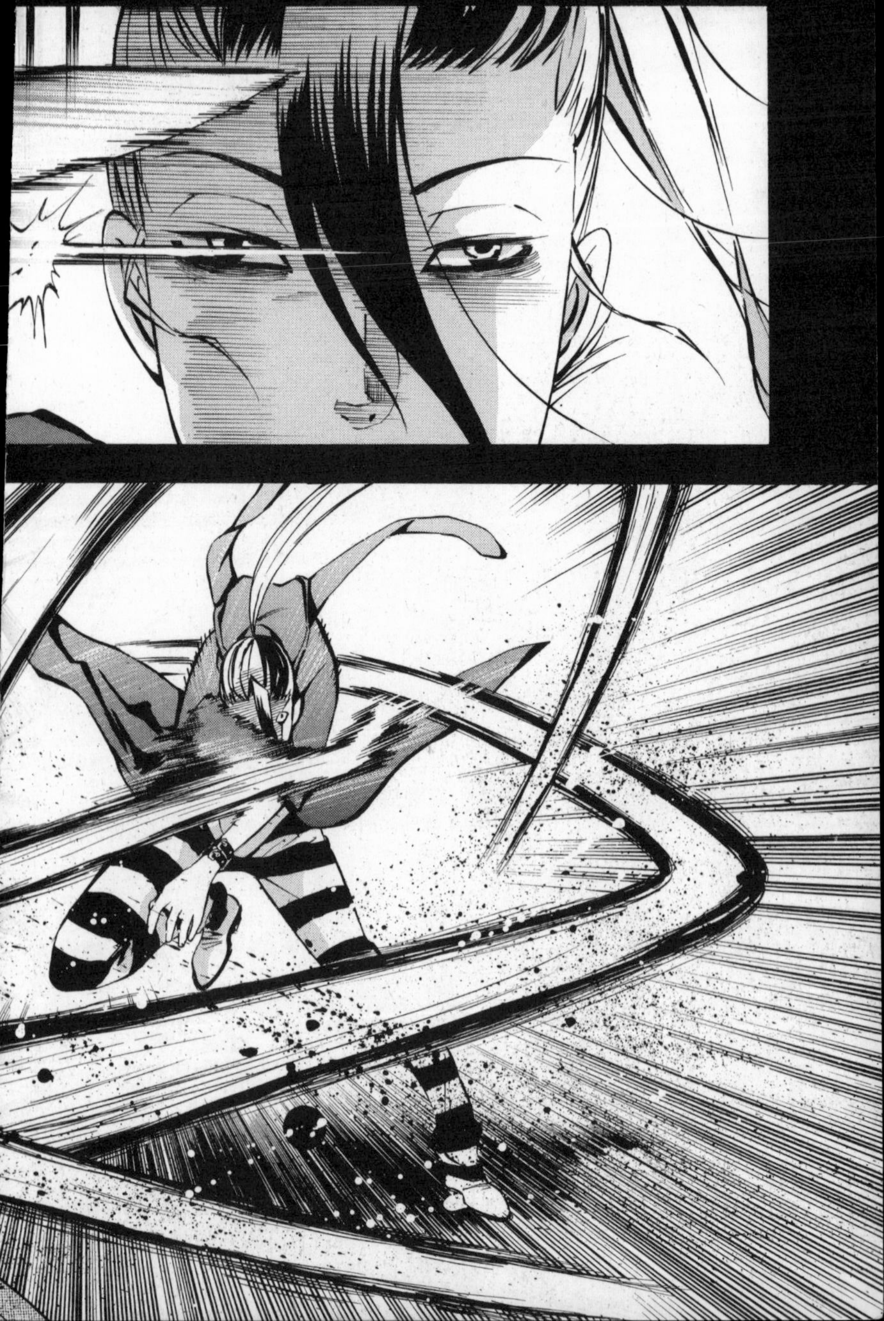

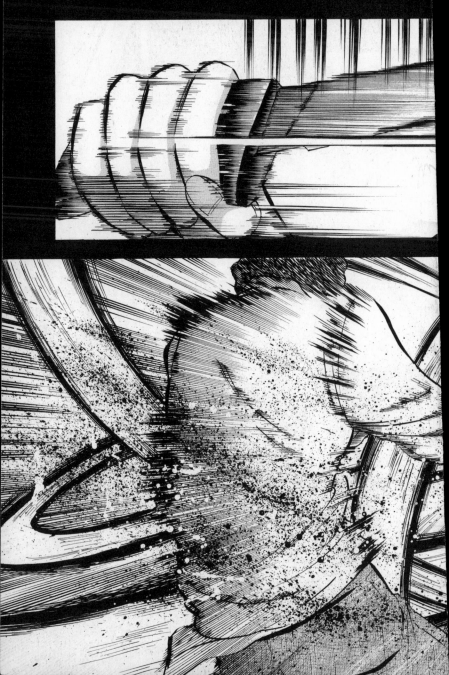

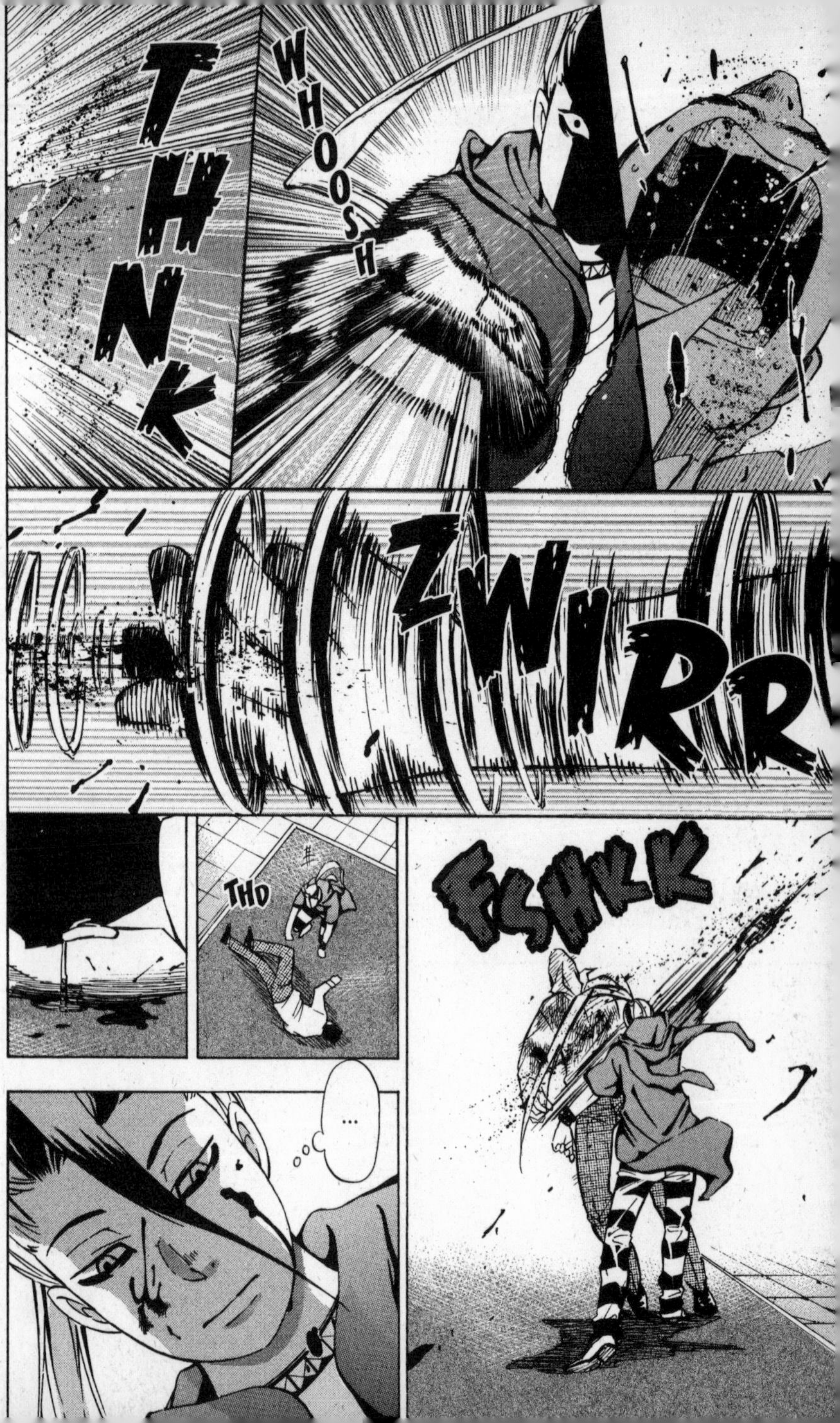
WHOOSH
THNK
ZWIRR
FSHLK
THD
...

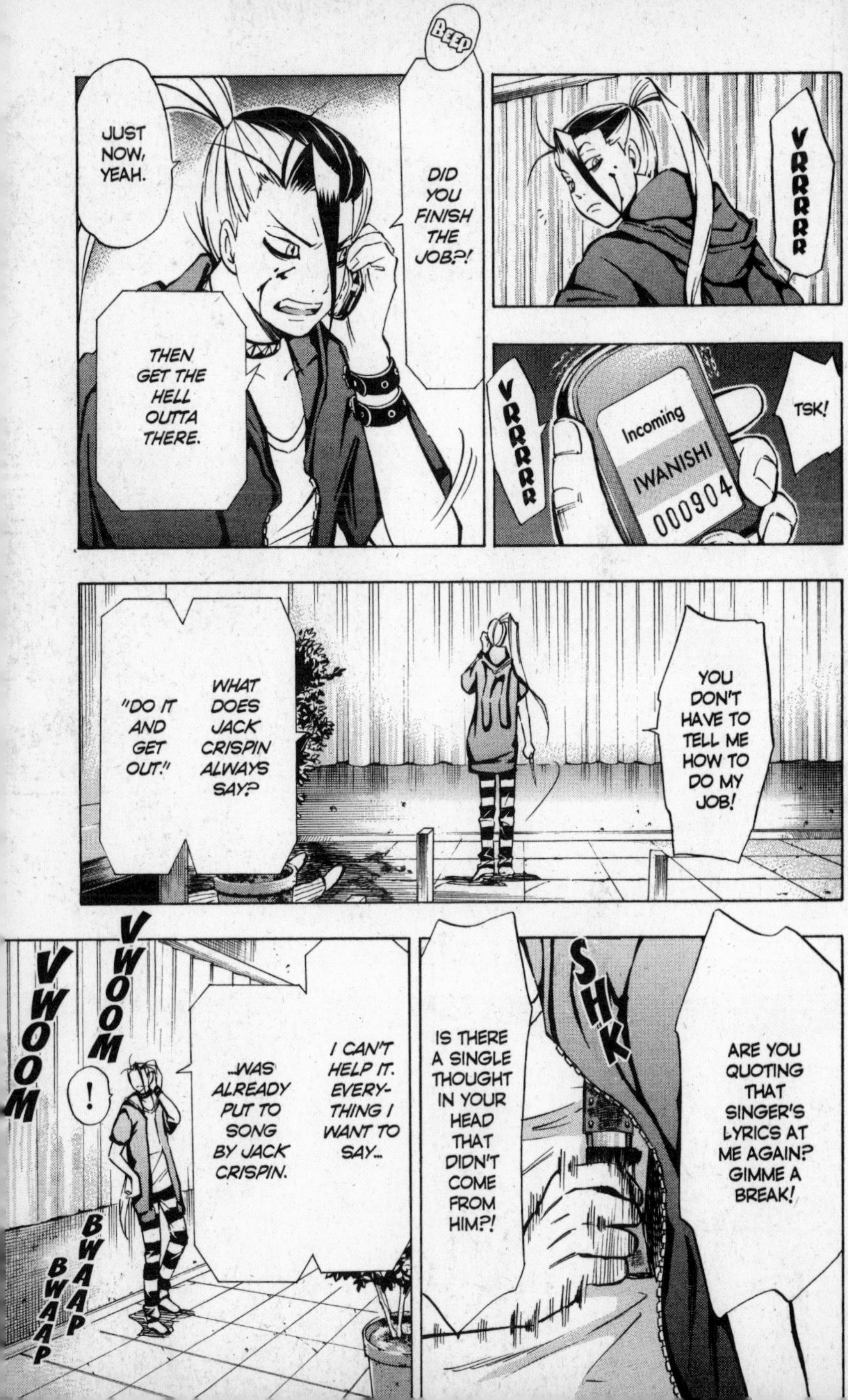
VRRRRR
TSK!
Incoming
IWANISHI
000904
VRRRRR
BEEP
DID YOU FINISH THE JOB?!
JUST NOW, YEAH.
THEN GET THE HELL OUTTA THERE.
YOU DON'T HAVE TO TELL ME HOW TO DO MY JOB!
WHAT DOES JACK CRISPIN ALWAYS SAY?
"DO IT AND GET OUT."
SHK
ARE YOU QUOTING THAT SINGER'S LYRICS AT ME AGAIN? GIMME A BREAK!
IS THERE A SINGLE THOUGHT IN YOUR HEAD THAT DIDN'T COME FROM HIM?!
I CAN'T HELP IT. EVERY-THING I WANT TO SAY...
...WAS ALREADY PUT TO SONG BY JACK CRISPIN.
VWOOM
VWOOM
!
BWAAP
BWAAP

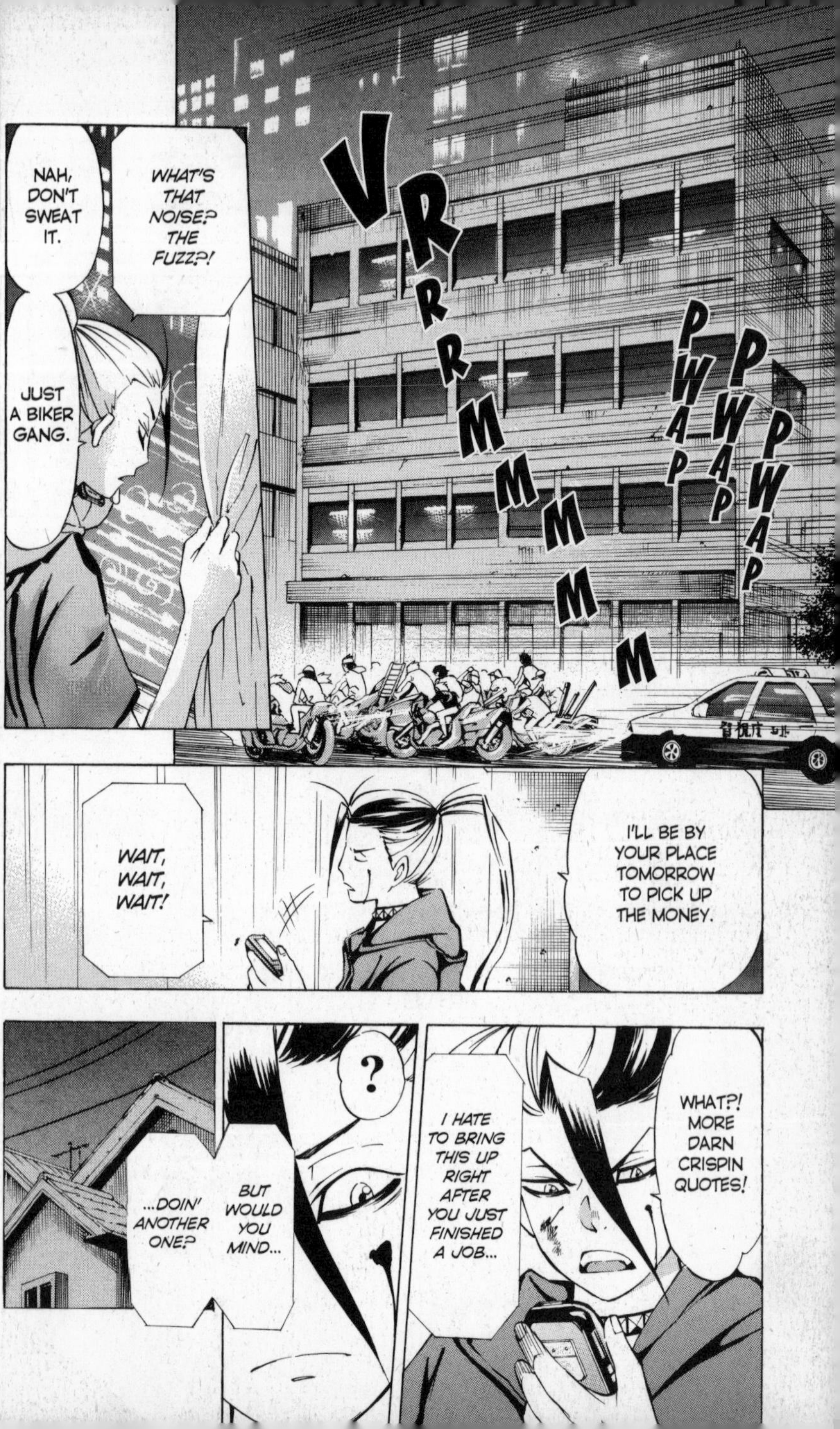
VRRRMMMMMM
PWAP PWAP PWAP
WHAT'S THAT NOISE? THE FUZZ?!
NAH, DON'T SWEAT IT.
JUST A BIKER GANG.
I'LL BE BY YOUR PLACE TOMORROW TO PICK UP THE MONEY.
WAIT, WAIT, WAIT!
WHAT?! MORE DARN CRISPIN QUOTES!
I HATE TO BRING THIS UP RIGHT AFTER YOU JUST FINISHED A JOB...
?
BUT WOULD YOU MIND...
...DOIN' ANOTHER ONE?

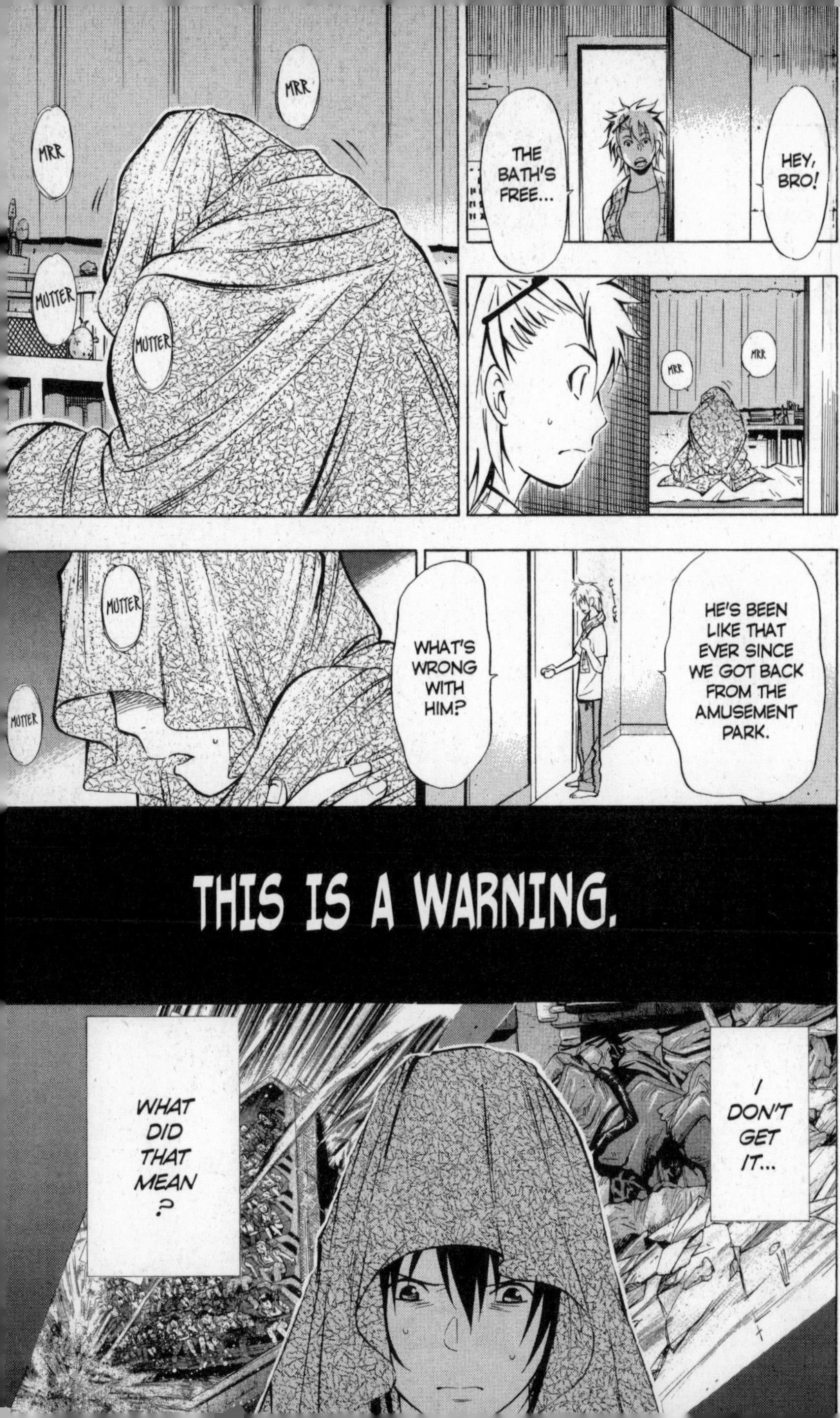
HEY, BRO!
THE BATH'S FREE...
MRR
MRR
MRR
MRR
MUTTER
MUTTER
HE'S BEEN LIKE THAT EVER SINCE WE GOT BACK FROM THE AMUSEMENT PARK.
CLICK
WHAT'S WRONG WITH HIM?
MUTTER
MUTTER
THIS IS A WARNING.
I DON'T GET IT...
WHAT DID THAT MEAN?

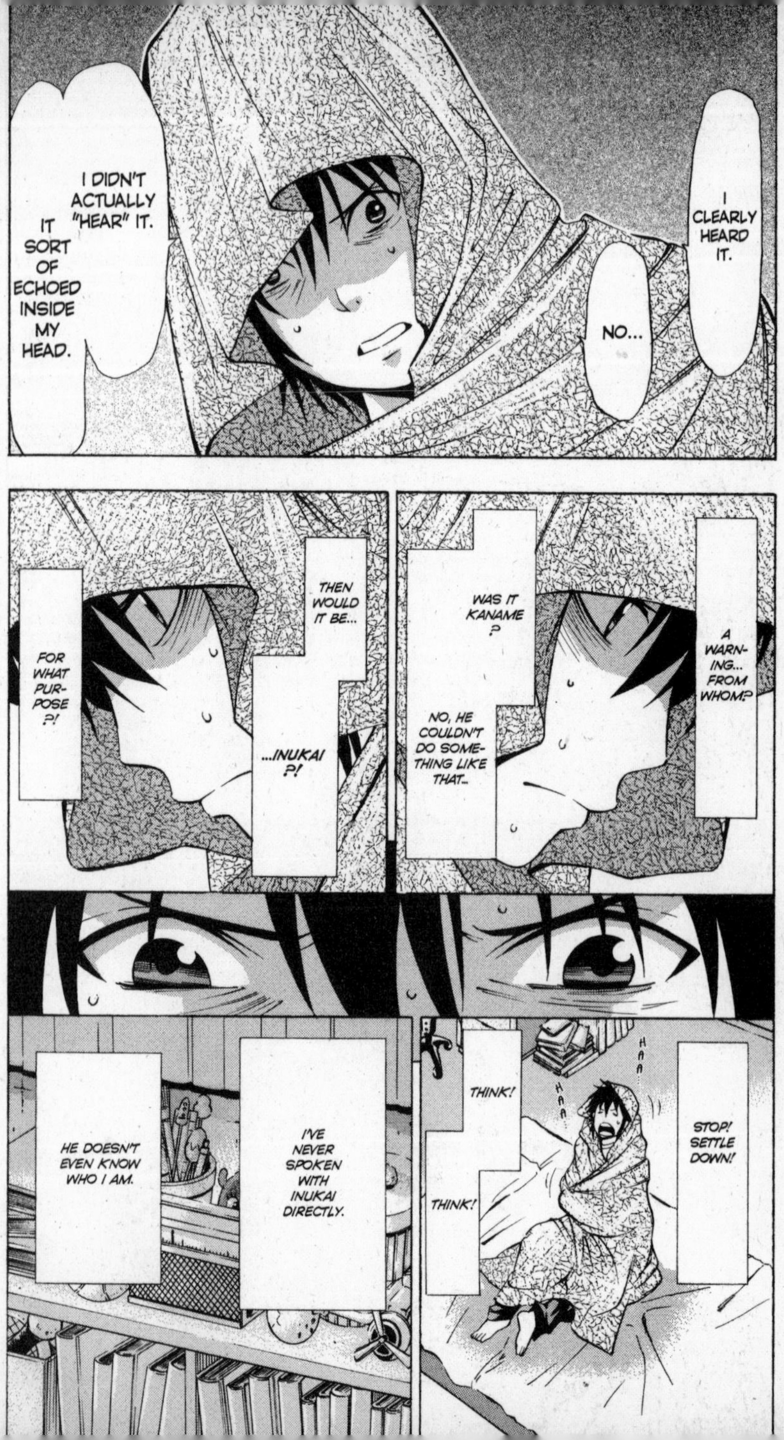
I CLEARLY HEARD IT.
NO...
I DIDN'T ACTUALLY "HEAR" IT.
IT SORT OF ECHOED INSIDE MY HEAD.
A WARNING... FROM WHOM?
WAS IT KANAME?
NO, HE COULDN'T DO SOMETHING LIKE THAT...
THEN WOULD IT BE...
...INUKAI?!
FOR WHAT PURPOSE?!
HAA
HAA
STOP! SETTLE DOWN!
THINK!
THINK!
I'VE NEVER SPOKEN WITH INUKAI DIRECTLY.
HE DOESN'T EVEN KNOW WHO I AM.

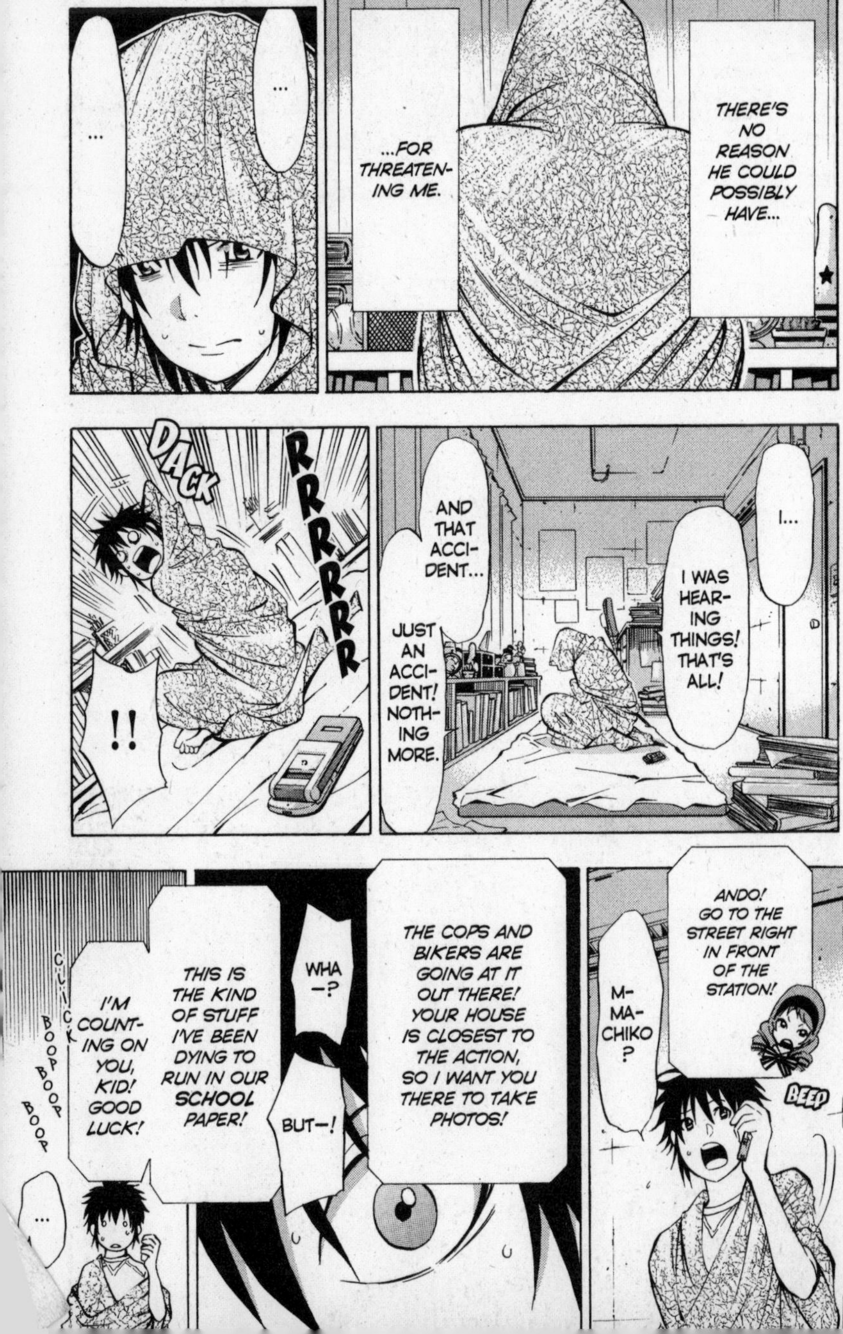
THERE'S NO REASON HE COULD POSSIBLY HAVE...
...FOR THREATENING ME.
...
...
I...
I WAS HEARING THINGS! THAT'S ALL!
AND THAT ACCIDENT...
JUST AN ACCIDENT! NOTHING MORE.
RRRRRRR
DACK
!!
BEEP
ANDO! GO TO THE STREET RIGHT IN FRONT OF THE STATION!
M-MACHIKO?
THE COPS AND BIKERS ARE GOING AT IT OUT THERE! YOUR HOUSE IS CLOSEST TO THE ACTION, SO I WANT YOU THERE TO TAKE PHOTOS!
WHA-?
BUT-!
THIS IS THE KIND OF STUFF I'VE BEEN DYING TO RUN IN OUR SCHOOL PAPER!
I'M COUNTING ON YOU, KID! GOOD LUCK!
CLICK
BOOP BOOP BOOP
...

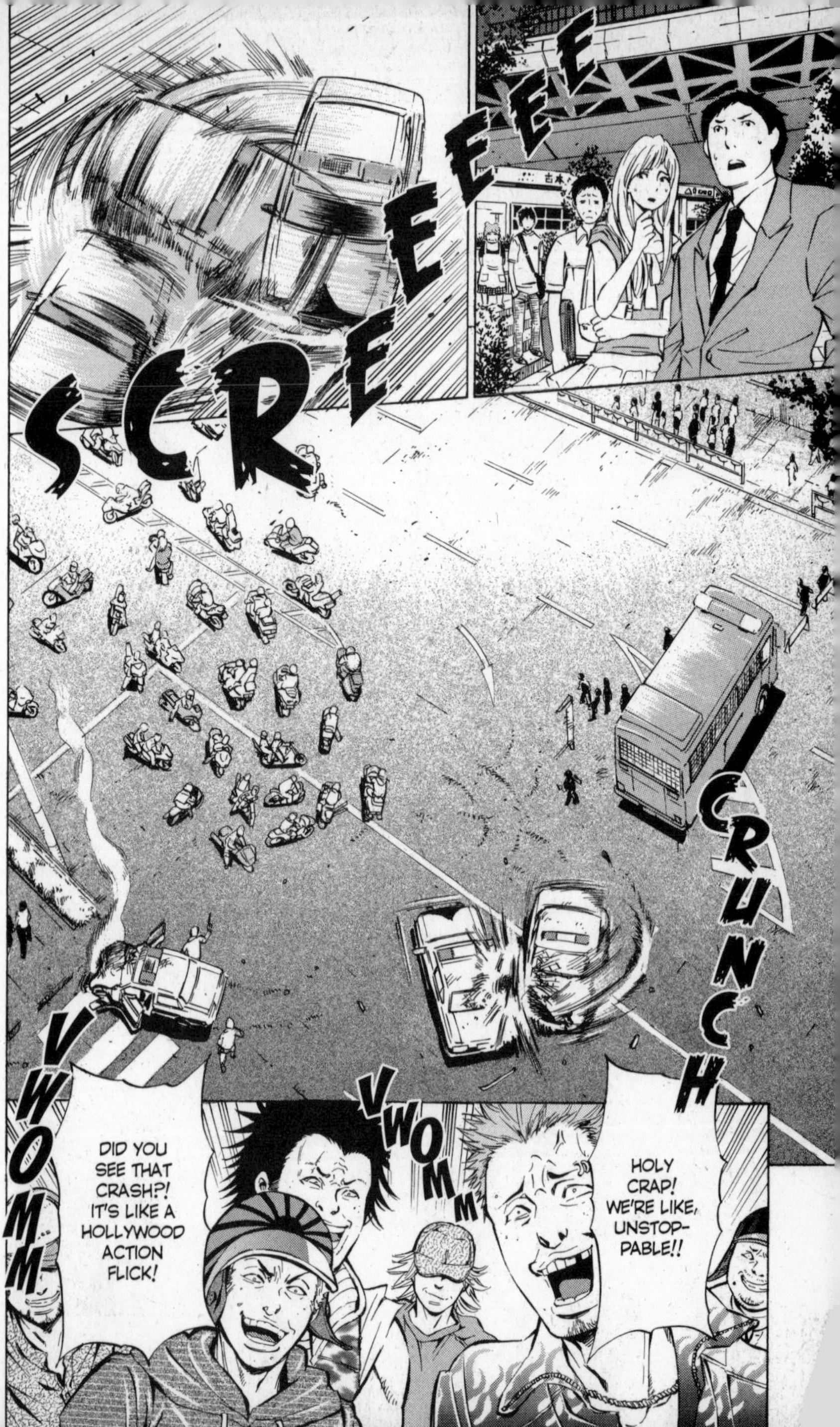
SCREEEEEE
CRUNCH
HOLY CRAP! WE'RE LIKE, UNSTOPPABLE!!
VWOMM
DID YOU SEE THAT CRASH?! IT'S LIKE A HOLLYWOOD ACTION FLICK!
VWOMM

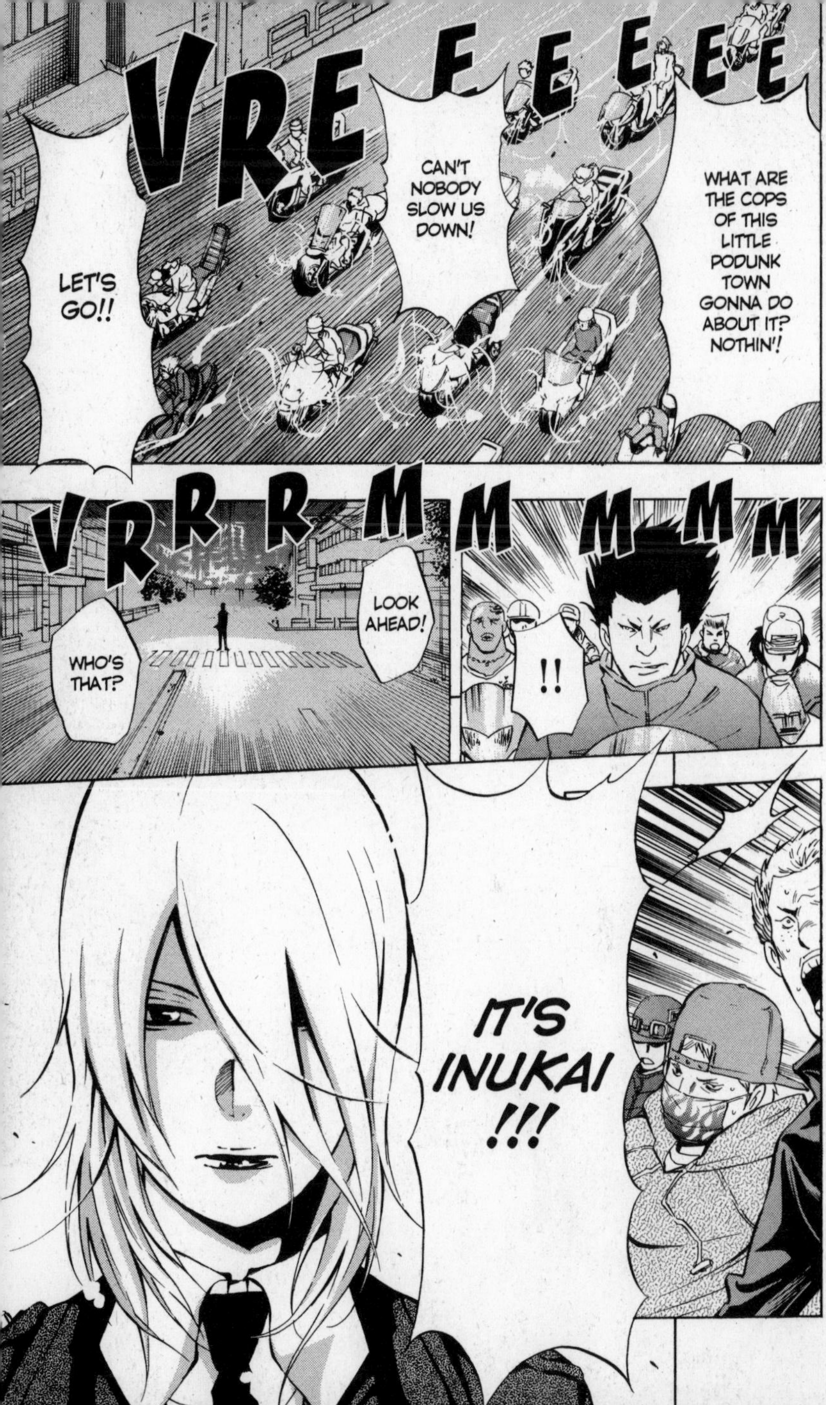
VREEEEEEE
WHAT ARE THE COPS OF THIS LITTLE PODUNK TOWN GONNA DO ABOUT IT? NOTHIN'!
CAN'T NOBODY SLOW US DOWN!
LET'S GO!!
VRRRMMMMM
!!
LOOK AHEAD!
WHO'S THAT?
IT'S INUKAI!!!

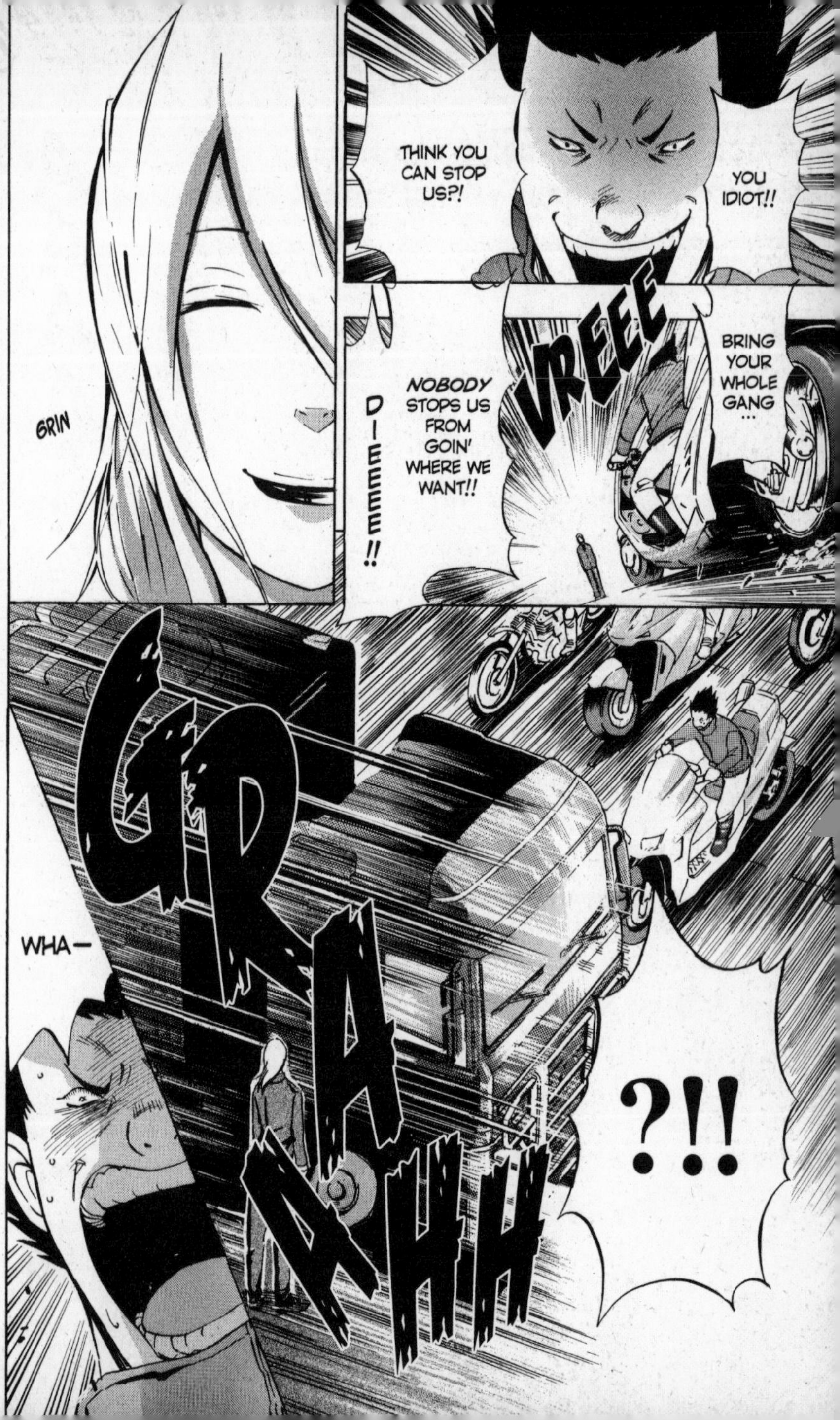
YOU IDIOT!!
THINK YOU CAN STOP US?!
BRING YOUR WHOLE GANG ...
VREEE
NOBODY STOPS US FROM GOIN' WHERE WE WANT!!
DIEEEE!!
GRIN
?!!
GRAAHHH
WHA—

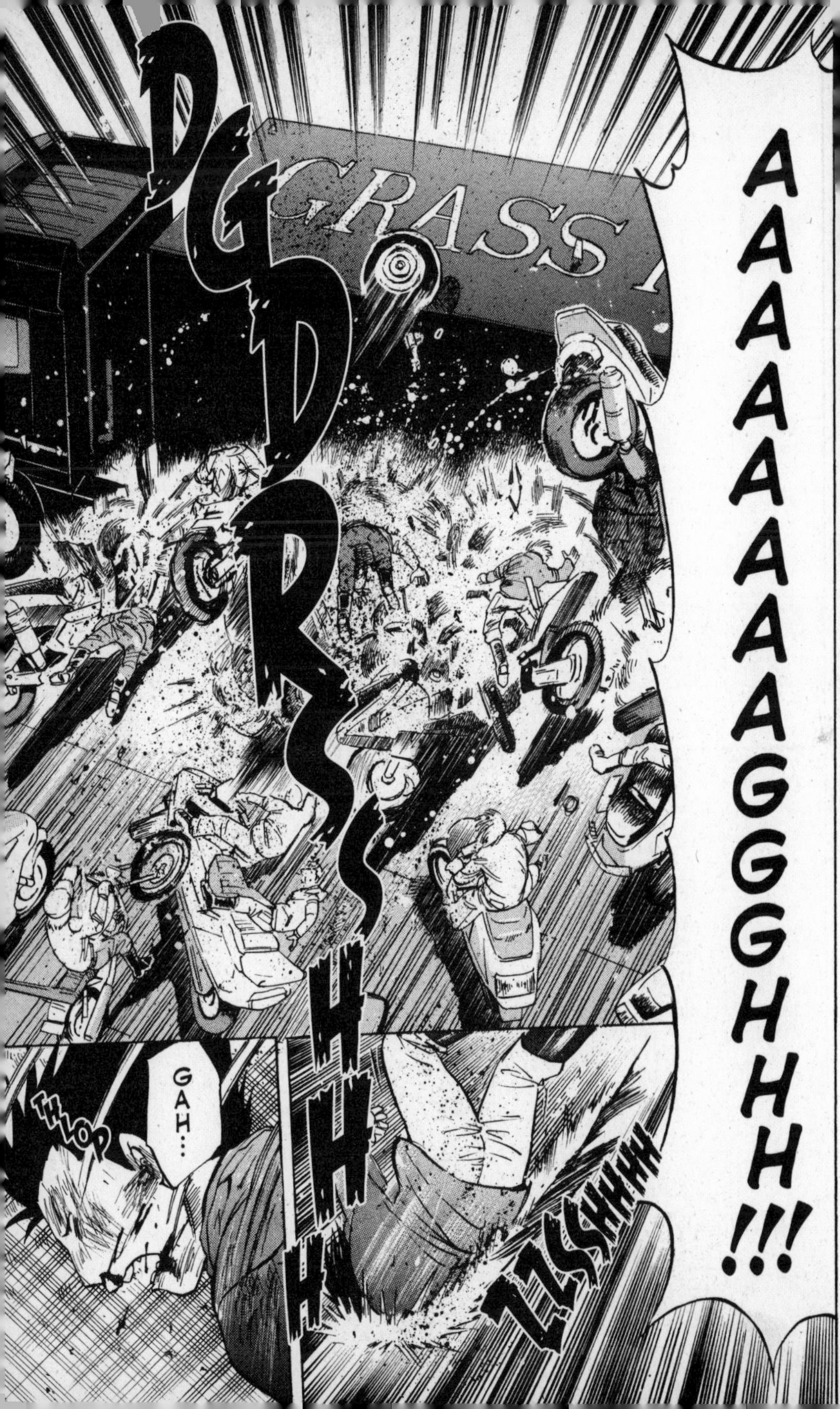
AAAAAAAAAGGGHHH!!!
DGDRSSHHHH
GAH...
THLOP
TSSSHHHH

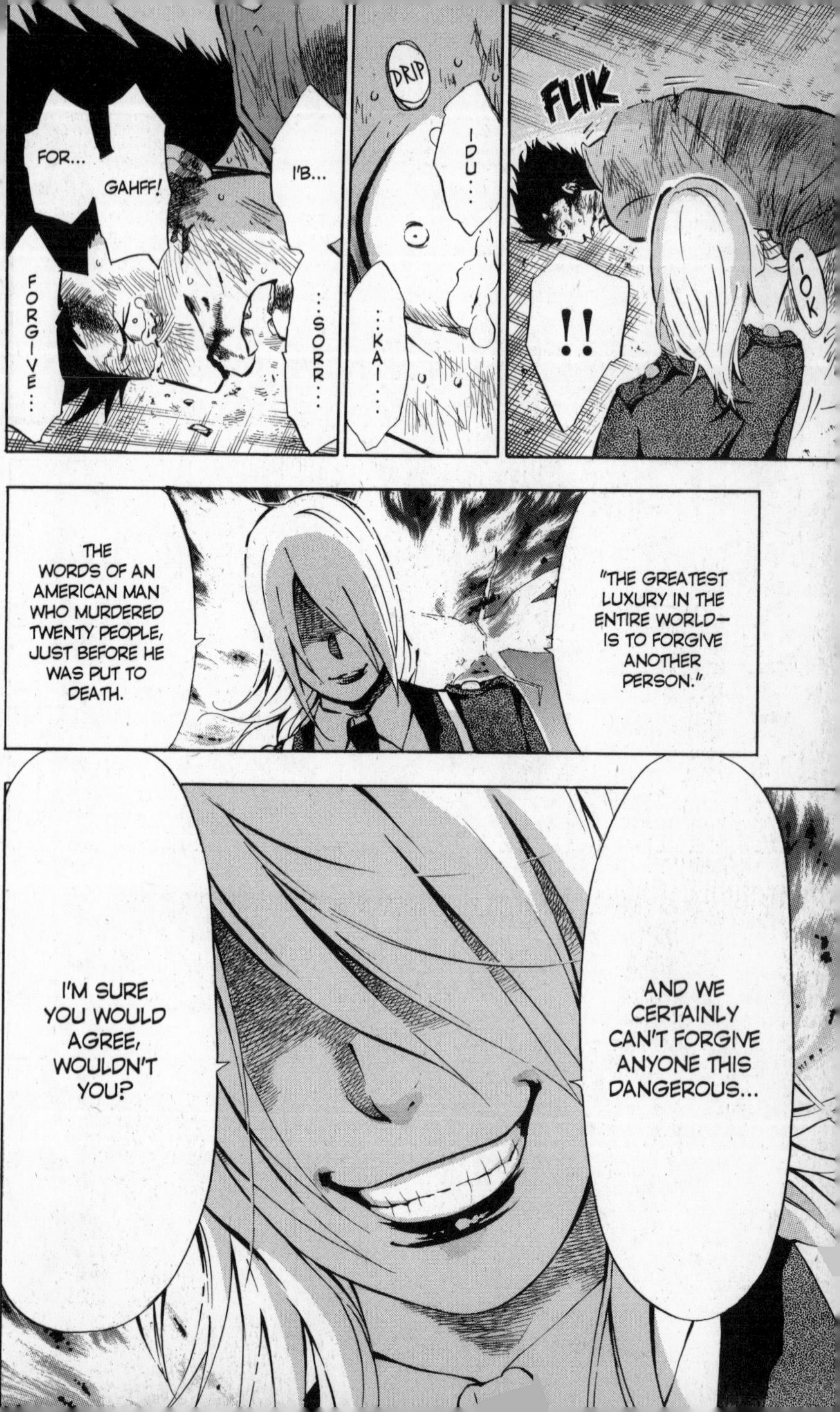
FLIK
TOK
!!
DRIP
IDU...
...KAI...
I'B...
...SORR...
FOR...
GAHFF!
FORGIVE...
"THE GREATEST LUXURY IN THE ENTIRE WORLD—IS TO FORGIVE ANOTHER PERSON."
THE WORDS OF AN AMERICAN MAN WHO MURDERED TWENTY PEOPLE, JUST BEFORE HE WAS PUT TO DEATH.
AND WE CERTAINLY CAN'T FORGIVE ANYONE THIS DANGEROUS...
I'M SURE YOU WOULD AGREE, WOULDN'T YOU?

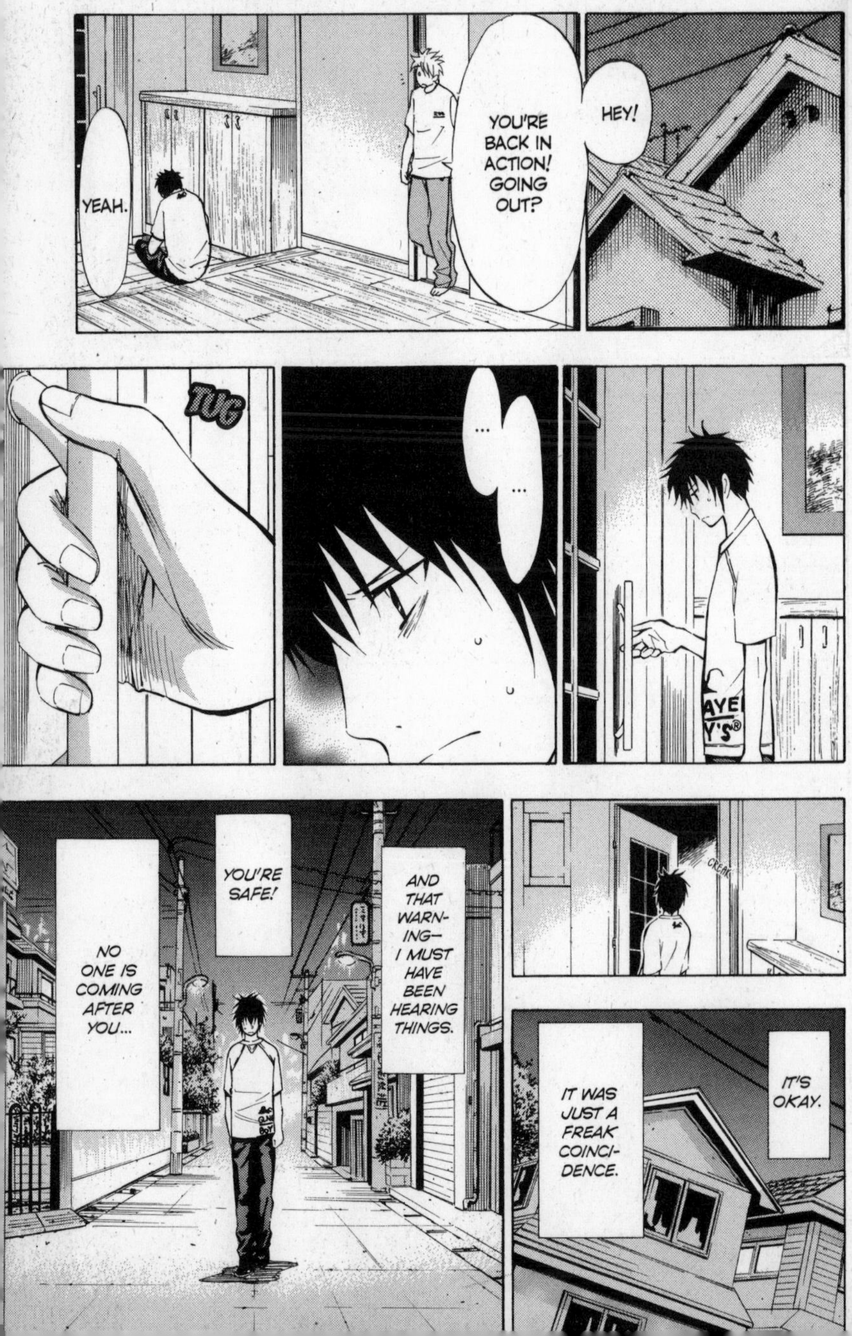
HEY!
YOU'RE BACK IN ACTION! GOING OUT?
YEAH.
...
...
TUG
CREAK
IT'S OKAY.
IT WAS JUST A FREAK COINCIDENCE.
AND THAT WARNING— I MUST HAVE BEEN HEARING THINGS.
YOU'RE SAFE!
NO ONE IS COMING AFTER YOU...

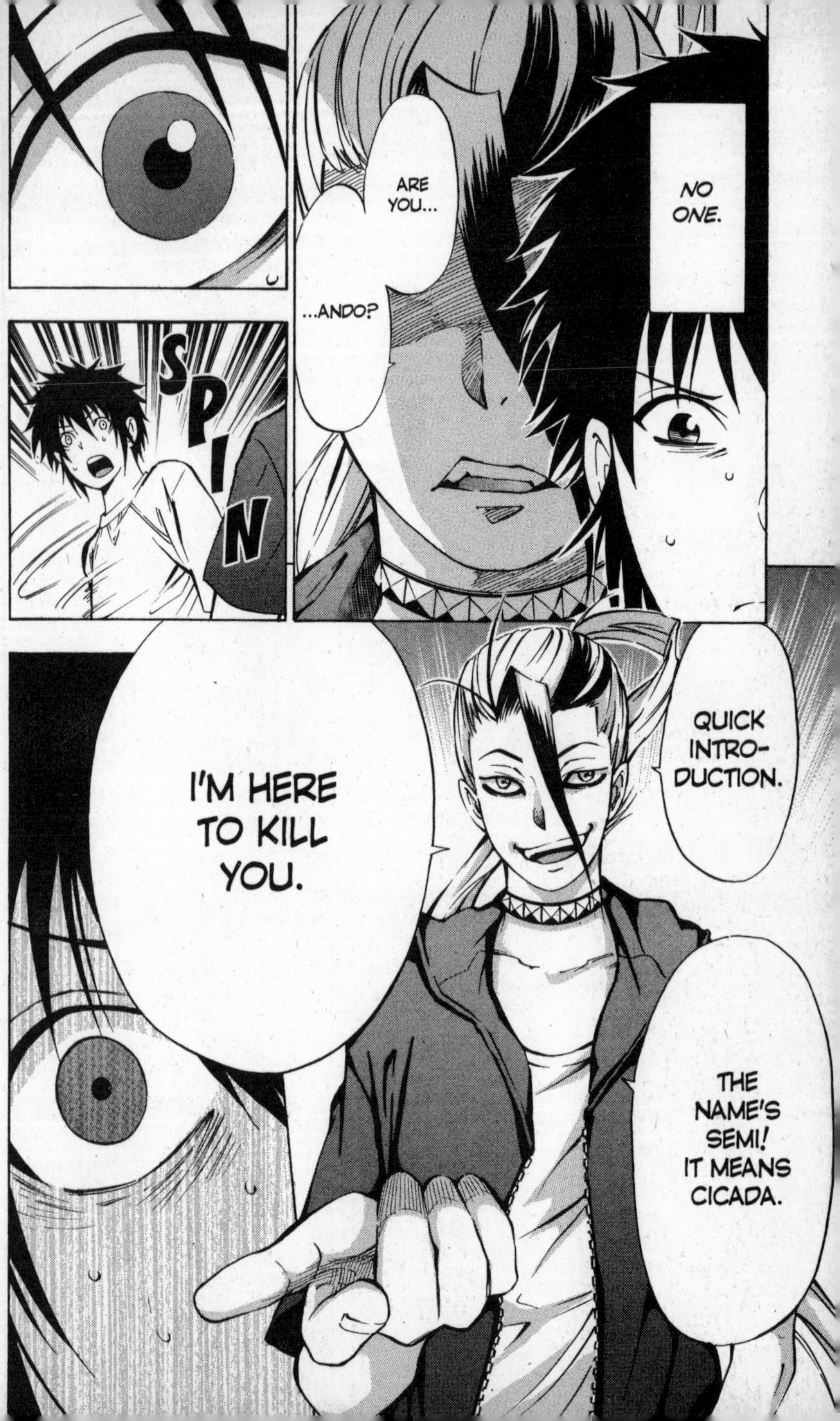
NO ONE.
ARE YOU...
...ANDO?
SPIN
QUICK INTRO-DUCTION.
THE NAME'S SEMI! IT MEANS CICADA.
I'M HERE TO KILL YOU.

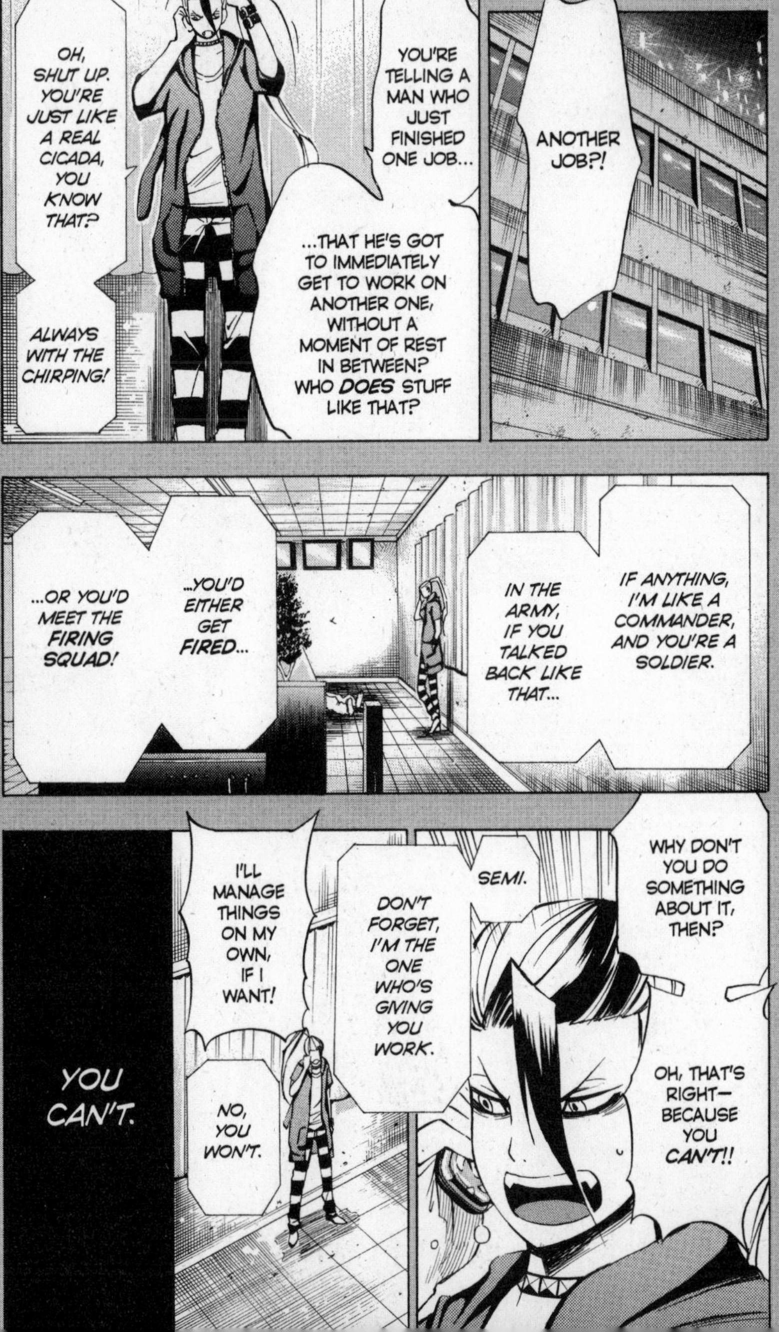
ANOTHER JOB?!
YOU'RE TELLING A MAN WHO JUST FINISHED ONE JOB...
...THAT HE'S GOT TO IMMEDIATELY GET TO WORK ON ANOTHER ONE, WITHOUT A MOMENT OF REST IN BETWEEN? WHO DOES STUFF LIKE THAT?
OH, SHUT UP. YOU'RE JUST LIKE A REAL CICADA, YOU KNOW THAT?
ALWAYS WITH THE CHIRPING!
IF ANYTHING, I'M LIKE A COMMANDER, AND YOU'RE A SOLDIER.
IN THE ARMY, IF YOU TALKED BACK LIKE THAT...
...YOU'D EITHER GET FIRED...
...OR YOU'D MEET THE FIRING SQUAD!
WHY DON'T YOU DO SOMETHING ABOUT IT, THEN?
OH, THAT'S RIGHT—BECAUSE YOU CAN'T!!
SEMI.
DON'T FORGET, I'M THE ONE WHO'S GIVING YOU WORK.
I'LL MANAGE THINGS ON MY OWN, IF I WANT!
NO, YOU WON'T.
YOU CAN'T.

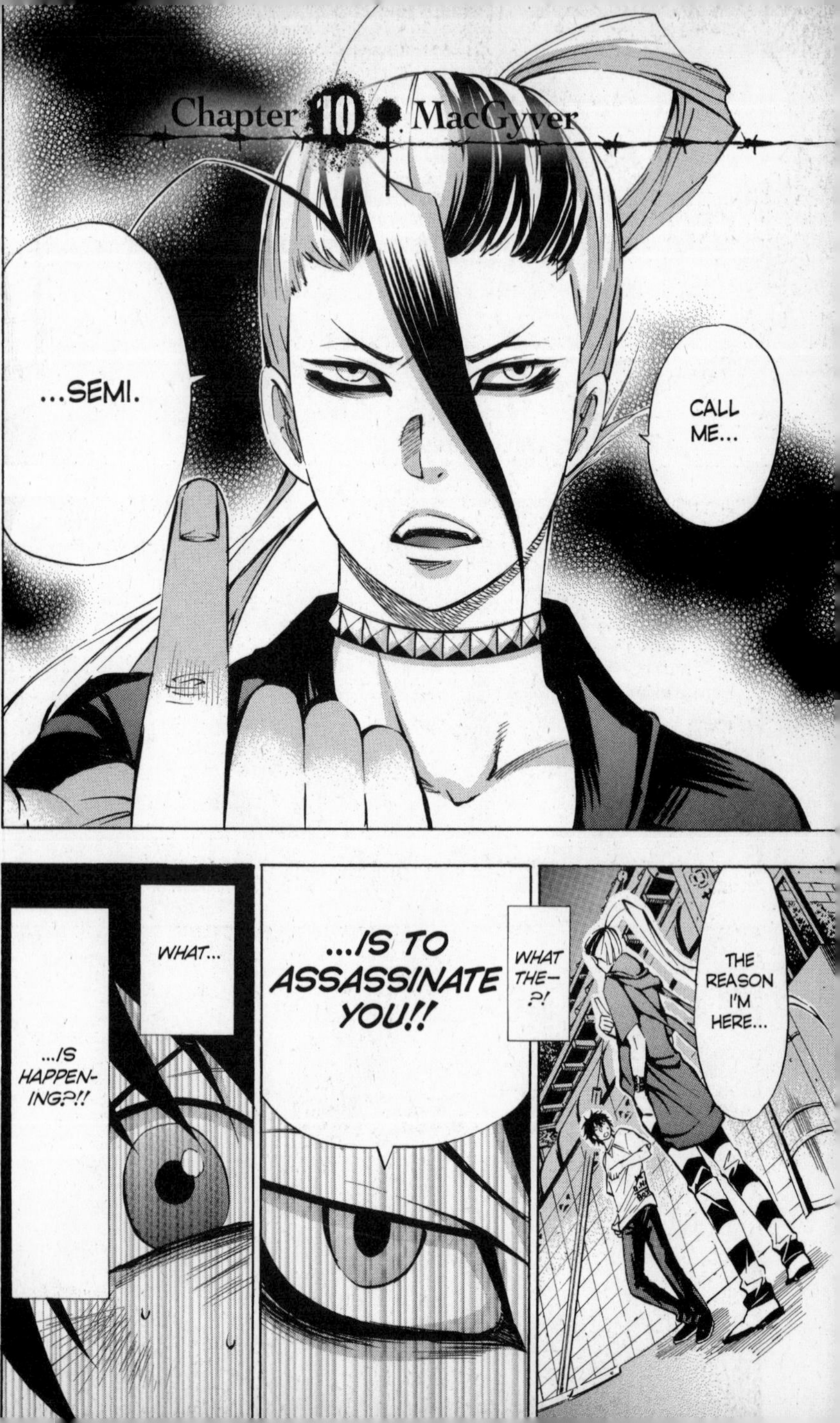
Chapter 10 • MacGyver
CALL ME...
...SEMI.
THE REASON I'M HERE...
WHAT THE—?!
...IS TO ASSASSINATE YOU!!
WHAT...
...IS HAPPENING?!!

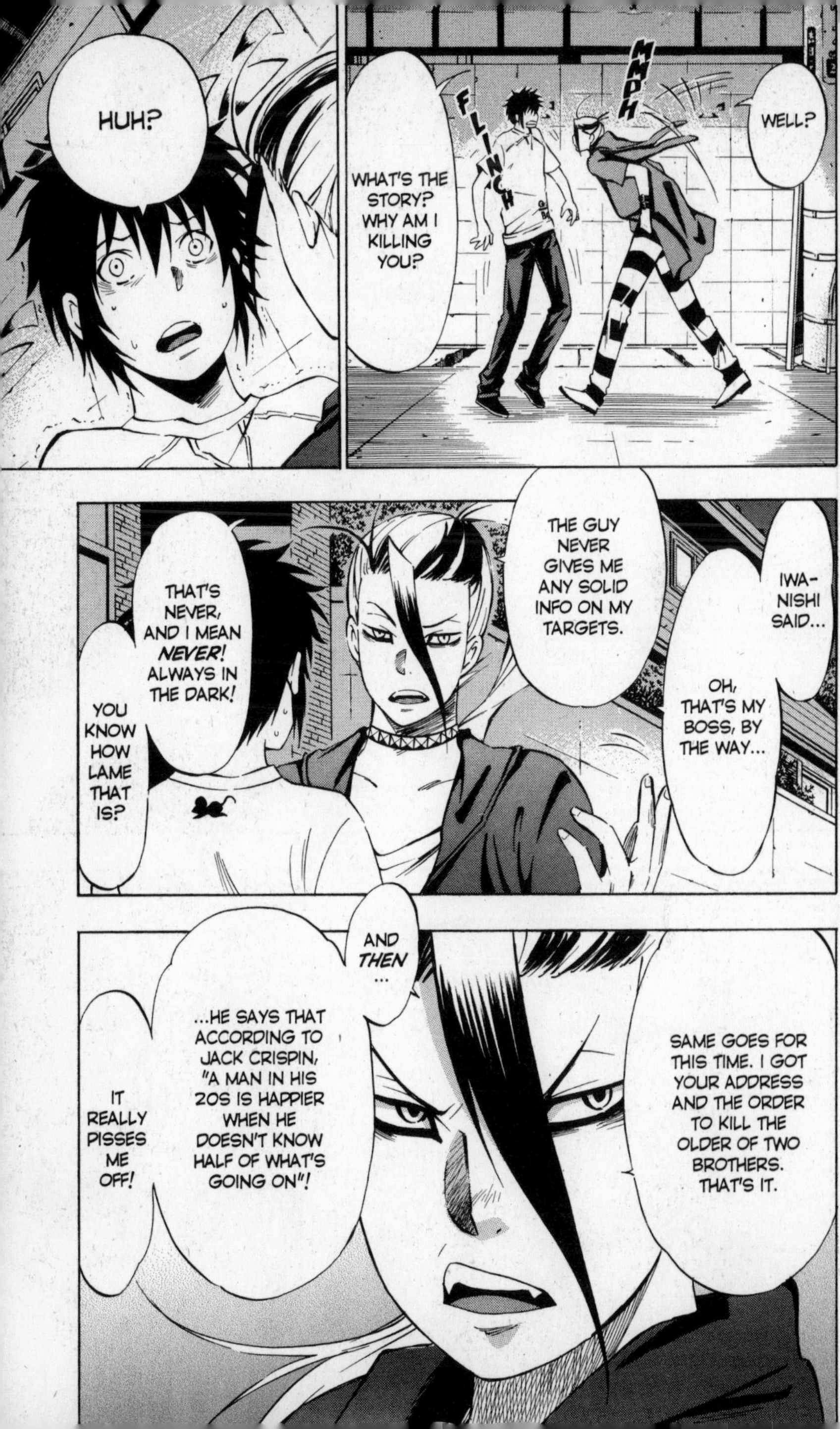
WELL?
MMPH
FLINCH
WHAT'S THE STORY? WHY AM I KILLING YOU?
HUH?
IWA-NISHI SAID...
OH, THAT'S MY BOSS, BY THE WAY...
THE GUY NEVER GIVES ME ANY SOLID INFO ON MY TARGETS.
THAT'S NEVER, AND I MEAN *NEVER*! ALWAYS IN THE DARK!
YOU KNOW HOW LAME THAT IS?
SAME GOES FOR THIS TIME. I GOT YOUR ADDRESS AND THE ORDER TO KILL THE OLDER OF TWO BROTHERS. THAT'S IT.
AND *THEN*...
...HE SAYS THAT ACCORDING TO JACK CRISPIN, "A MAN IN HIS 20S IS HAPPIER WHEN HE DOESN'T KNOW HALF OF WHAT'S GOING ON"!
IT REALLY PISSES ME OFF!

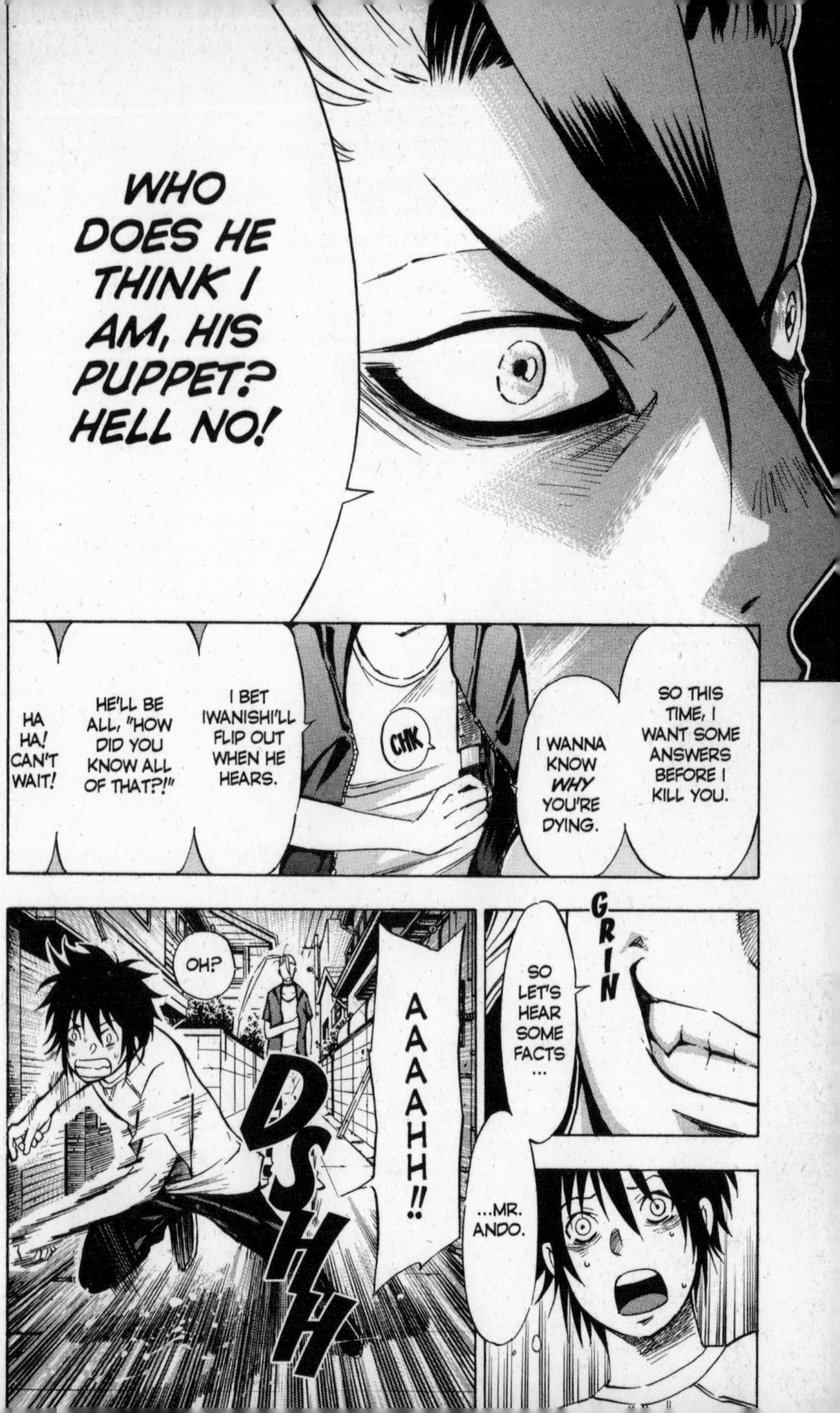
WHO DOES HE THINK I AM, HIS PUPPET? HELL NO!
SO THIS TIME, I WANT SOME ANSWERS BEFORE I KILL YOU.
I WANNA KNOW *WHY* YOU'RE DYING.
CHK
I BET IWANISHI'LL FLIP OUT WHEN HE HEARS.
HE'LL BE ALL, "HOW DID YOU KNOW ALL OF THAT?!"
HA HA! CAN'T WAIT!
GRIN
SO LET'S HEAR SOME FACTS...
...MR. ANDO.
AAAAAHH!!
DSHH
OH?

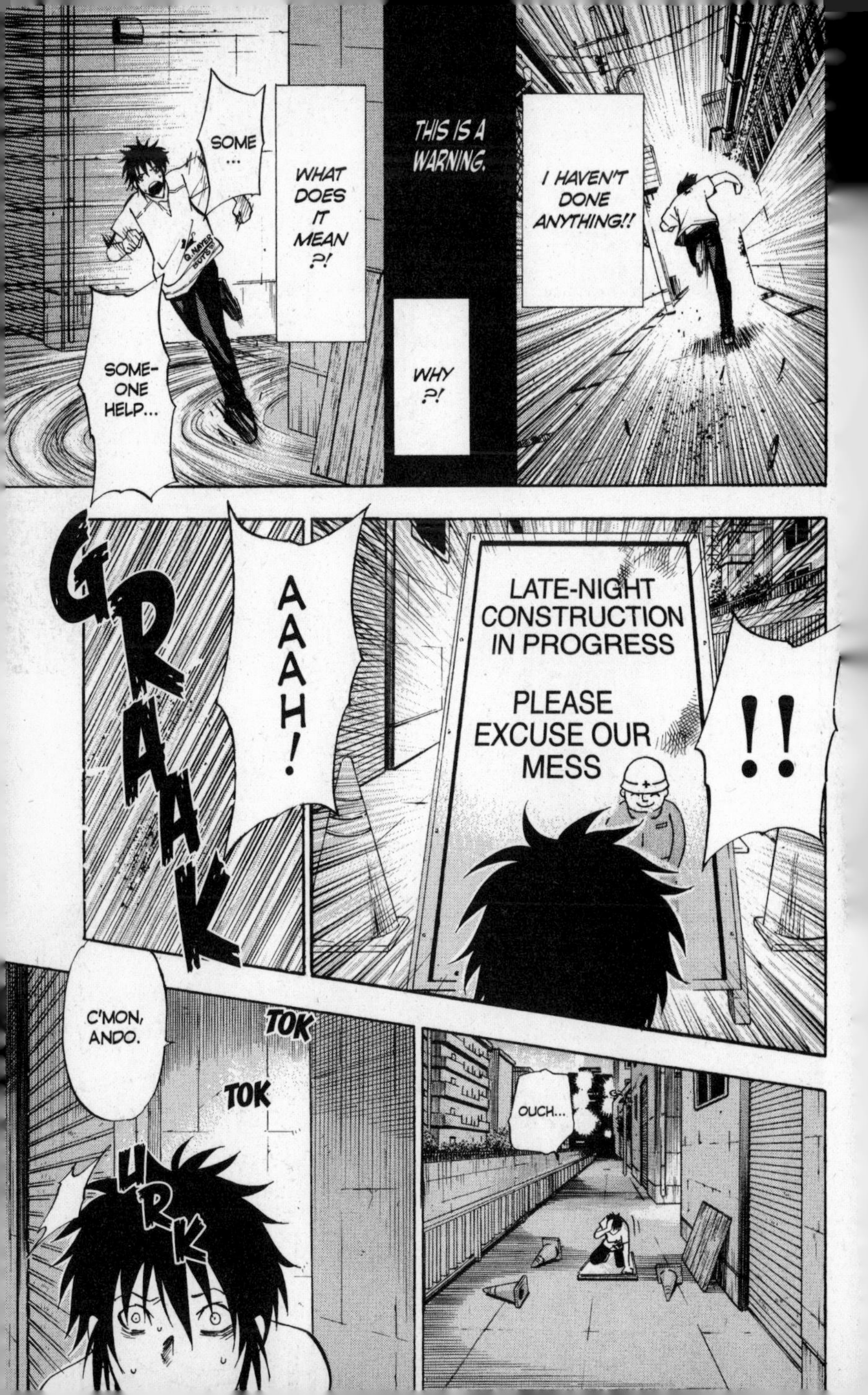
I HAVEN'T DONE ANYTHING!!
THIS IS A WARNING.
WHY ?!
WHAT DOES IT MEAN ?!
SOME ...
SOME-ONE HELP...
!!
LATE-NIGHT CONSTRUCTION IN PROGRESS
PLEASE EXCUSE OUR MESS
AAAH!
GRAAK
OUCH...
C'MON, ANDO.
TOK
TOK
URK

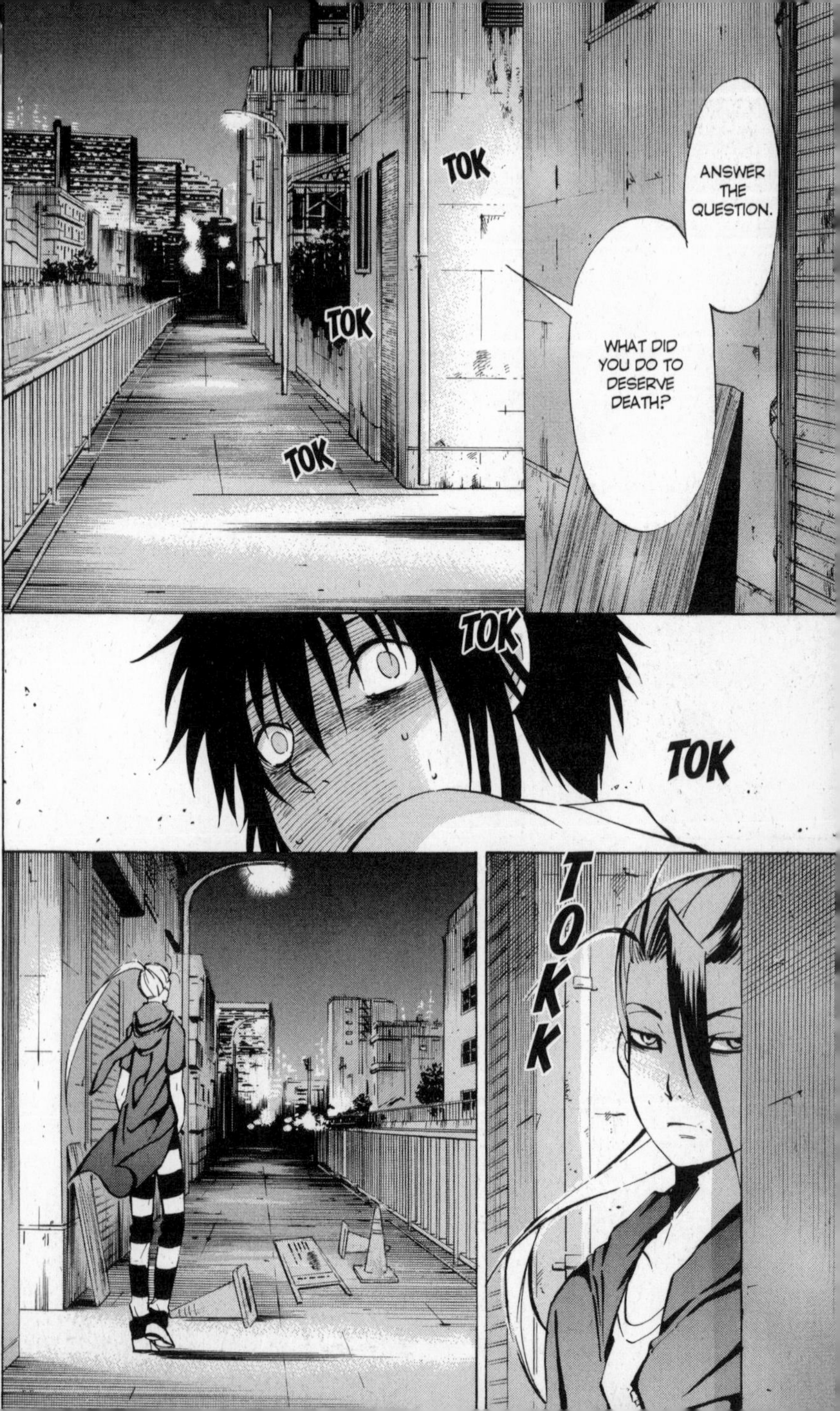
ANSWER THE QUESTION.
WHAT DID YOU DO TO DESERVE DEATH?
TOK
TOK
TOK
TOK
TOK
TOKK

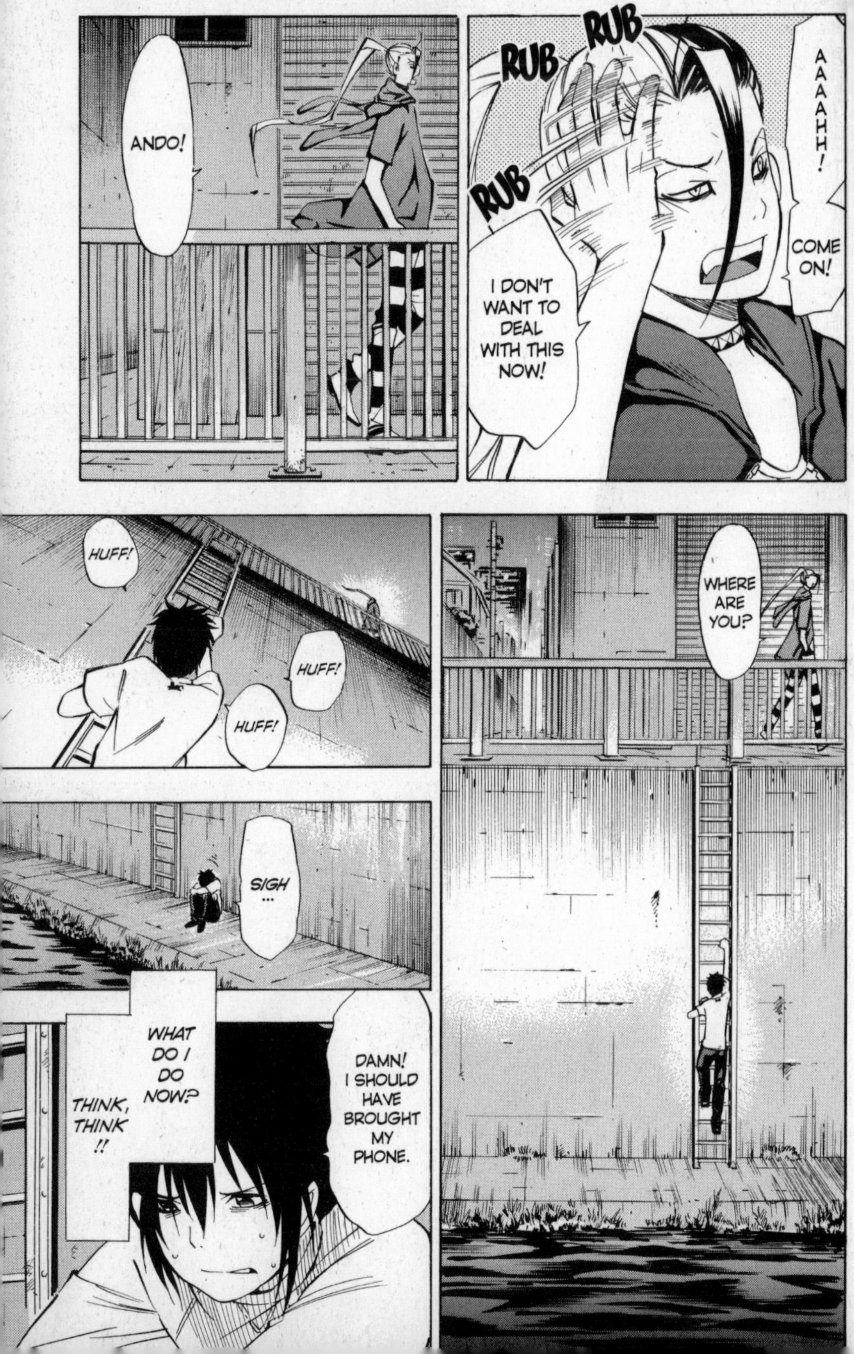
AAAAAHH!
RUB RUB
COME ON!
RUB
I DON'T WANT TO DEAL WITH THIS NOW!
ANDO!
WHERE ARE YOU?
HUFF!
HUFF!
HUFF!
SIGH...
DAMN! I SHOULD HAVE BROUGHT MY PHONE.
WHAT DO I DO NOW?
THINK, THINK!!

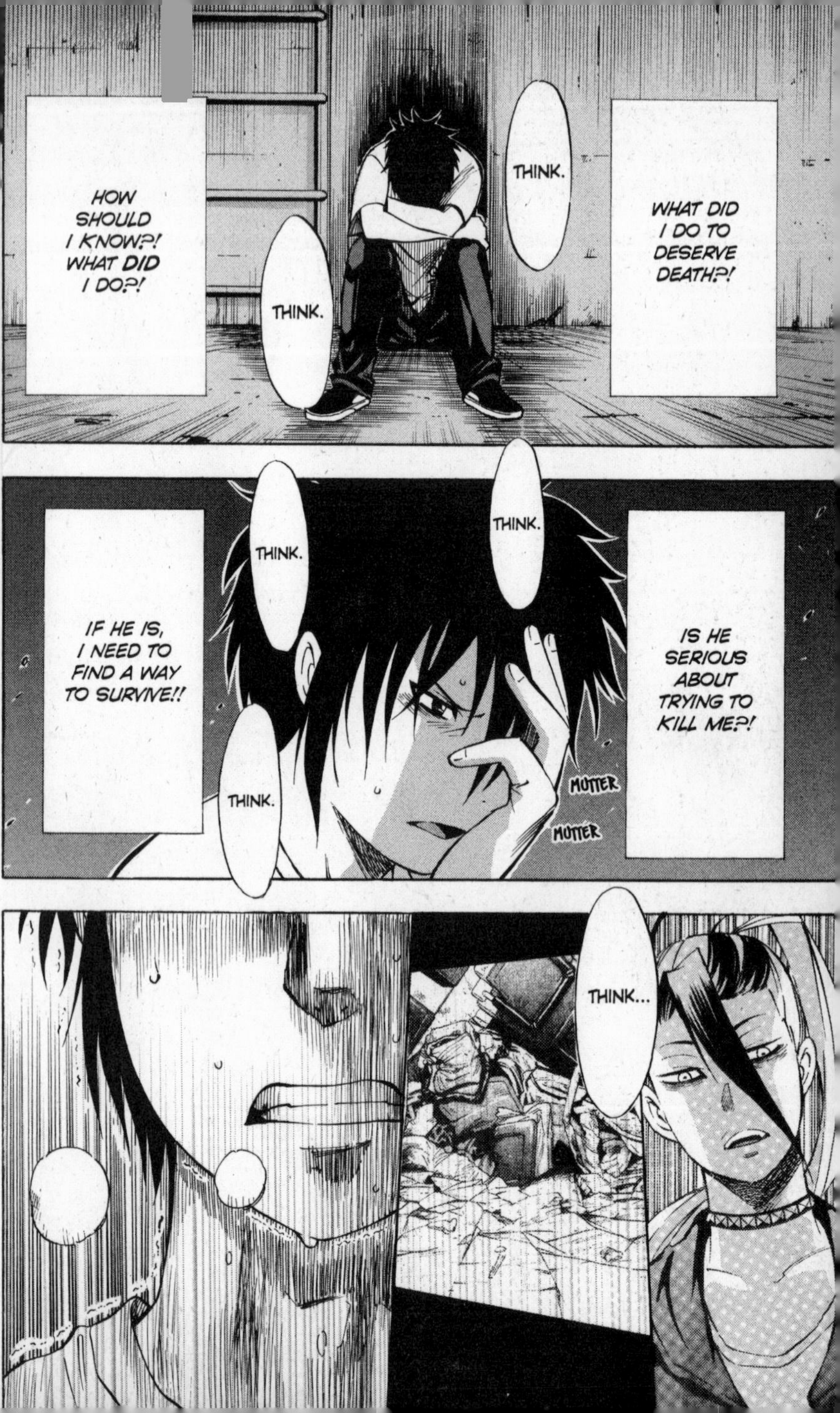
WHAT DID I DO TO DESERVE DEATH?!
THINK.
THINK.
HOW SHOULD I KNOW?! WHAT **DID** I DO?!
IS HE SERIOUS ABOUT TRYING TO KILL ME?!
THINK.
MUTTER
MUTTER
THINK.
IF HE IS, I NEED TO FIND A WAY TO SURVIVE!!
THINK.
THINK...

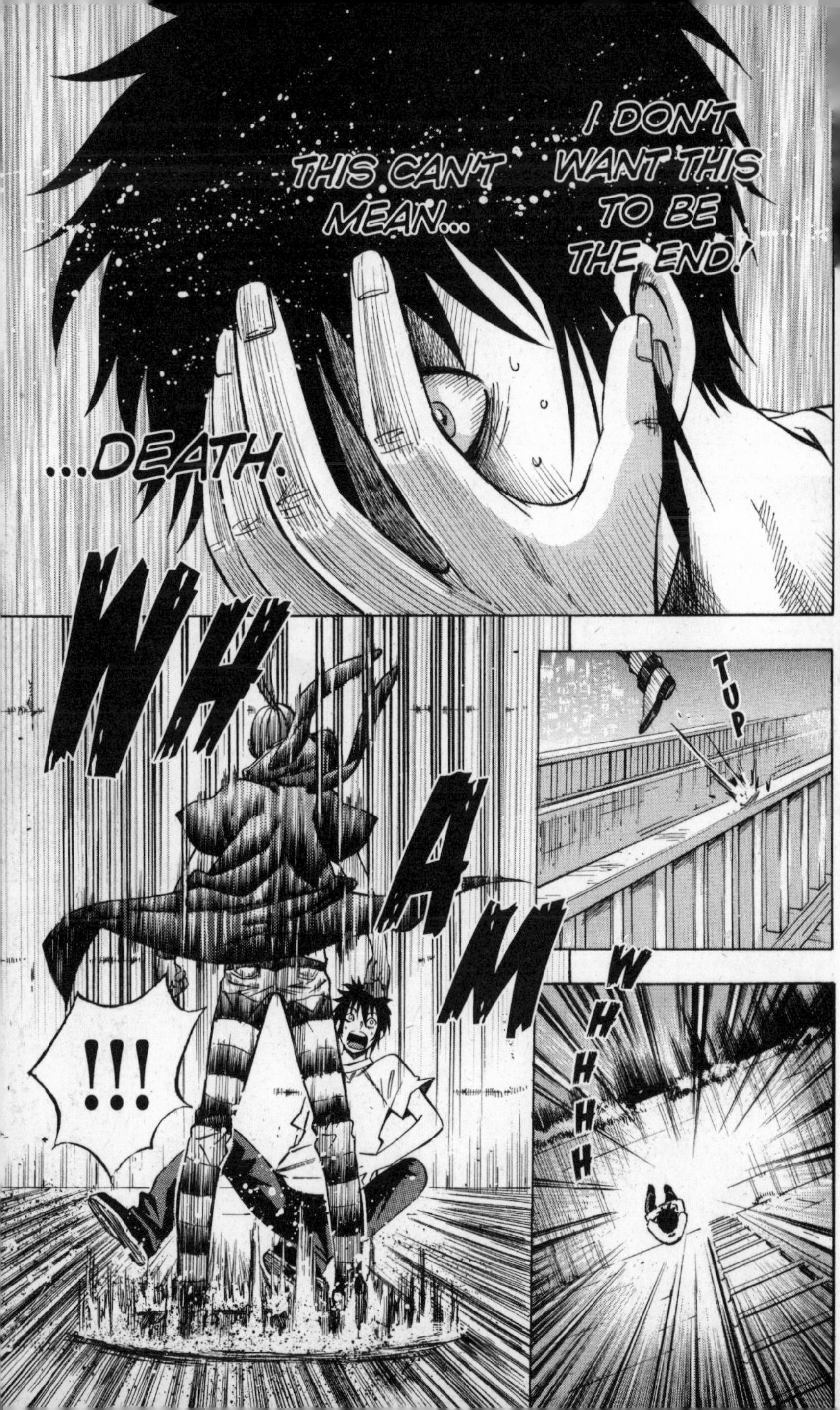
I DON'T WANT THIS TO BE THE END!
THIS CAN'T MEAN...
...DEATH.
TUP
WHHHHHH
WHAM
!!!

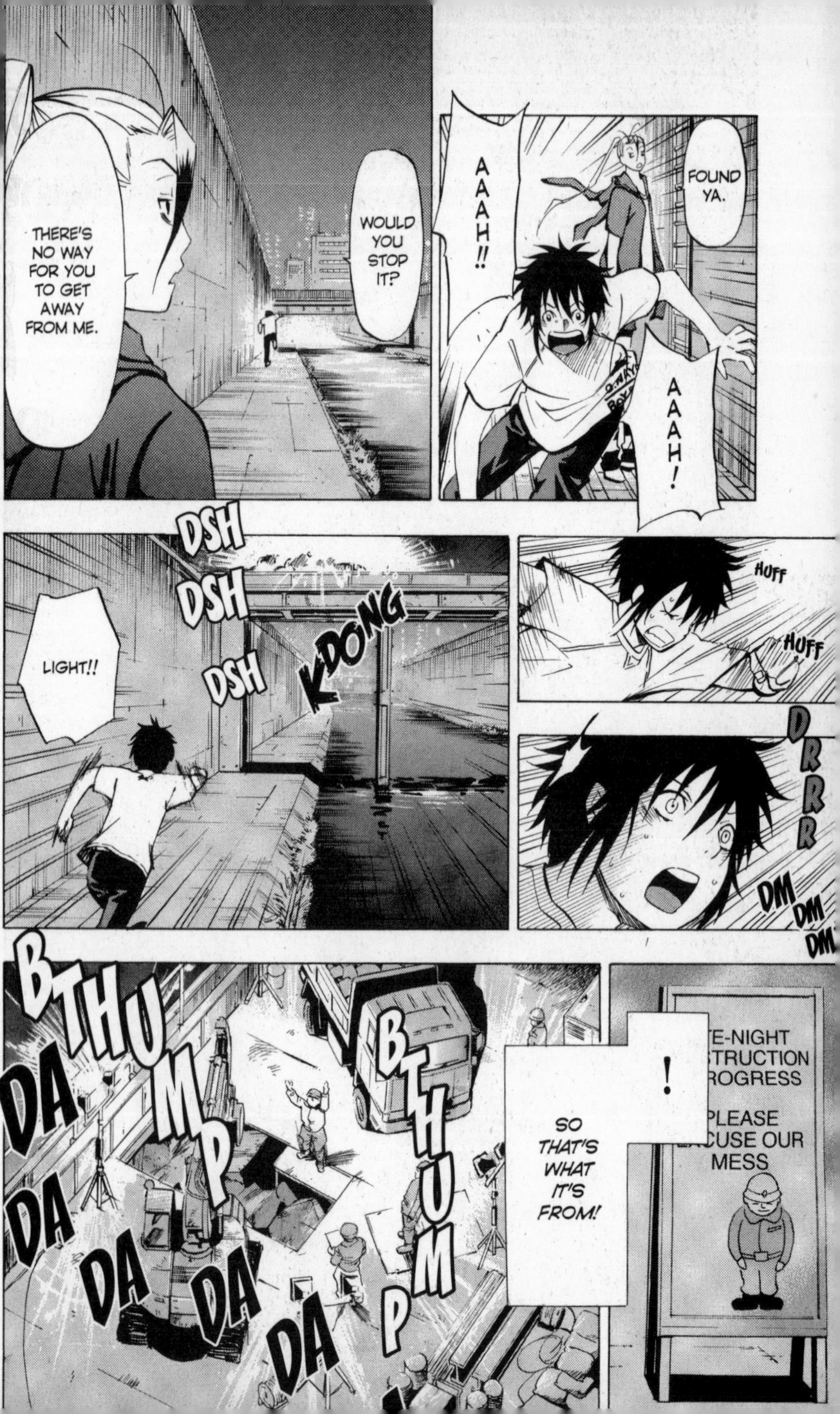
FOUND YA.
AAAH!!
AAAH!
WOULD YOU STOP IT?
THERE'S NO WAY FOR YOU TO GET AWAY FROM ME.
HUFF
HUFF
DRRR
DM DM DM
DSH DSH DSH
KDONG
LIGHT!!
TE-NIGHT
STRUCTION
ROGRESS
PLEASE
CUSE OUR
MESS
!
SO THAT'S WHAT IT'S FROM!
BTHUMP
DA DA DA DA DA
BTHUMP

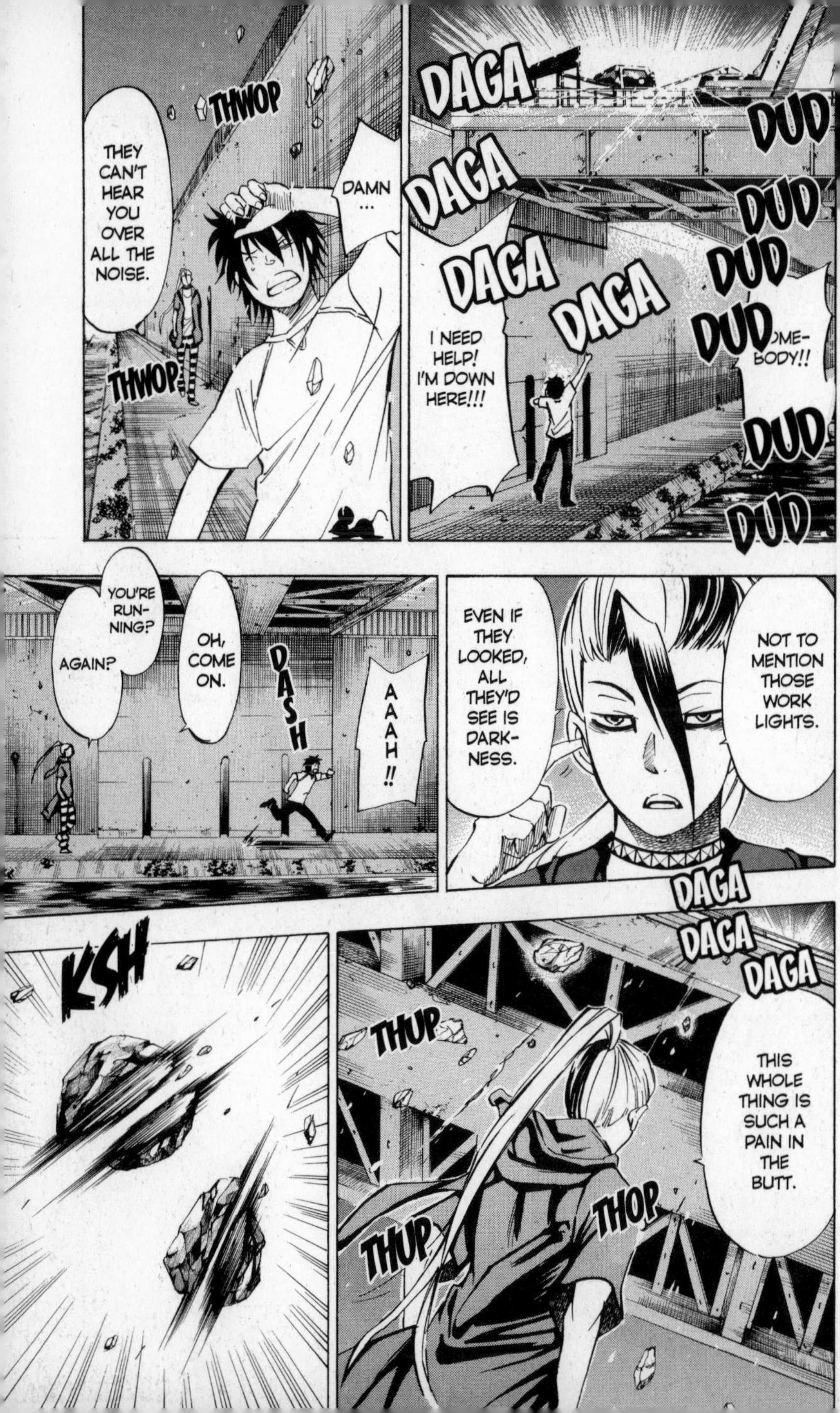
DAGA
DAGA
DAGA
DAGA
DUD
DUD
DUD
DUD
DUD
DUD
I NEED HELP! I'M DOWN HERE!!!
OME-BODY!!
THWOP
DAMN ...
THEY CAN'T HEAR YOU OVER ALL THE NOISE.
THWOP
NOT TO MENTION THOSE WORK LIGHTS.
EVEN IF THEY LOOKED, ALL THEY'D SEE IS DARKNESS.
AAAH!!
DASH
OH, COME ON.
YOU'RE RUN-NING?
AGAIN?
DAGA
DAGA
DAGA
THIS WHOLE THING IS SUCH A PAIN IN THE BUTT.
THUP
THOP
THUP
KSH

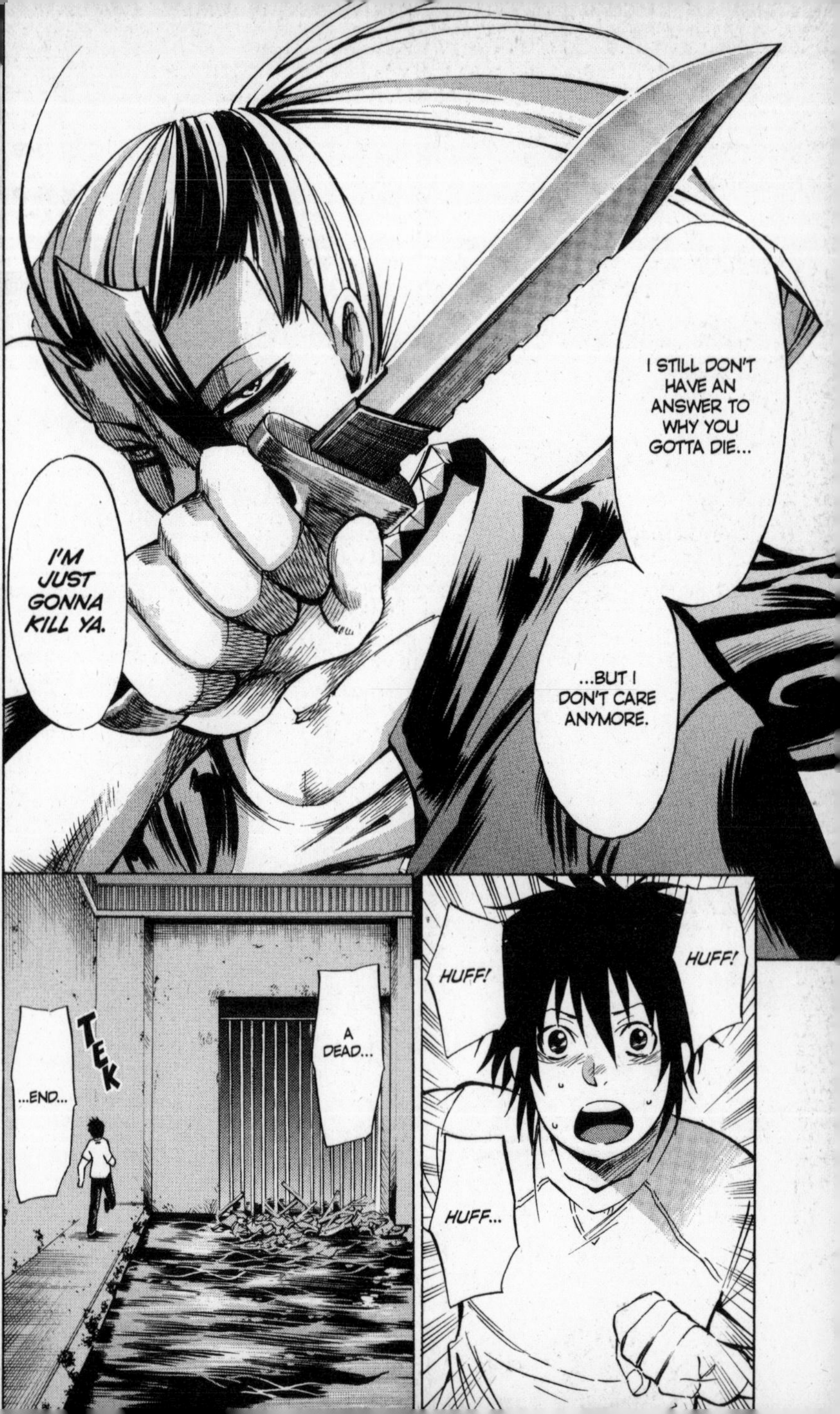
I STILL DON'T HAVE AN ANSWER TO WHY YOU GOTTA DIE...
...BUT I DON'T CARE ANYMORE.
I'M JUST GONNA KILL YA.
HUFF!
HUFF!
HUFF...
A DEAD...
TEK
...END...

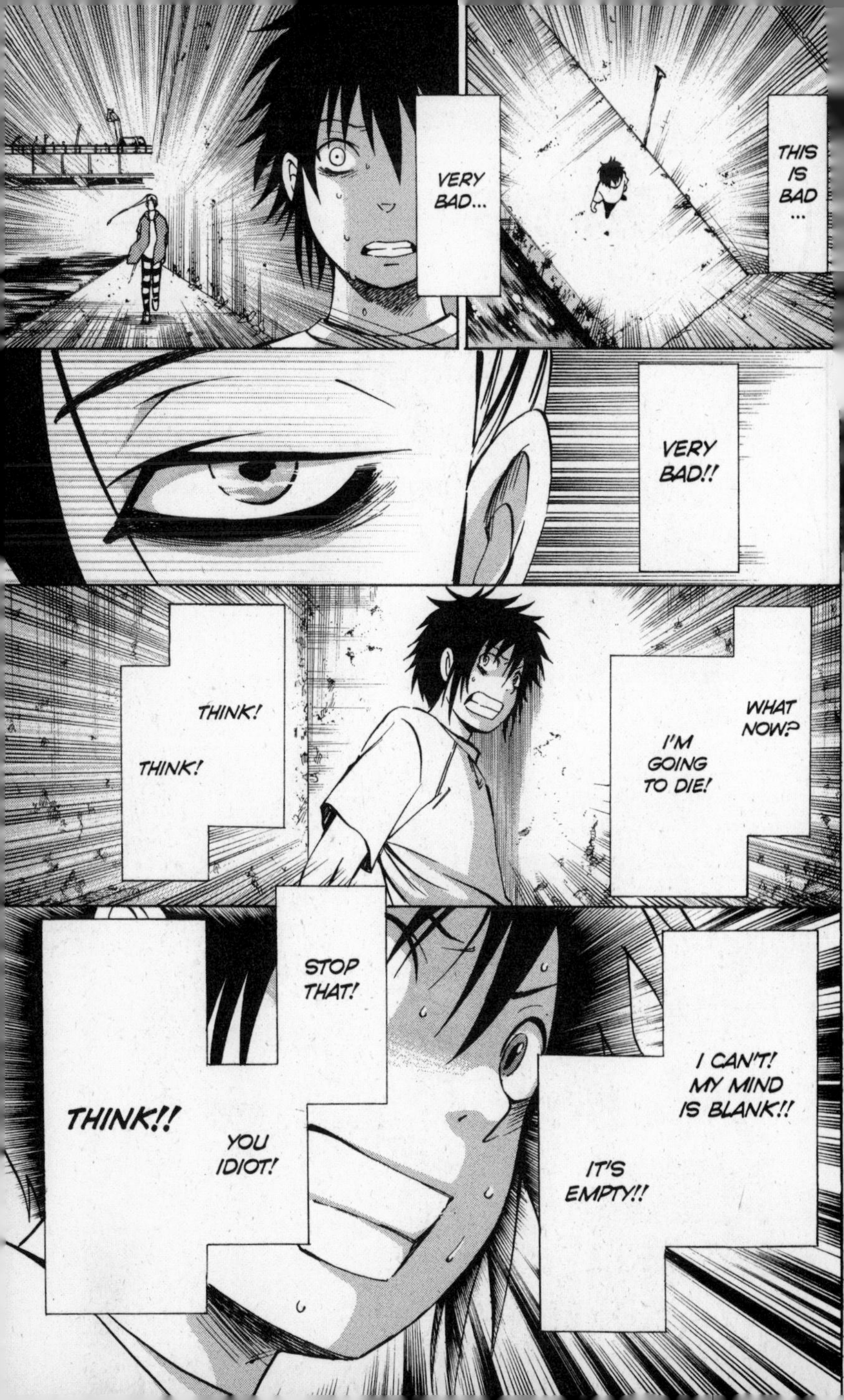
THIS IS BAD ...
VERY BAD...
VERY BAD!!
WHAT NOW?
I'M GOING TO DIE!
THINK!
THINK!
I CAN'T! MY MIND IS BLANK!!
IT'S EMPTY!!
STOP THAT!
YOU IDIOT!
THINK!!

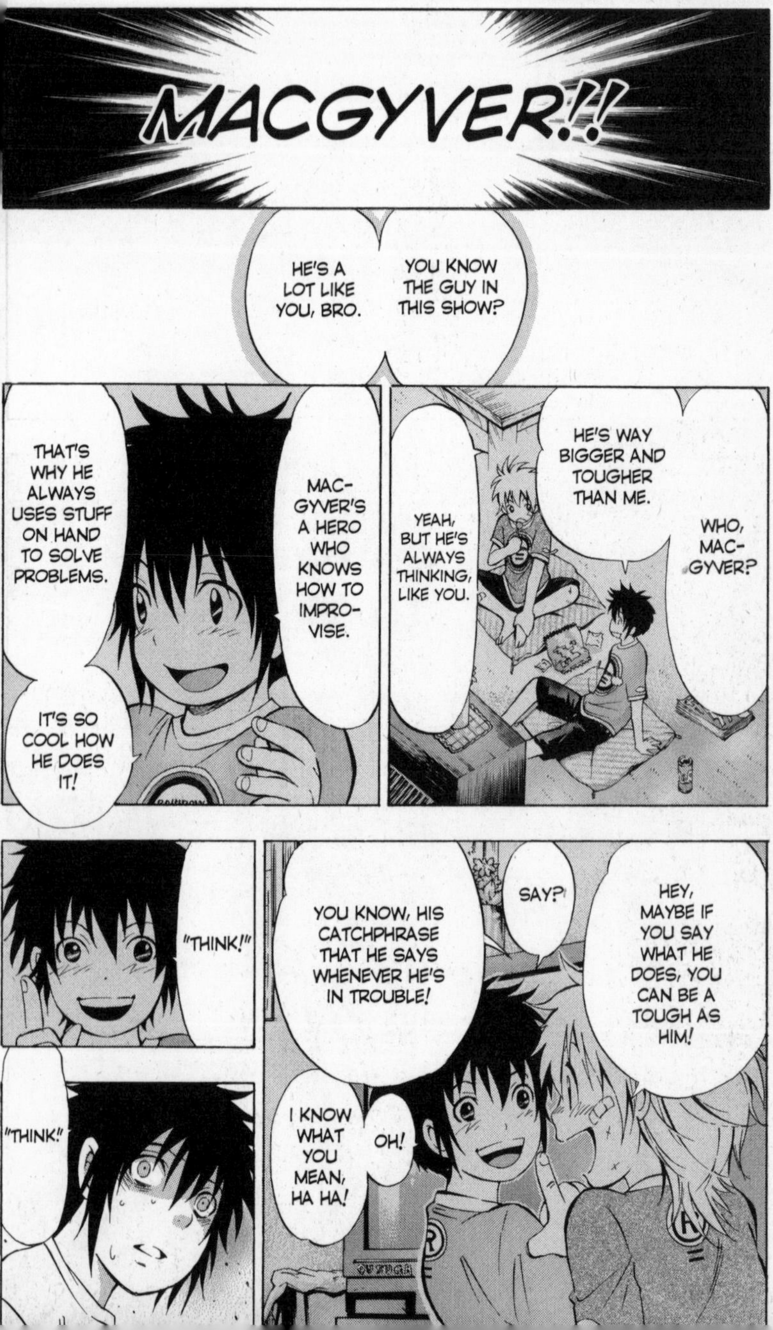
MACGYVER!!
YOU KNOW THE GUY IN THIS SHOW?
HE'S A LOT LIKE YOU, BRO.
WHO, MAC-GYVER?
HE'S WAY BIGGER AND TOUGHER THAN ME.
YEAH, BUT HE'S ALWAYS THINKING, LIKE YOU.
MAC-GYVER'S A HERO WHO KNOWS HOW TO IMPRO-VISE.
THAT'S WHY HE ALWAYS USES STUFF ON HAND TO SOLVE PROBLEMS.
IT'S SO COOL HOW HE DOES IT!
HEY, MAYBE IF YOU SAY WHAT HE DOES, YOU CAN BE A TOUGH AS HIM!
SAY?
YOU KNOW, HIS CATCHPHRASE THAT HE SAYS WHENEVER HE'S IN TROUBLE!
OH!
I KNOW WHAT YOU MEAN, HA HA!
"THINK!"
"THINK!"

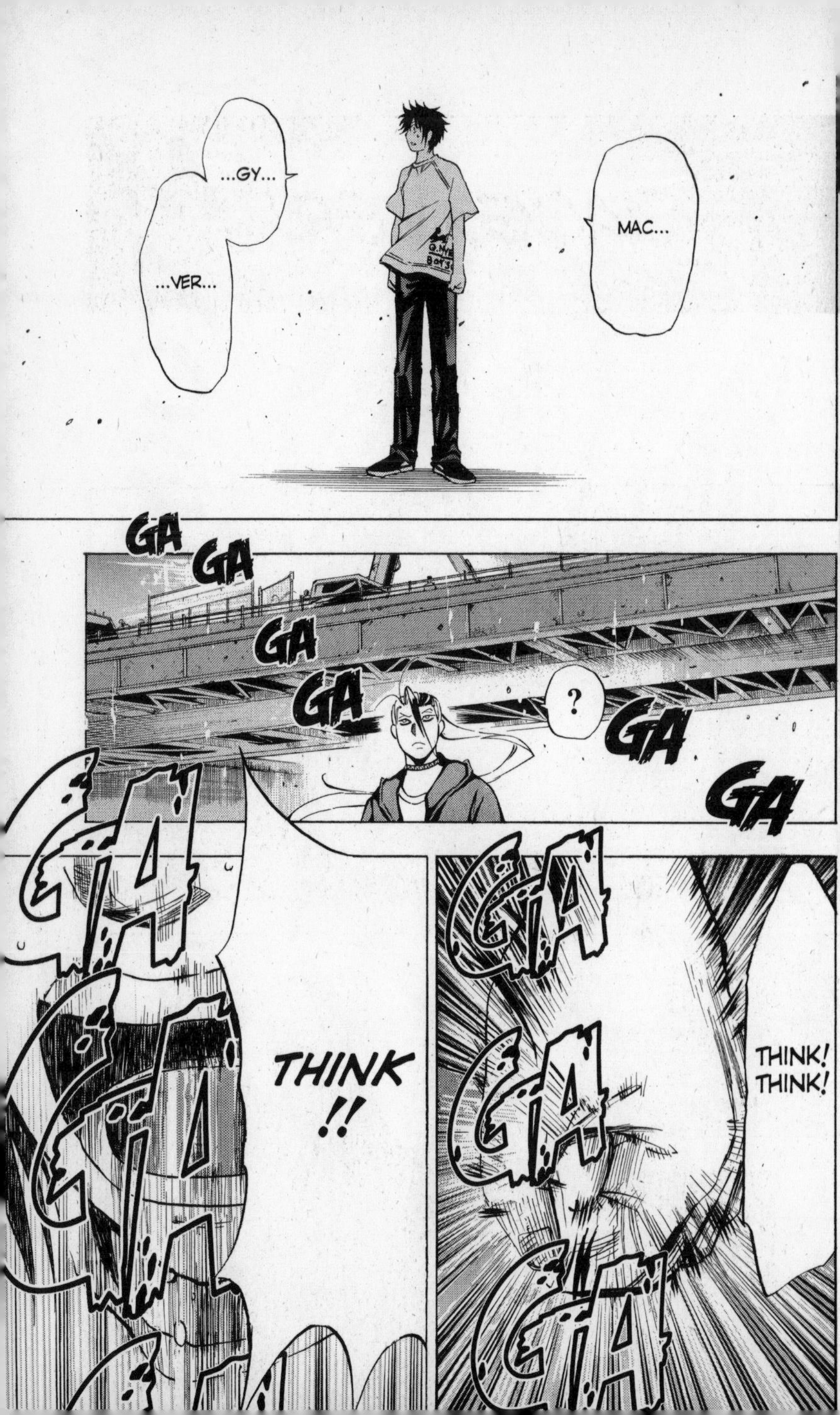
MAC...
...GY...
...VER...
GA
GA
GA
GA
?
GA
GA
THINK! THINK!
GA
GA
GA
THINK !!
GA
GA

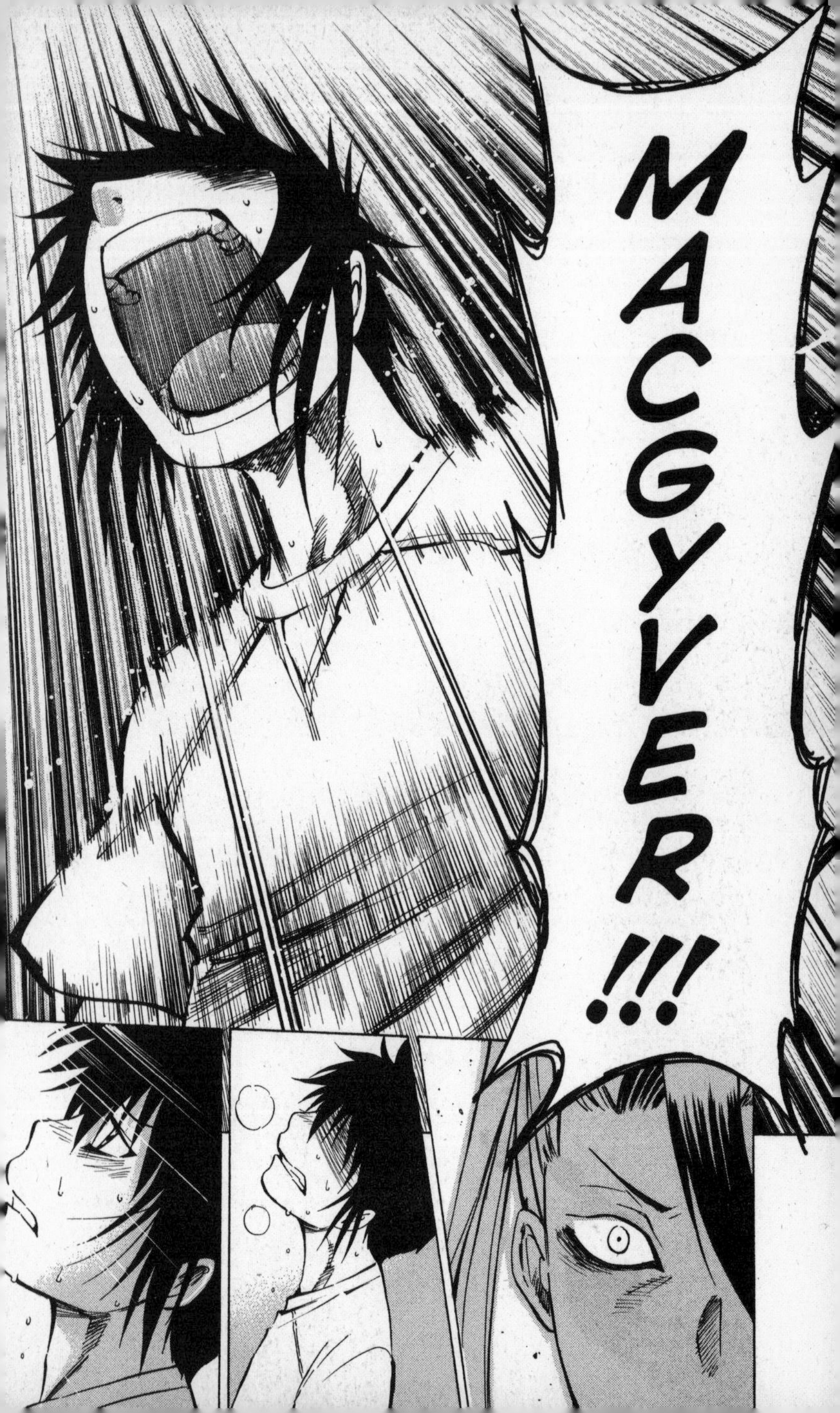
MACGYVER!!!

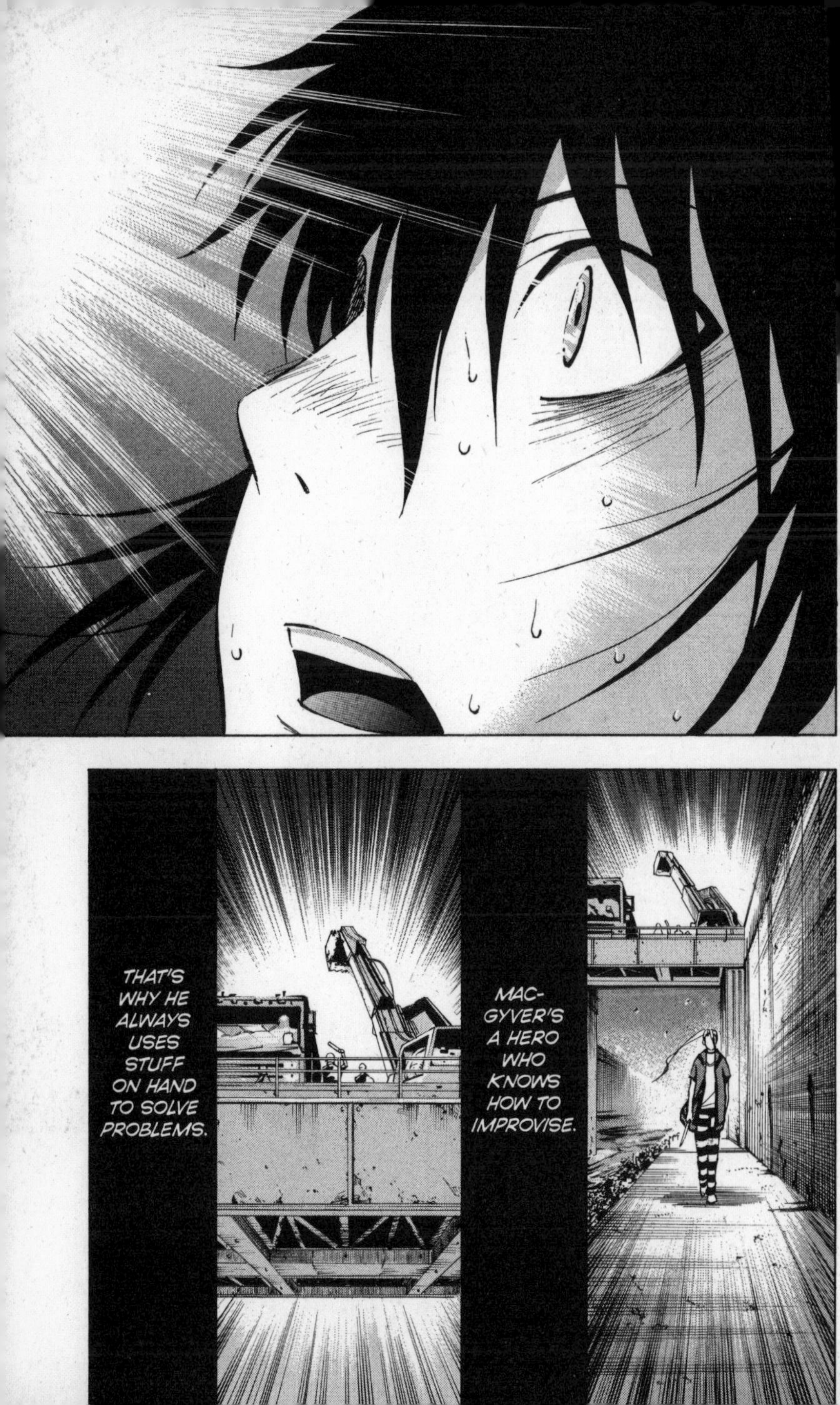
MAC-GYVER'S A HERO WHO KNOWS HOW TO IMPROVISE.
THAT'S WHY HE ALWAYS USES STUFF ON HAND TO SOLVE PROBLEMS.

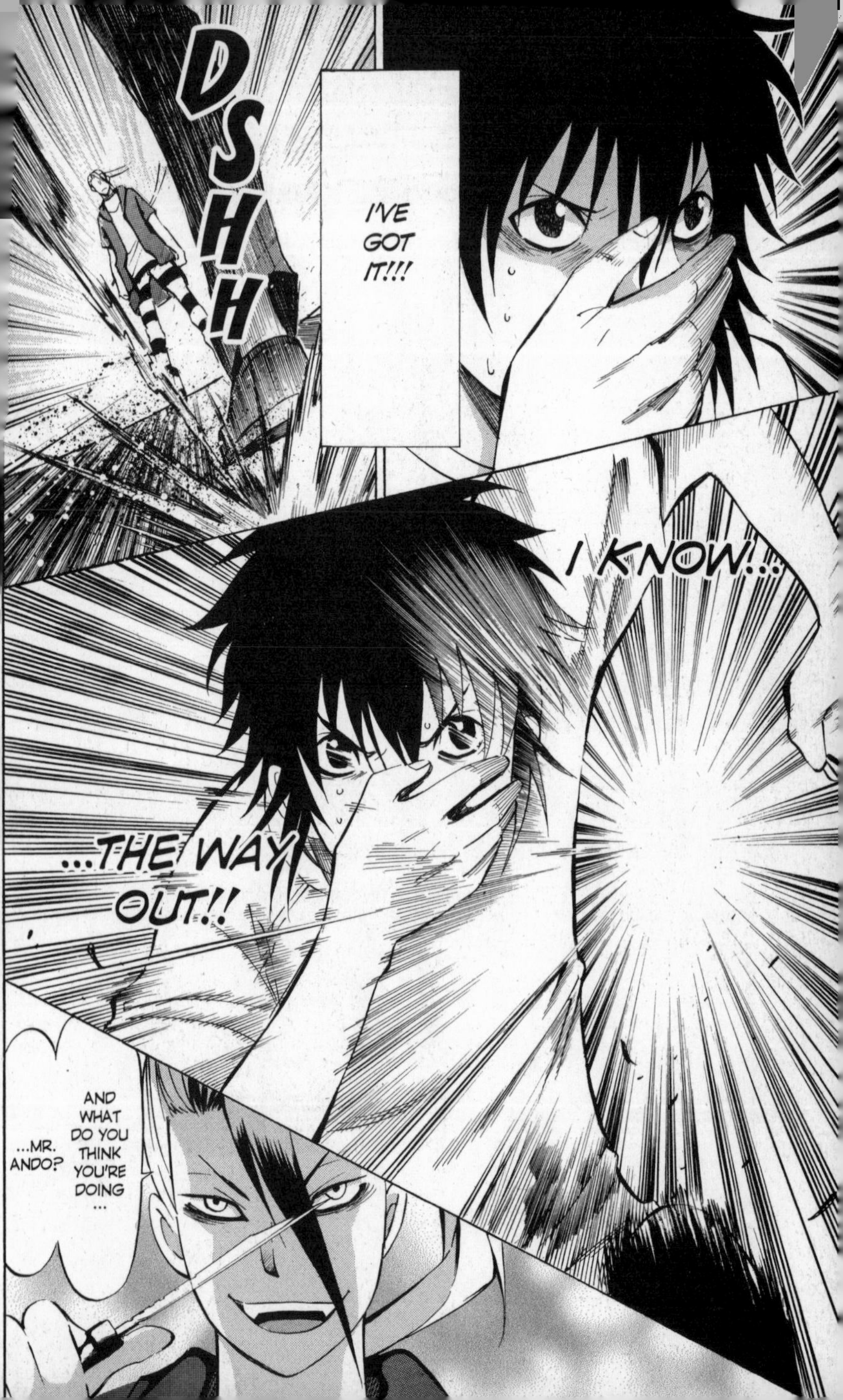
I'VE GOT IT!!!
DSHH
I KNOW...
...THE WAY OUT!!
AND WHAT DO YOU THINK YOU'RE DOING ...
...MR. ANDO?

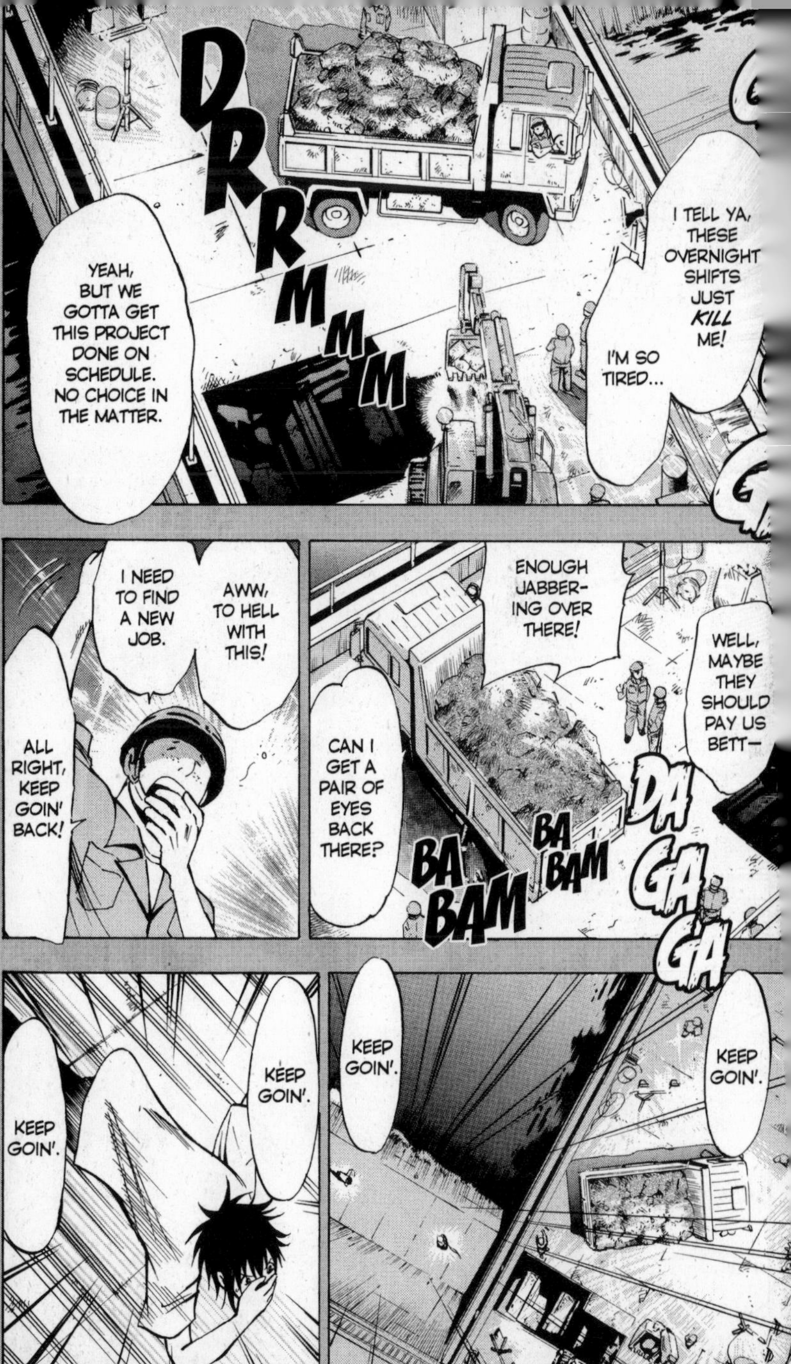
I TELL YA, THESE OVERNIGHT SHIFTS JUST KILL ME!
I'M SO TIRED...
DRRMMMM
YEAH, BUT WE GOTTA GET THIS PROJECT DONE ON SCHEDULE. NO CHOICE IN THE MATTER.
ENOUGH JABBERING OVER THERE!
WELL, MAYBE THEY SHOULD PAY US BETT—
DAGAGA
BABAM
BABAM
CAN I GET A PAIR OF EYES BACK THERE?
AWW, TO HELL WITH THIS!
I NEED TO FIND A NEW JOB.
ALL RIGHT, KEEP GOIN' BACK!
KEEP GOIN'.
KEEP GOIN'.
KEEP GOIN'.
KEEP GOIN'.

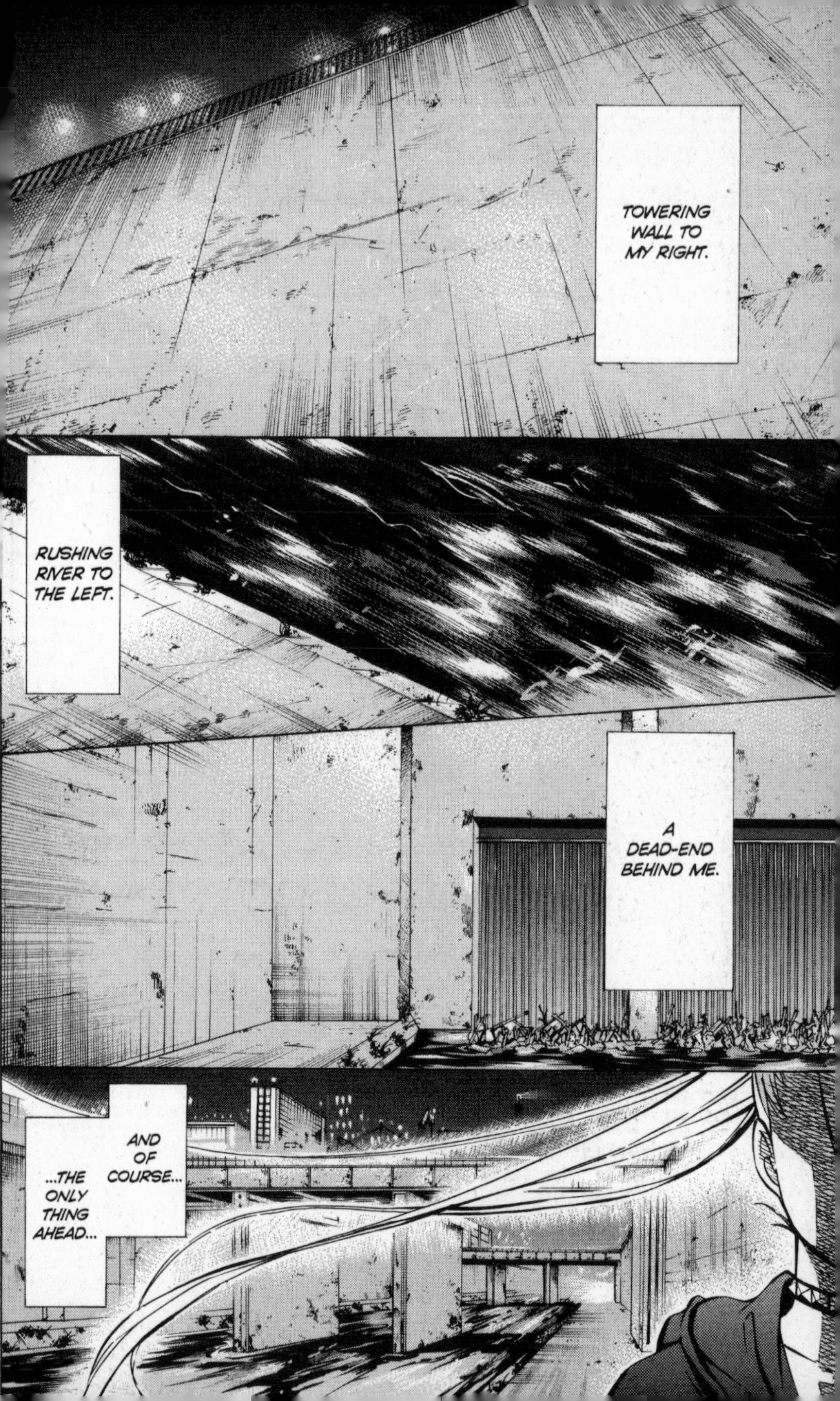
TOWERING WALL TO MY RIGHT.
RUSHING RIVER TO THE LEFT.
A DEAD-END BEHIND ME.
AND OF COURSE...
...THE ONLY THING AHEAD...

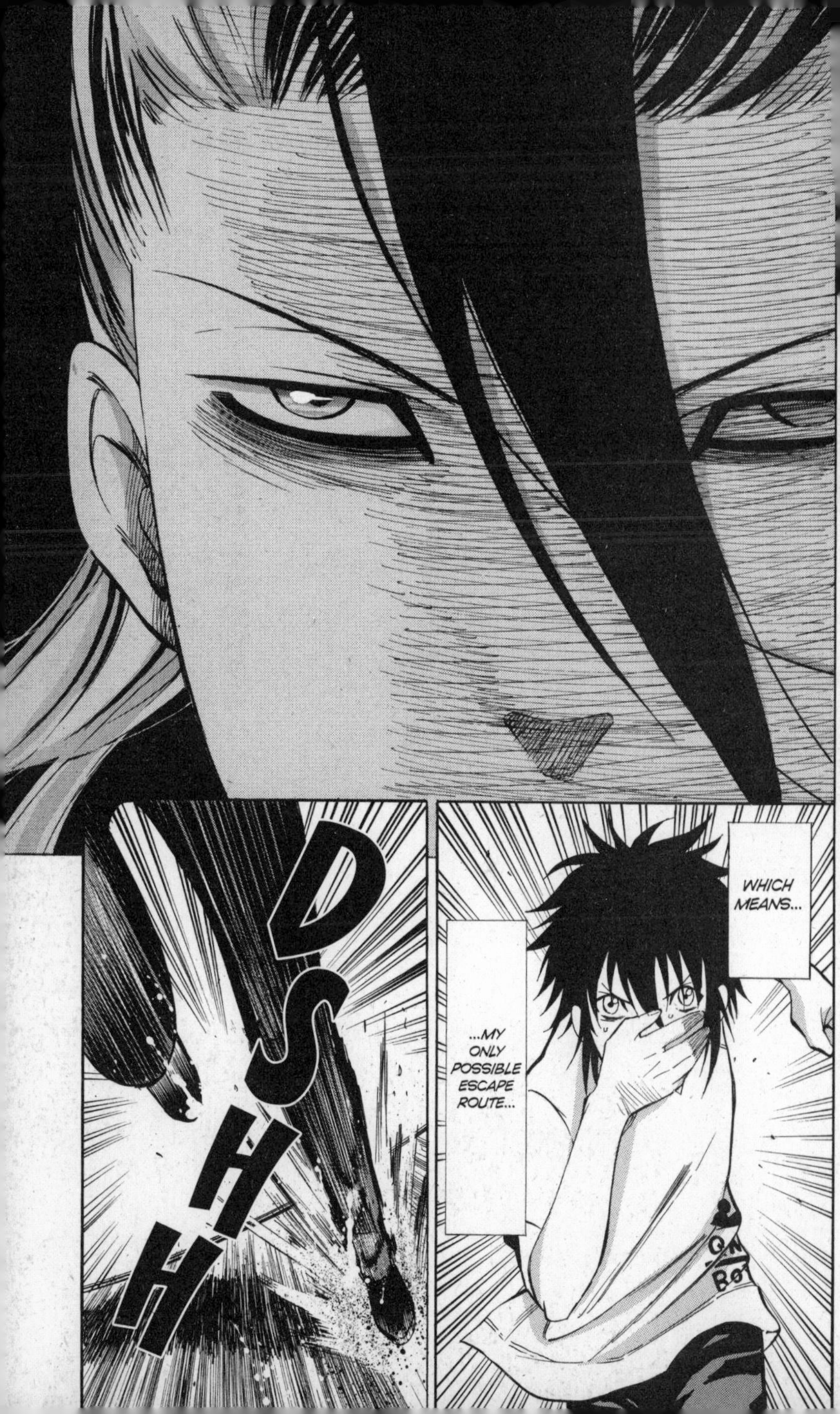

WHICH MEANS...
...MY ONLY POSSIBLE ESCAPE ROUTE...
DSHHH

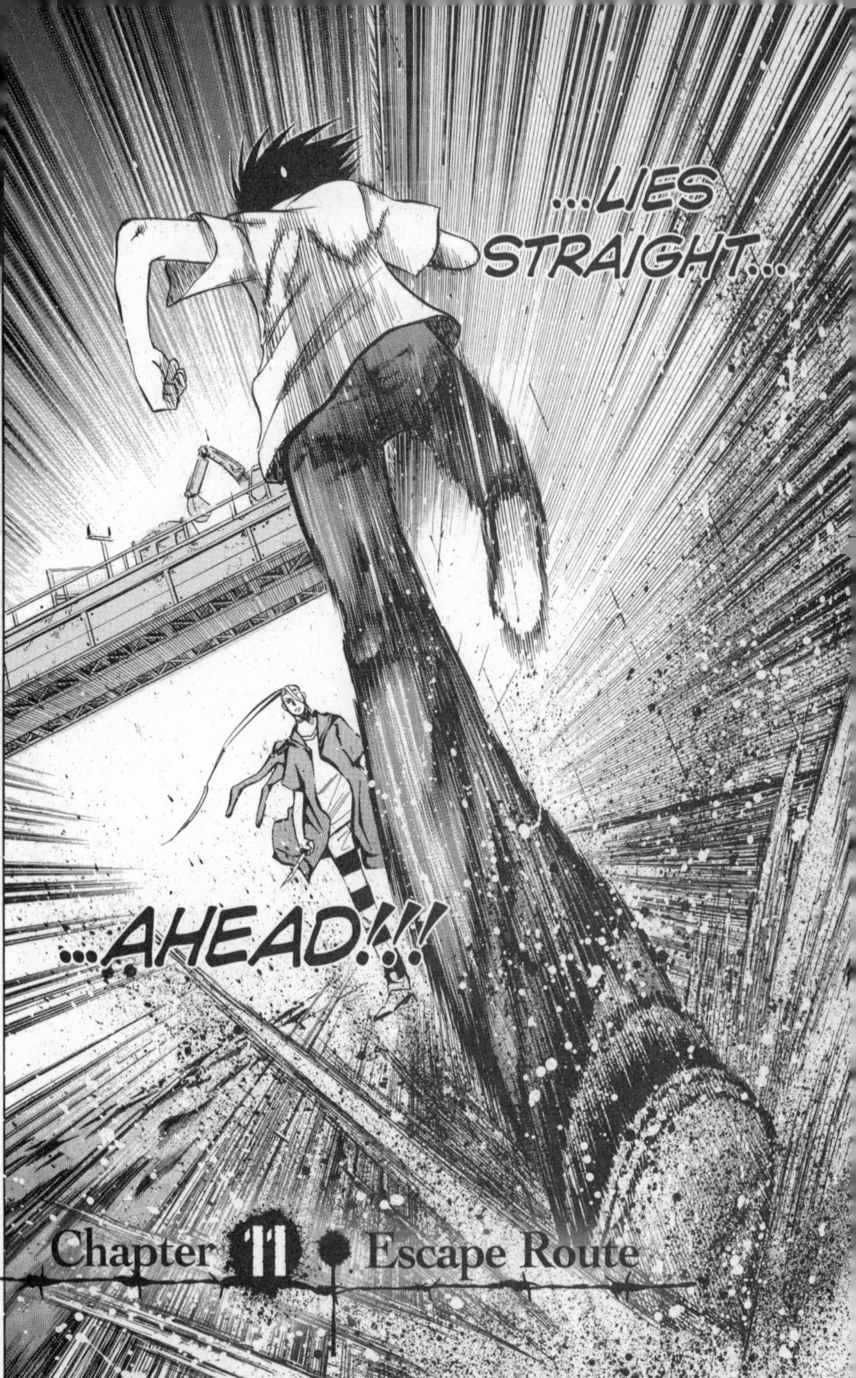
...LIES STRAIGHT...
...AHEAD!!!

Chapter 11 • Escape Route

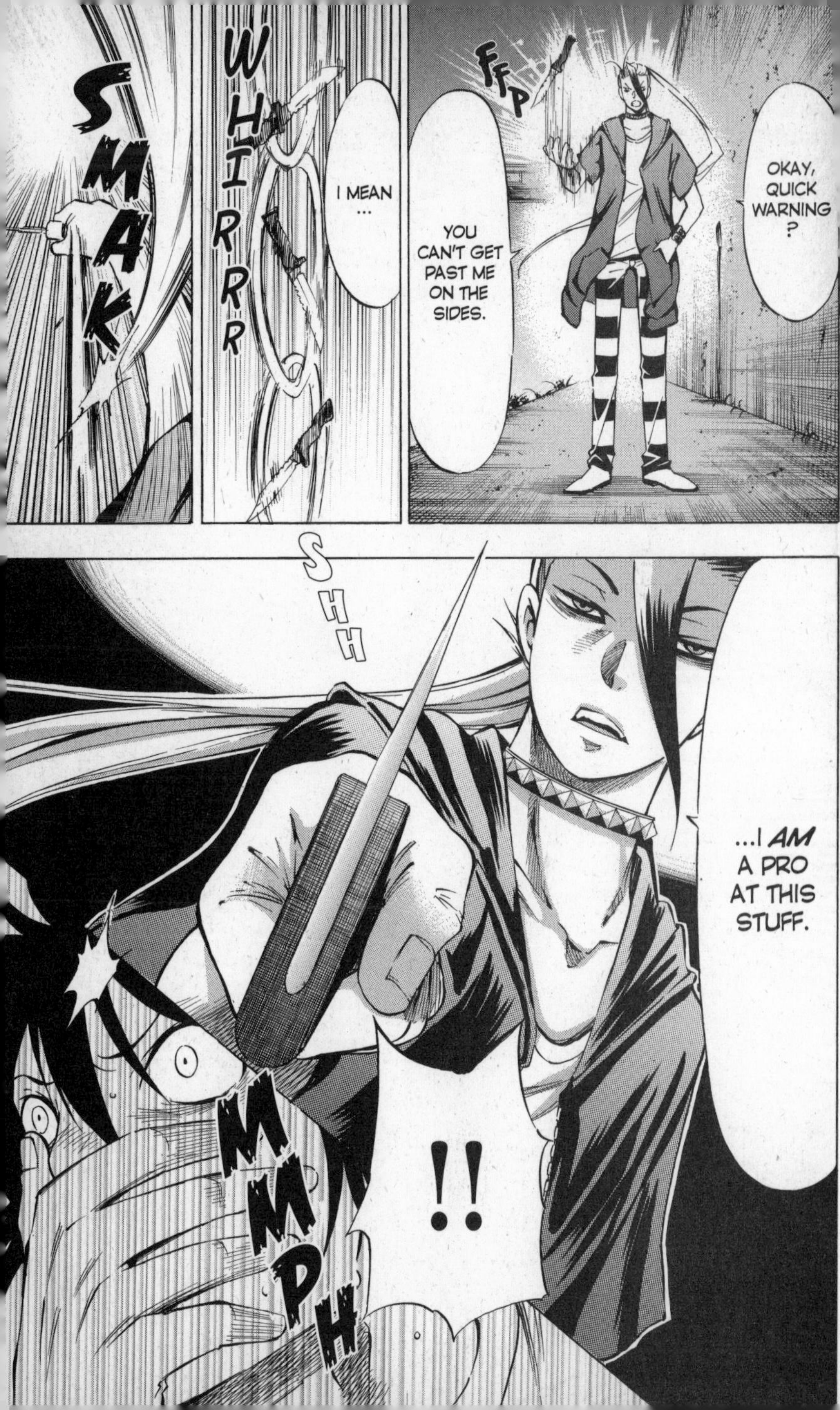
OKAY, QUICK WARNING?
FFP
YOU CAN'T GET PAST ME ON THE SIDES.
I MEAN ...
WHIRRR
SMAK
...I *AM* A PRO AT THIS STUFF.
SHH
!!
MMPH

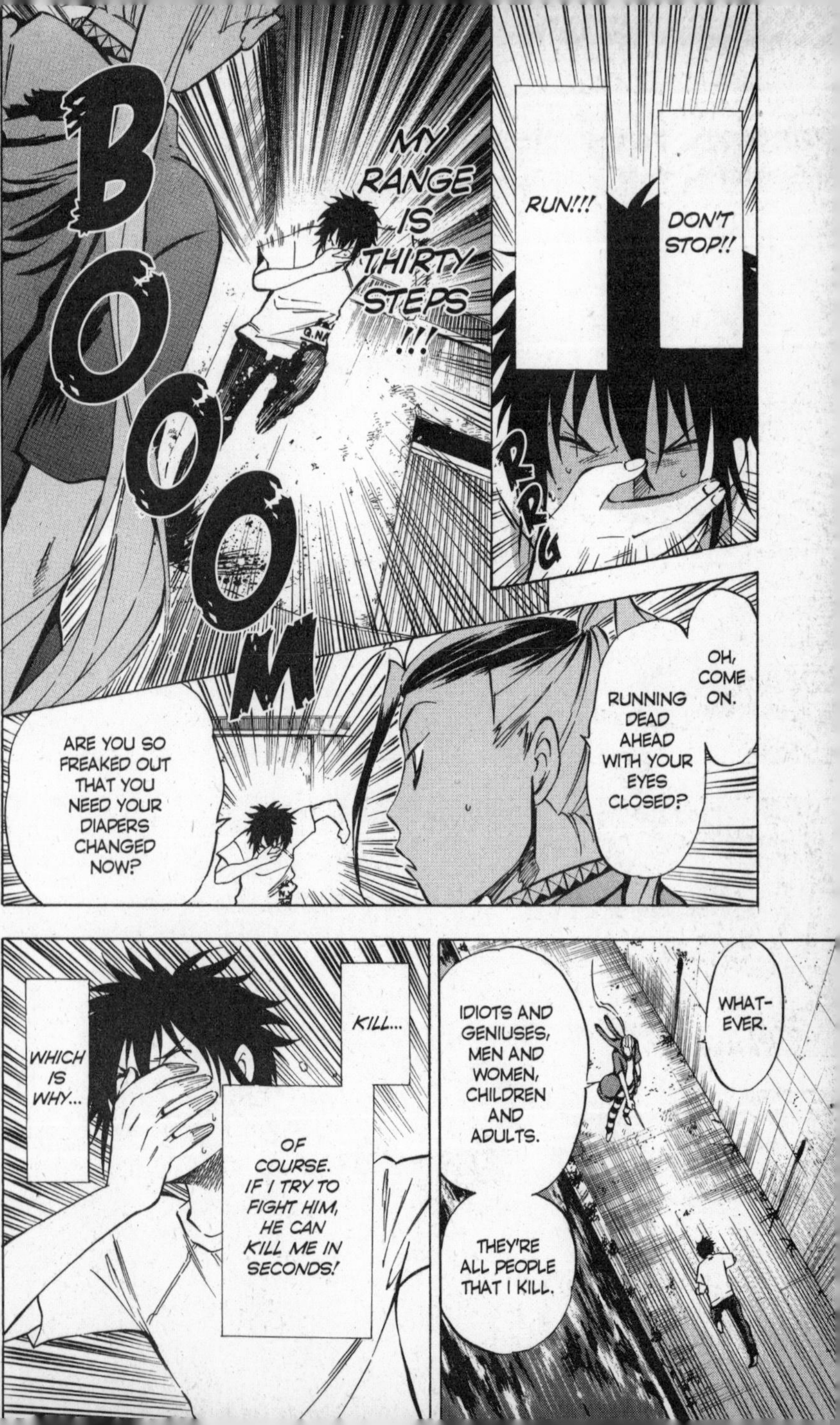
DON'T STOP!!
RUN!!!
RRG
BOOOOM
MY RANGE IS THIRTY STEPS!!!
OH, COME ON.
RUNNING DEAD AHEAD WITH YOUR EYES CLOSED?
ARE YOU SO FREAKED OUT THAT YOU NEED YOUR DIAPERS CHANGED NOW?
WHAT-EVER.
IDIOTS AND GENIUSES, MEN AND WOMEN, CHILDREN AND ADULTS.
THEY'RE ALL PEOPLE THAT I KILL.
KILL...
OF COURSE. IF I TRY TO FIGHT HIM, HE CAN KILL ME IN SECONDS!
WHICH IS WHY...

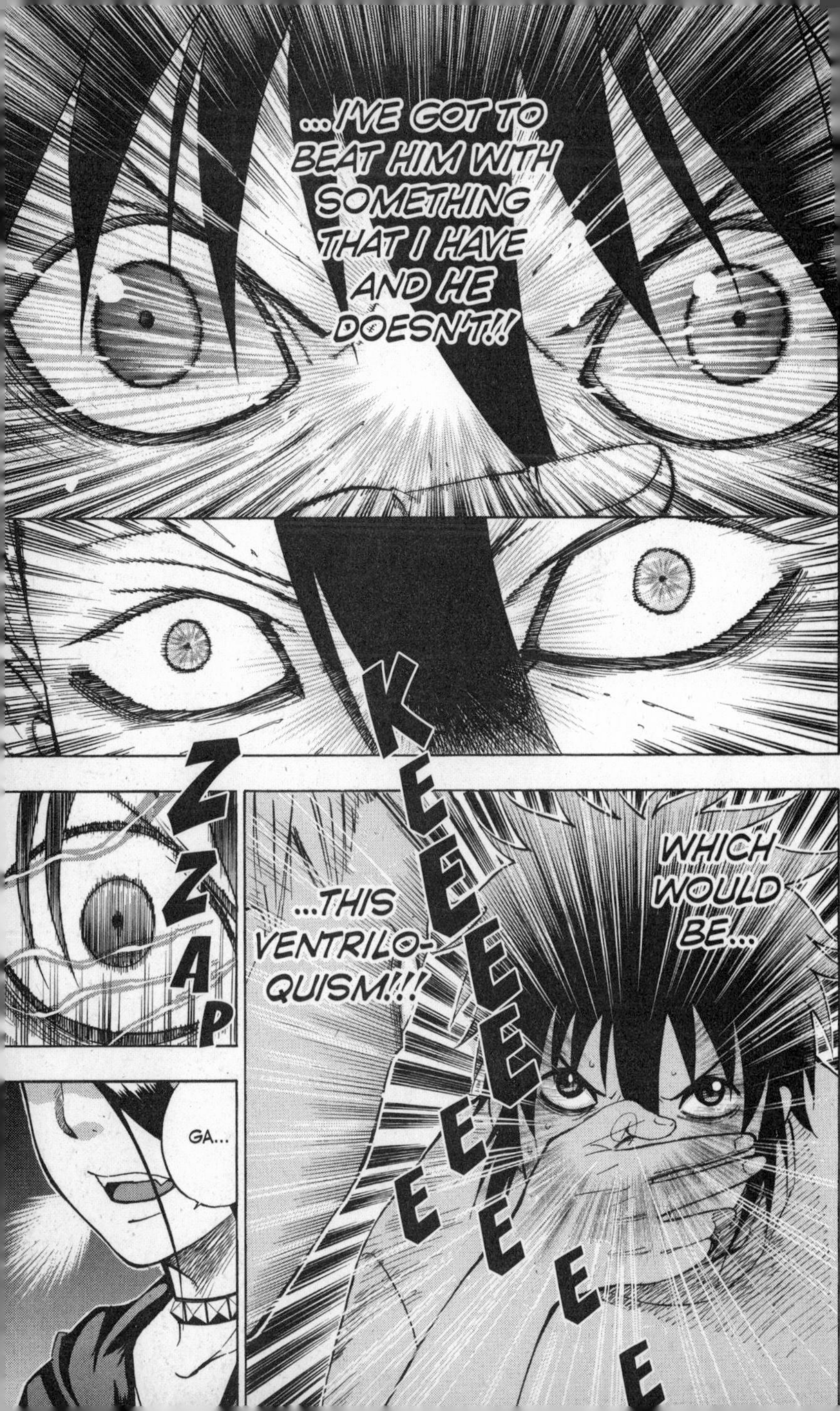
...I'VE GOT TO BEAT HIM WITH SOMETHING THAT I HAVE AND HE DOESN'T!!
WHICH WOULD BE...
...THIS VENTRILO-QUISM!!
KEEEEEEEEEEE
ZZAP
GA...

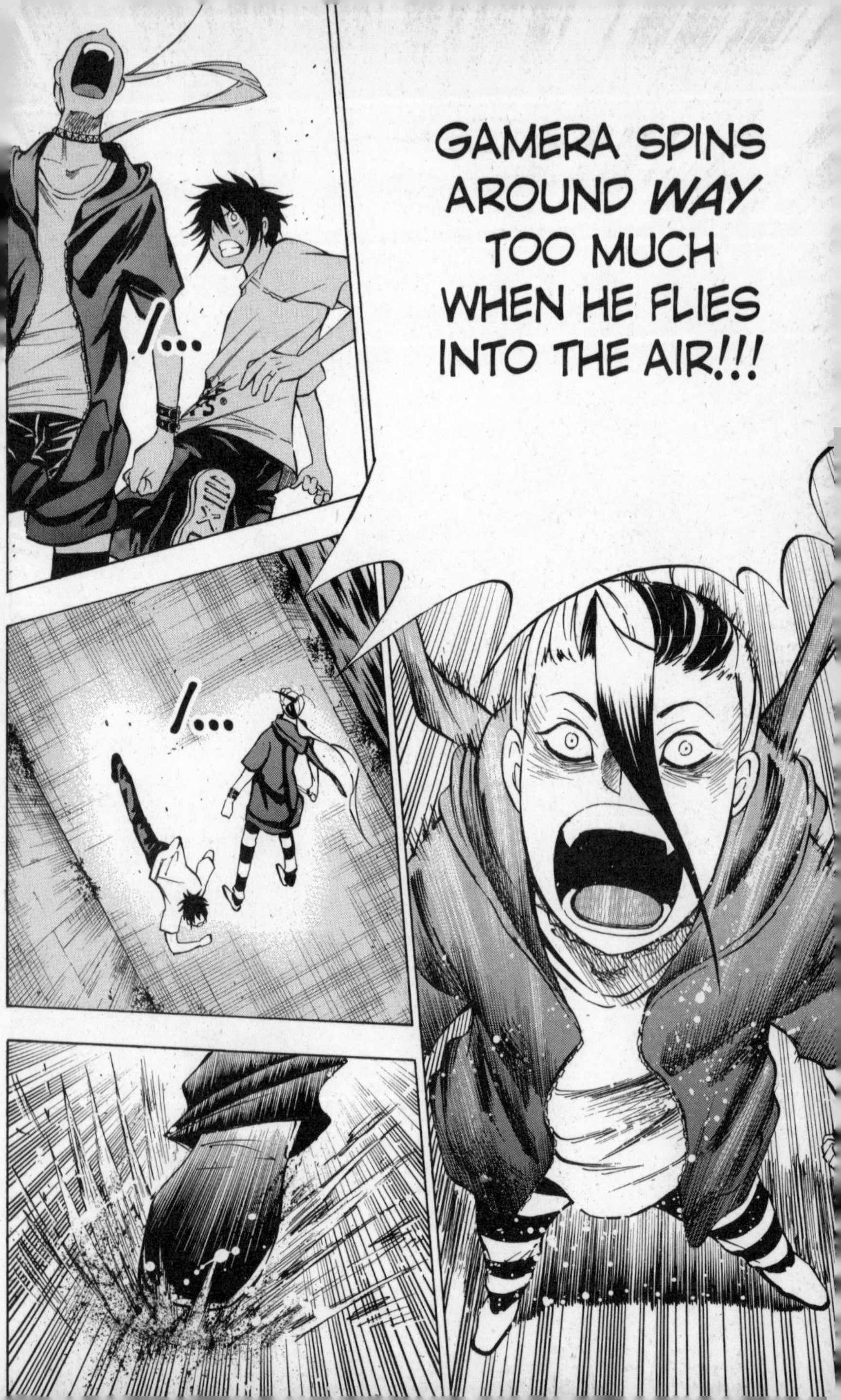

GAMERA SPINS AROUND *WAY* TOO MUCH WHEN HE FLIES INTO THE AIR!!!
/...
/...

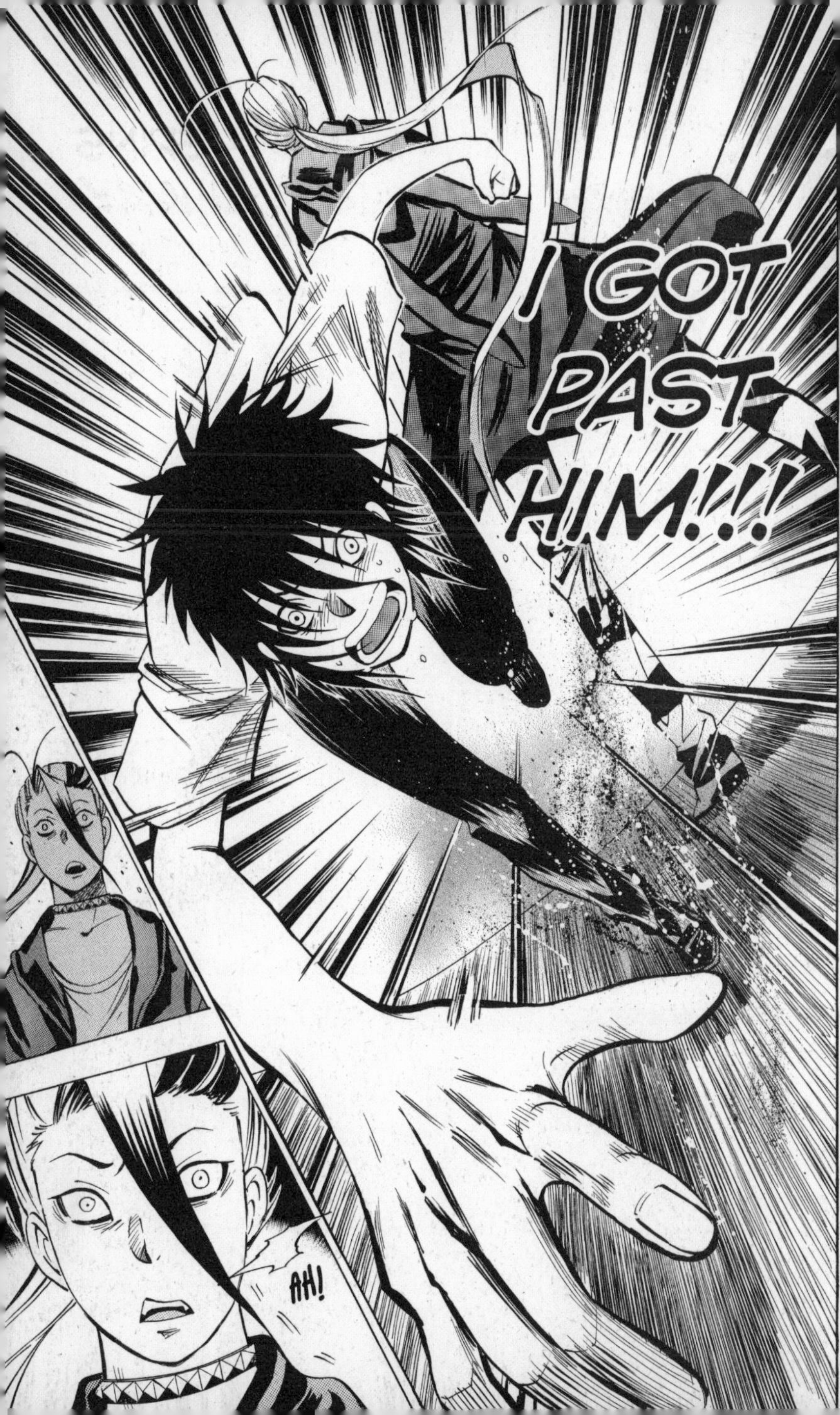
I GOT PAST HIM!!!
AH!

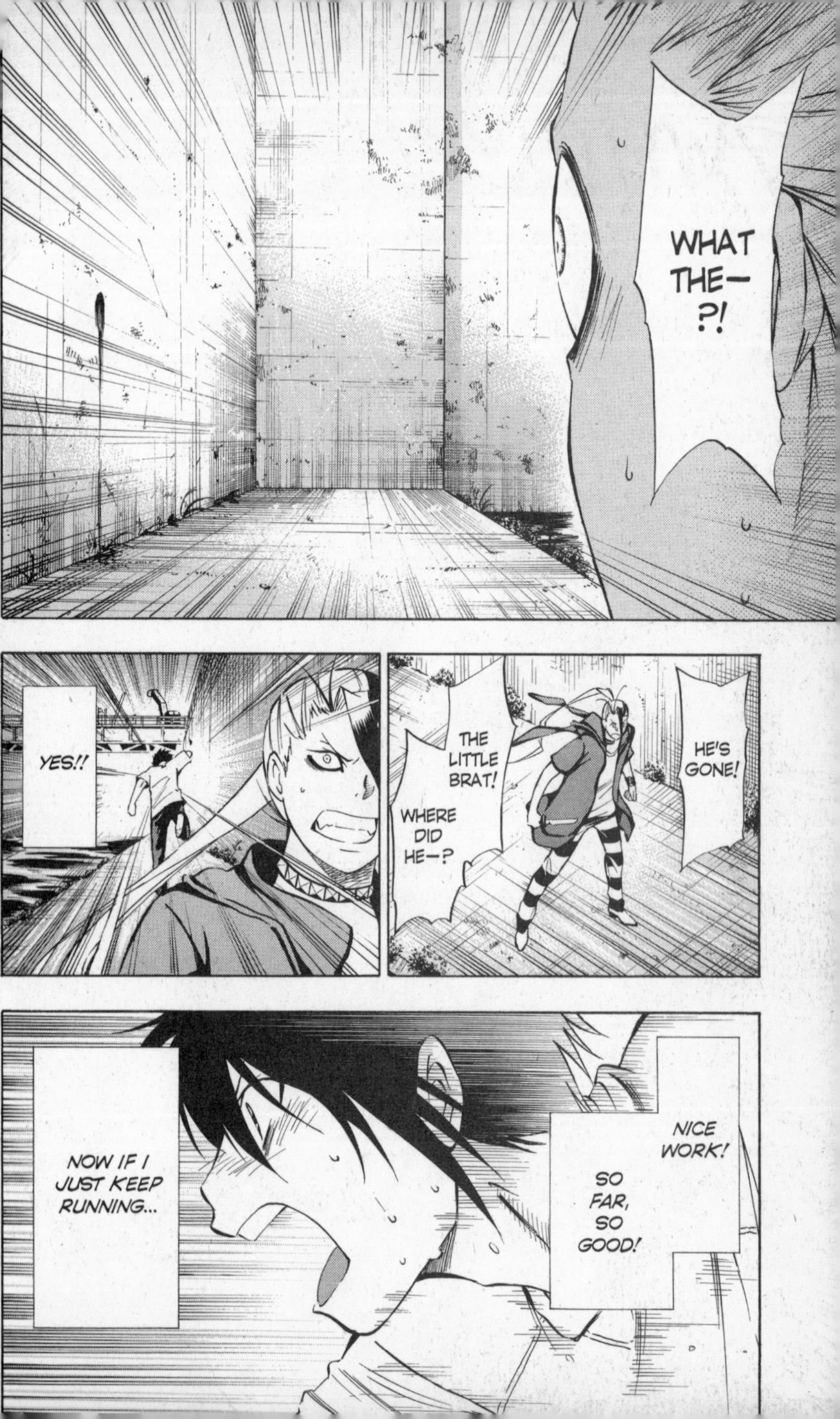
WHAT THE—?!
HE'S GONE!
THE LITTLE BRAT!
WHERE DID HE—?
YES!!
NICE WORK!
SO FAR, SO GOOD!
NOW IF I JUST KEEP RUNNING...

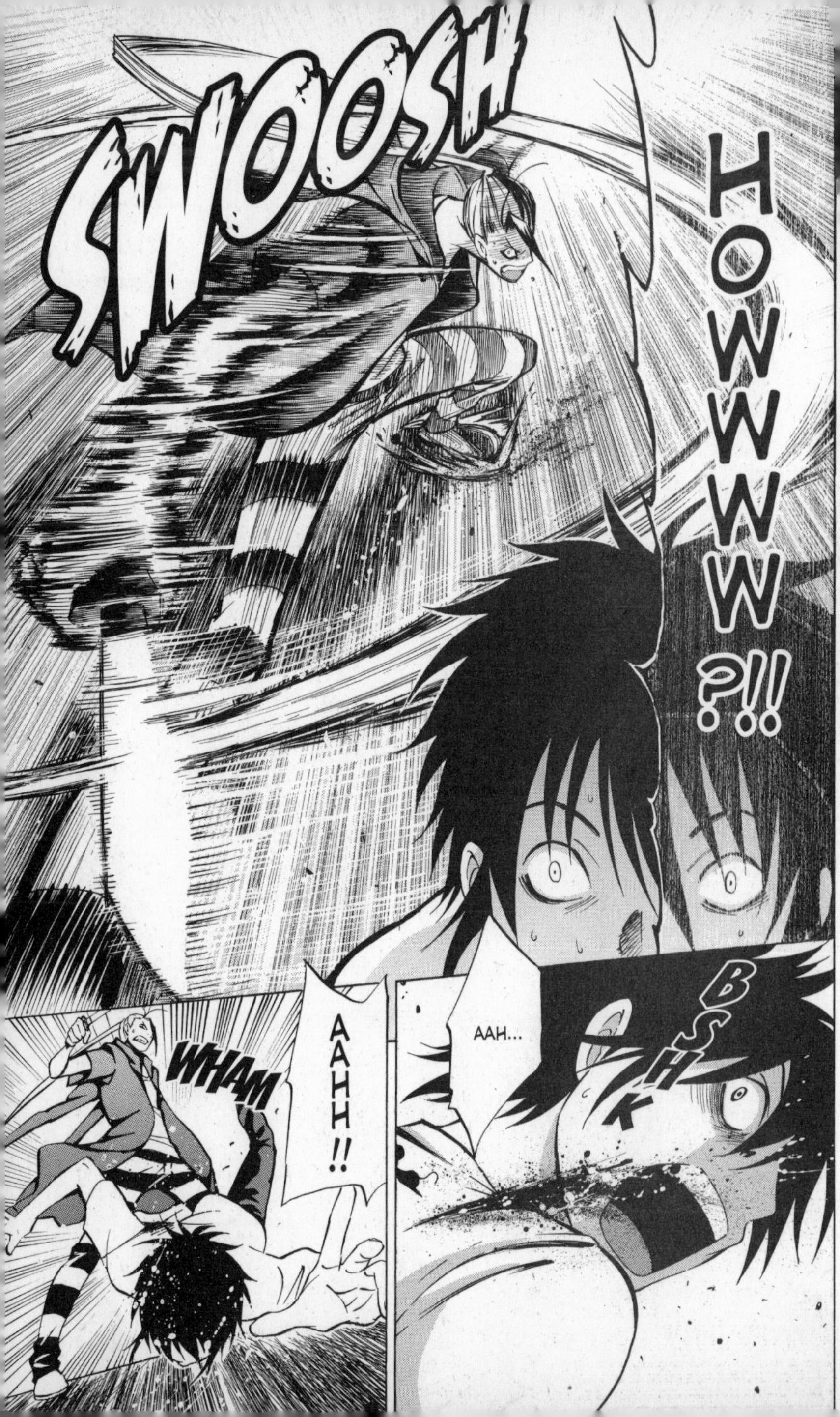
HOWWWW?!!
SWOOSH
BSHK
AAH...
AAHH!!
WHAM

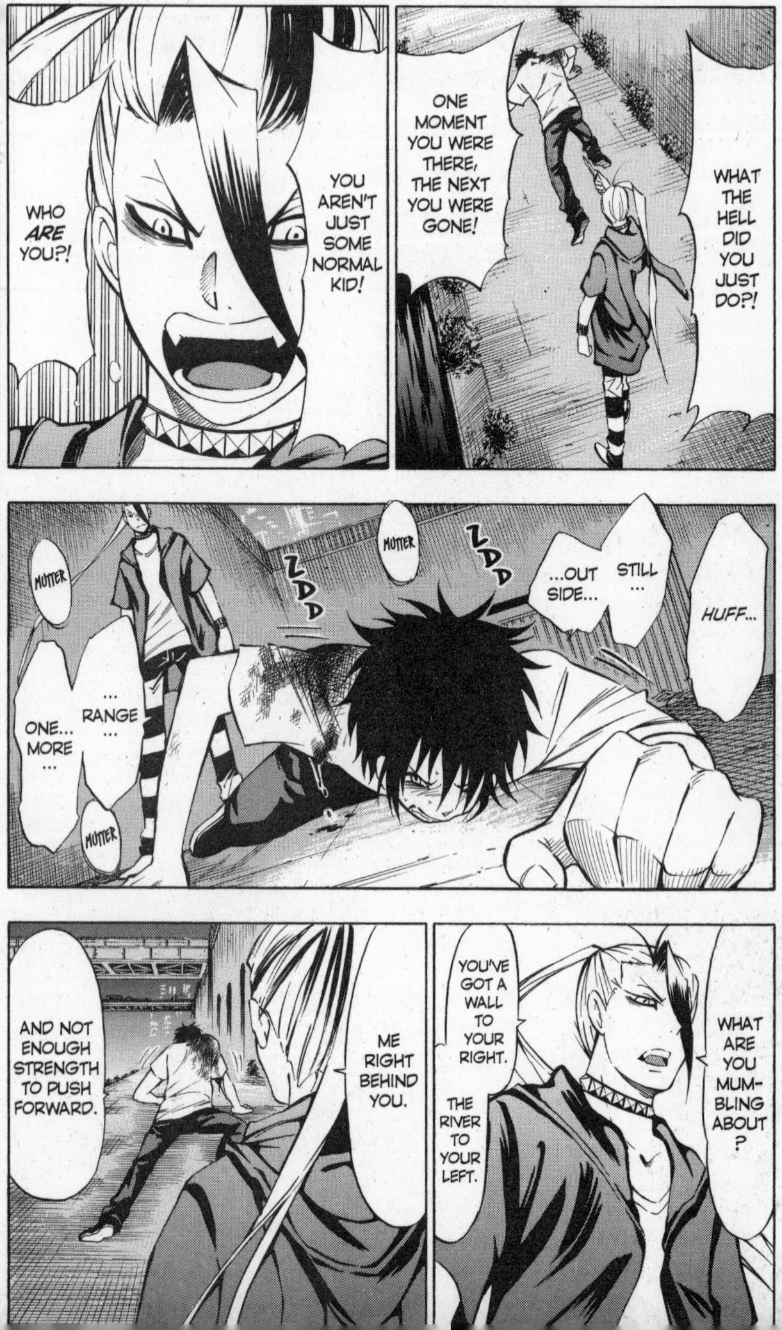
WHAT THE HELL DID YOU JUST DO?!
ONE MOMENT YOU WERE THERE, THE NEXT YOU WERE GONE!
YOU AREN'T JUST SOME NORMAL KID!
WHO *ARE* YOU?!
HUFF...
STILL...
...OUT SIDE...
ZDD
MUTTER
ZDD
MUTTER
...RANGE...
ONE... MORE...
MUTTER
WHAT ARE YOU MUMBLING ABOUT?
YOU'VE GOT A WALL TO YOUR RIGHT.
THE RIVER TO YOUR LEFT.
ME RIGHT BEHIND YOU.
AND NOT ENOUGH STRENGTH TO PUSH FORWARD.

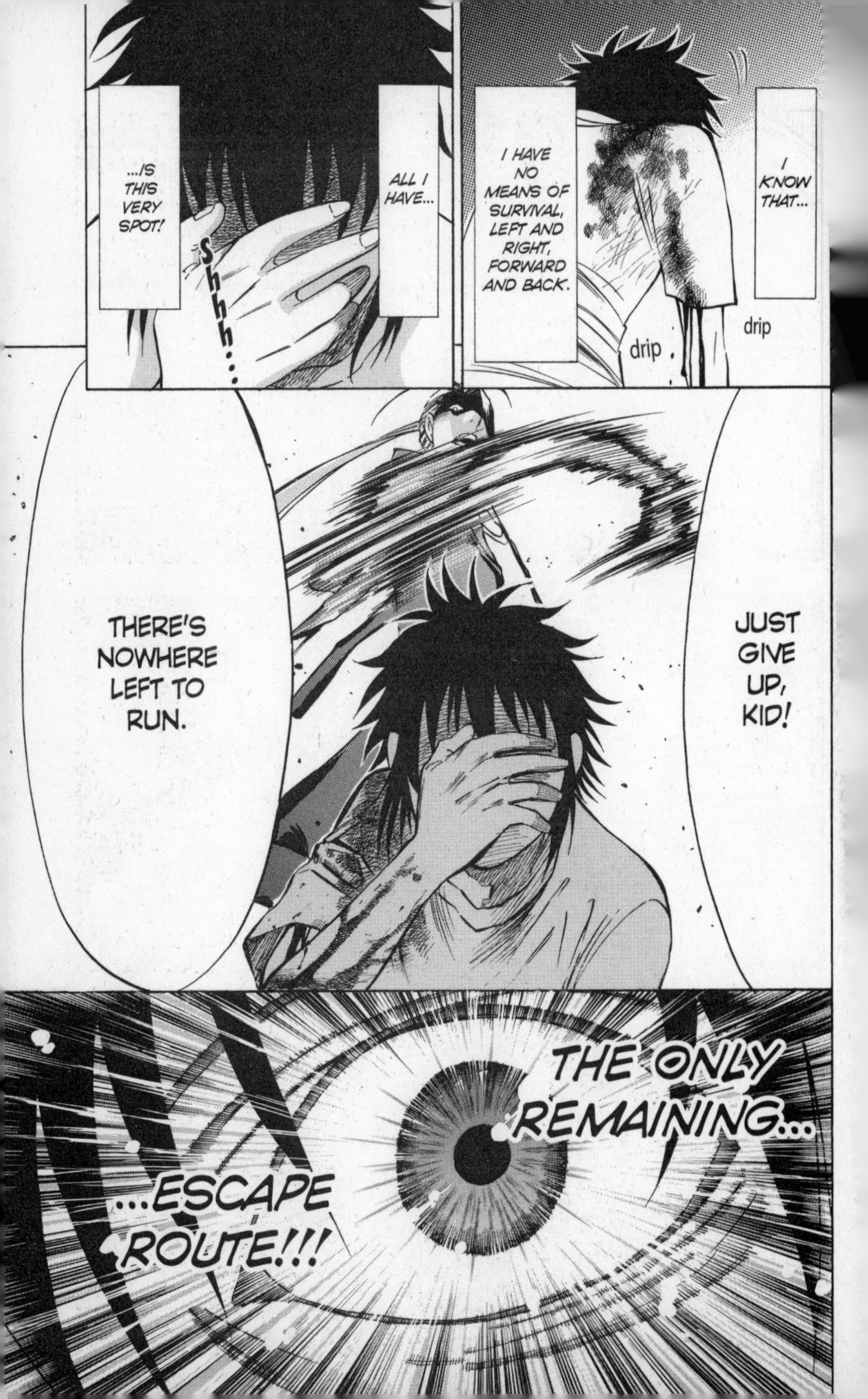
I KNOW THAT...
I HAVE NO MEANS OF SURVIVAL, LEFT AND RIGHT, FORWARD AND BACK.
drip
drip
ALL I HAVE...
Shhh...
...IS THIS VERY SPOT!
JUST GIVE UP, KID!
THERE'S NOWHERE LEFT TO RUN.
THE ONLY REMAINING...
...ESCAPE ROUTE!!!

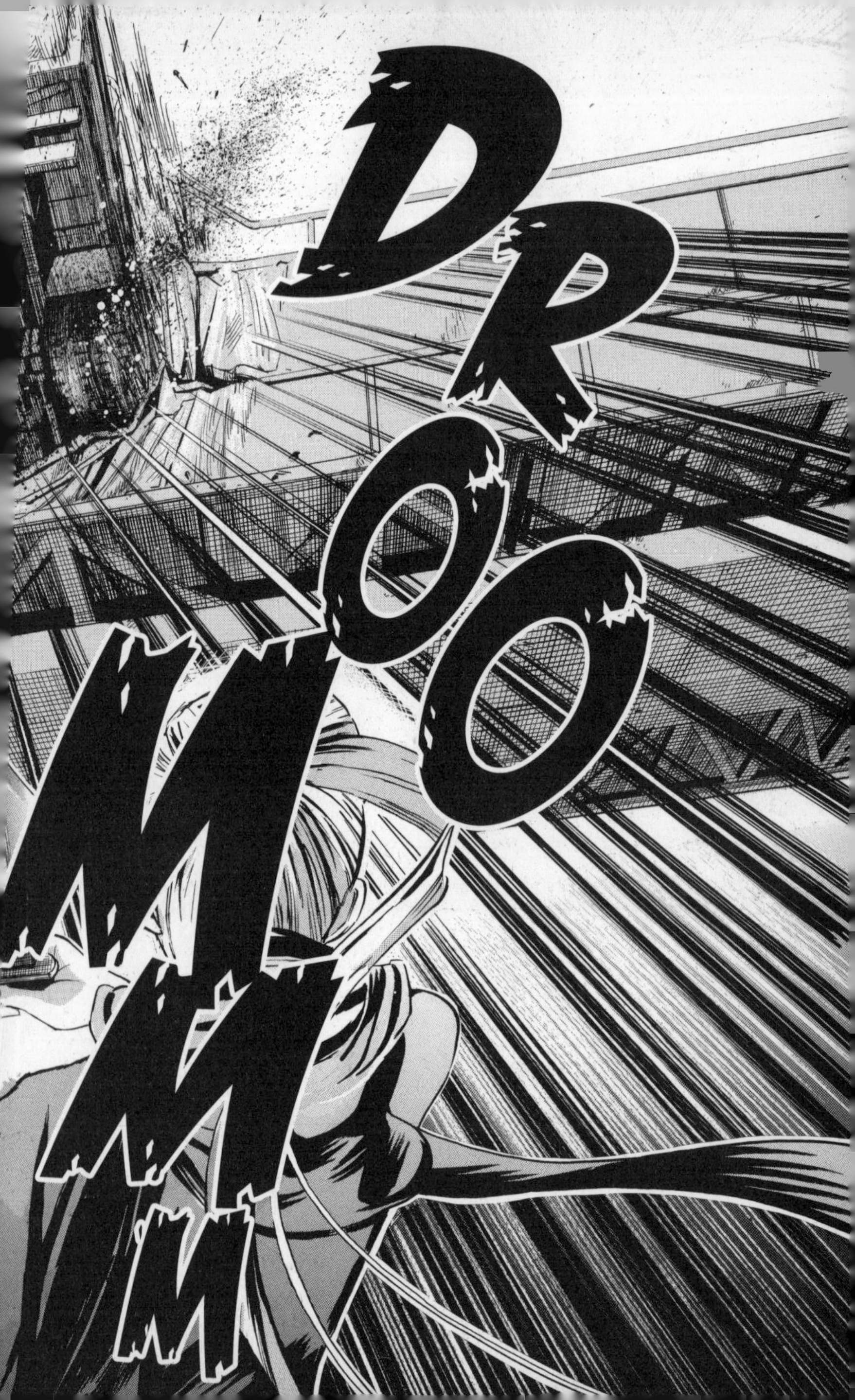
DROOMMM

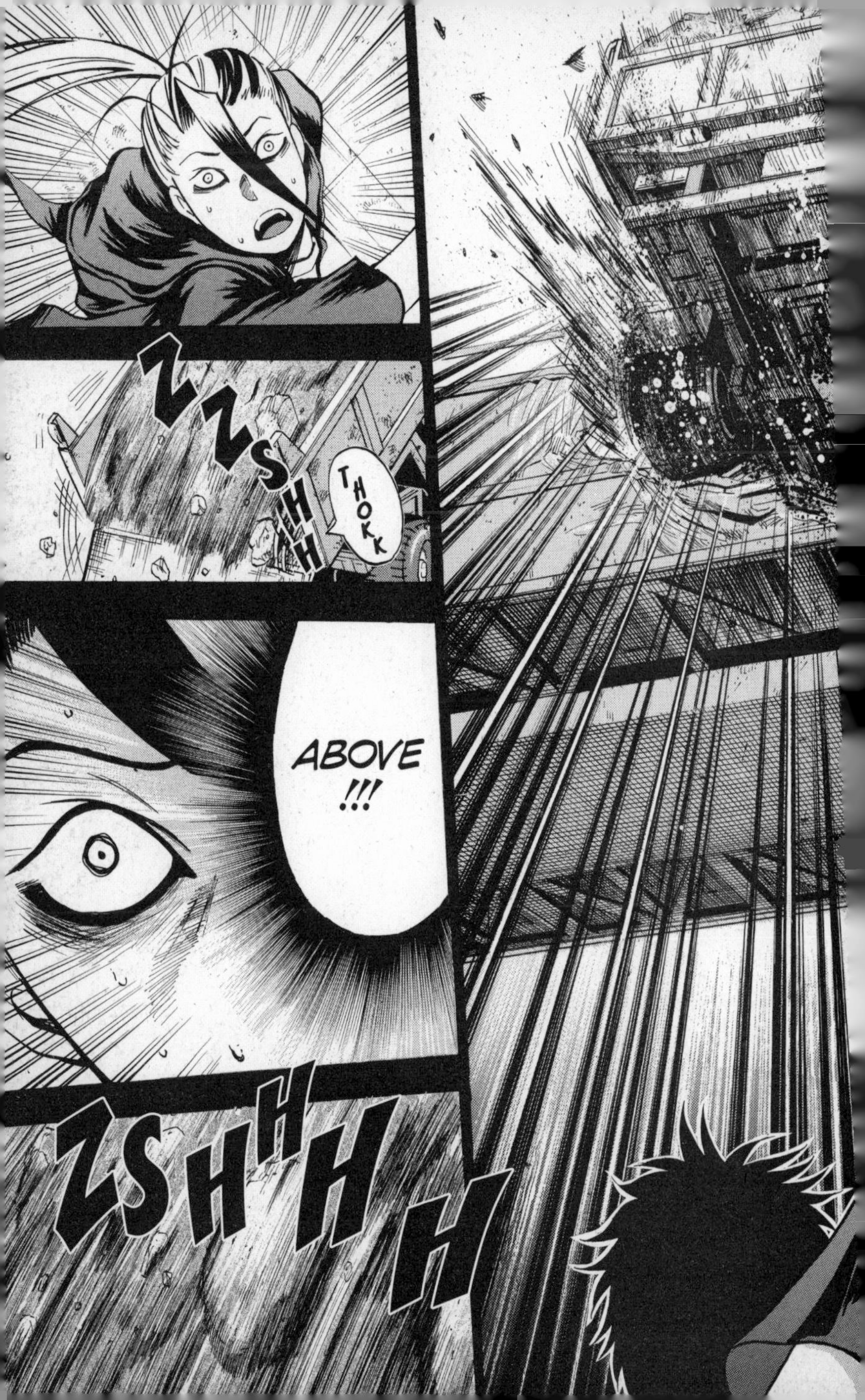
THOKK
ZZSHHH
ABOVE !!!
ZSHHHH

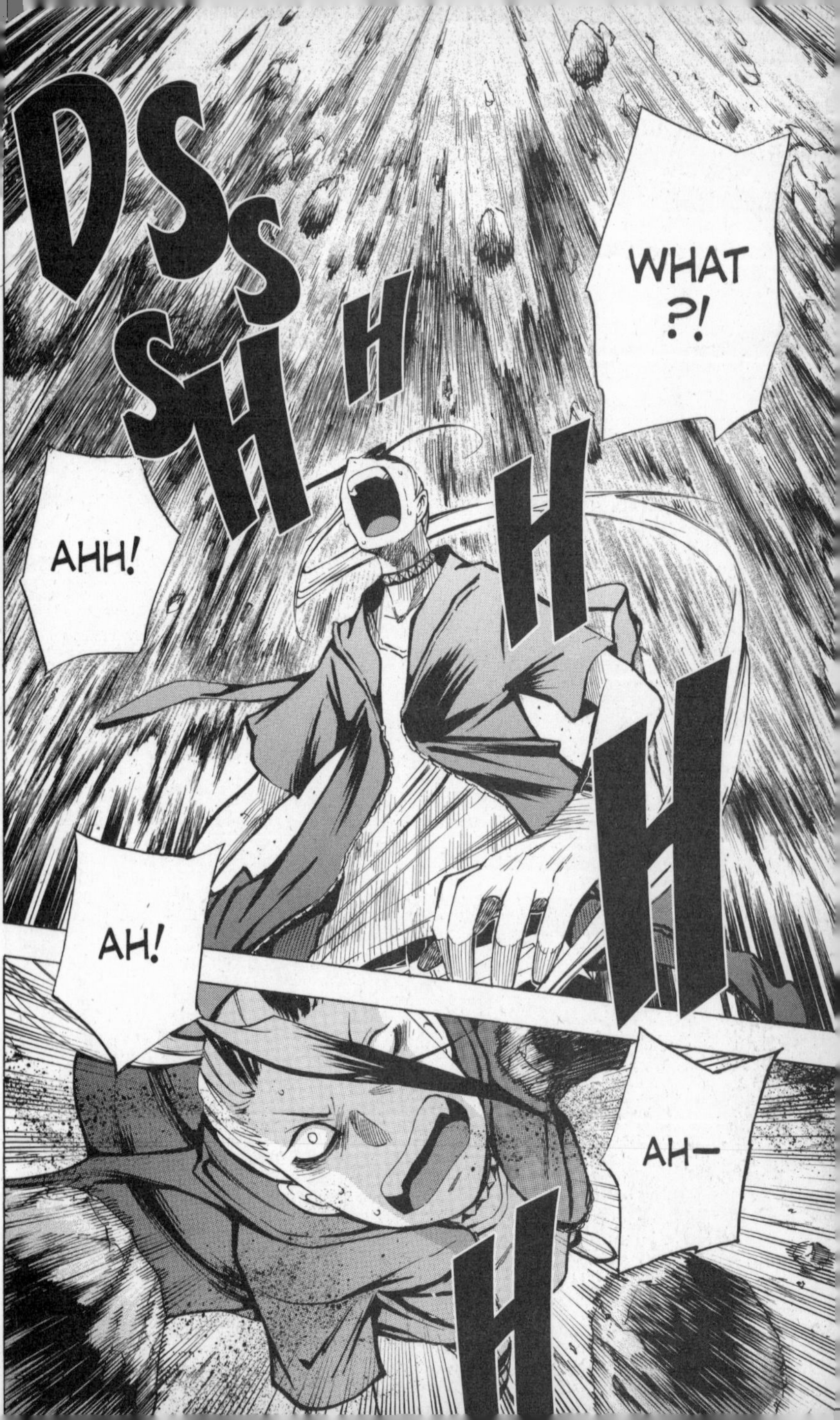
WHAT ?!
DSSSHHHHHH
AHH!
AH!
AH—

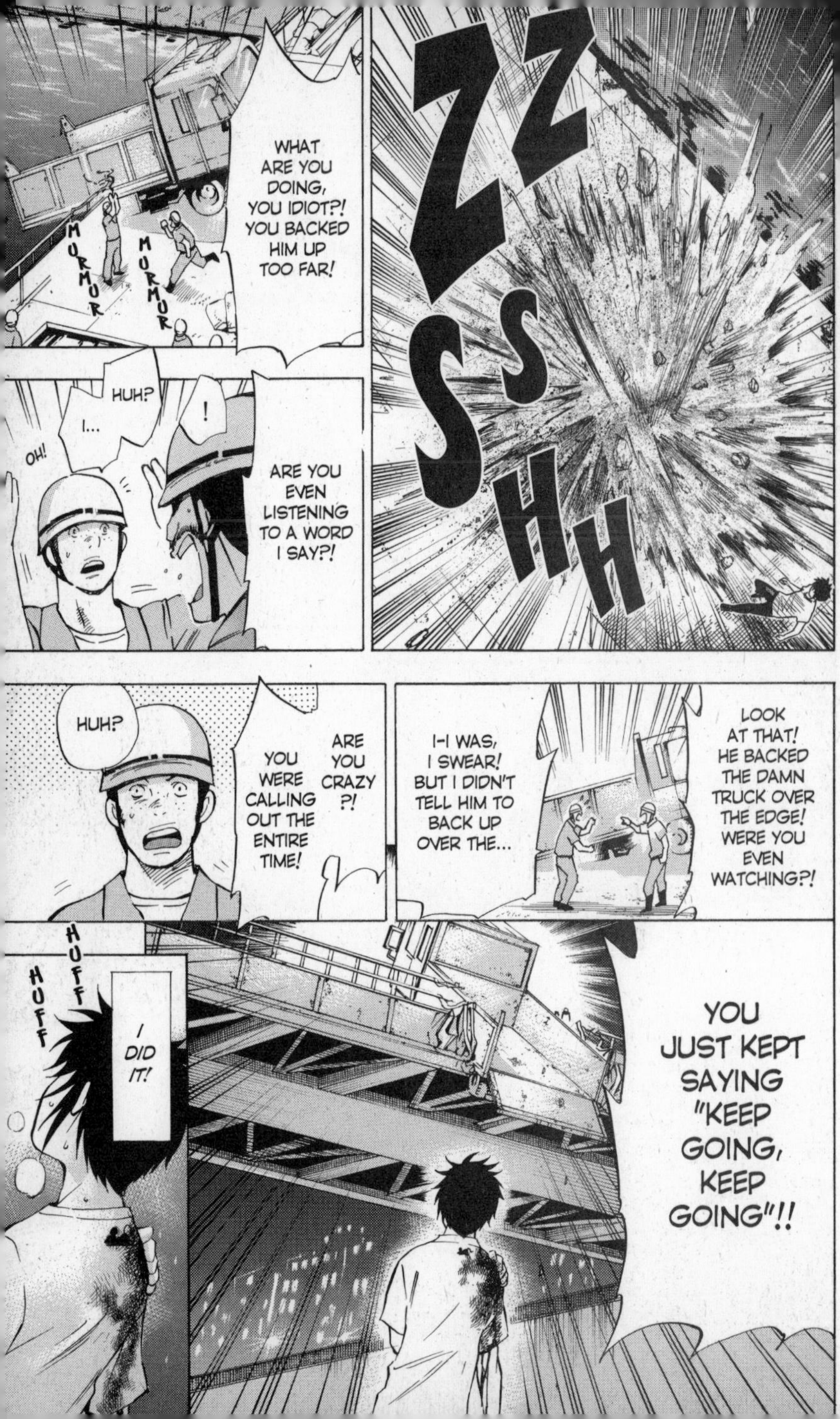
ZZSSHH
WHAT ARE YOU DOING, YOU IDIOT?! YOU BACKED HIM UP TOO FAR!
MURMUR
MURMUR
!
ARE YOU EVEN LISTENING TO A WORD I SAY?!
HUH? I...
OH!
LOOK AT THAT! HE BACKED THE DAMN TRUCK OVER THE EDGE! WERE YOU EVEN WATCHING?!
I-I WAS, I SWEAR! BUT I DIDN'T TELL HIM TO BACK UP OVER THE...
ARE YOU CRAZY?!
YOU WERE CALLING OUT THE ENTIRE TIME!
HUH?
YOU JUST KEPT SAYING "KEEP GOING, KEEP GOING"!!
HUFF
I DID IT!
HUFF

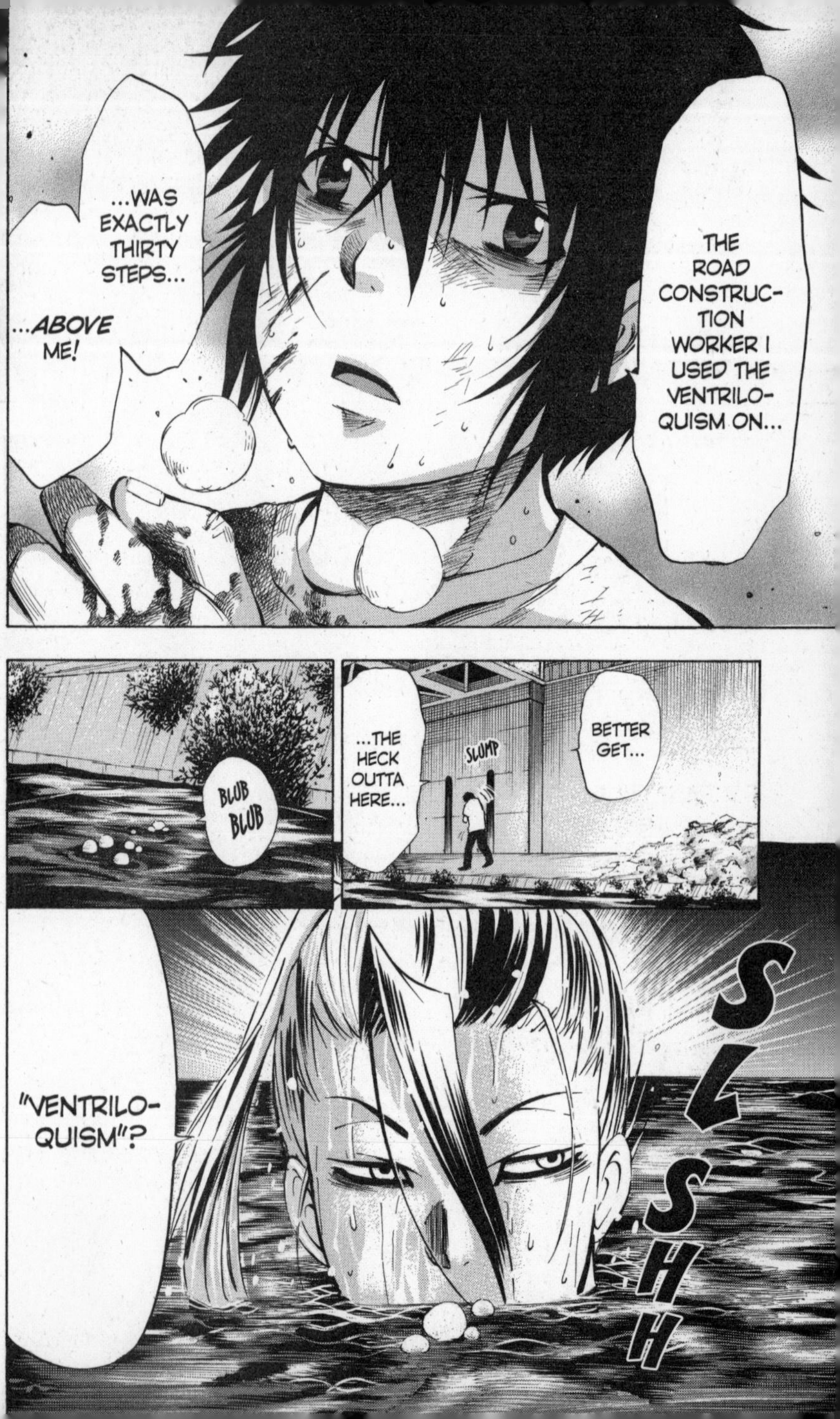
THE ROAD CONSTRUCTION WORKER I USED THE VENTRILOQUISM ON...
...WAS EXACTLY THIRTY STEPS...
...*ABOVE* ME!
BETTER GET...
SLUMP
...THE HECK OUTTA HERE...
BLUB BLUB
SLSHH
"VENTRILOQUISM"?

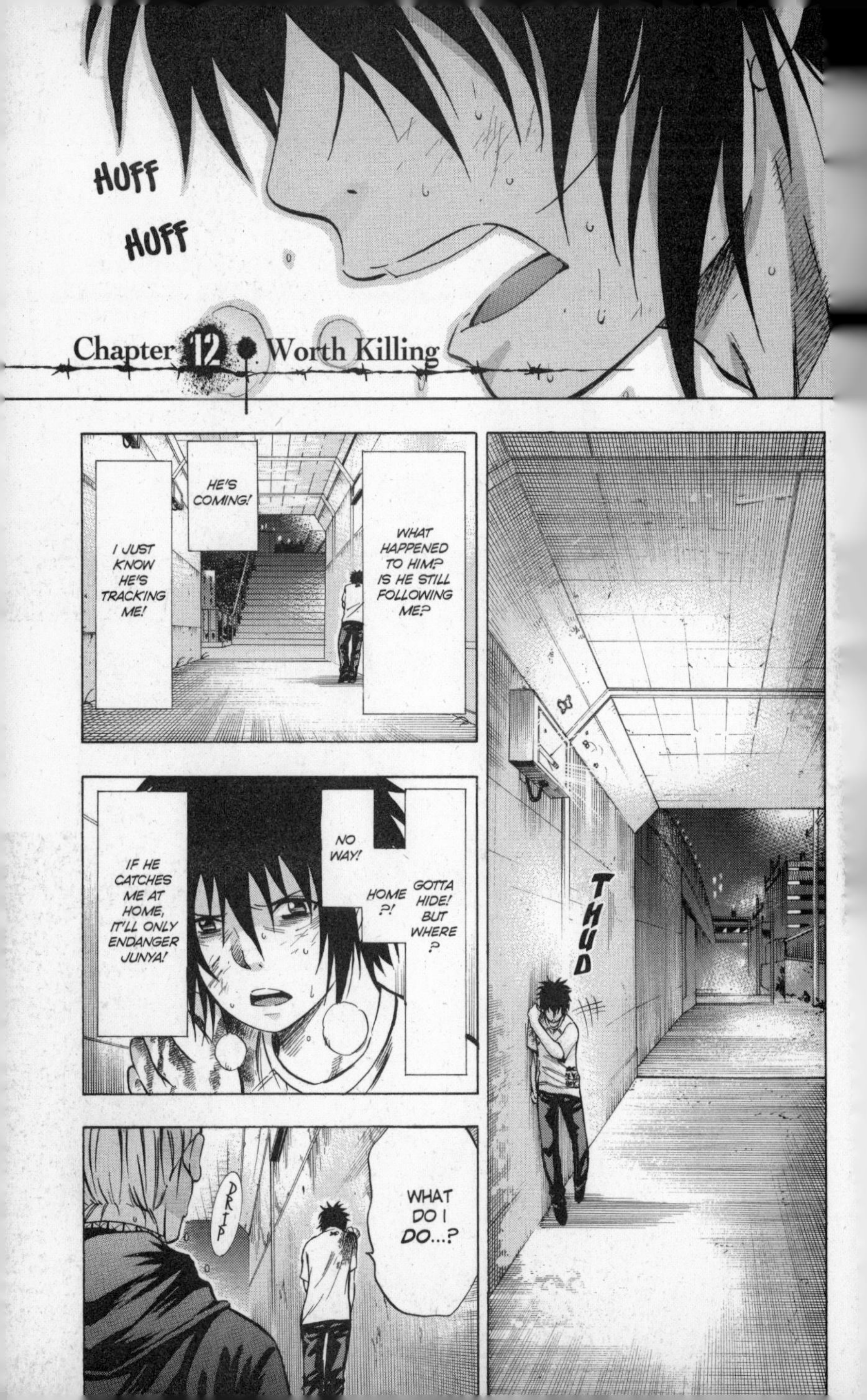
HUFF
HUFF
Chapter 12 Worth Killing
THUD
WHAT HAPPENED TO HIM? IS HE STILL FOLLOWING ME?
HE'S COMING!
I JUST KNOW HE'S TRACKING ME!
GOTTA HIDE! BUT WHERE?
HOME?!
NO WAY!
IF HE CATCHES ME AT HOME, IT'LL ONLY ENDANGER JUNYA!
WHAT DO I DO...?
DRIP

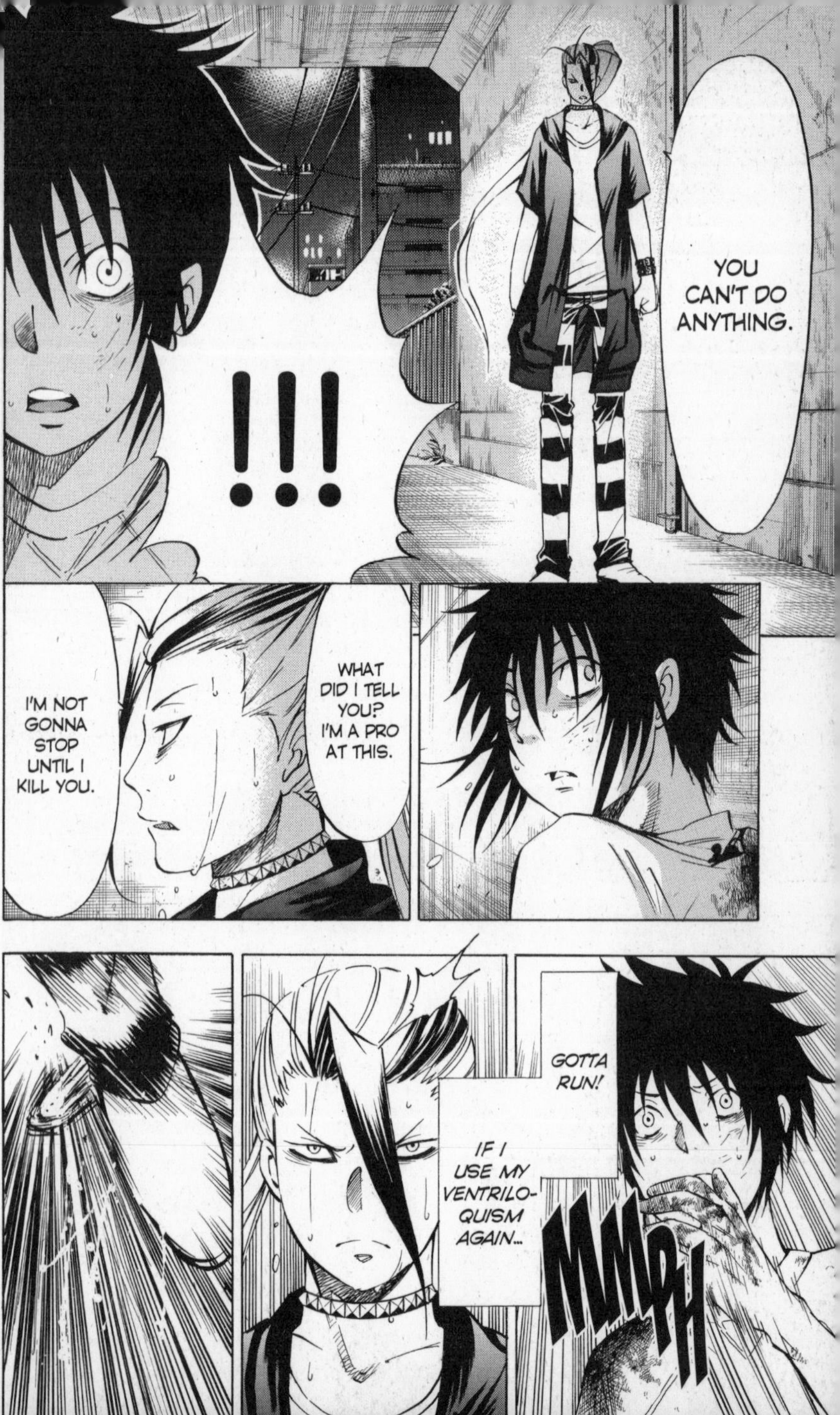
YOU CAN'T DO ANYTHING.
!!!
WHAT DID I TELL YOU? I'M A PRO AT THIS.
I'M NOT GONNA STOP UNTIL I KILL YOU.
GOTTA RUN!
IF I USE MY VENTRILO-QUISM AGAIN...
MMMPH

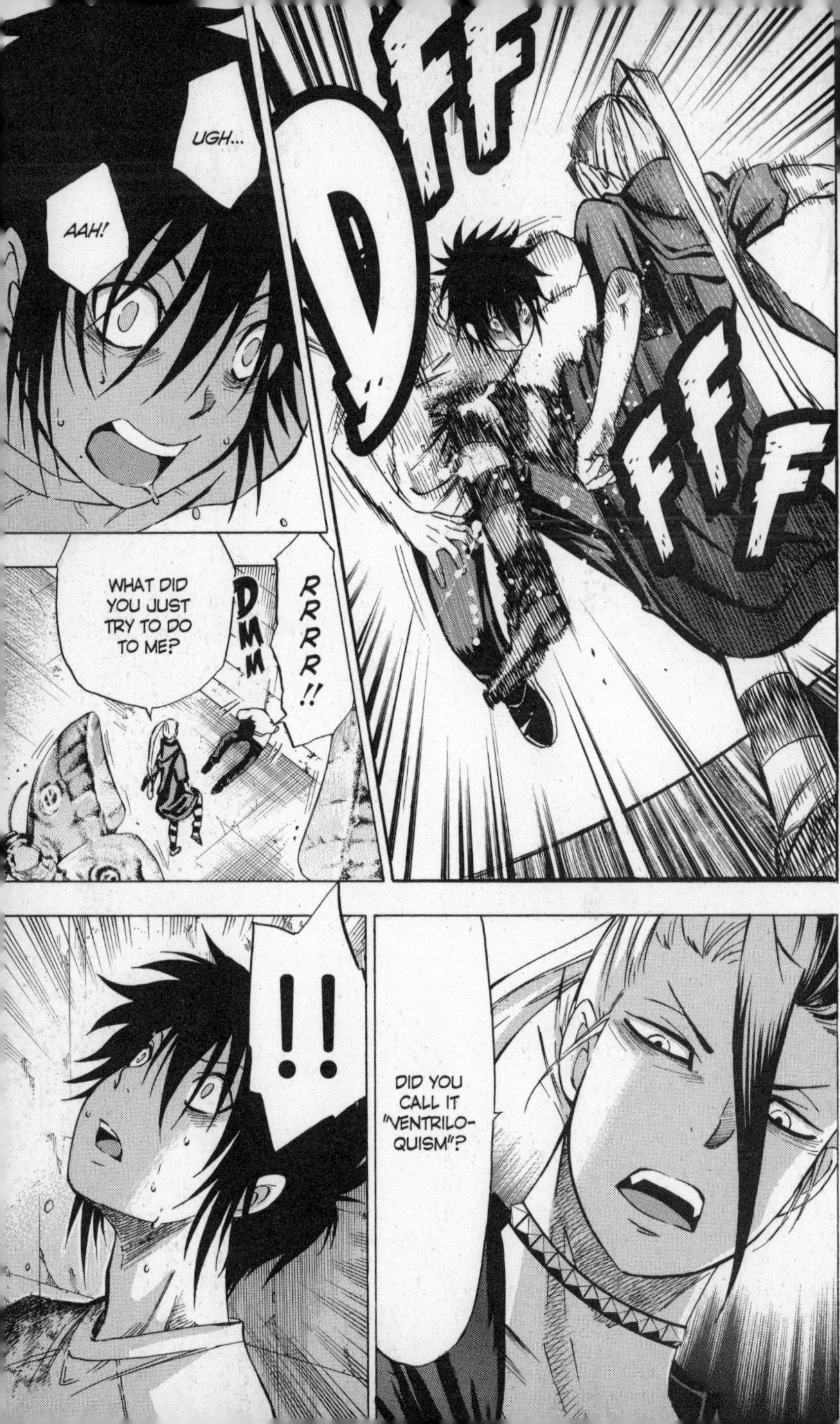

FF
D
FFF
UGH...
AAH!
RRRR!!
DMM
WHAT DID YOU JUST TRY TO DO TO ME?
DID YOU CALL IT "VENTRILO-QUISM"?
!!

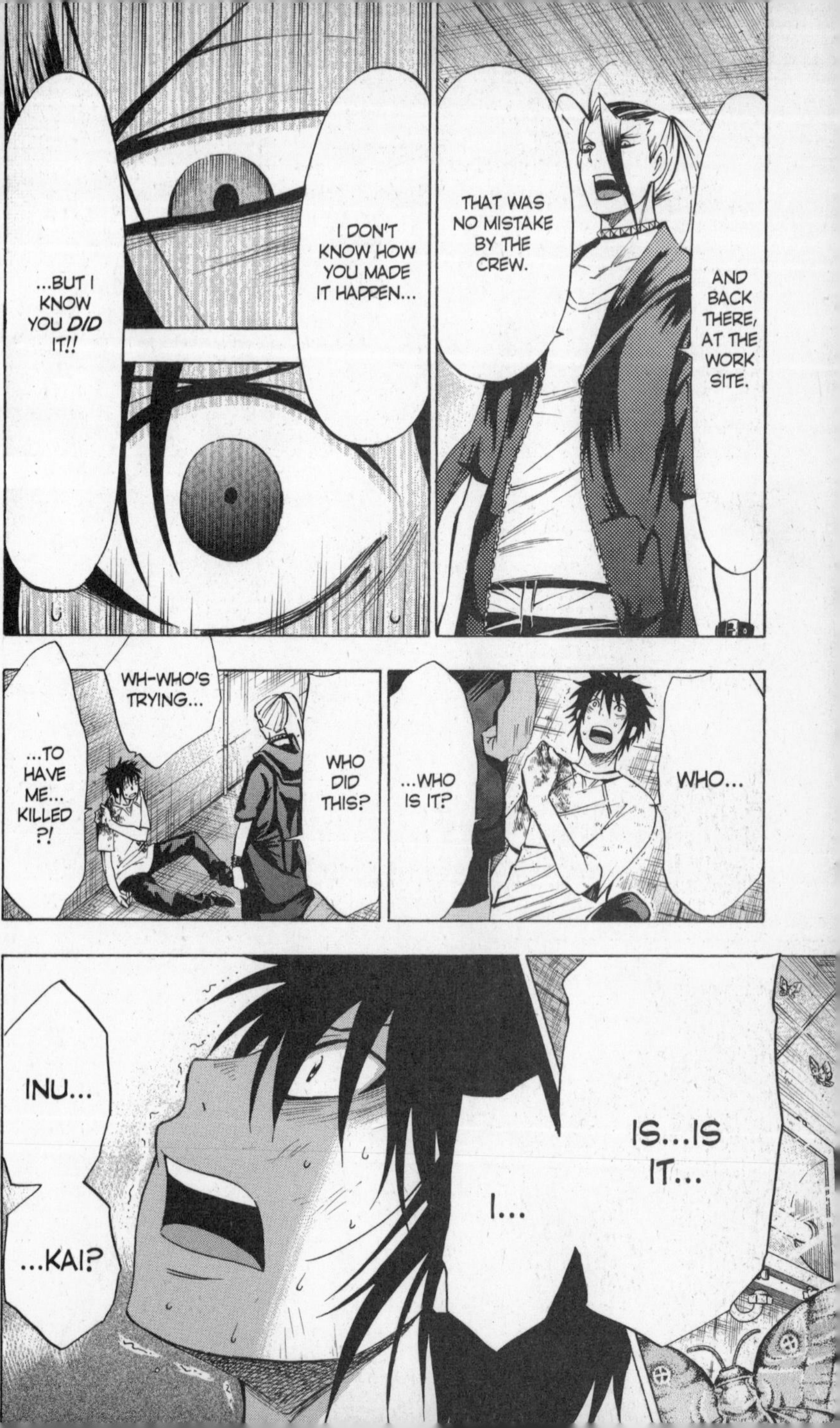
AND BACK THERE, AT THE WORK SITE.
THAT WAS NO MISTAKE BY THE CREW.
I DON'T KNOW HOW YOU MADE IT HAPPEN...
...BUT I KNOW YOU *DID* IT!!
WHO...
...WHO IS IT?
WHO DID THIS?
WH-WHO'S TRYING...
...TO HAVE ME... KILLED?!
IS...IS IT...
I...
INU...
...KAI?

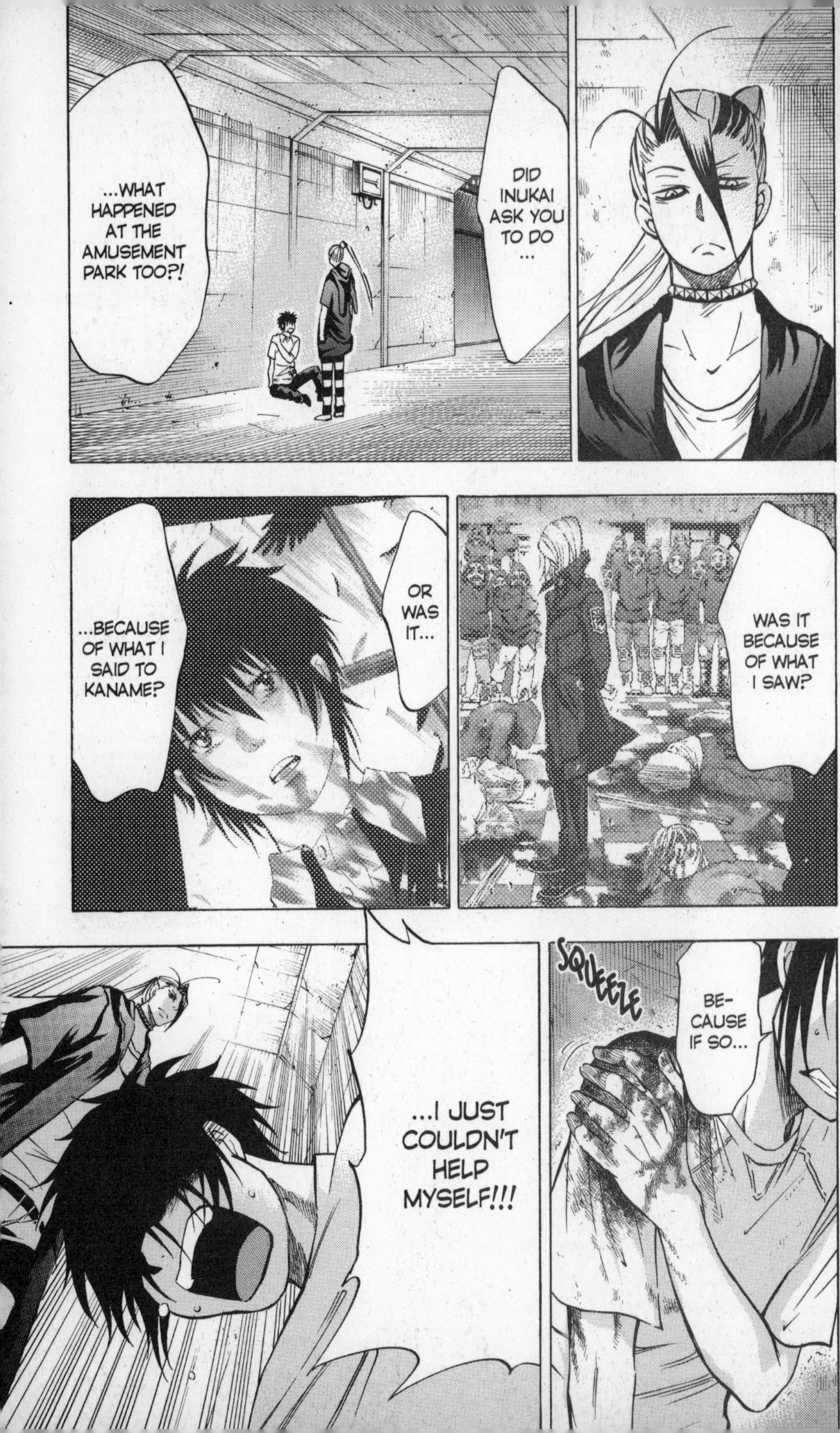
DID INUKAI ASK YOU TO DO ...
...WHAT HAPPENED AT THE AMUSEMENT PARK TOO?!
WAS IT BECAUSE OF WHAT I SAW?
OR WAS IT...
...BECAUSE OF WHAT I SAID TO KANAME?
SQUEEZE
BE-CAUSE IF SO...
...I JUST COULDN'T HELP MYSELF!!!

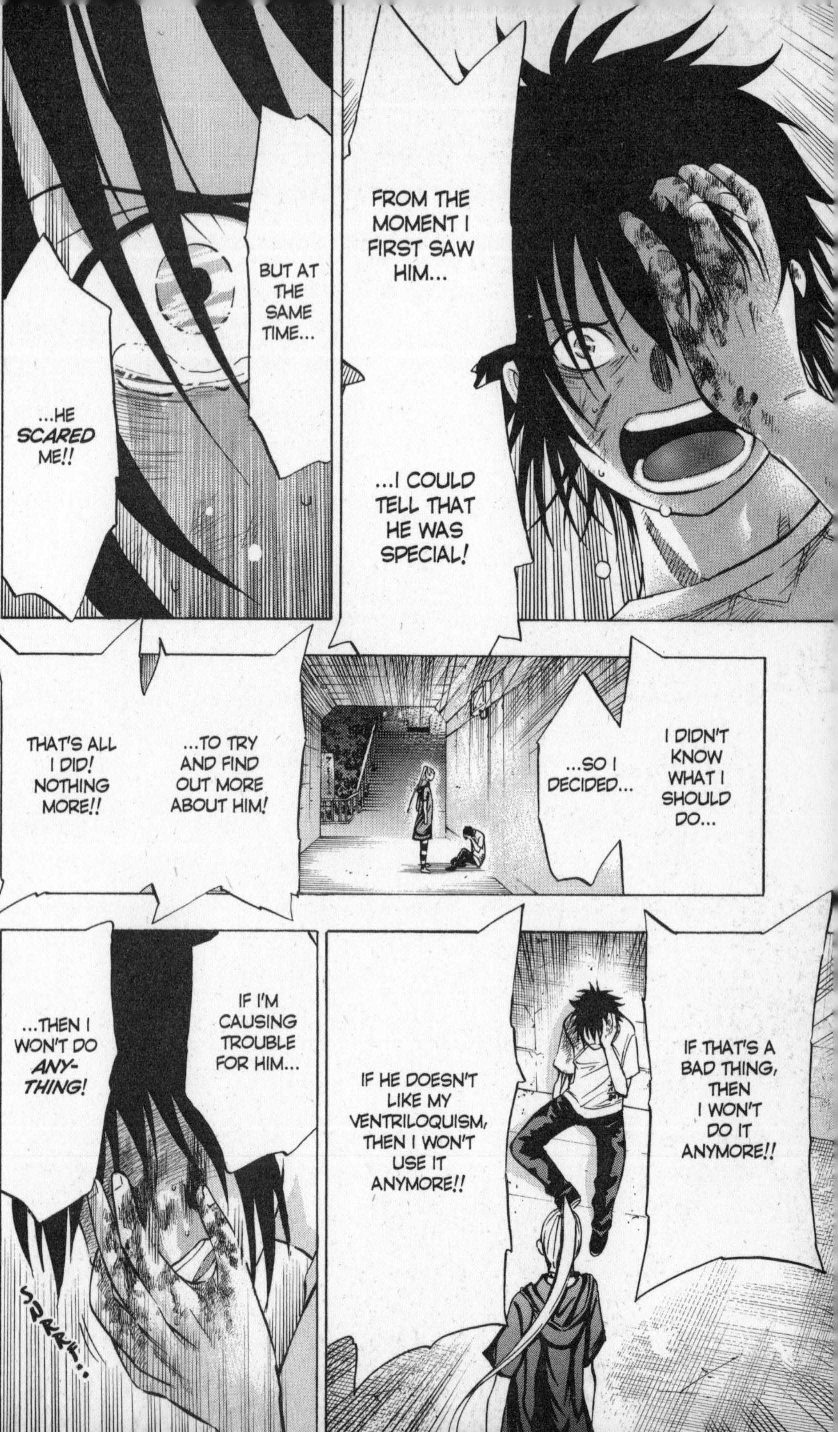
FROM THE MOMENT I FIRST SAW HIM...
...I COULD TELL THAT HE WAS SPECIAL!
BUT AT THE SAME TIME...
...HE *SCARED* ME!!
I DIDN'T KNOW WHAT I SHOULD DO...
...SO I DECIDED...
...TO TRY AND FIND OUT MORE ABOUT HIM!
THAT'S ALL I DID! NOTHING MORE!!
IF THAT'S A BAD THING, THEN I WON'T DO IT ANYMORE!!
IF HE DOESN'T LIKE MY VENTRILOQUISM, THEN I WON'T USE IT ANYMORE!!
IF I'M CAUSING TROUBLE FOR HIM...
...THEN I WON'T DO *ANY-THING*!
SNRRF..

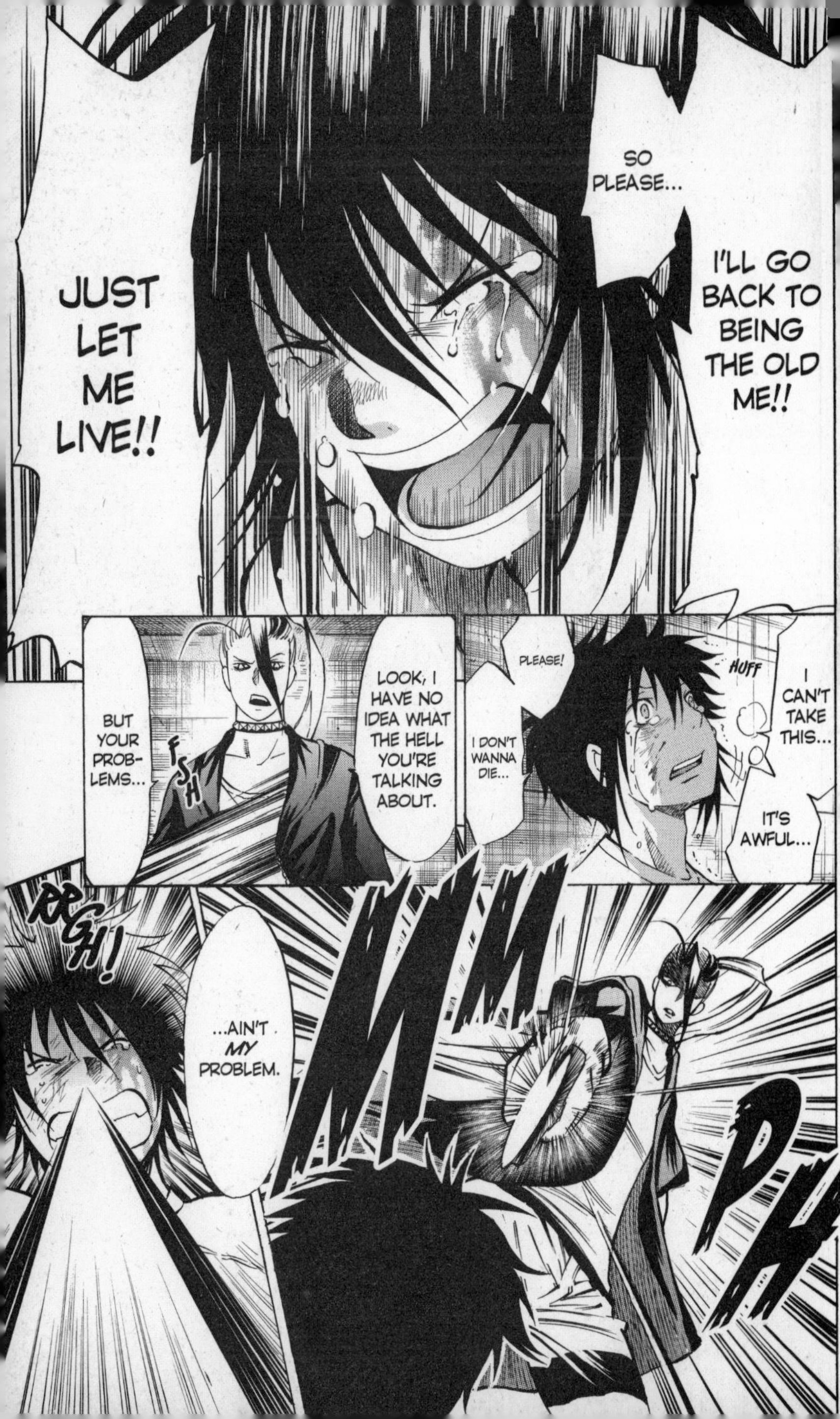
SO PLEASE...
I'LL GO BACK TO BEING THE OLD ME!!
JUST LET ME LIVE!!
I CAN'T TAKE THIS...
HUFF
IT'S AWFUL...
PLEASE!
I DON'T WANNA DIE...
LOOK, I HAVE NO IDEA WHAT THE HELL YOU'RE TALKING ABOUT.
FSH
BUT YOUR PROBLEMS...
...AIN'T MY PROBLEM.

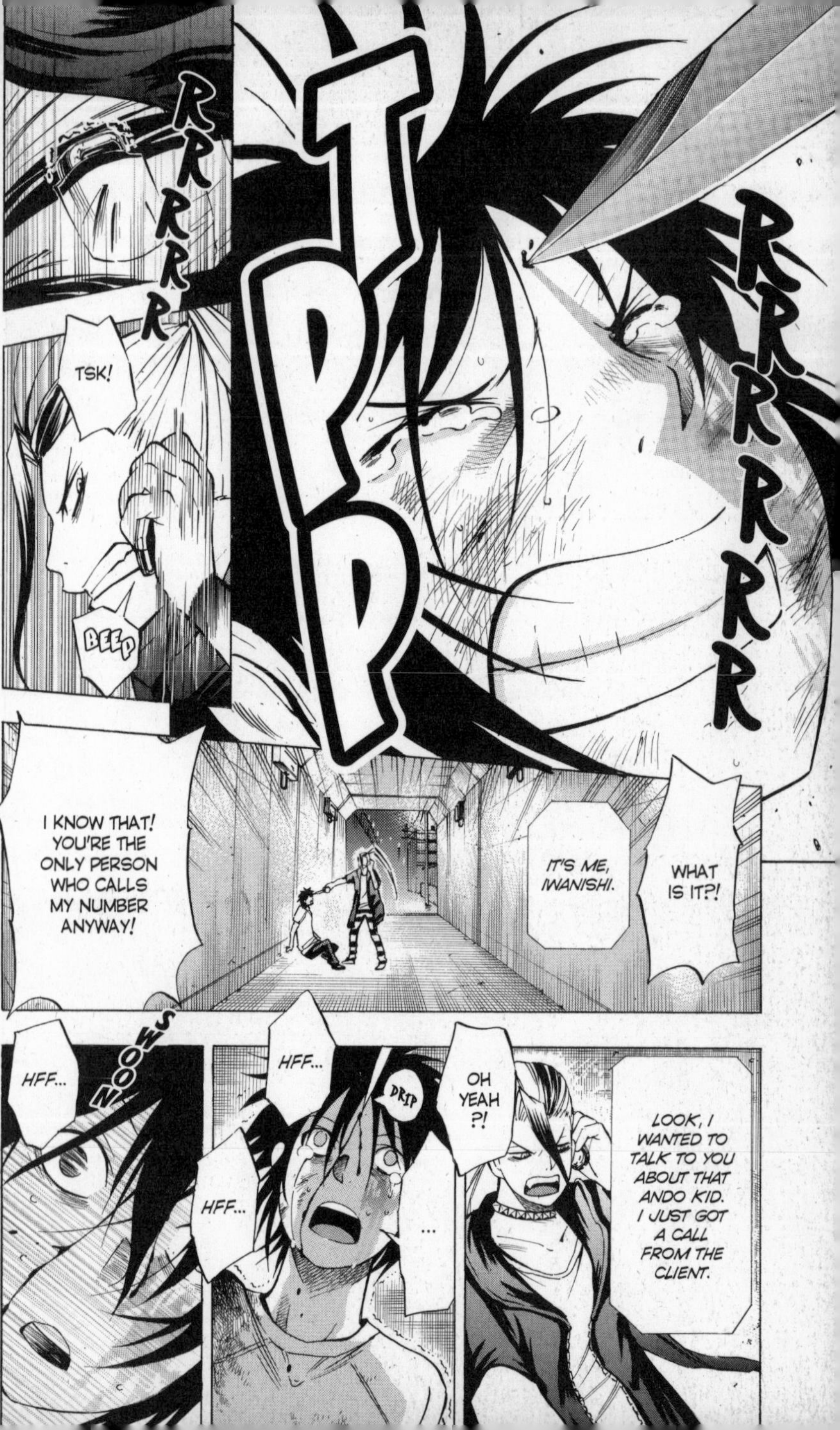

RRRRRR
TIP
RRRR
TSK!
BEEP
WHAT IS IT?!
IT'S ME, IWANISHI.
I KNOW THAT! YOU'RE THE ONLY PERSON WHO CALLS MY NUMBER ANYWAY!
LOOK, I WANTED TO TALK TO YOU ABOUT THAT ANDO KID. I JUST GOT A CALL FROM THE CLIENT.
OH YEAH?!
HFF...
DRIP
HFF...
...
HFF...
SWOON

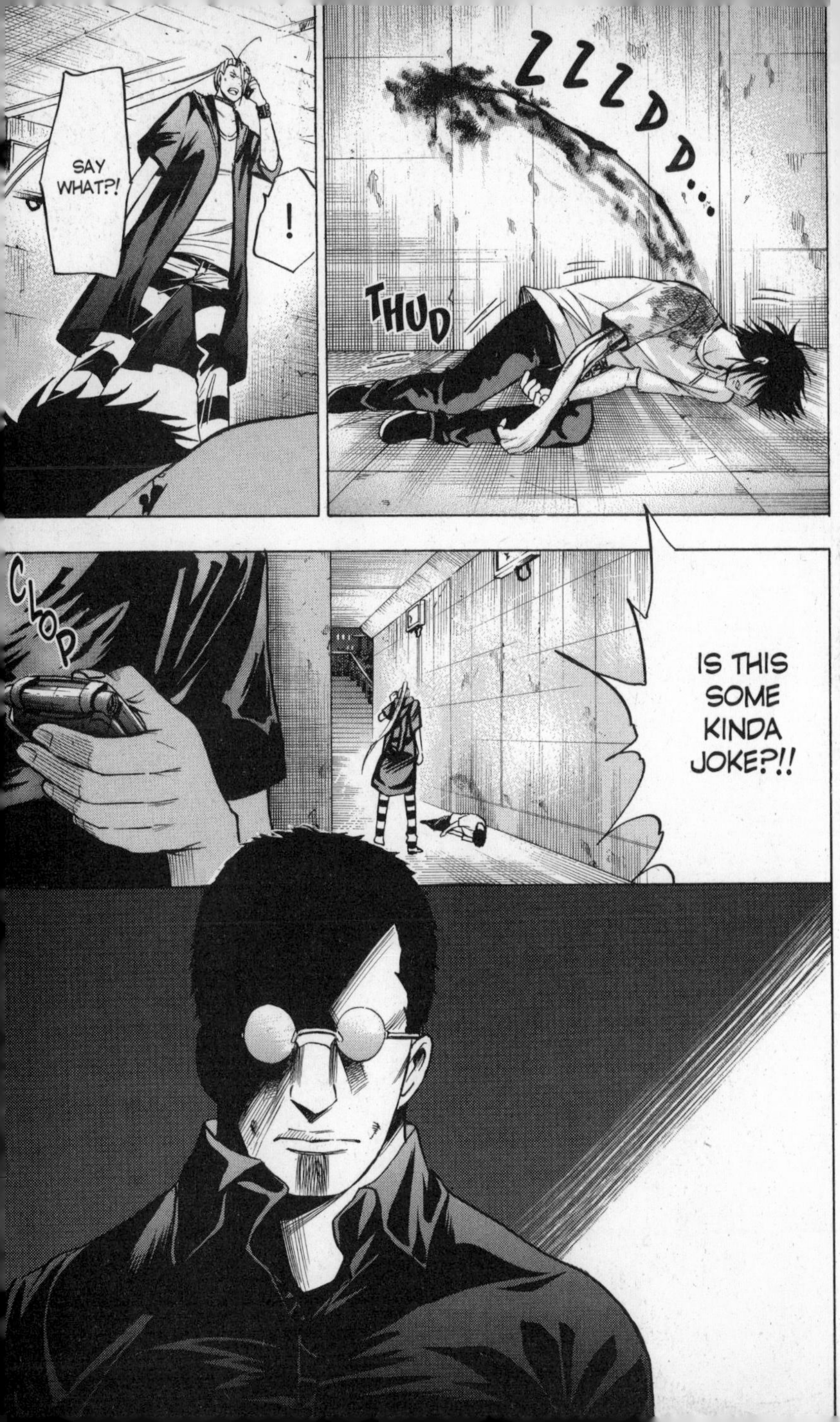
ZZZDD...
THUD
!
SAY WHAT?!
IS THIS SOME KINDA JOKE?!!
CLOP

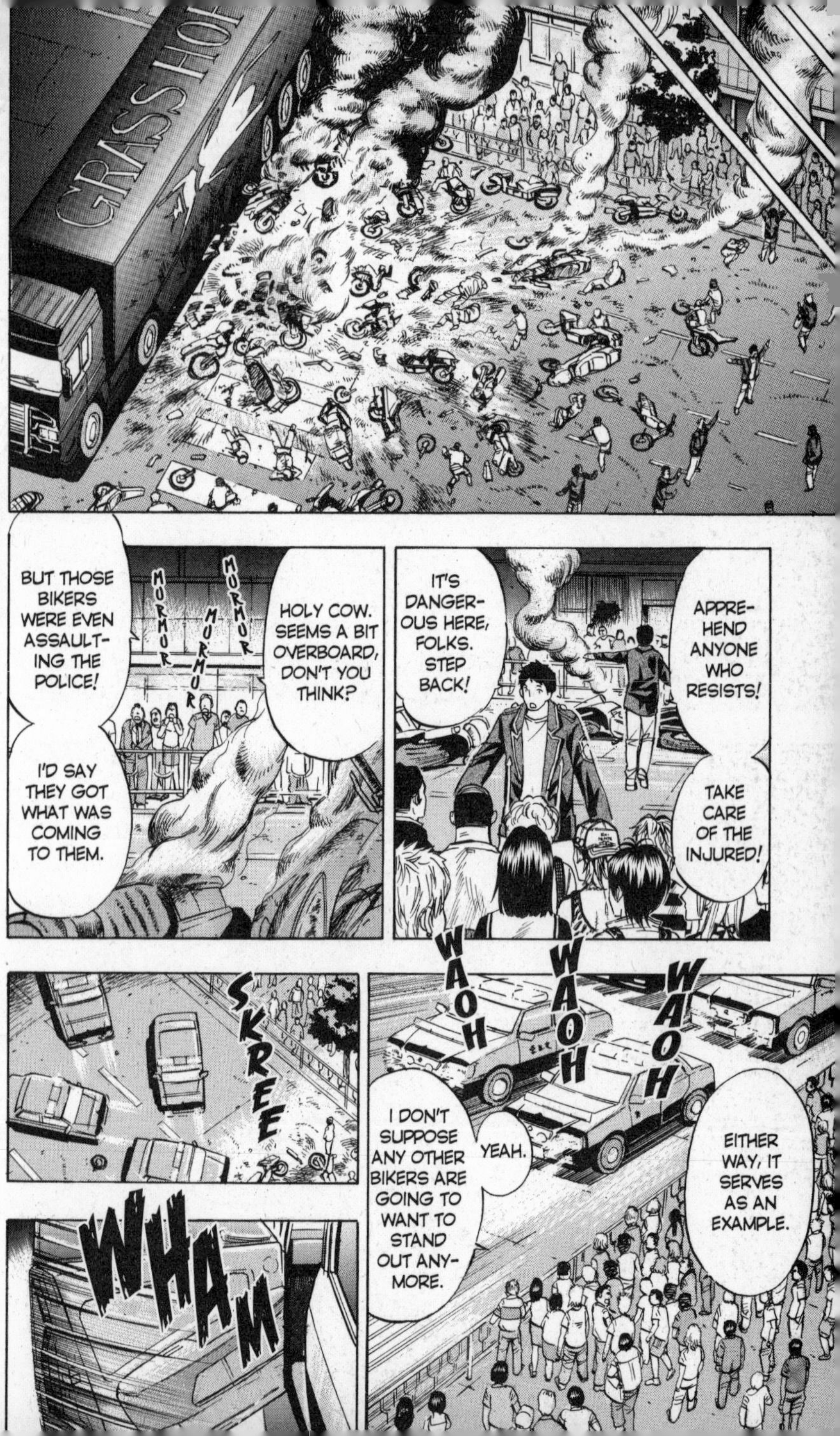

GRASS HO
APPREHEND ANYONE WHO RESISTS!
TAKE CARE OF THE INJURED!
IT'S DANGEROUS HERE, FOLKS. STEP BACK!
HOLY COW. SEEMS A BIT OVERBOARD, DON'T YOU THINK?
MURMUR
MURMUR
MURMUR
BUT THOSE BIKERS WERE EVEN ASSAULTING THE POLICE!
I'D SAY THEY GOT WHAT WAS COMING TO THEM.
WAOH
WAOH
WAOH
EITHER WAY, IT SERVES AS AN EXAMPLE.
YEAH.
I DON'T SUPPOSE ANY OTHER BIKERS ARE GOING TO WANT TO STAND OUT ANYMORE.
SKREE
WHAM

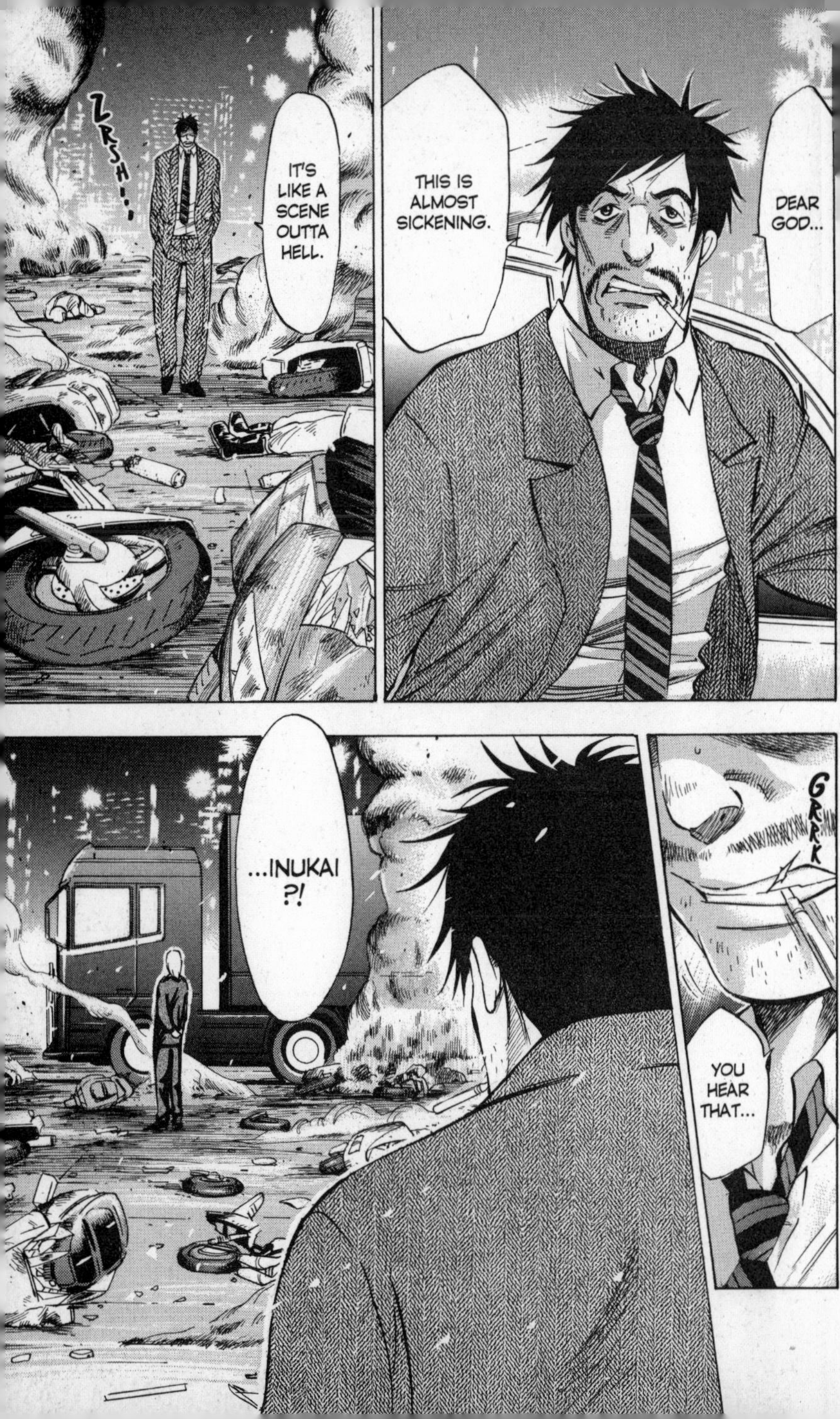
DEAR GOD...
THIS IS ALMOST SICKENING.
IT'S LIKE A SCENE OUTTA HELL.
ZRSH...
GRRK
YOU HEAR THAT...
...INUKAI ?!

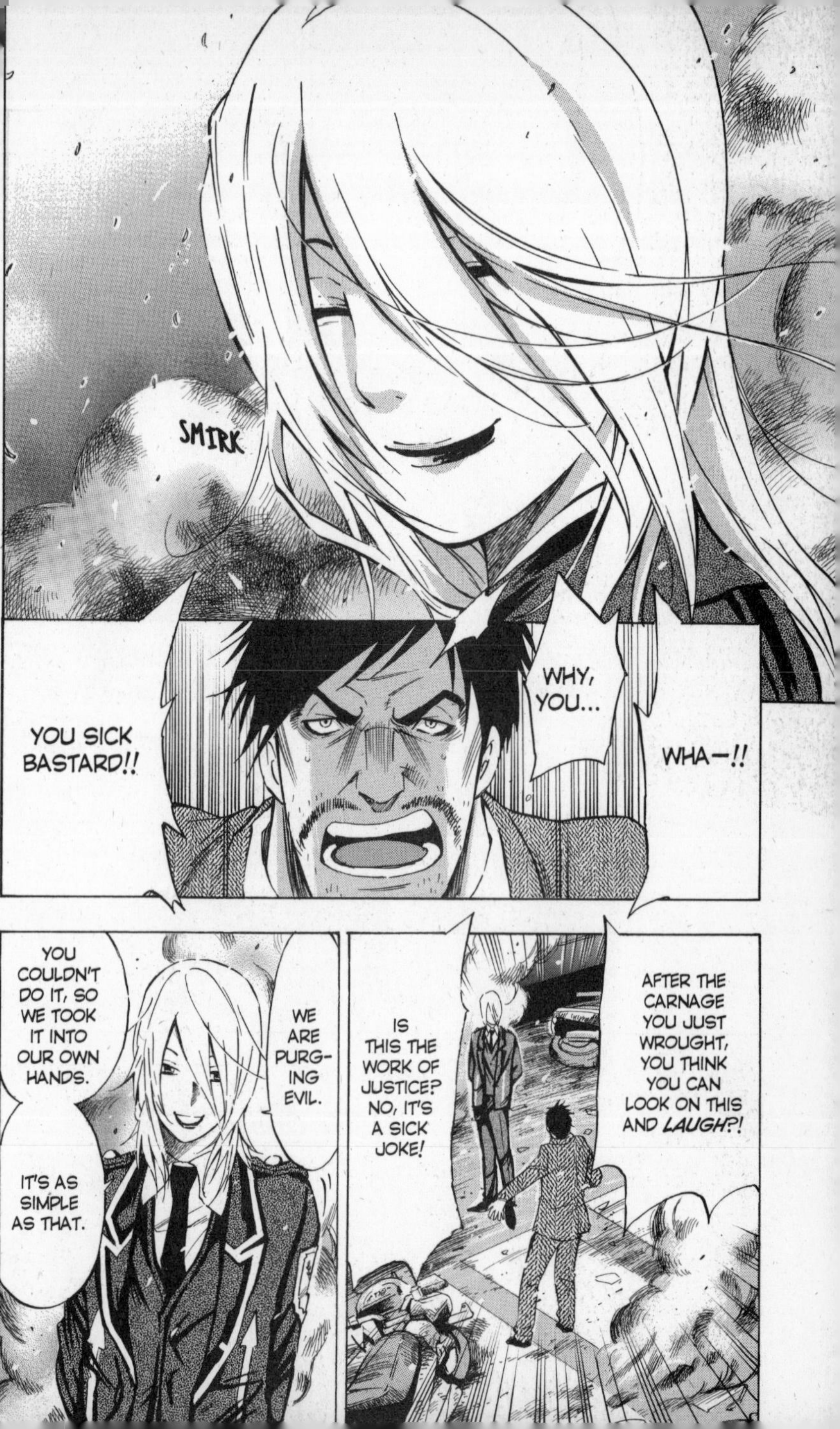
SMIRK
WHA—!!
WHY, YOU...
YOU SICK BASTARD!!
AFTER THE CARNAGE YOU JUST WROUGHT, YOU THINK YOU CAN LOOK ON THIS AND *LAUGH*?!
IS THIS THE WORK OF JUSTICE? NO, IT'S A SICK JOKE!
WE ARE PURG-ING EVIL.
YOU COULDN'T DO IT, SO WE TOOK IT INTO OUR OWN HANDS.
IT'S AS SIMPLE AS THAT.

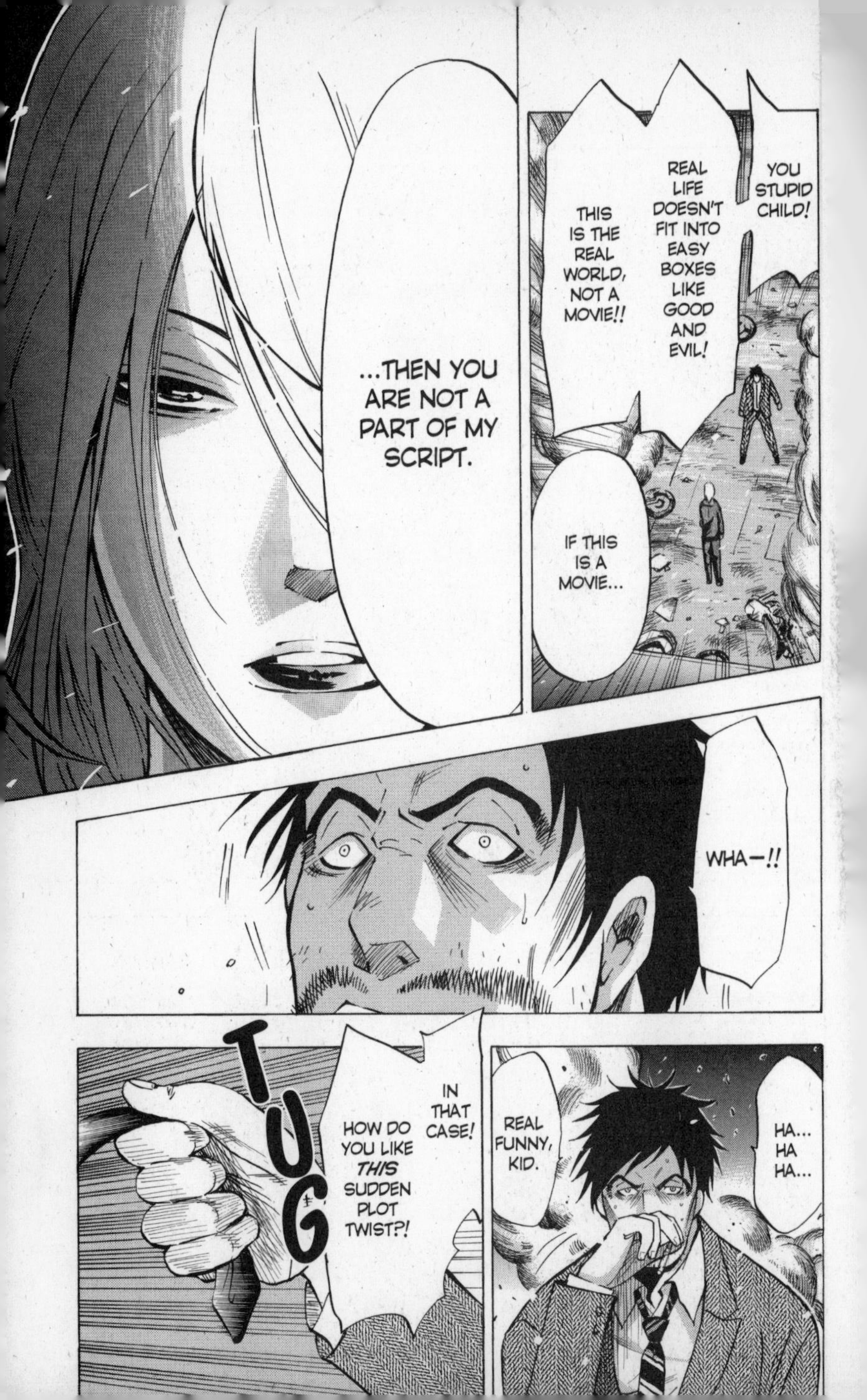
YOU STUPID CHILD!
REAL LIFE DOESN'T FIT INTO EASY BOXES LIKE GOOD AND EVIL!
THIS IS THE REAL WORLD, NOT A MOVIE!!
IF THIS IS A MOVIE...
...THEN YOU ARE NOT A PART OF MY SCRIPT.
WHA—!!
HA... HA HA...
REAL FUNNY, KID.
IN THAT CASE!
HOW DO YOU LIKE *THIS* SUDDEN PLOT TWIST?!
TUG

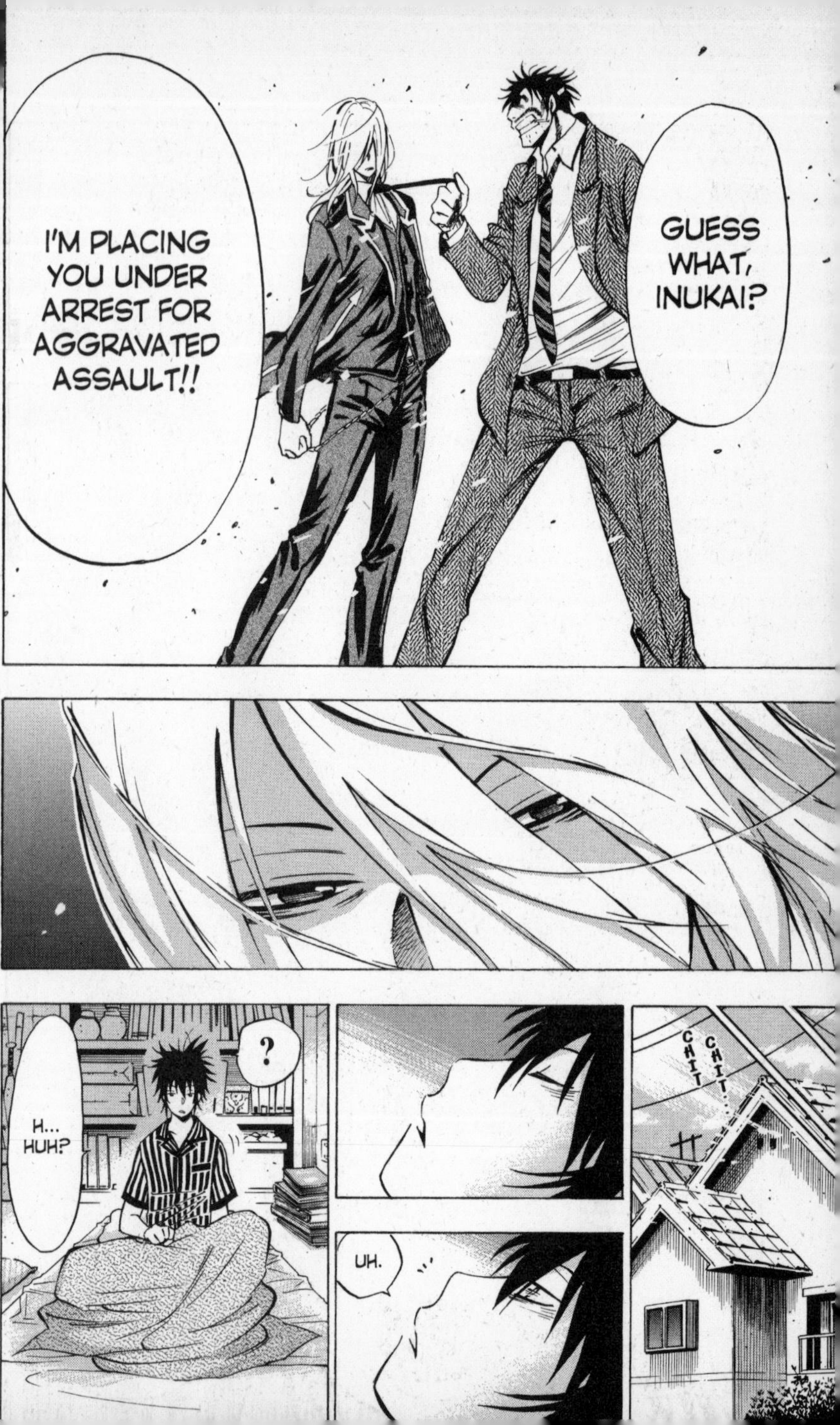
GUESS WHAT, INUKAI?
I'M PLACING YOU UNDER ARREST FOR AGGRAVATED ASSAULT!!
CHIT CHIT...
UH.
?
H... HUH?

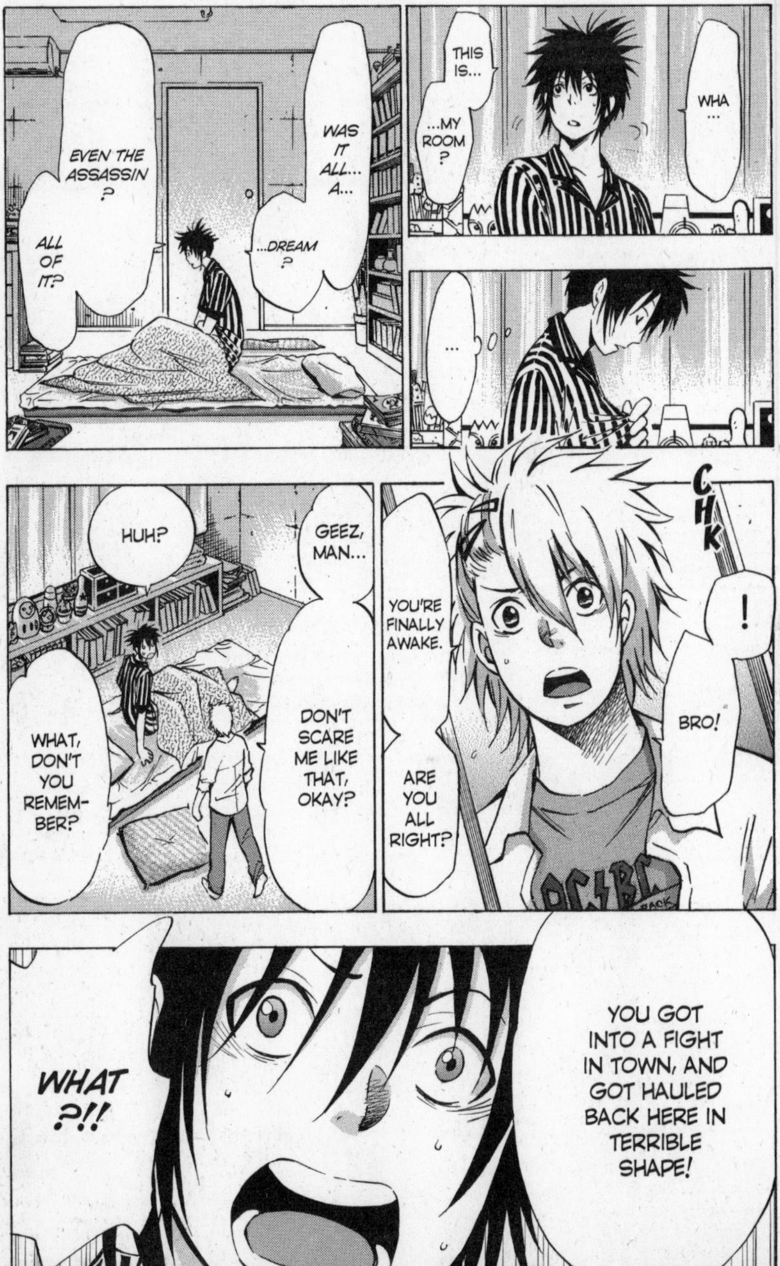
WHA...
THIS IS...
...MY ROOM?
...
WAS IT ALL... A...
...DREAM?
EVEN THE ASSASSIN?
ALL OF IT?
CHK
!
BRO!
YOU'RE FINALLY AWAKE.
ARE YOU ALL RIGHT?
GEEZ, MAN...
DON'T SCARE ME LIKE THAT, OKAY?
HUH?
WHAT, DON'T YOU REMEMBER?
YOU GOT INTO A FIGHT IN TOWN, AND GOT HAULED BACK HERE IN TERRIBLE SHAPE!
WHAT?!!

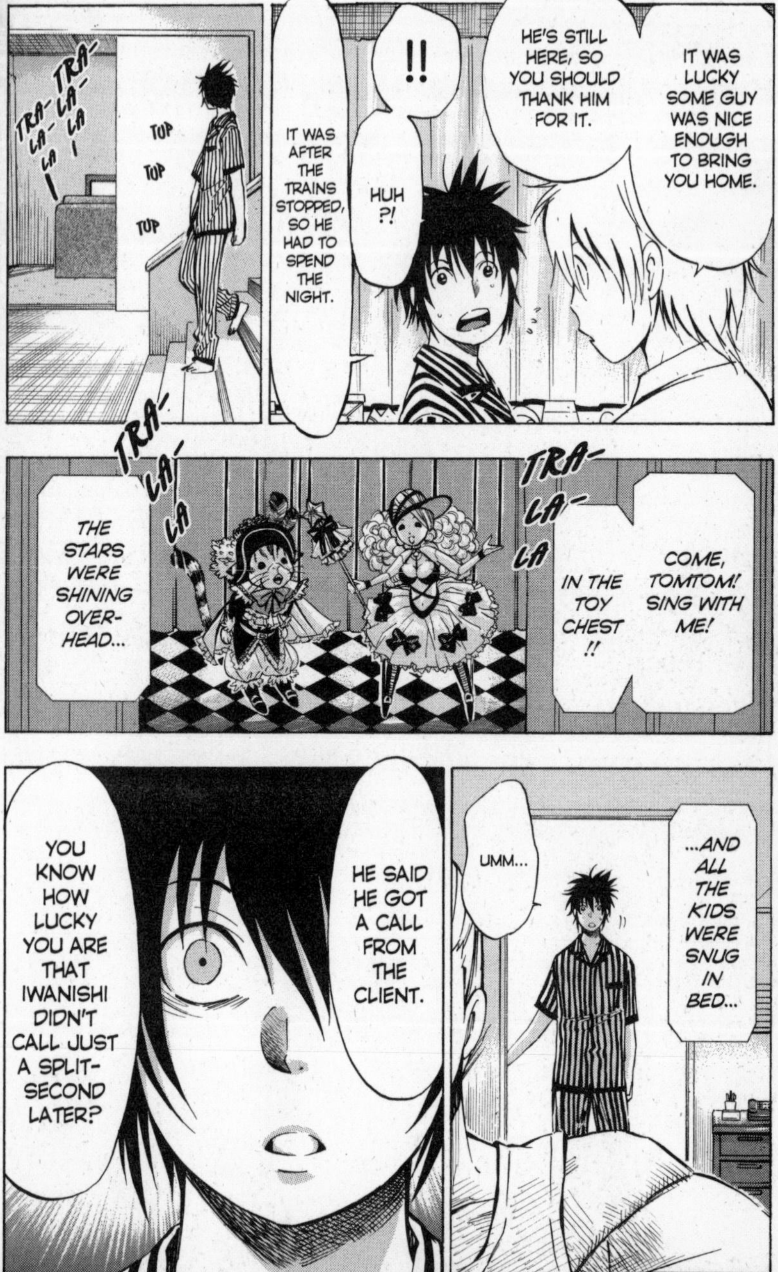
IT WAS LUCKY SOME GUY WAS NICE ENOUGH TO BRING YOU HOME.
HE'S STILL HERE, SO YOU SHOULD THANK HIM FOR IT.
!!
HUH?!
IT WAS AFTER THE TRAINS STOPPED, SO HE HAD TO SPEND THE NIGHT.
TRA-LA-LA
TRA-LA-LA
TUP
TUP
TUP
TRA-LA-LA
COME, TOMTOM! SING WITH ME!
IN THE TOY CHEST!!
TRA-LA-LA
THE STARS WERE SHINING OVERHEAD...
...AND ALL THE KIDS WERE SNUG IN BED...
UMM...
HE SAID HE GOT A CALL FROM THE CLIENT.
YOU KNOW HOW LUCKY YOU ARE THAT IWANISHI DIDN'T CALL JUST A SPLIT-SECOND LATER?

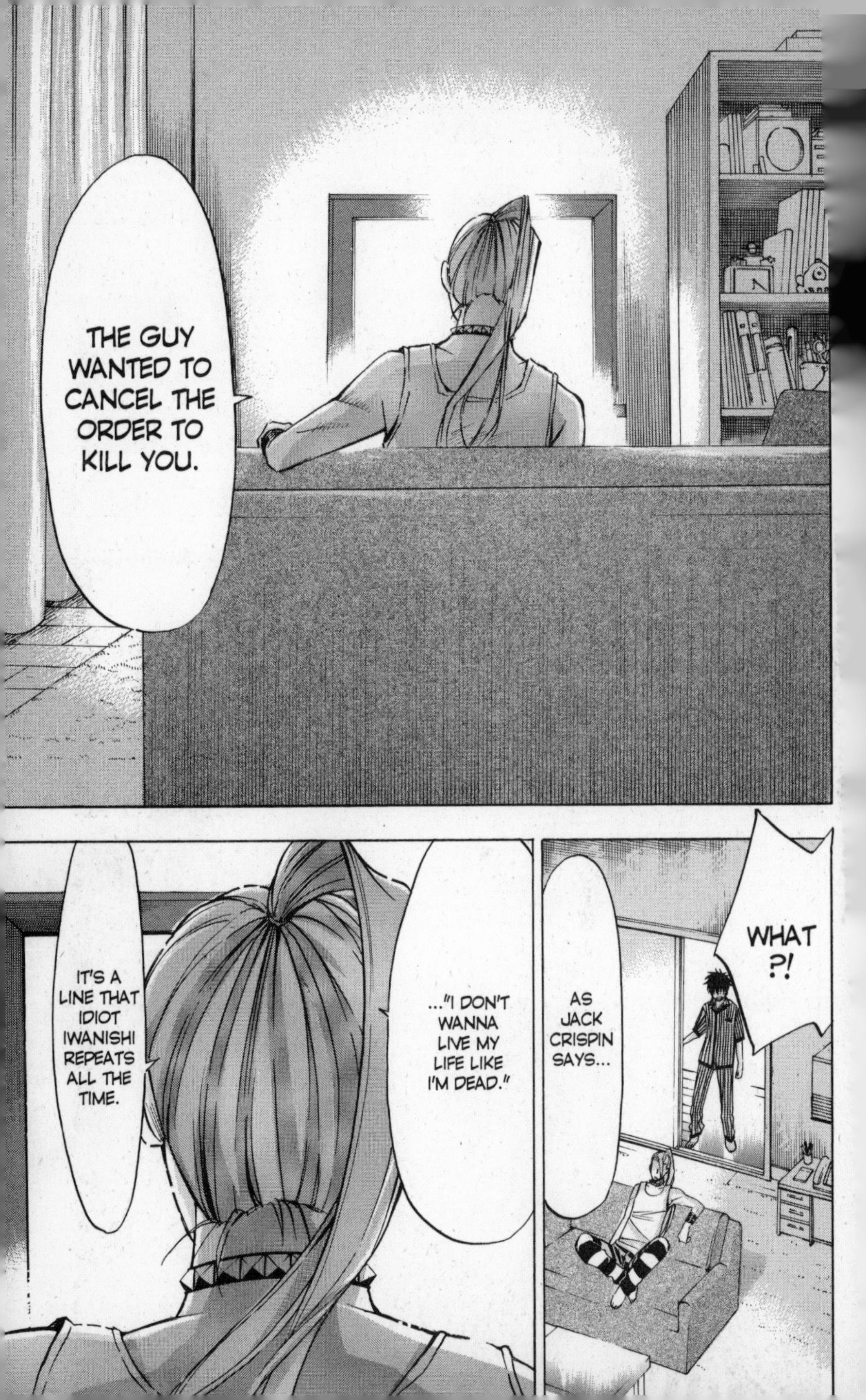
THE GUY WANTED TO CANCEL THE ORDER TO KILL YOU.
WHAT?!
AS JACK CRISPIN SAYS...
..."I DON'T WANNA LIVE MY LIFE LIKE I'M DEAD."
IT'S A LINE THAT IDIOT IWANISHI REPEATS ALL THE TIME.

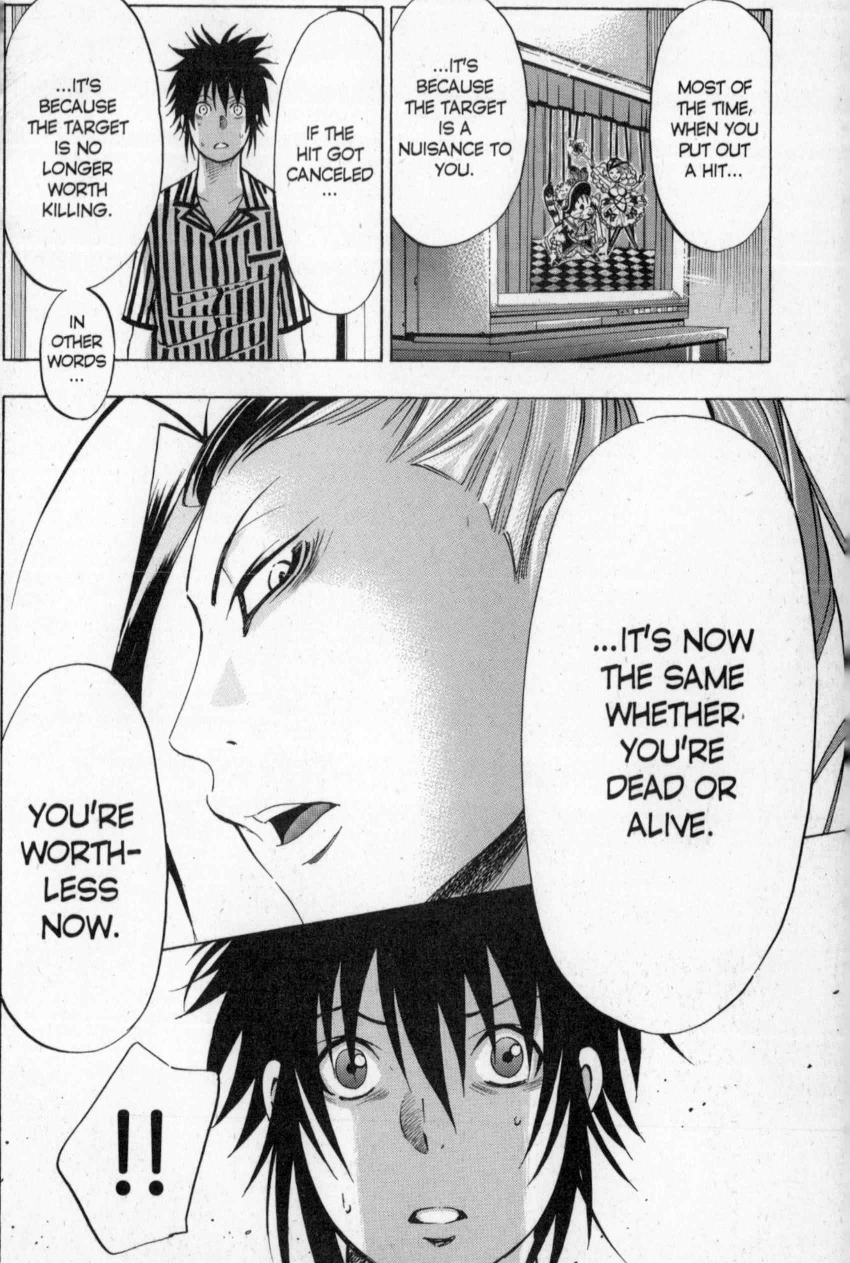
MOST OF THE TIME, WHEN YOU PUT OUT A HIT...
...IT'S BECAUSE THE TARGET IS A NUISANCE TO YOU.
IF THE HIT GOT CANCELED...
...IT'S BECAUSE THE TARGET IS NO LONGER WORTH KILLING.
IN OTHER WORDS...
...IT'S NOW THE SAME WHETHER YOU'RE DEAD OR ALIVE.
YOU'RE WORTH-LESS NOW.
!!

Chapter 13 • Reason

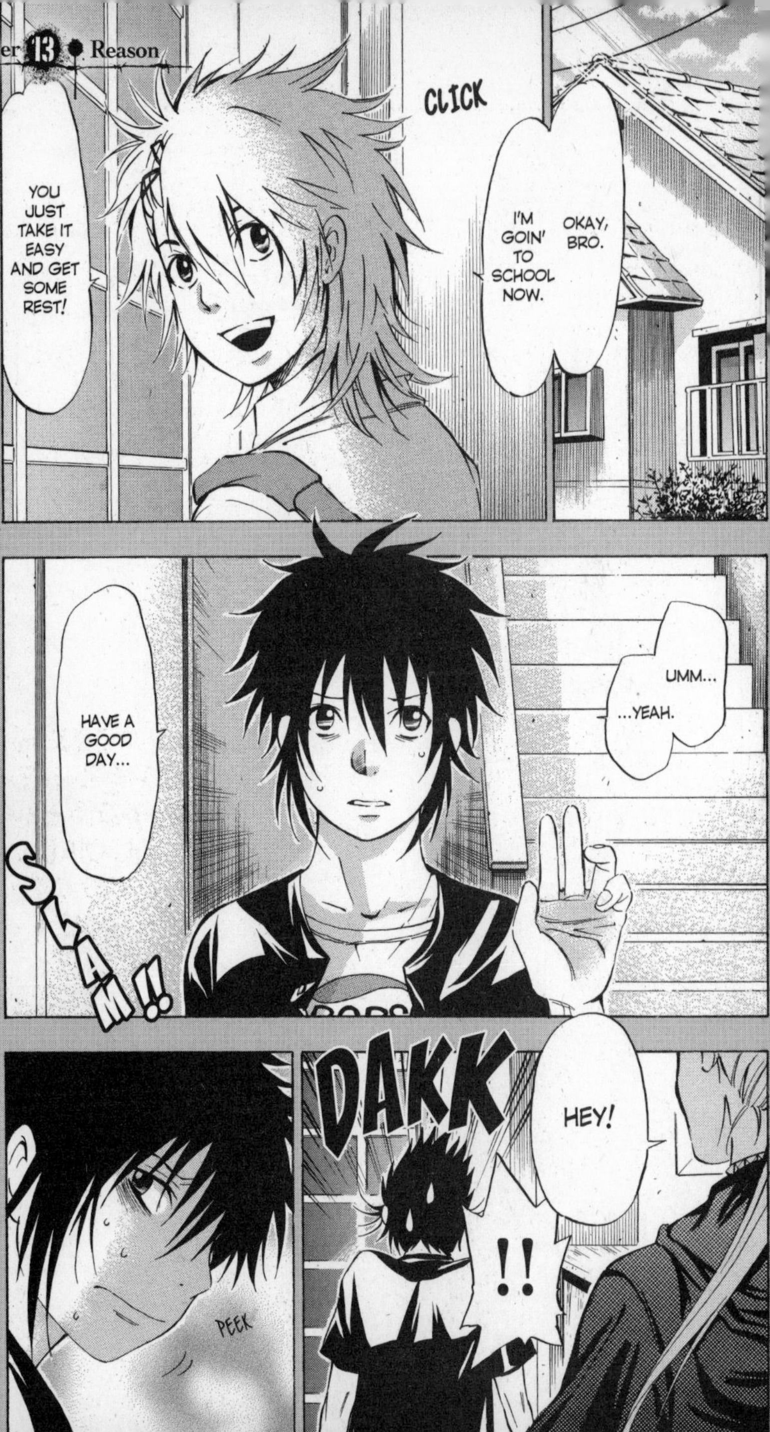

OKAY, BRO.
I'M GOIN' TO SCHOOL NOW.
CLICK
YOU JUST TAKE IT EASY AND GET SOME REST!
UMM...
...YEAH.
HAVE A GOOD DAY...
SLAM!!
HEY!
DAKK
!!
PEEK

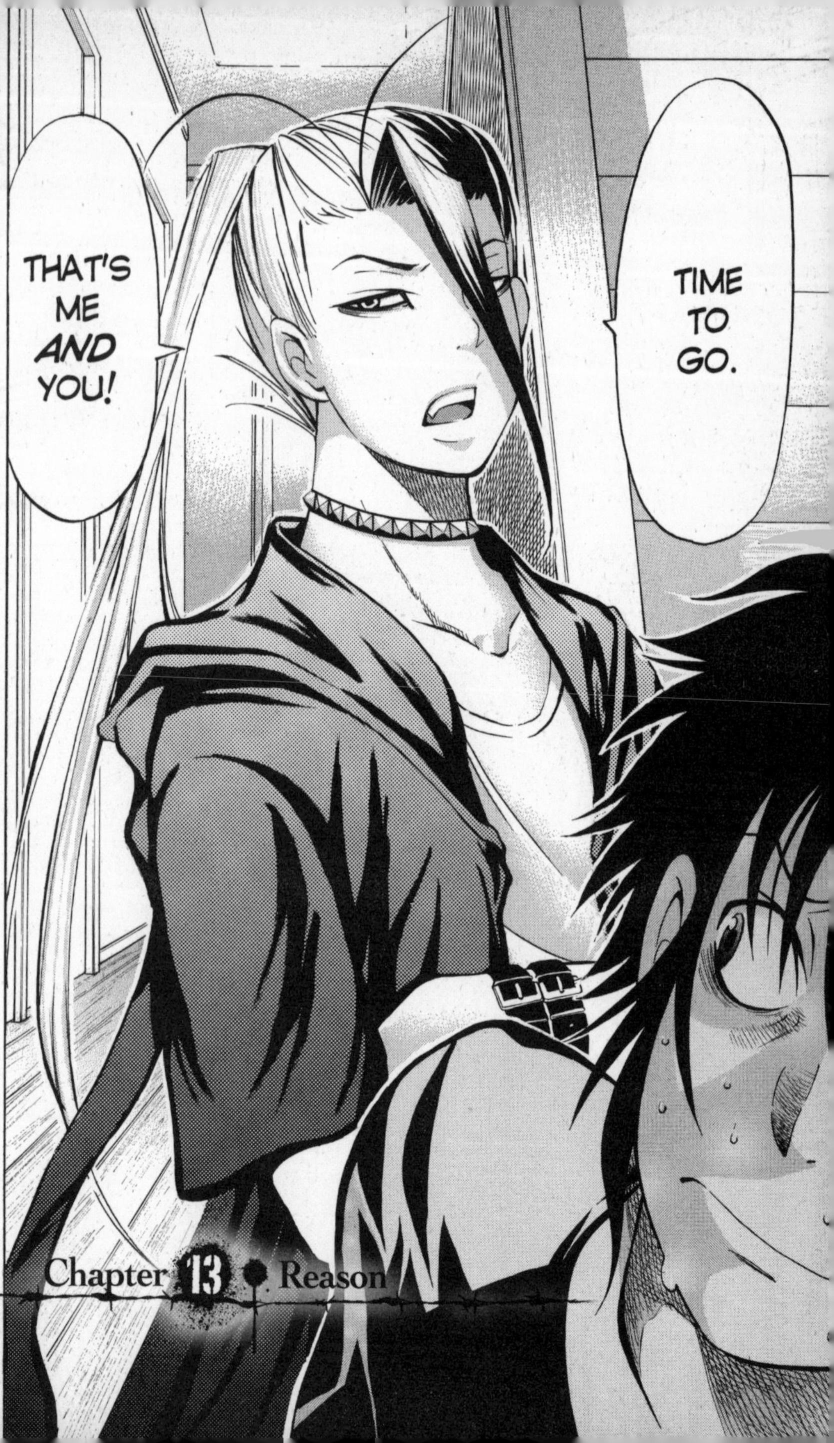
TIME TO GO.
THAT'S ME *AND* YOU!
Chapter 13 Reason

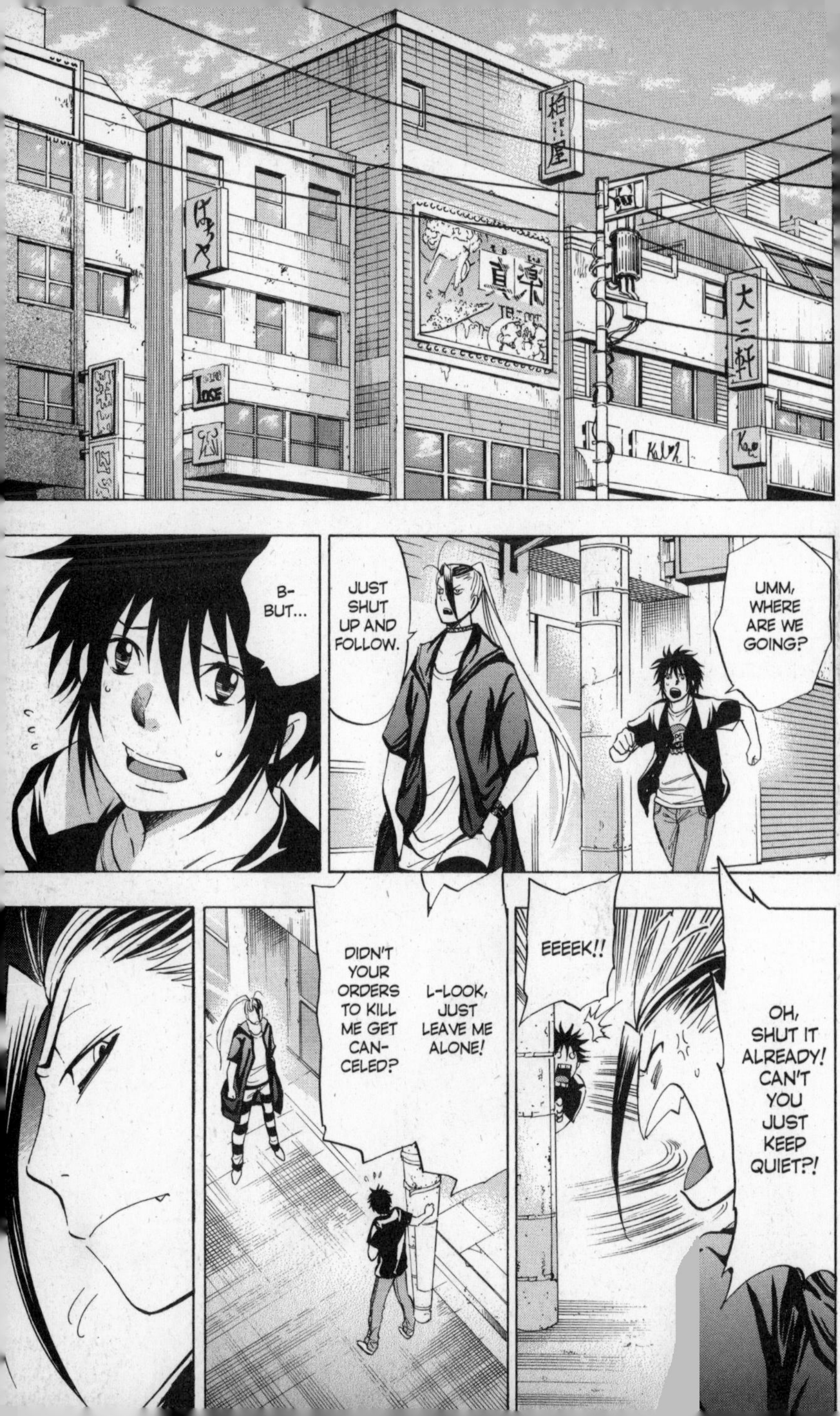
UMM, WHERE ARE WE GOING?
JUST SHUT UP AND FOLLOW.
B-BUT...
OH, SHUT IT ALREADY! CAN'T YOU JUST KEEP QUIET?!
EEEEK!!
L-LOOK, JUST LEAVE ME ALONE!
DIDN'T YOUR ORDERS TO KILL ME GET CAN-CELED?

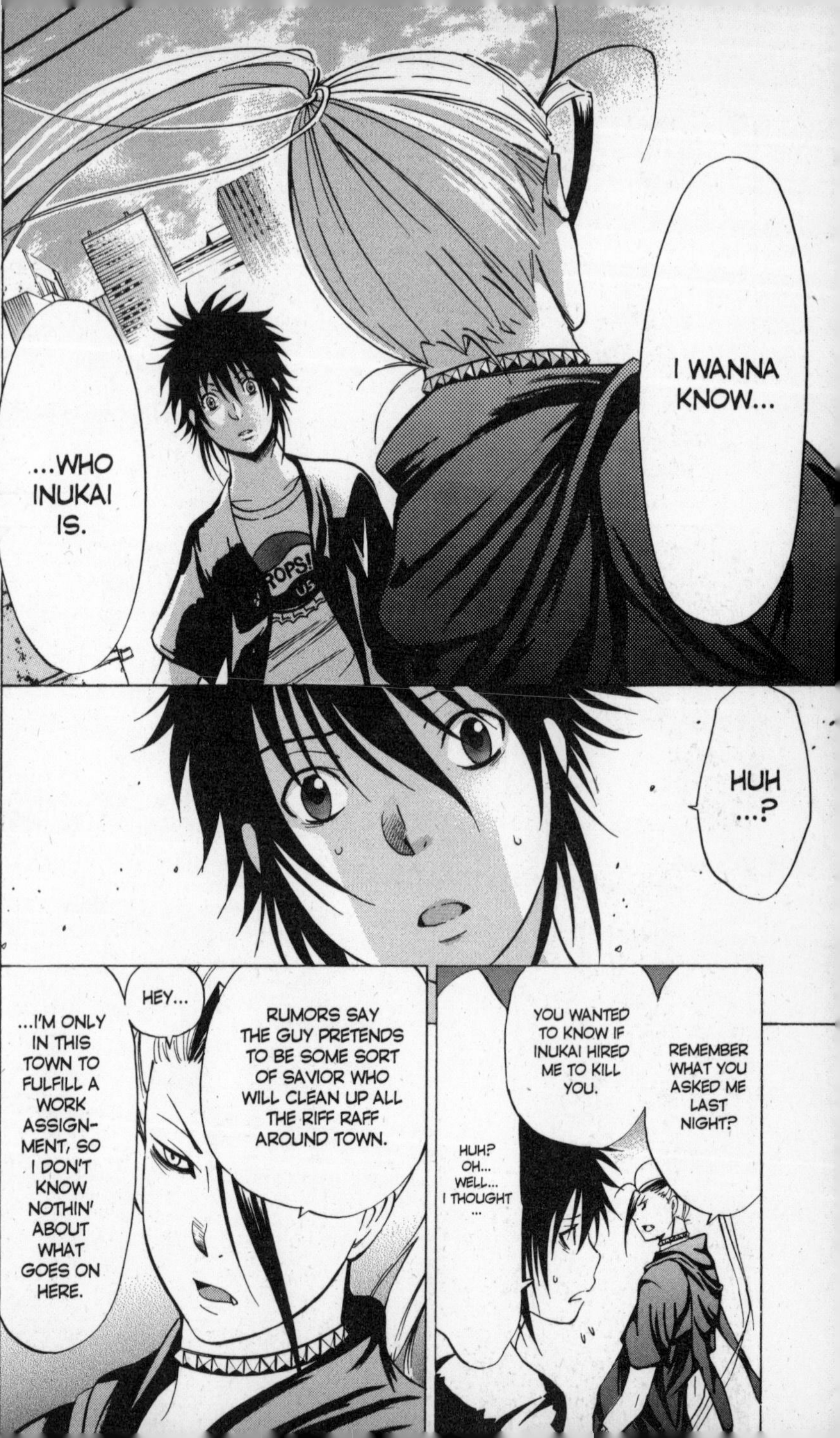
I WANNA KNOW...
...WHO INUKAI IS.
HUH ...?
REMEMBER WHAT YOU ASKED ME LAST NIGHT?
YOU WANTED TO KNOW IF INUKAI HIRED ME TO KILL YOU.
HUH? OH... WELL... I THOUGHT ...
HEY...
RUMORS SAY THE GUY PRETENDS TO BE SOME SORT OF SAVIOR WHO WILL CLEAN UP ALL THE RIFF RAFF AROUND TOWN.
...I'M ONLY IN THIS TOWN TO FULFILL A WORK ASSIGN-MENT, SO I DON'T KNOW NOTHIN' ABOUT WHAT GOES ON HERE.

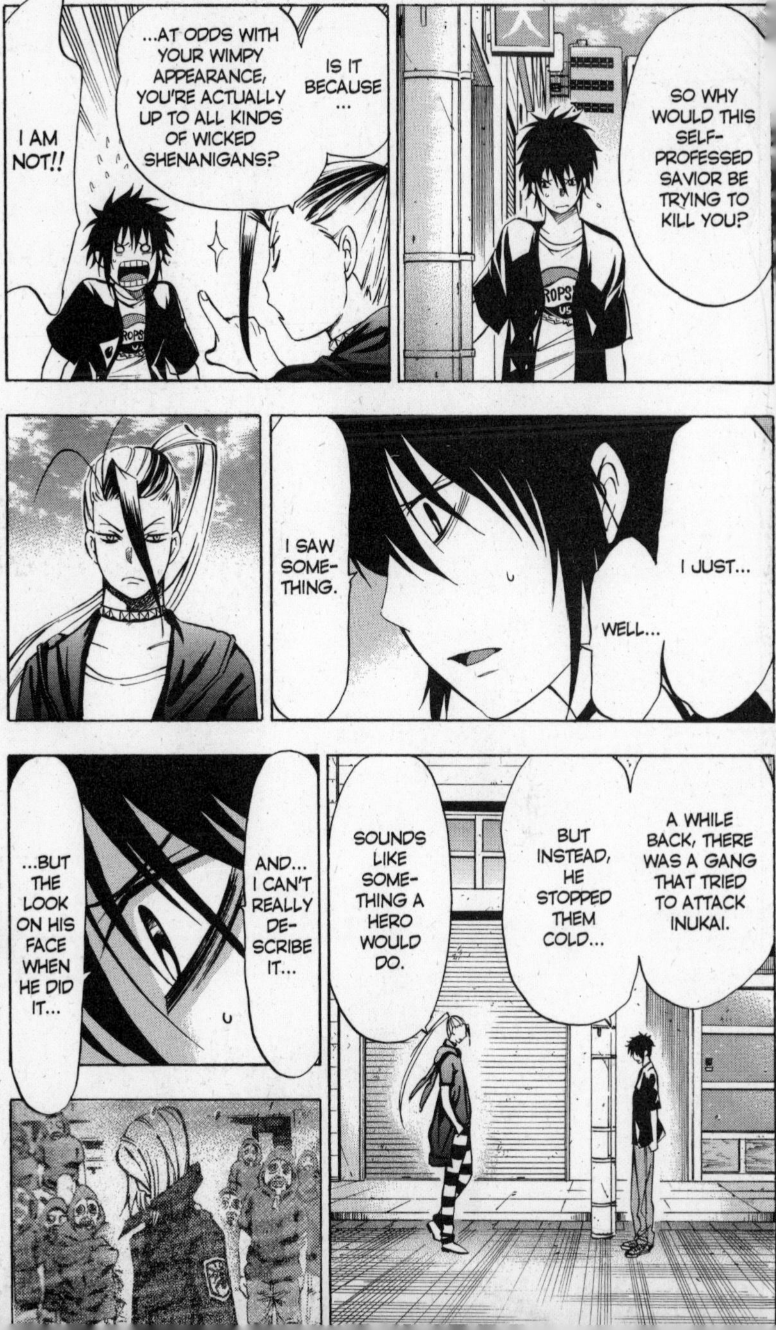
SO WHY WOULD THIS SELF-PROFESSED SAVIOR BE TRYING TO KILL YOU?
IS IT BECAUSE ...
...AT ODDS WITH YOUR WIMPY APPEARANCE, YOU'RE ACTUALLY UP TO ALL KINDS OF WICKED SHENANIGANS?
I AM NOT!!
I JUST...
WELL...
I SAW SOMETHING.
A WHILE BACK, THERE WAS A GANG THAT TRIED TO ATTACK INUKAI.
BUT INSTEAD, HE STOPPED THEM COLD...
SOUNDS LIKE SOMETHING A HERO WOULD DO.
AND... I CAN'T REALLY DESCRIBE IT...
...BUT THE LOOK ON HIS FACE WHEN HE DID IT...

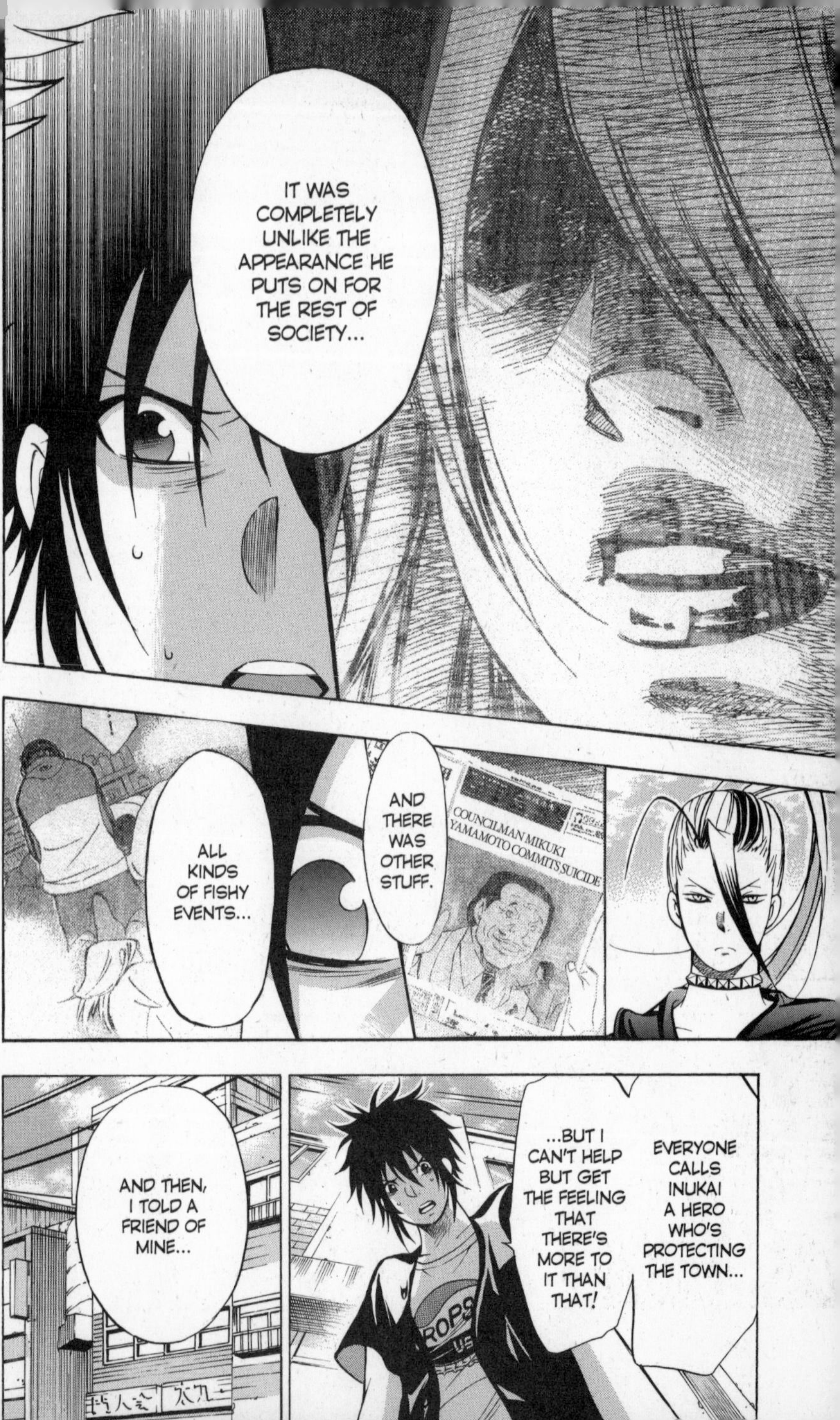
IT WAS COMPLETELY UNLIKE THE APPEARANCE HE PUTS ON FOR THE REST OF SOCIETY...
COUNCILMAN MIKUKI YAMAMOTO COMMITS SUICIDE
AND THERE WAS OTHER STUFF.
ALL KINDS OF FISHY EVENTS...
EVERYONE CALLS INUKAI A HERO WHO'S PROTECTING THE TOWN...
...BUT I CAN'T HELP BUT GET THE FEELING THAT THERE'S MORE TO IT THAN THAT!
AND THEN, I TOLD A FRIEND OF MINE...

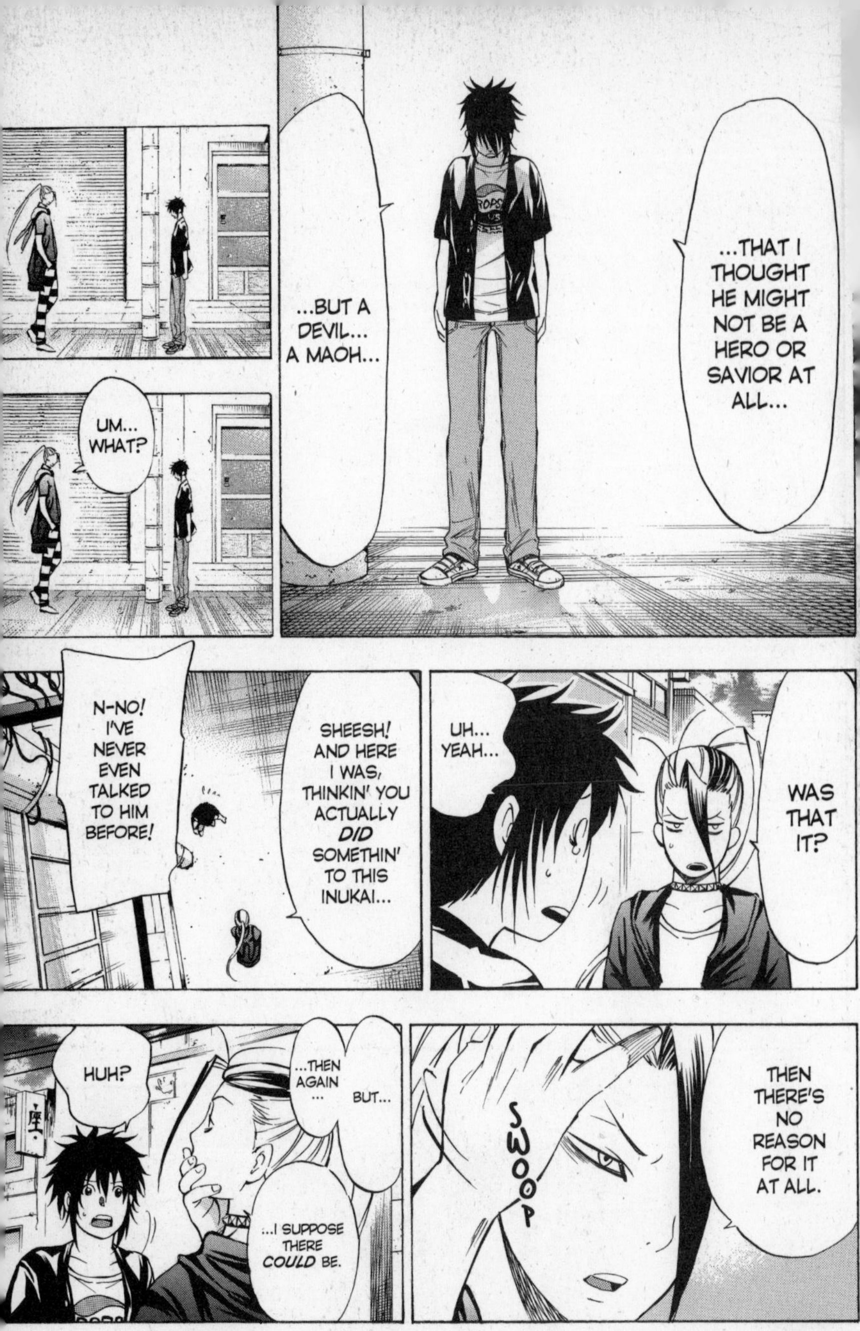
...THAT I THOUGHT HE MIGHT NOT BE A HERO OR SAVIOR AT ALL...
...BUT A DEVIL... A MAOH...
UM... WHAT?
WAS THAT IT?
UH... YEAH...
SHEESH! AND HERE I WAS, THINKIN' YOU ACTUALLY *DID* SOMETHIN' TO THIS INUKAI...
N-NO! I'VE NEVER EVEN TALKED TO HIM BEFORE!
THEN THERE'S NO REASON FOR IT AT ALL.
SWOOP
BUT...
...THEN AGAIN...
...I SUPPOSE THERE *COULD* BE.
HUH?

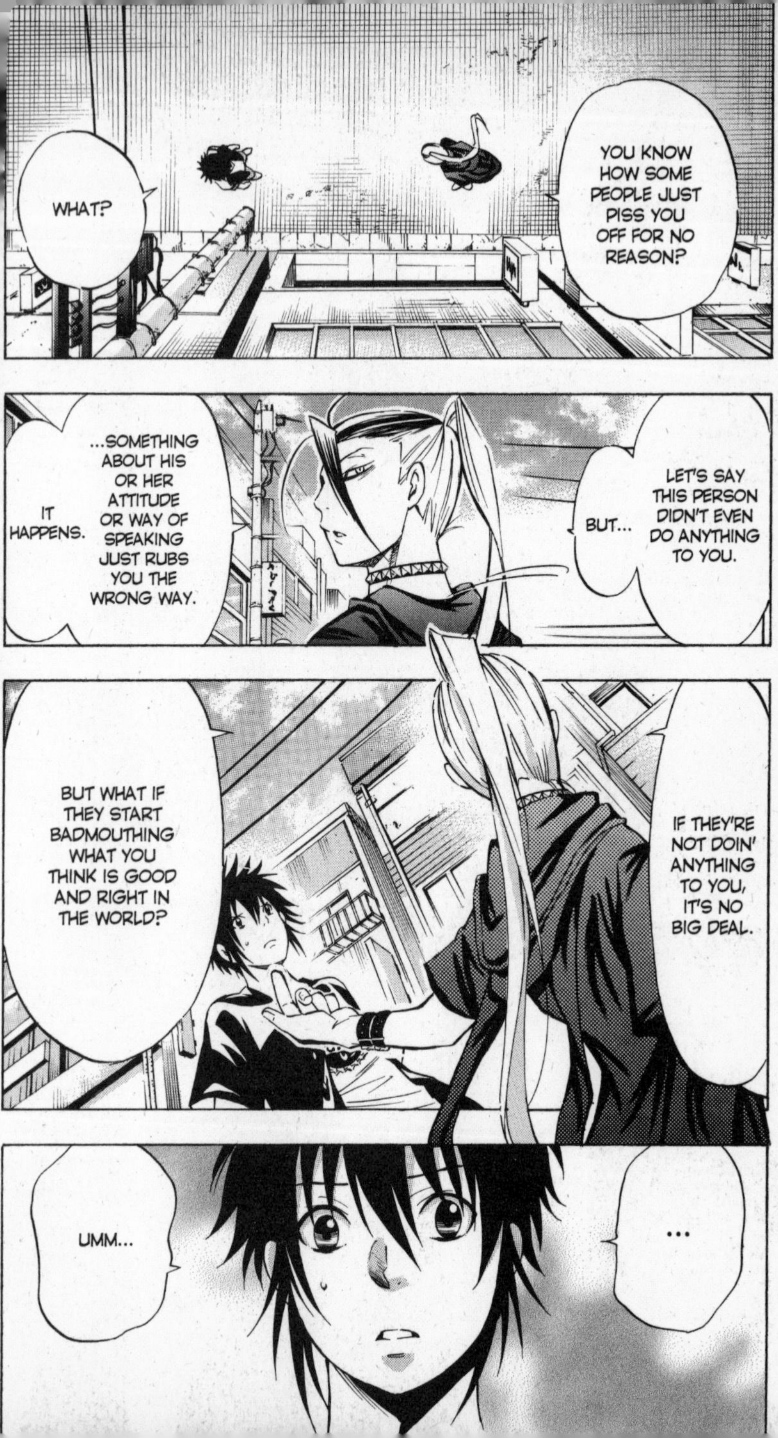

YOU KNOW HOW SOME PEOPLE JUST PISS YOU OFF FOR NO REASON?
WHAT?
BUT... LET'S SAY THIS PERSON DIDN'T EVEN DO ANYTHING TO YOU.
IT HAPPENS. ...SOMETHING ABOUT HIS OR HER ATTITUDE OR WAY OF SPEAKING JUST RUBS YOU THE WRONG WAY.
IF THEY'RE NOT DOIN' ANYTHING TO YOU, IT'S NO BIG DEAL.
BUT WHAT IF THEY START BADMOUTHING WHAT YOU THINK IS GOOD AND RIGHT IN THE WORLD?
...
UMM...

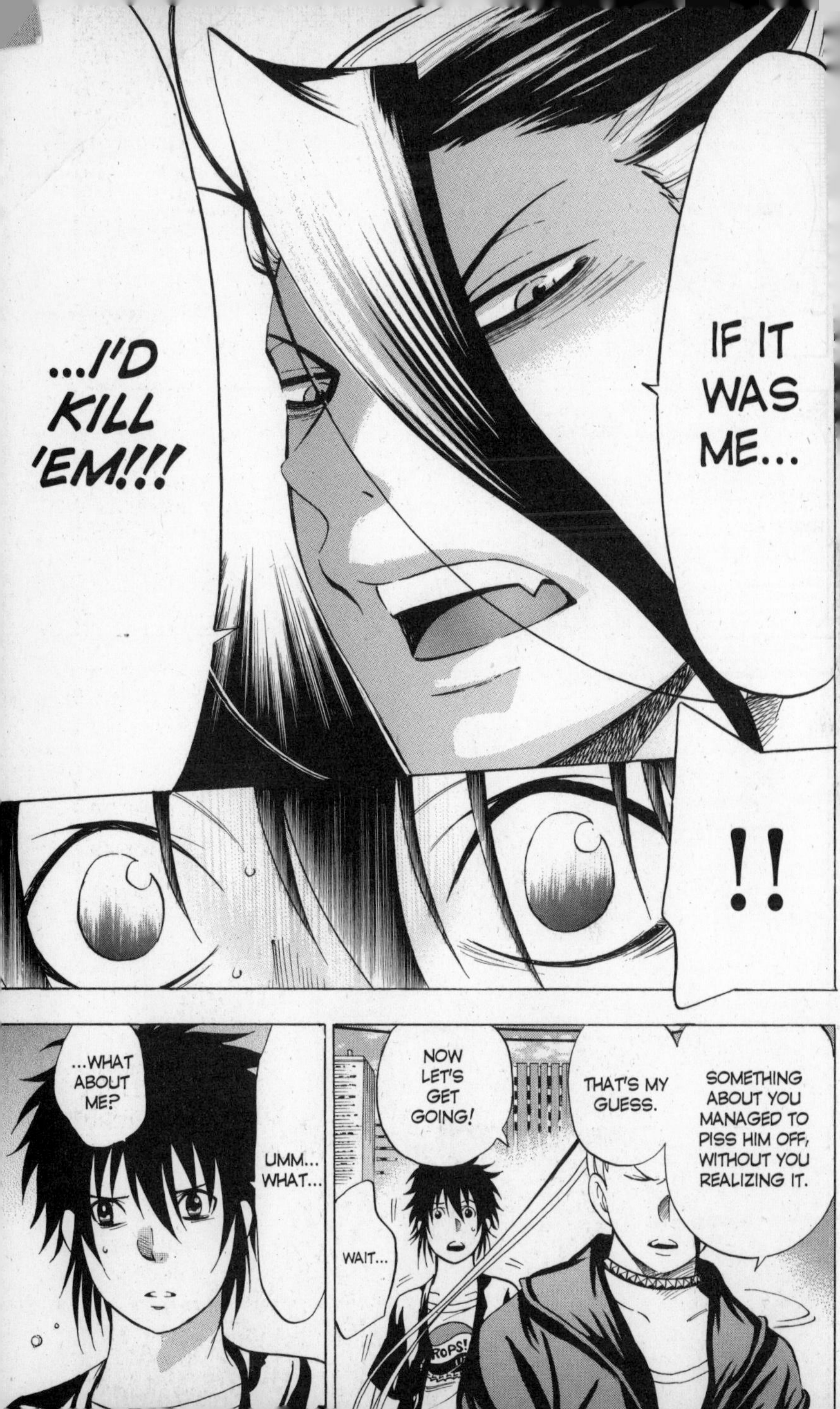
IF IT WAS ME...
...I'D KILL 'EM!!!
!!
SOMETHING ABOUT YOU MANAGED TO PISS HIM OFF, WITHOUT YOU REALIZING IT.
THAT'S MY GUESS.
NOW LET'S GET GOING!
WAIT...
UMM... WHAT...
...WHAT ABOUT ME?

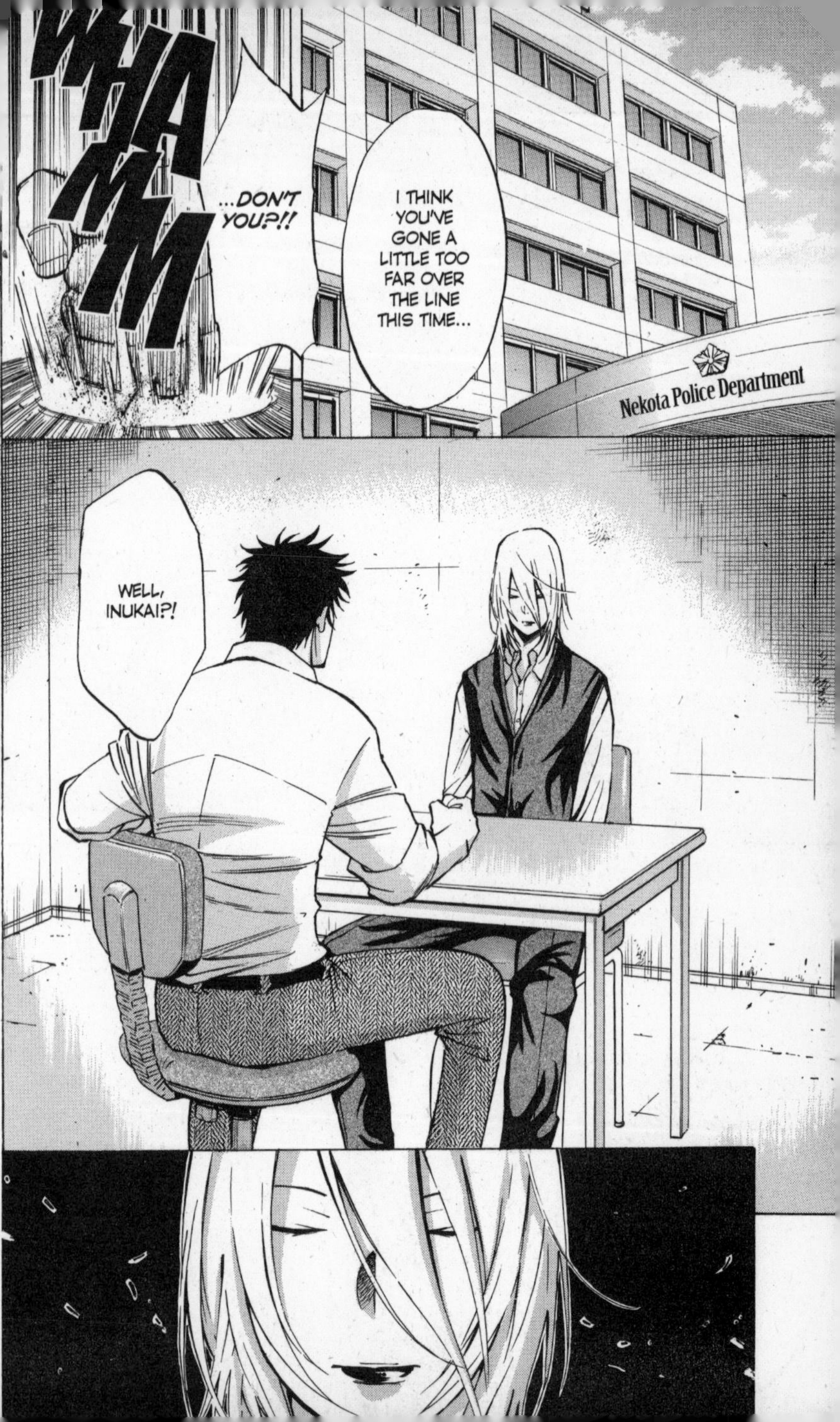

Nekota Police Department
I THINK YOU'VE GONE A LITTLE TOO FAR OVER THE LINE THIS TIME...
...DON'T YOU?!!
WHAMM
WELL, INUKAI?!

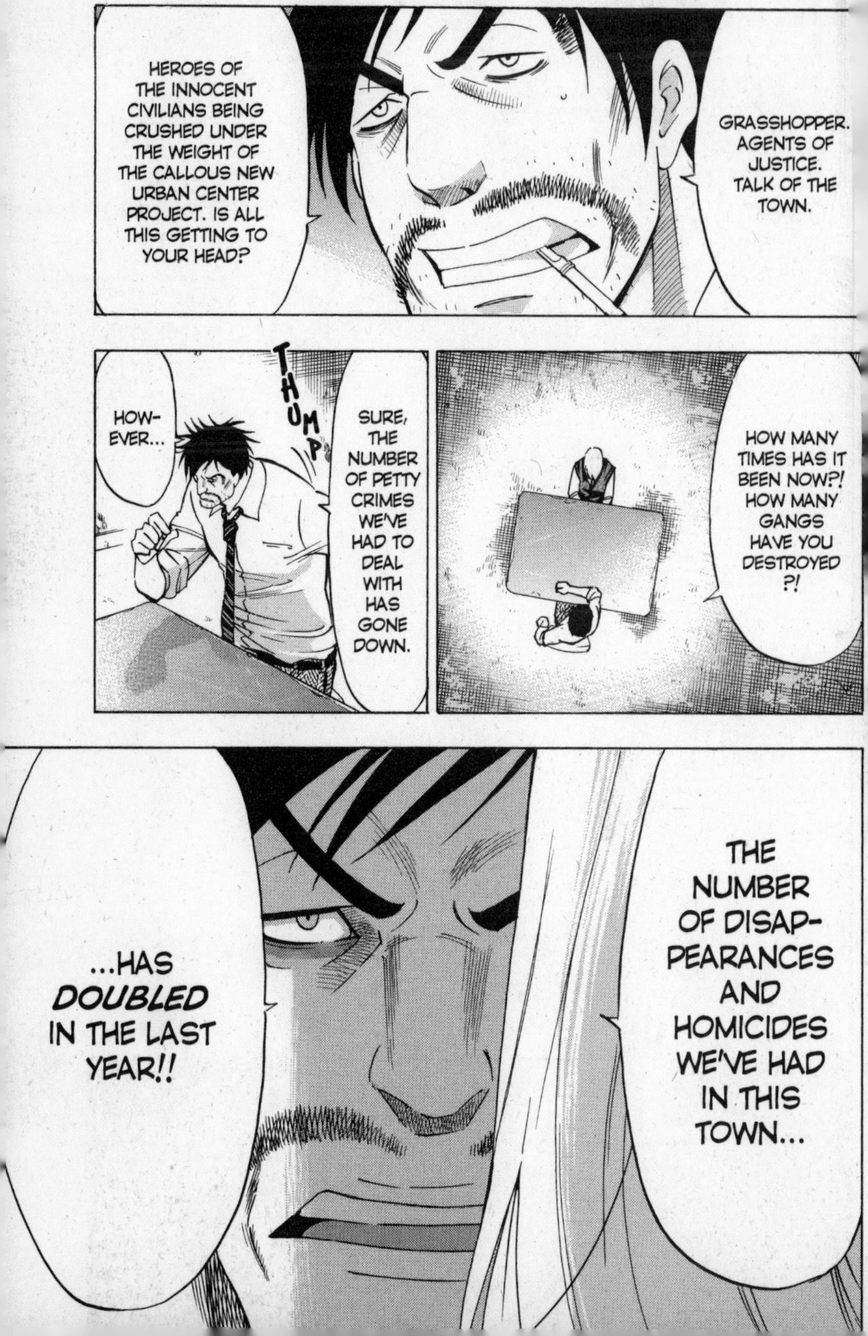
GRASSHOPPER. AGENTS OF JUSTICE. TALK OF THE TOWN.
HEROES OF THE INNOCENT CIVILIANS BEING CRUSHED UNDER THE WEIGHT OF THE CALLOUS NEW URBAN CENTER PROJECT. IS ALL THIS GETTING TO YOUR HEAD?
HOW MANY TIMES HAS IT BEEN NOW?! HOW MANY GANGS HAVE YOU DESTROYED ?!
SURE, THE NUMBER OF PETTY CRIMES WE'VE HAD TO DEAL WITH HAS GONE DOWN.
THUMP
HOW-EVER...
THE NUMBER OF DISAP-PEARANCES AND HOMICIDES WE'VE HAD IN THIS TOWN...
...HAS *DOUBLED* IN THE LAST YEAR!!

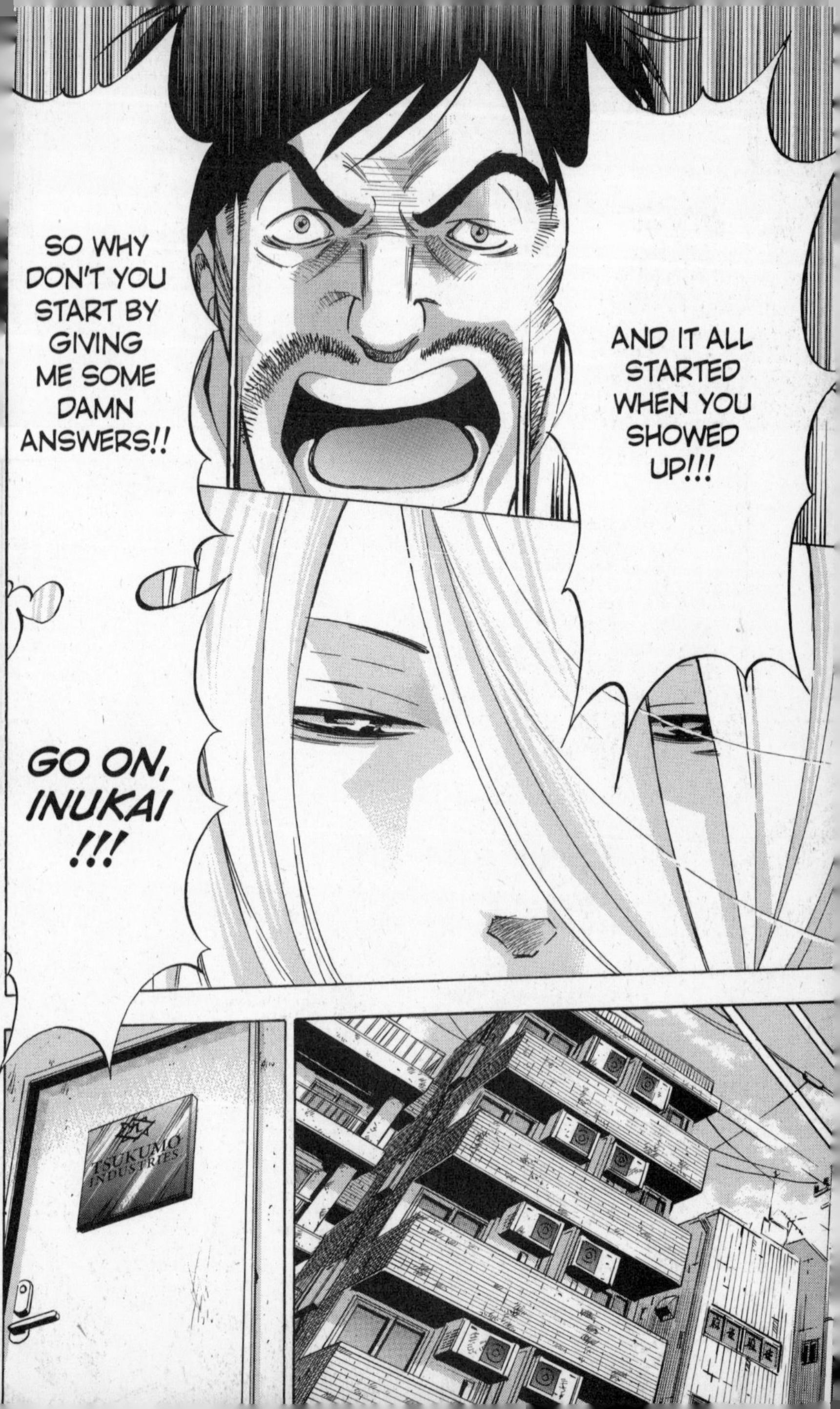
AND IT ALL STARTED WHEN YOU SHOWED UP!!!
SO WHY DON'T YOU START BY GIVING ME SOME DAMN ANSWERS!!
GO ON, INUKAI !!!
TSUKUMO INDUSTRIES

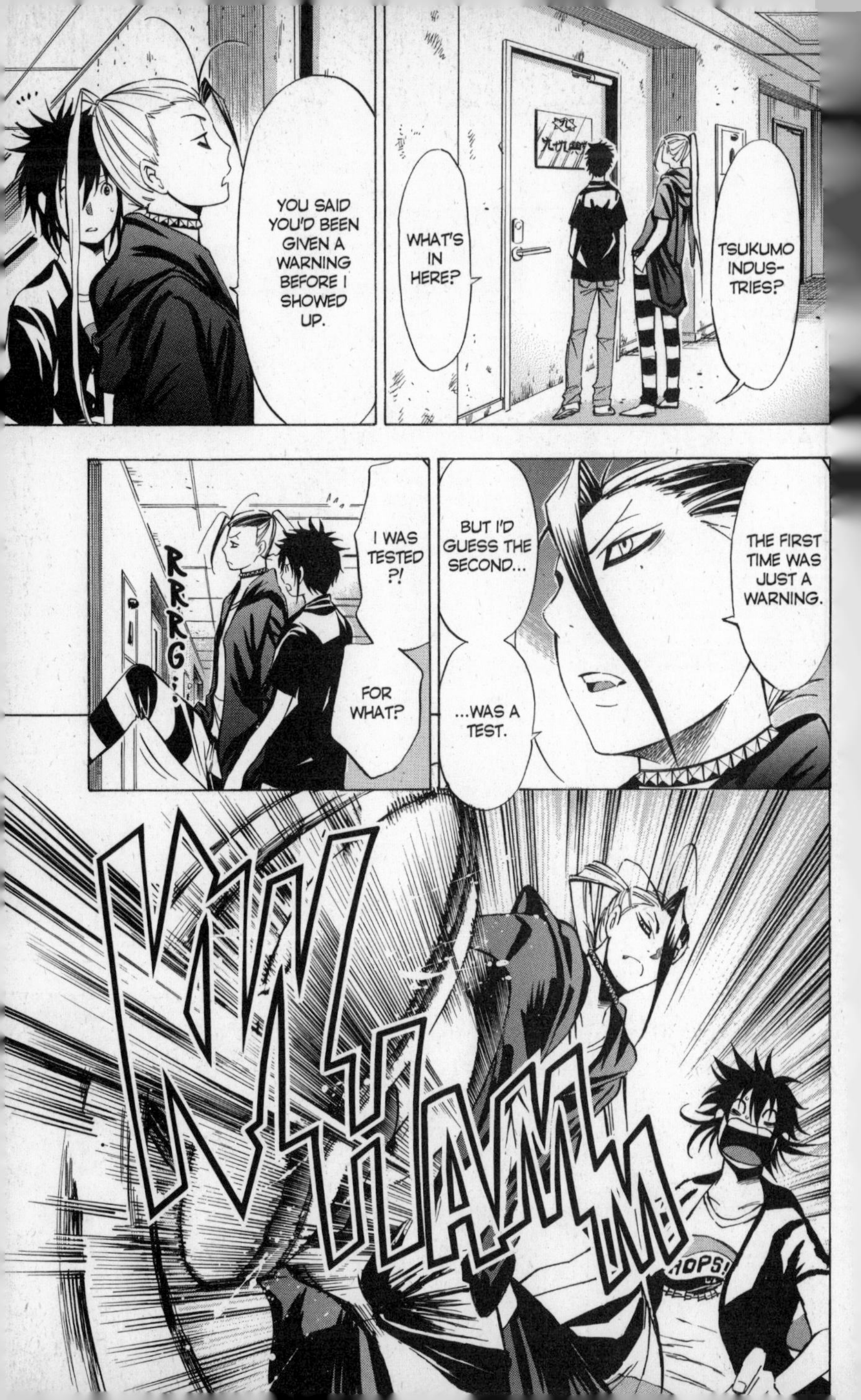

TSUKUMO INDUS-TRIES?
WHAT'S IN HERE?
YOU SAID YOU'D BEEN GIVEN A WARNING BEFORE I SHOWED UP.
THE FIRST TIME WAS JUST A WARNING.
BUT I'D GUESS THE SECOND...
...WAS A TEST.
I WAS TESTED?!
FOR WHAT?
RRRG...
WHAM

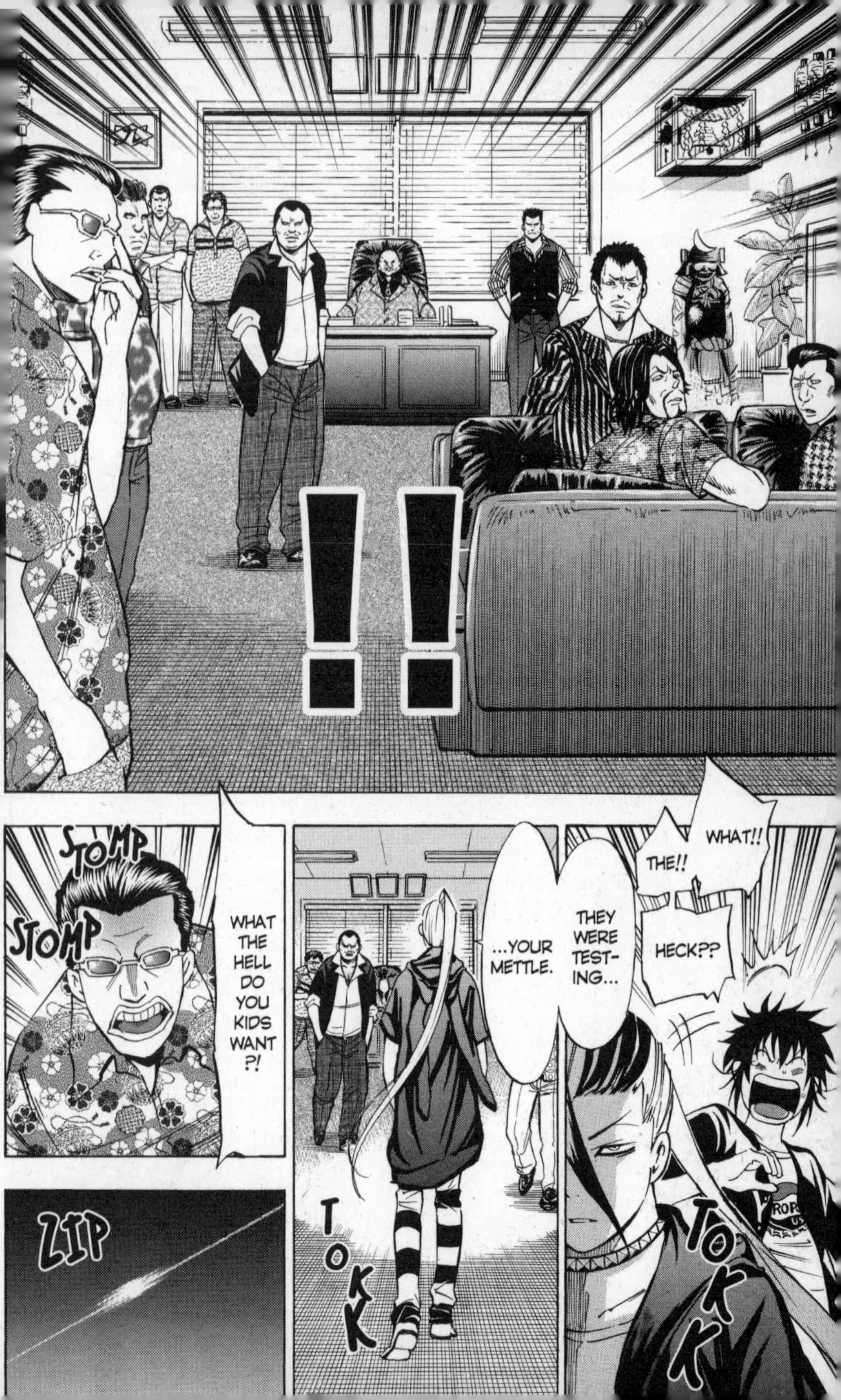
!!
WHAT!!
THE!!
HECK??
TOKK
THEY WERE TESTING...
...YOUR METTLE.
TOKK
STOMP
STOMP
WHAT THE HELL DO YOU KIDS WANT?!
ZIP

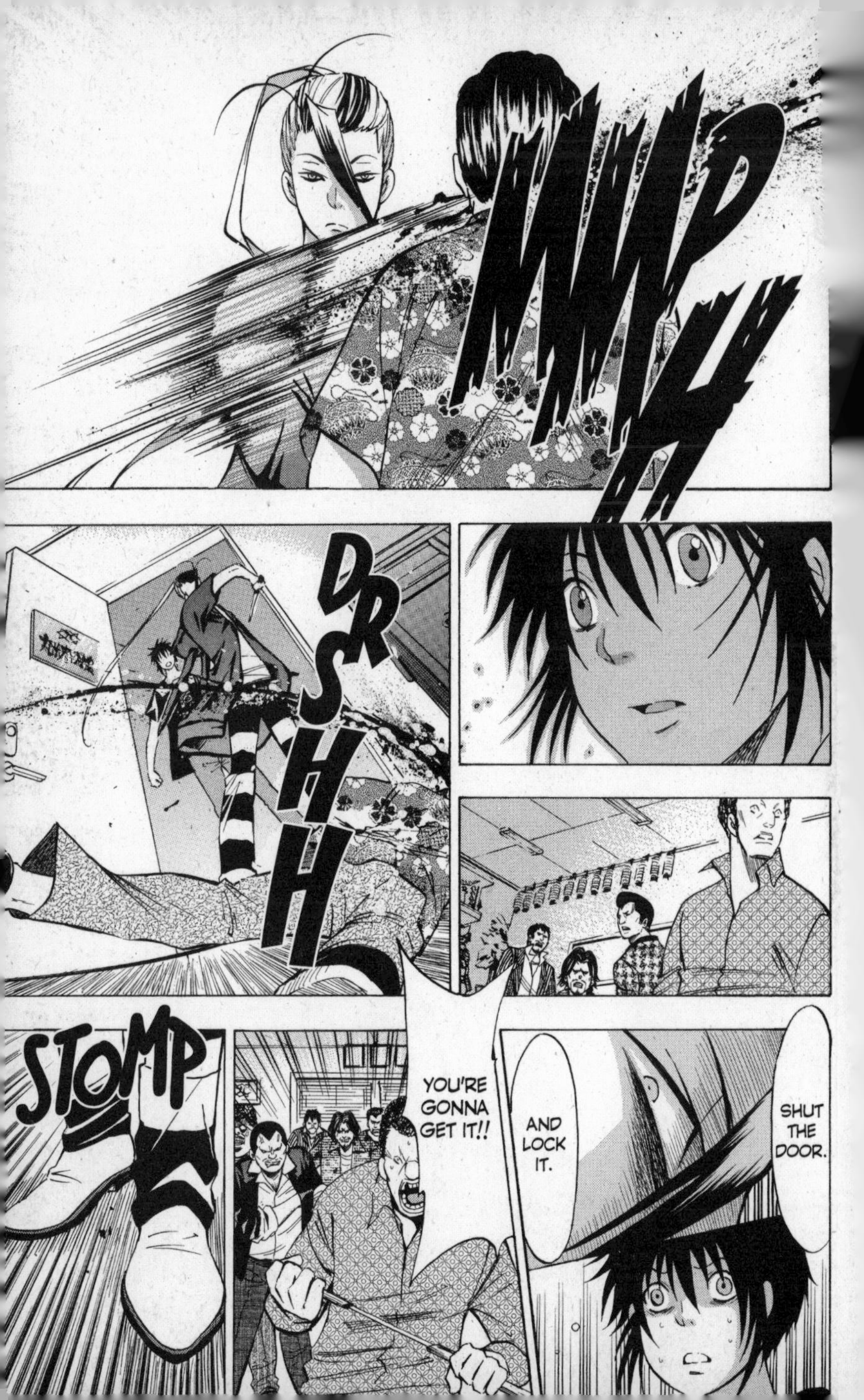
DRSHHH
SHUT THE DOOR.
AND LOCK IT.
YOU'RE GONNA GET IT!!
STOMP

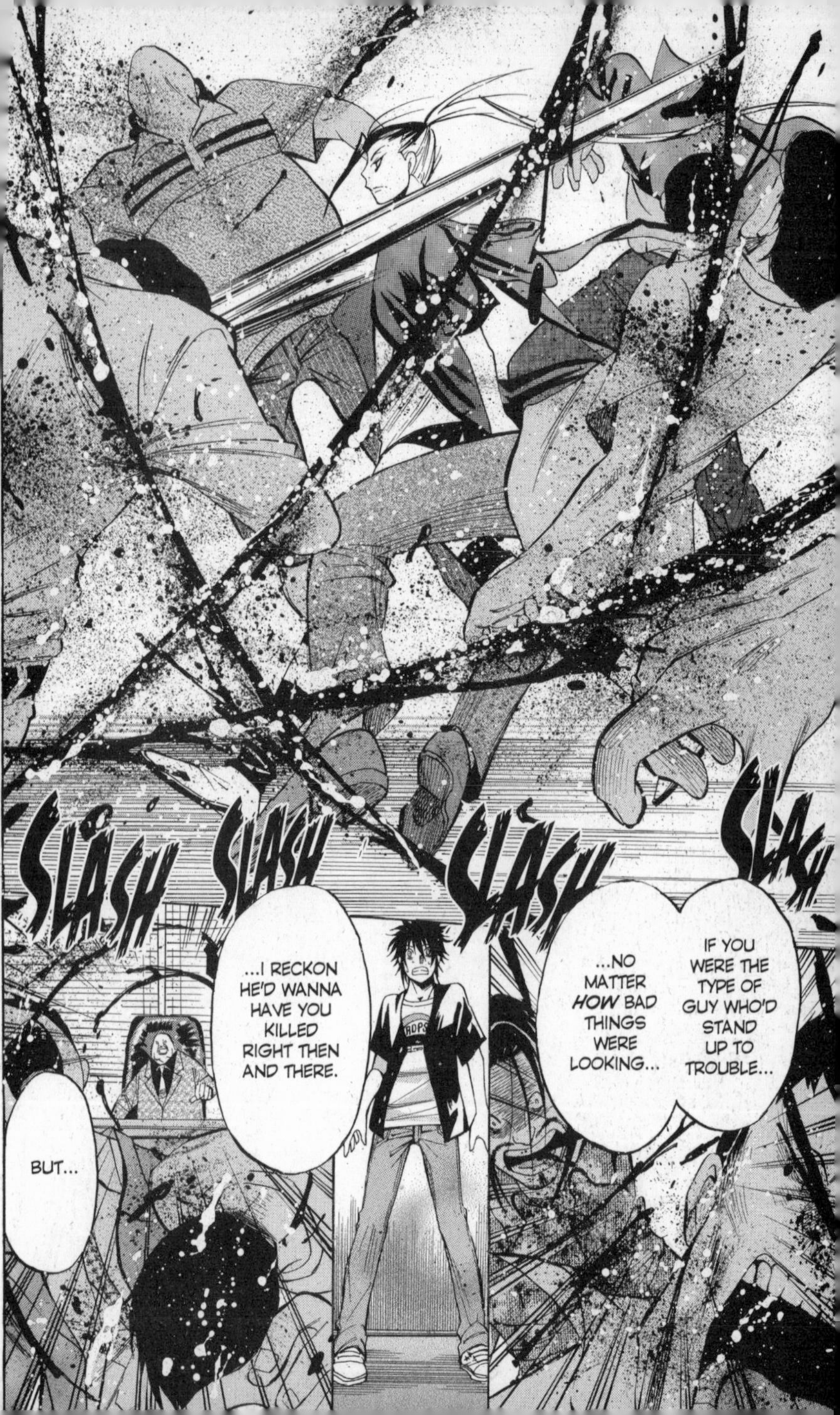
SLASH
SLASH
SLASH
SLASH
IF YOU WERE THE TYPE OF GUY WHO'D STAND UP TO TROUBLE...
...NO MATTER *HOW* BAD THINGS WERE LOOKING...
...I RECKON HE'D WANNA HAVE YOU KILLED RIGHT THEN AND THERE.
BUT...

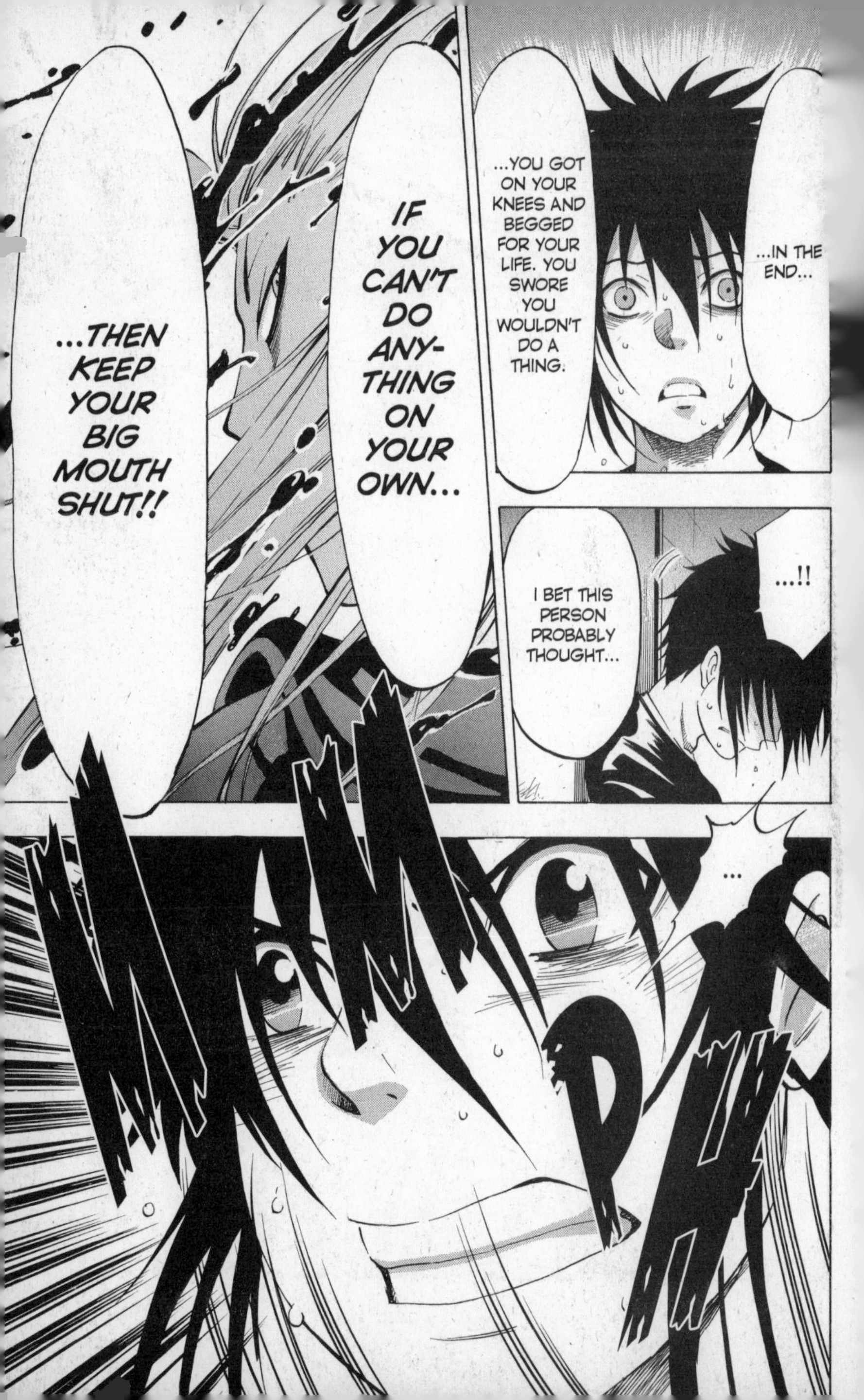
...IN THE END...
...YOU GOT ON YOUR KNEES AND BEGGED FOR YOUR LIFE. YOU SWORE YOU WOULDN'T DO A THING.
...!!
I BET THIS PERSON PROBABLY THOUGHT...
IF YOU CAN'T DO ANY-THING ON YOUR OWN...
...THEN KEEP YOUR BIG MOUTH SHUT!!
...

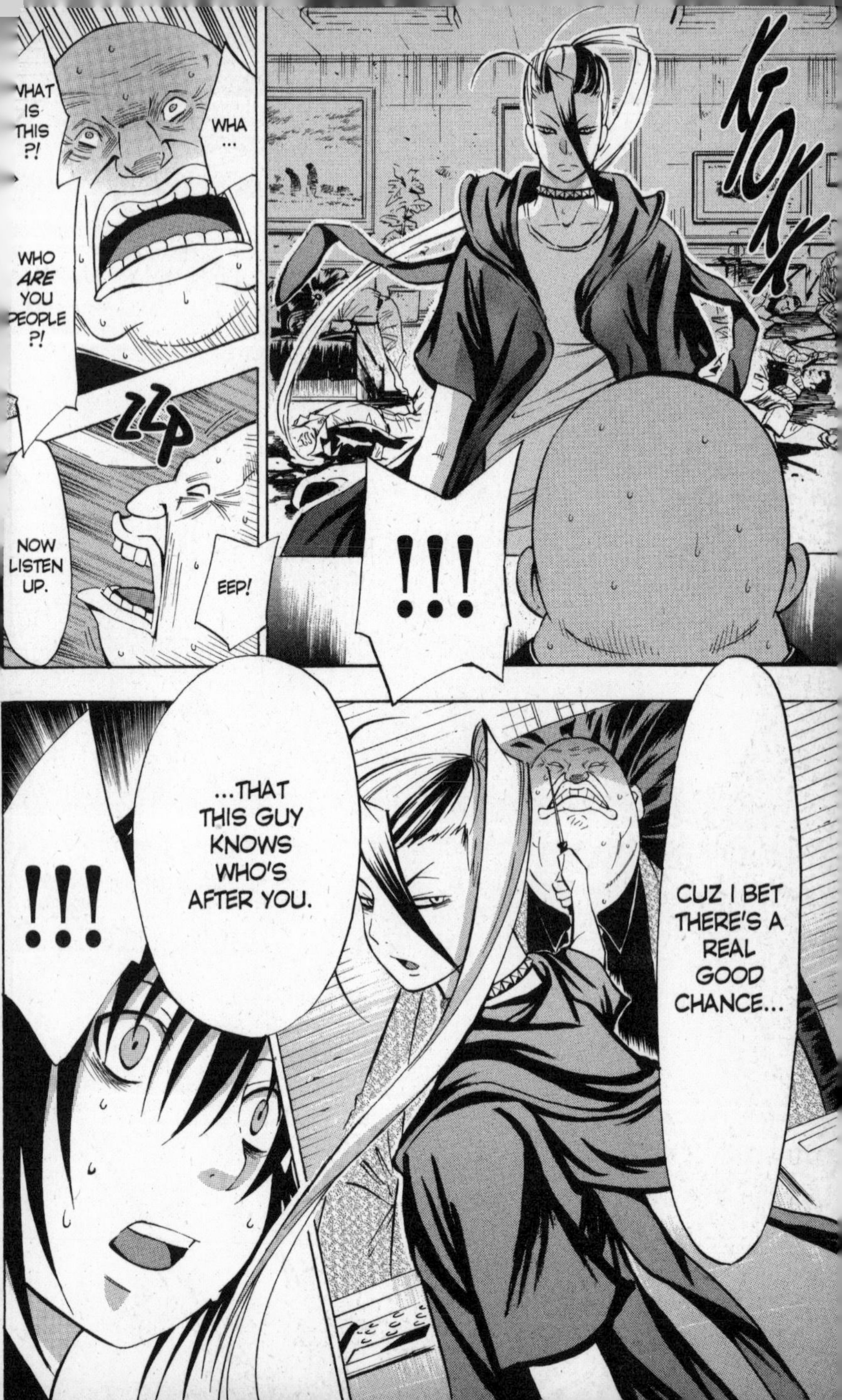
!!!
WHA...
WHAT IS THIS?!
WHO ARE YOU PEOPLE?!
EEP!
ZZP
NOW LISTEN UP.
CUZ I BET THERE'S A REAL GOOD CHANCE...
...THAT THIS GUY KNOWS WHO'S AFTER YOU.
!!!

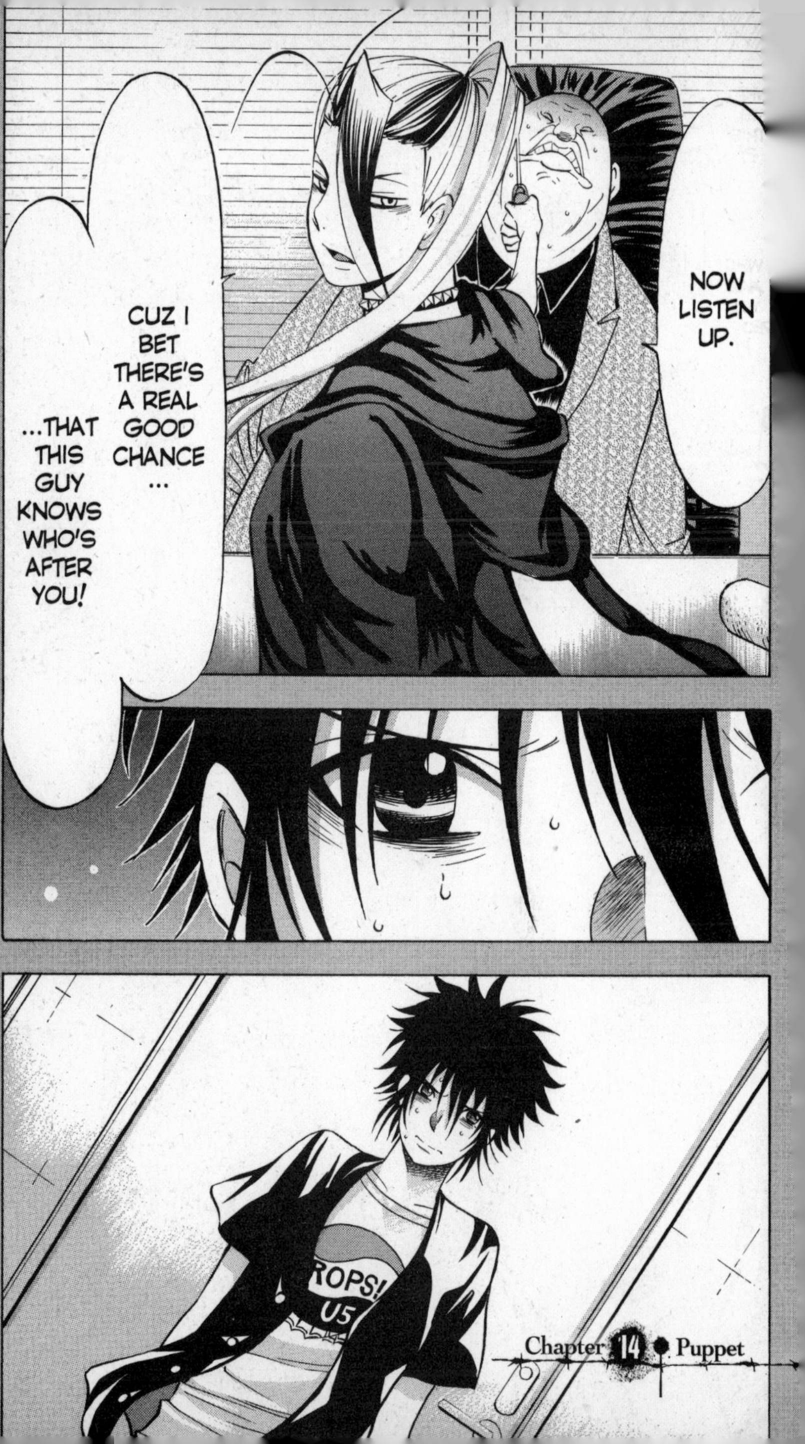
NOW LISTEN UP.
CUZ I BET THERE'S A REAL GOOD CHANCE ...
...THAT THIS GUY KNOWS WHO'S AFTER YOU!
ROPS! U5
Chapter 14 Puppet

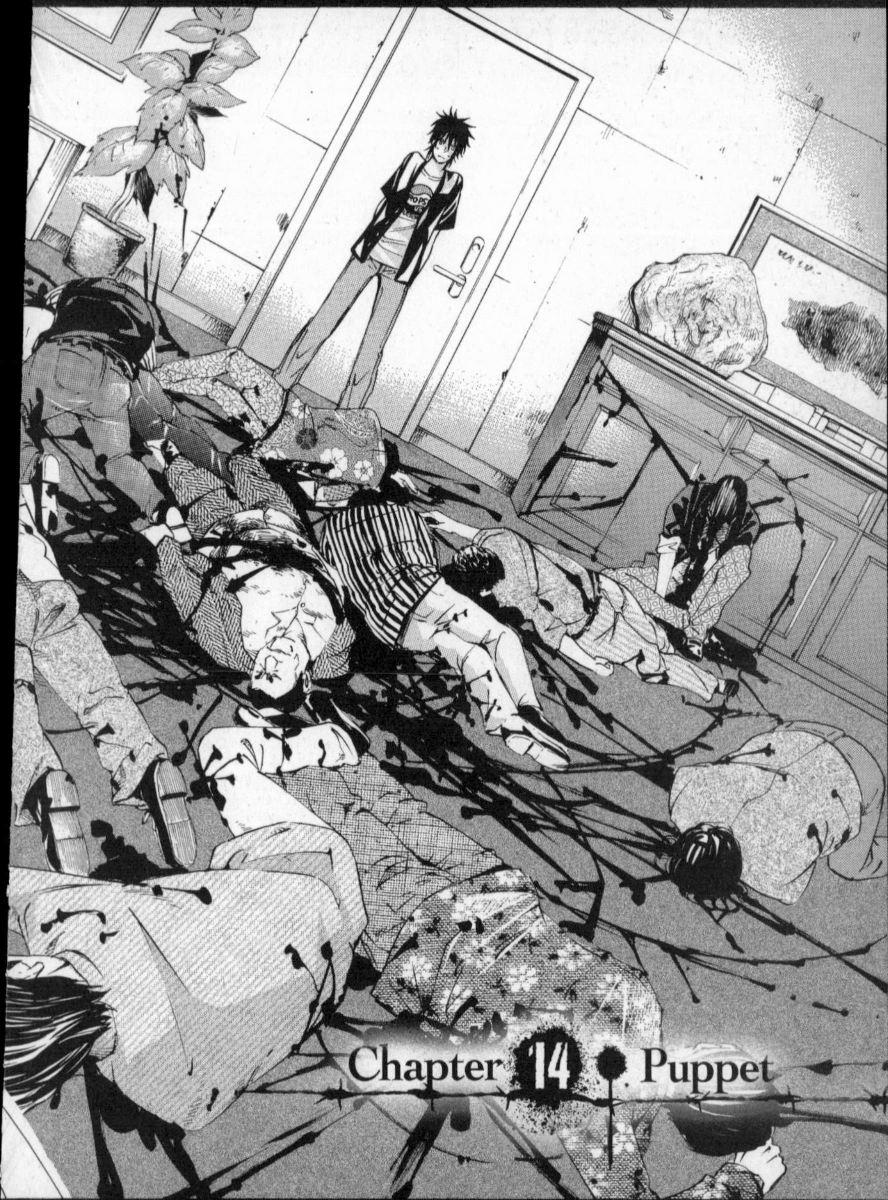
Chapter 14 Puppet

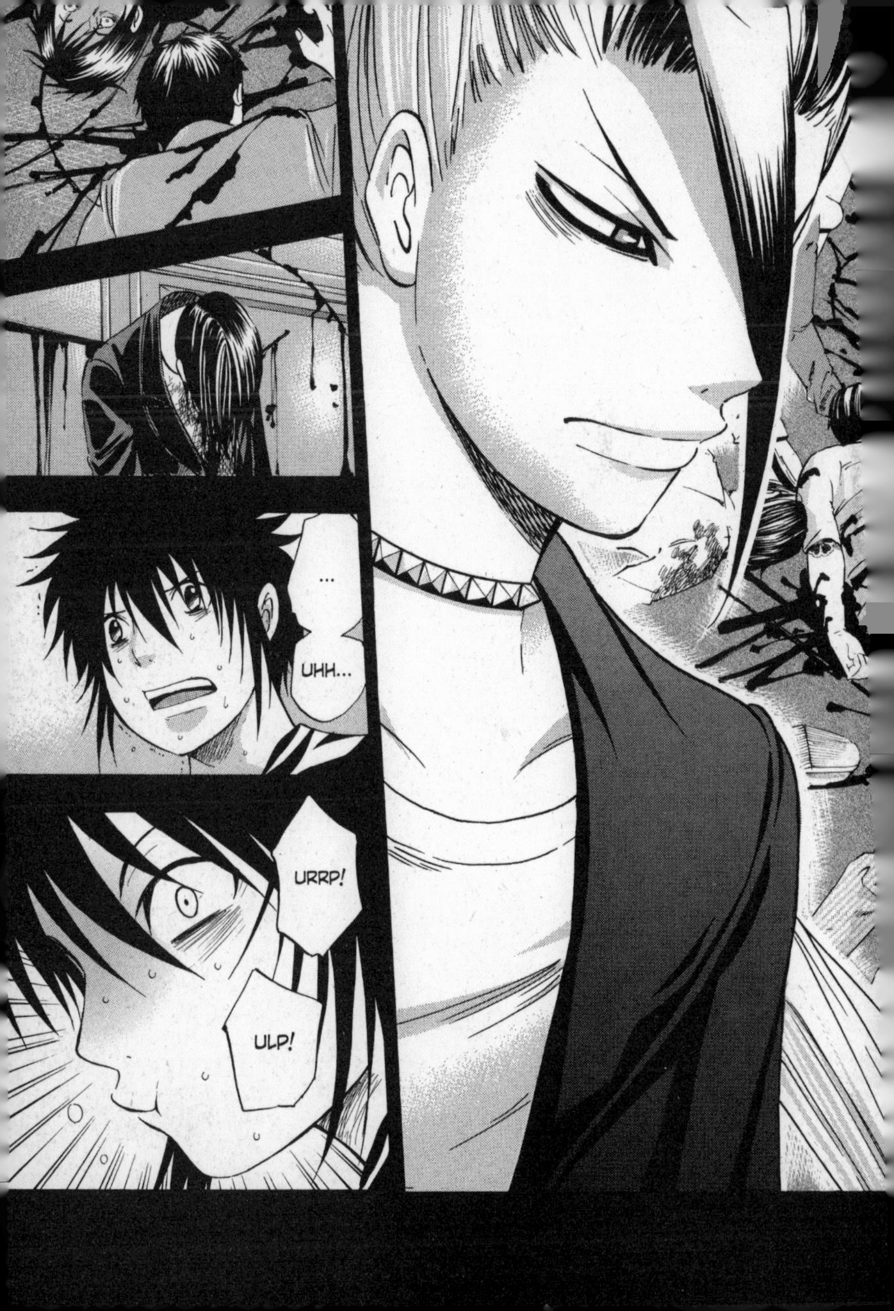
...
UHH...
URRP!
ULP!

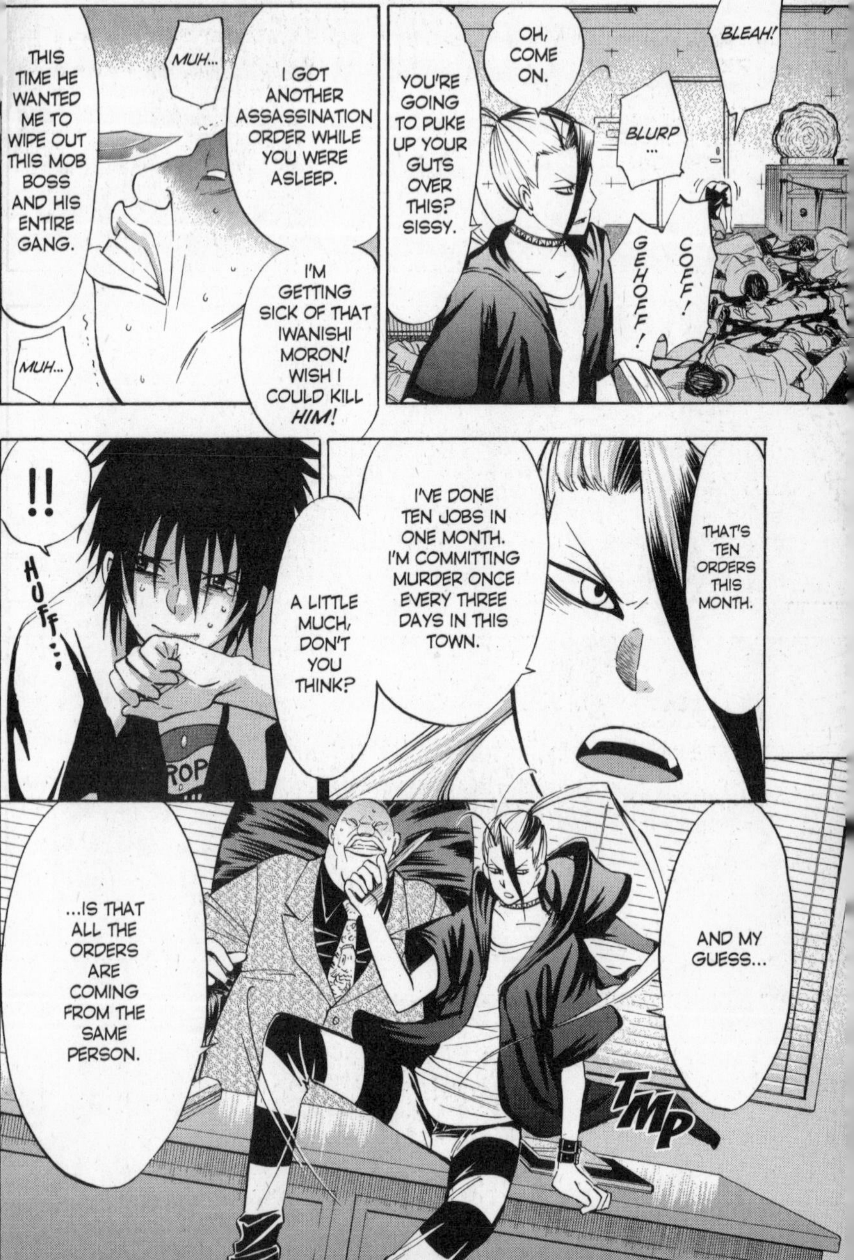
BLEAH!
BLURP...
COFF!
GEHOFF!
OH, COME ON.
YOU'RE GOING TO PUKE UP YOUR GUTS OVER THIS? SISSY.
I GOT ANOTHER ASSASSINATION ORDER WHILE YOU WERE ASLEEP.
I'M GETTING SICK OF THAT IWANISHI MORON! WISH I COULD KILL *HIM*!
MUH...
THIS TIME HE WANTED ME TO WIPE OUT THIS MOB BOSS AND HIS ENTIRE GANG.
MUH...
THAT'S TEN ORDERS THIS MONTH.
I'VE DONE TEN JOBS IN ONE MONTH. I'M COMMITTING MURDER ONCE EVERY THREE DAYS IN THIS TOWN.
A LITTLE MUCH, DON'T YOU THINK?
!!
HUFF...
AND MY GUESS...
TMP
...IS THAT ALL THE ORDERS ARE COMING FROM THE SAME PERSON.

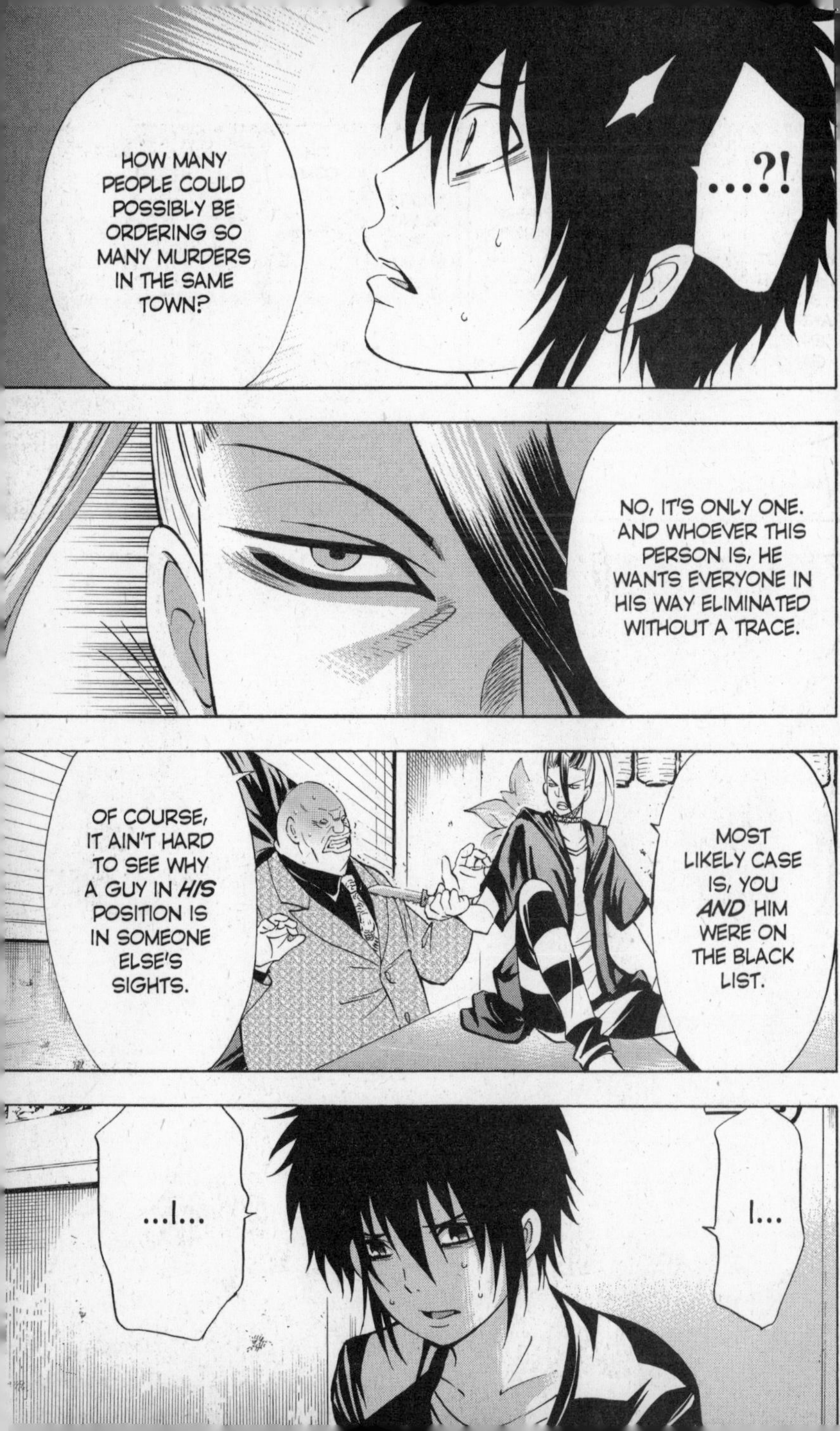
...?!
HOW MANY PEOPLE COULD POSSIBLY BE ORDERING SO MANY MURDERS IN THE SAME TOWN?
NO, IT'S ONLY ONE. AND WHOEVER THIS PERSON IS, HE WANTS EVERYONE IN HIS WAY ELIMINATED WITHOUT A TRACE.
MOST LIKELY CASE IS, YOU *AND* HIM WERE ON THE BLACK LIST.
OF COURSE, IT AIN'T HARD TO SEE WHY A GUY IN *HIS* POSITION IS IN SOMEONE ELSE'S SIGHTS.
I...
...I...

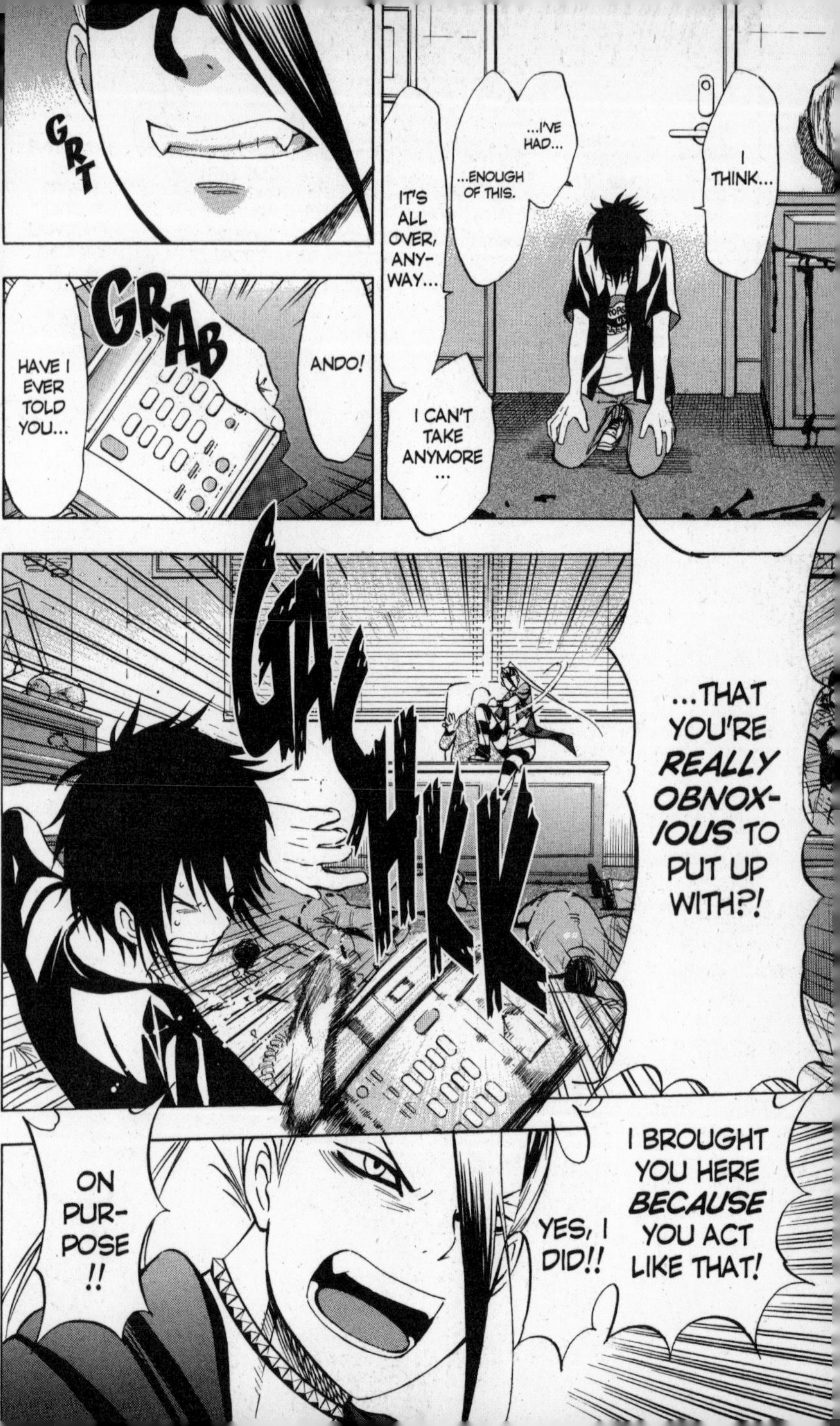
I THINK...
...I'VE HAD...
...ENOUGH OF THIS.
IT'S ALL OVER, ANYWAY...
I CAN'T TAKE ANYMORE...
GRT
ANDO!
GRAB
HAVE I EVER TOLD YOU...
...THAT YOU'RE REALLY OBNOXIOUS TO PUT UP WITH?!
GAHKK
I BROUGHT YOU HERE BECAUSE YOU ACT LIKE THAT!
YES, I DID!!
ON PURPOSE!!

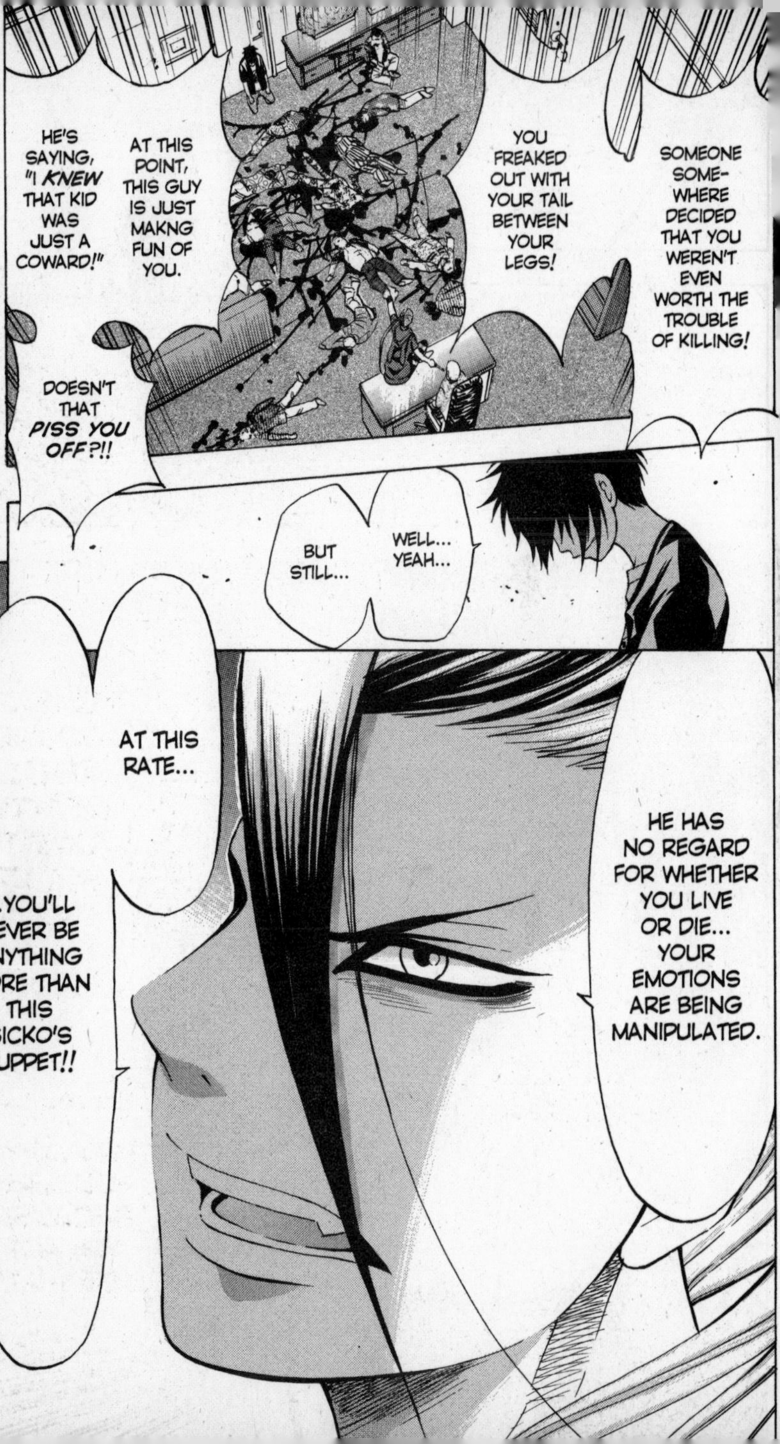
SOMEONE SOMEWHERE DECIDED THAT YOU WEREN'T EVEN WORTH THE TROUBLE OF KILLING!
YOU FREAKED OUT WITH YOUR TAIL BETWEEN YOUR LEGS!
AT THIS POINT, THIS GUY IS JUST MAKNG FUN OF YOU.
HE'S SAYING, "I KNEW THAT KID WAS JUST A COWARD!"
DOESN'T THAT PISS YOU OFF?!!
WELL... YEAH...
BUT STILL...
HE HAS NO REGARD FOR WHETHER YOU LIVE OR DIE... YOUR EMOTIONS ARE BEING MANIPULATED.
AT THIS RATE...
...YOU'LL NEVER BE ANYTHING MORE THAN THIS SICKO'S PUPPET!!

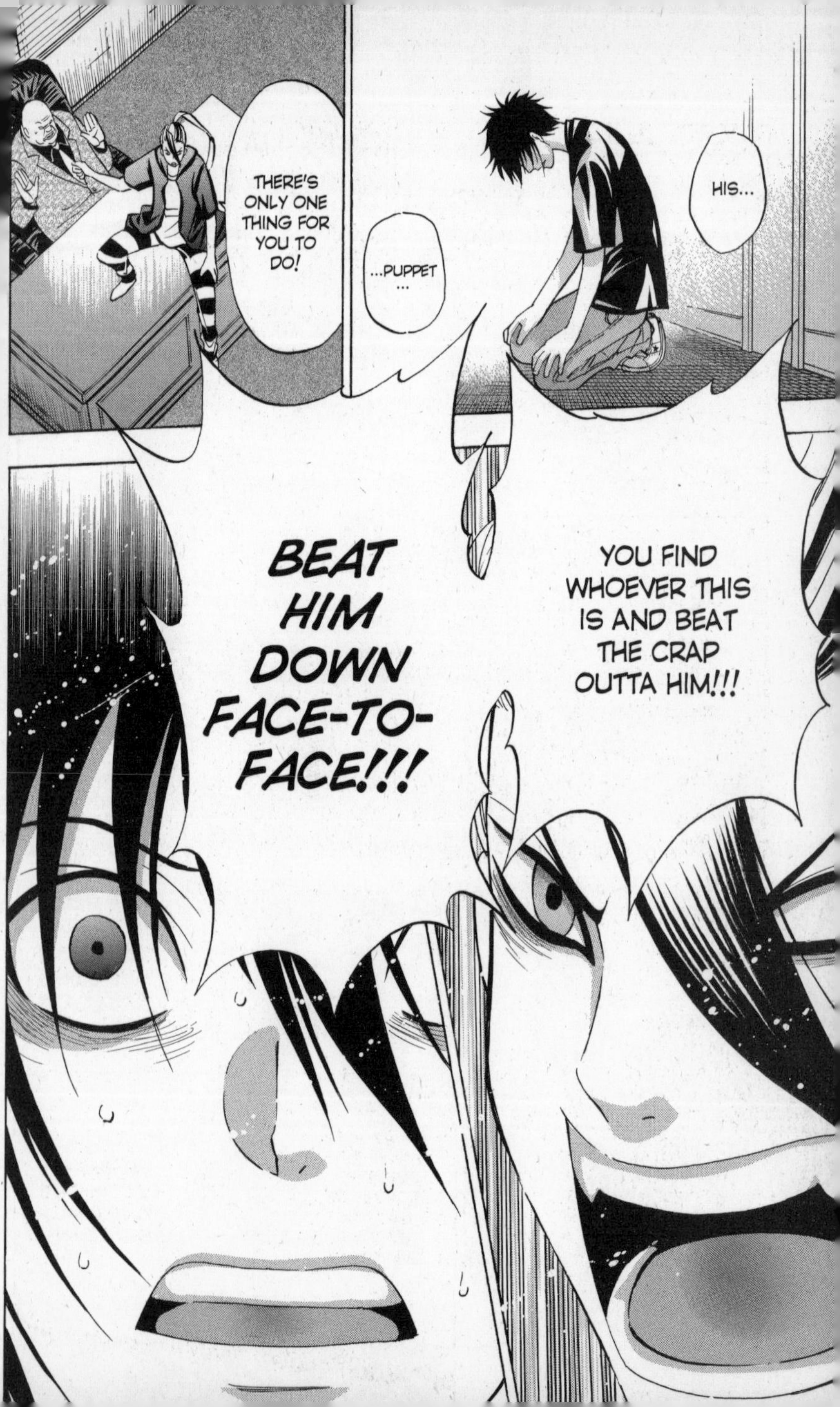
HIS...
...PUPPET ...
THERE'S ONLY ONE THING FOR YOU TO DO!
YOU FIND WHOEVER THIS IS AND BEAT THE CRAP OUTTA HIM!!!
BEAT HIM DOWN FACE-TO-FACE!!!

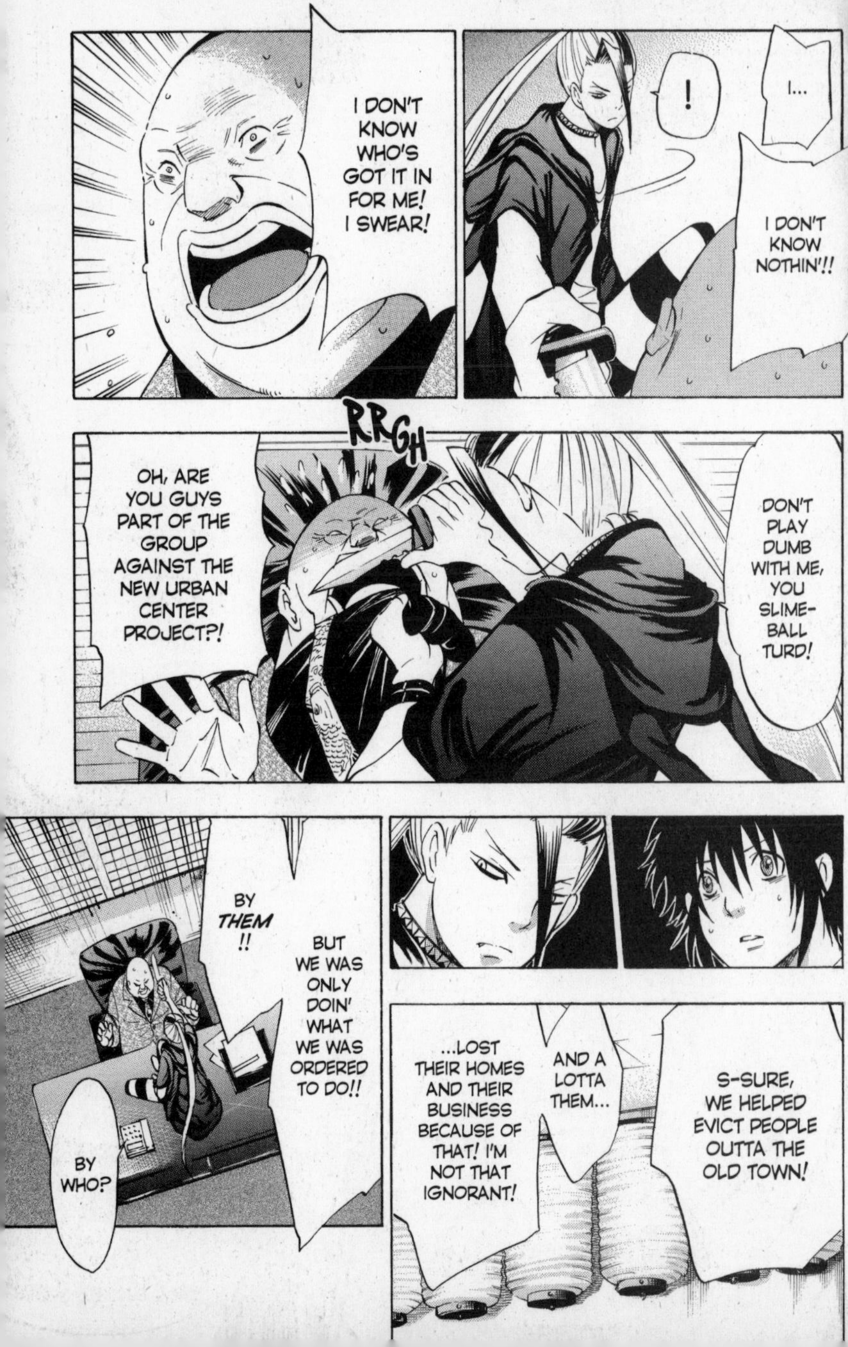
I...
!
I DON'T KNOW NOTHIN'!!
I DON'T KNOW WHO'S GOT IT IN FOR ME! I SWEAR!
RRGH
DON'T PLAY DUMB WITH ME, YOU SLIME-BALL TURD!
OH, ARE YOU GUYS PART OF THE GROUP AGAINST THE NEW URBAN CENTER PROJECT?!
S-SURE, WE HELPED EVICT PEOPLE OUTTA THE OLD TOWN!
AND A LOTTA THEM...
...LOST THEIR HOMES AND THEIR BUSINESS BECAUSE OF THAT! I'M NOT THAT IGNORANT!
BUT WE WAS ONLY DOIN' WHAT WE WAS ORDERED TO DO!!
BY WHO?
BY *THEM*!!

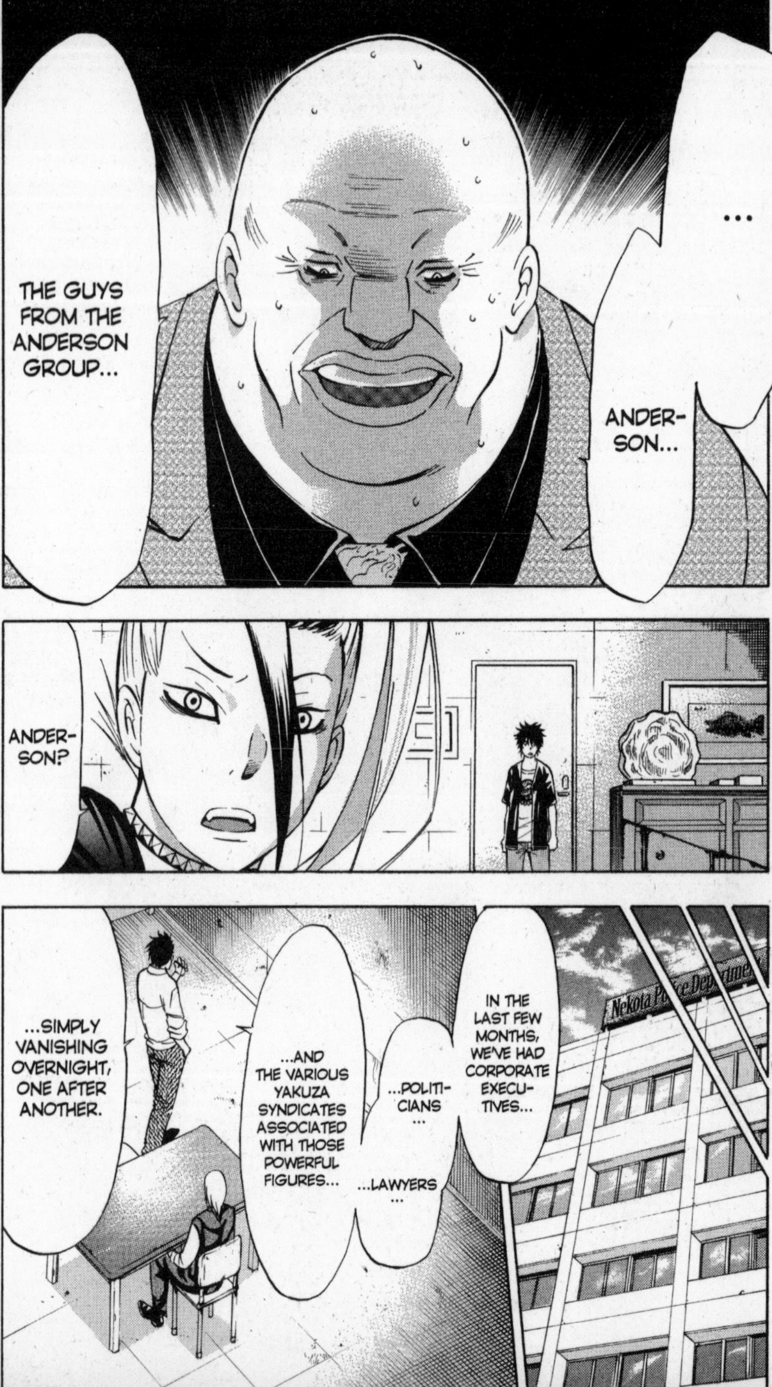
...
ANDER-SON...
THE GUYS FROM THE ANDERSON GROUP...
ANDER-SON?
IN THE LAST FEW MONTHS, WE'VE HAD CORPORATE EXECU-TIVES...
...POLITI-CIANS...
...LAWYERS...
...AND THE VARIOUS YAKUZA SYNDICATES ASSOCIATED WITH THOSE POWERFUL FIGURES...
...SIMPLY VANISHING OVERNIGHT, ONE AFTER ANOTHER.

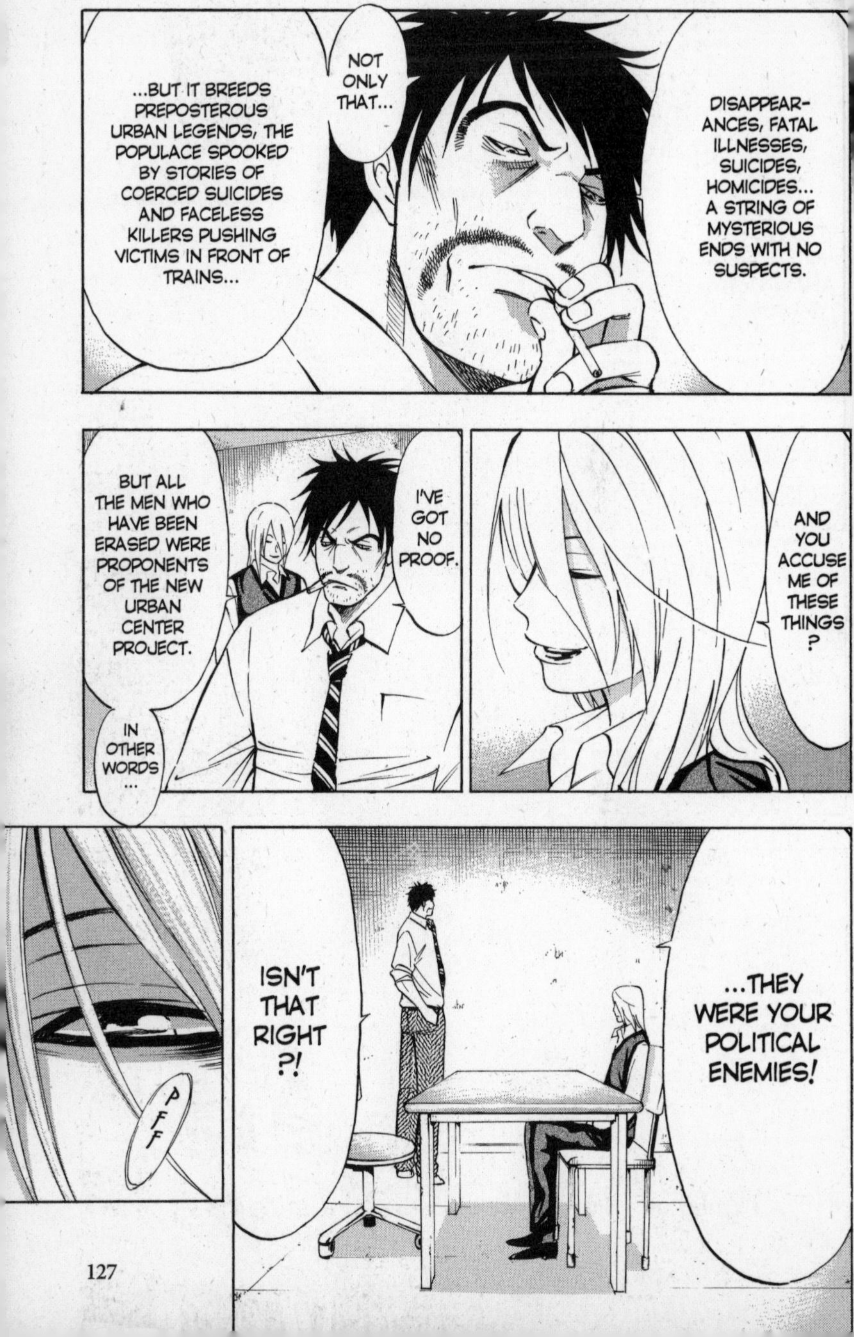
DISAPPEAR-ANCES, FATAL ILLNESSES, SUICIDES, HOMICIDES... A STRING OF MYSTERIOUS ENDS WITH NO SUSPECTS.
NOT ONLY THAT...
...BUT IT BREEDS PREPOSTEROUS URBAN LEGENDS, THE POPULACE SPOOKED BY STORIES OF COERCED SUICIDES AND FACELESS KILLERS PUSHING VICTIMS IN FRONT OF TRAINS...
AND YOU ACCUSE ME OF THESE THINGS?
I'VE GOT NO PROOF.
BUT ALL THE MEN WHO HAVE BEEN ERASED WERE PROPONENTS OF THE NEW URBAN CENTER PROJECT.
IN OTHER WORDS...
...THEY WERE YOUR POLITICAL ENEMIES!
ISN'T THAT RIGHT?!
PFF

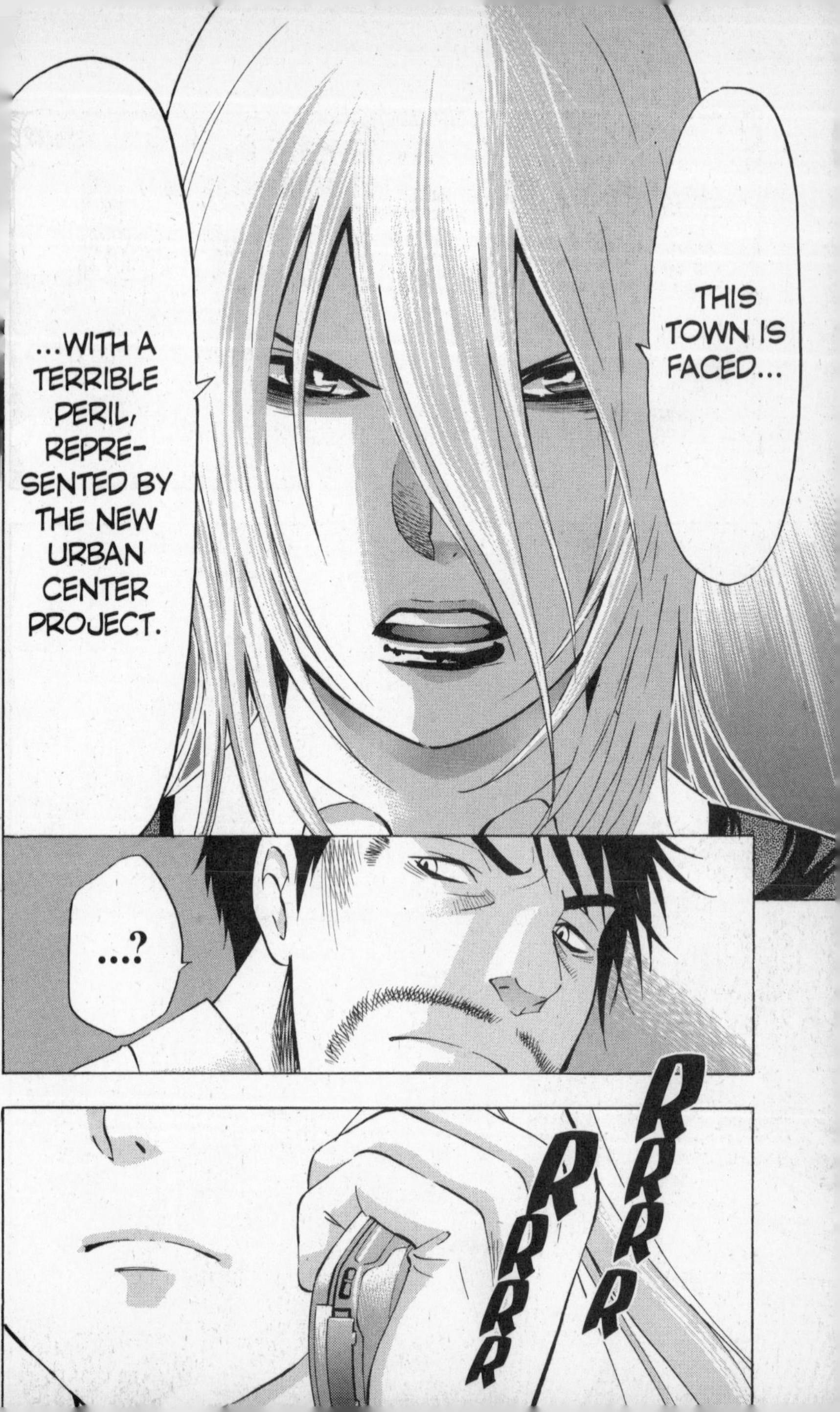
THIS TOWN IS FACED...
...WITH A TERRIBLE PERIL, REPRESENTED BY THE NEW URBAN CENTER PROJECT.
...?
RRRRR
RRRRRR

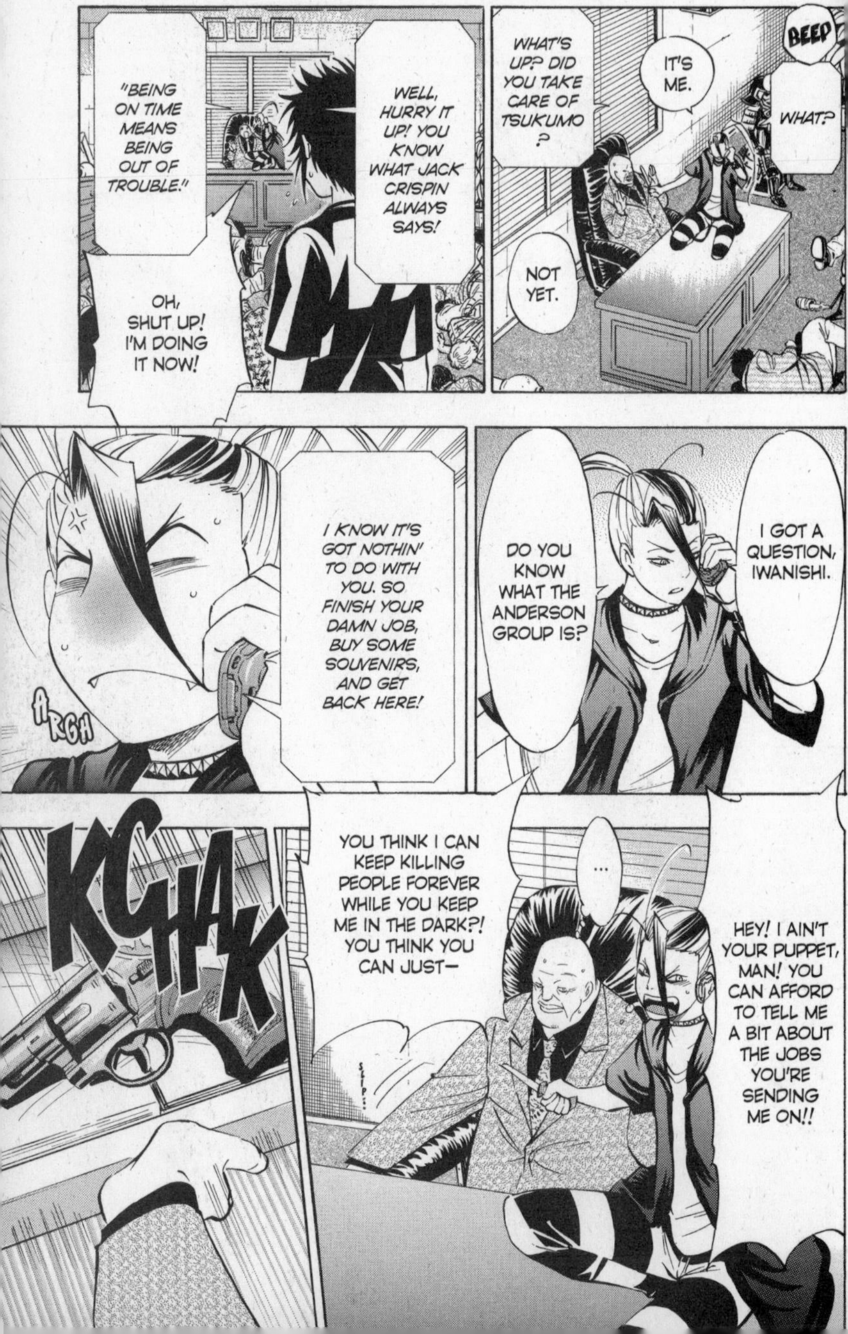
BEEP
WHAT?
IT'S ME.
WHAT'S UP? DID YOU TAKE CARE OF TSUKUMO?
NOT YET.
WELL, HURRY IT UP! YOU KNOW WHAT JACK CRISPIN ALWAYS SAYS!
"BEING ON TIME MEANS BEING OUT OF TROUBLE."
OH, SHUT UP! I'M DOING IT NOW!
I GOT A QUESTION, IWANISHI.
DO YOU KNOW WHAT THE ANDERSON GROUP IS?
I KNOW IT'S GOT NOTHIN' TO DO WITH YOU. SO FINISH YOUR DAMN JOB, BUY SOME SOUVENIRS, AND GET BACK HERE!
ARGH
HEY! I AIN'T YOUR PUPPET, MAN! YOU CAN AFFORD TO TELL ME A BIT ABOUT THE JOBS YOU'RE SENDING ME ON!!
...
YOU THINK I CAN KEEP KILLING PEOPLE FOREVER WHILE YOU KEEP ME IN THE DARK?! YOU THINK YOU CAN JUST—
KCHAK

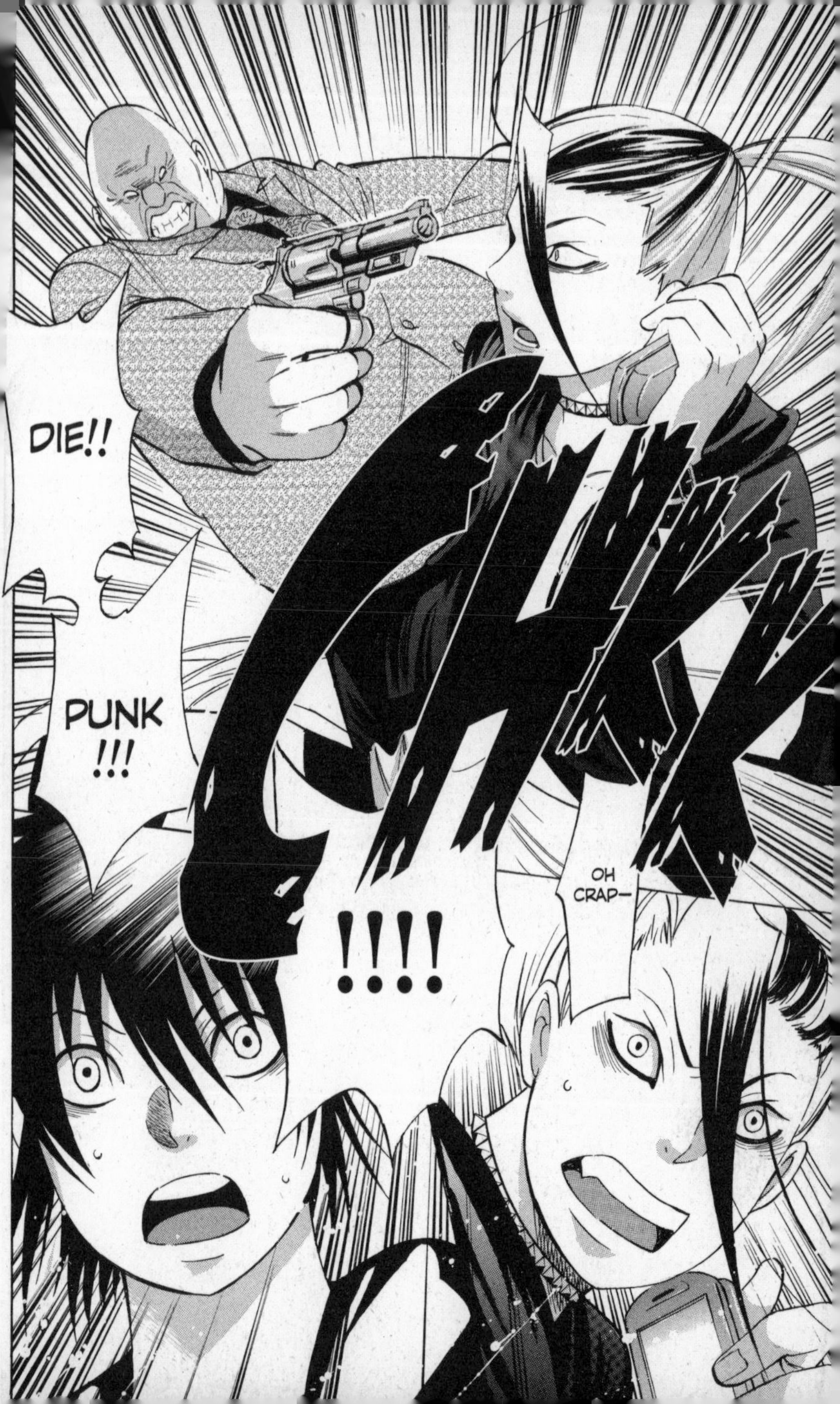
DIE!!
PUNK!!!
OH CRAP—
!!!!

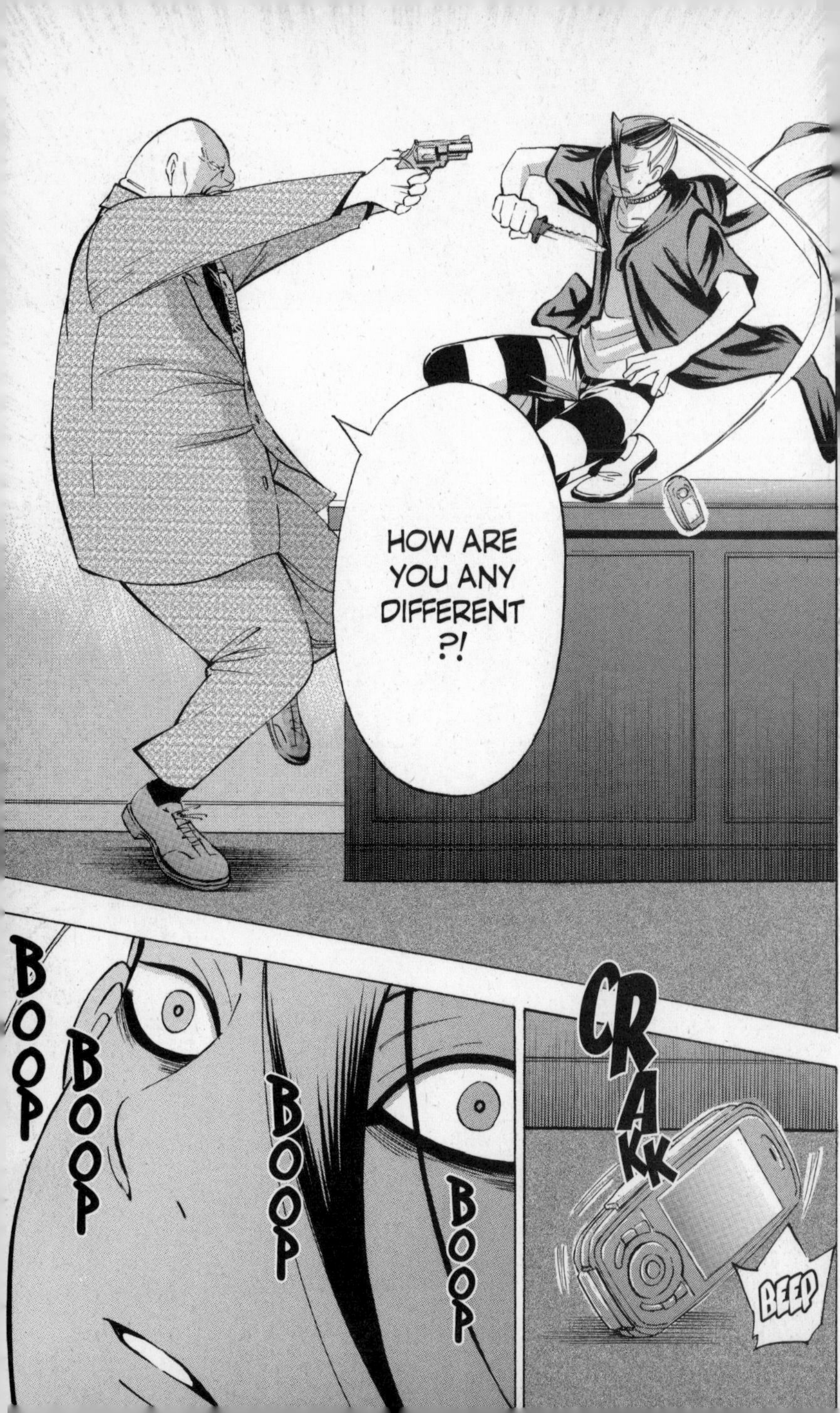
HOW ARE YOU ANY DIFFERENT ?!
CRAKK
BEEP
BOOP
BOOP
BOOP
BOOP

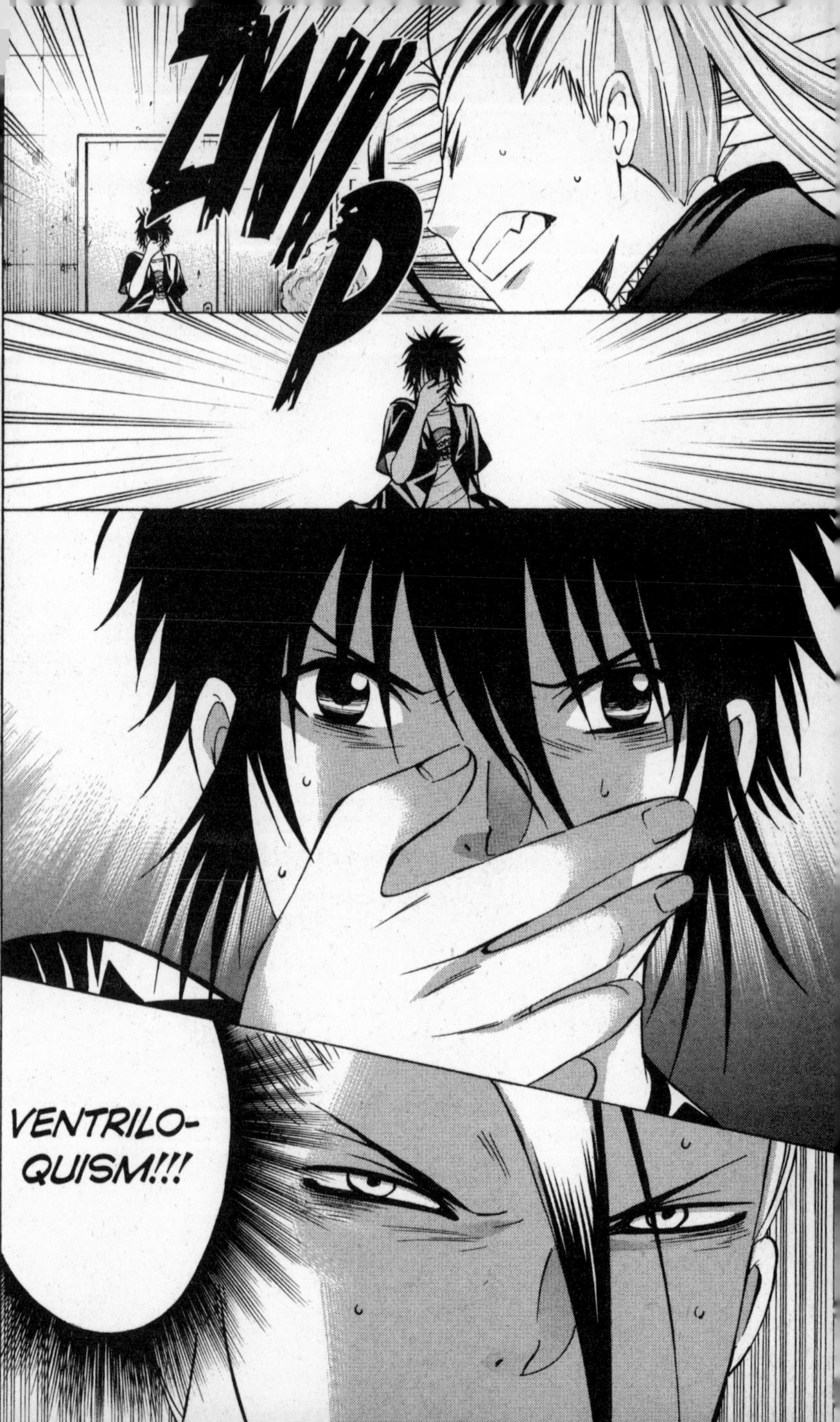
ZWIP
VENTRILO-
QUISM!!!

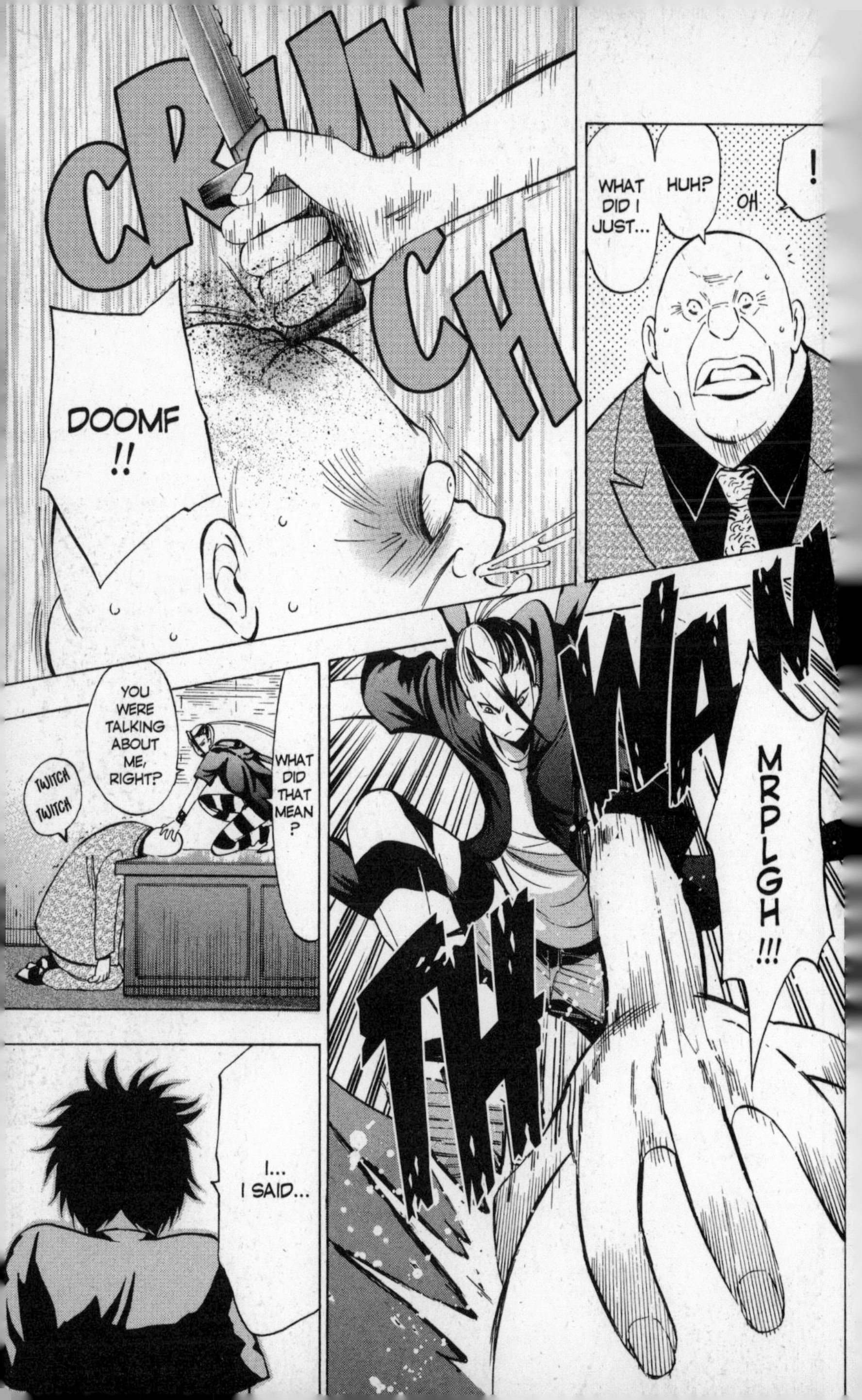
!
OH
HUH?
WHAT DID I JUST...
CRUNCH
DOOMF !!
THWAM
MRPLGH !!!
YOU WERE TALKING ABOUT ME, RIGHT?
WHAT DID THAT MEAN?
TWITCH TWITCH
I... I SAID...

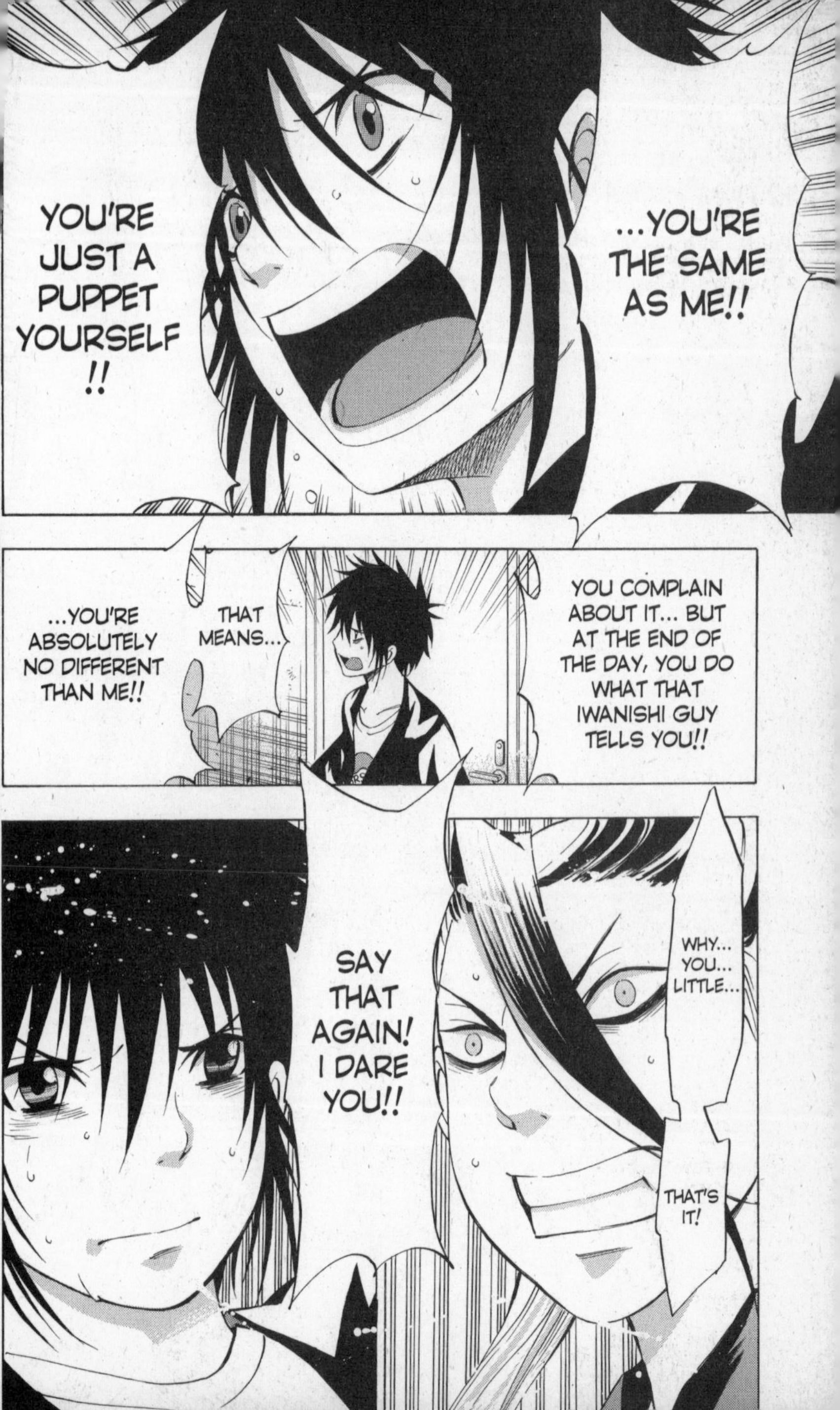
...YOU'RE THE SAME AS ME!!
YOU'RE JUST A PUPPET YOURSELF!!
YOU COMPLAIN ABOUT IT... BUT AT THE END OF THE DAY, YOU DO WHAT THAT IWANISHI GUY TELLS YOU!!
THAT MEANS...
...YOU'RE ABSOLUTELY NO DIFFERENT THAN ME!!
WHY... YOU... LITTLE...
THAT'S IT!
SAY THAT AGAIN! I DARE YOU!!

Chapter 15 • Freedom By Any Other Name

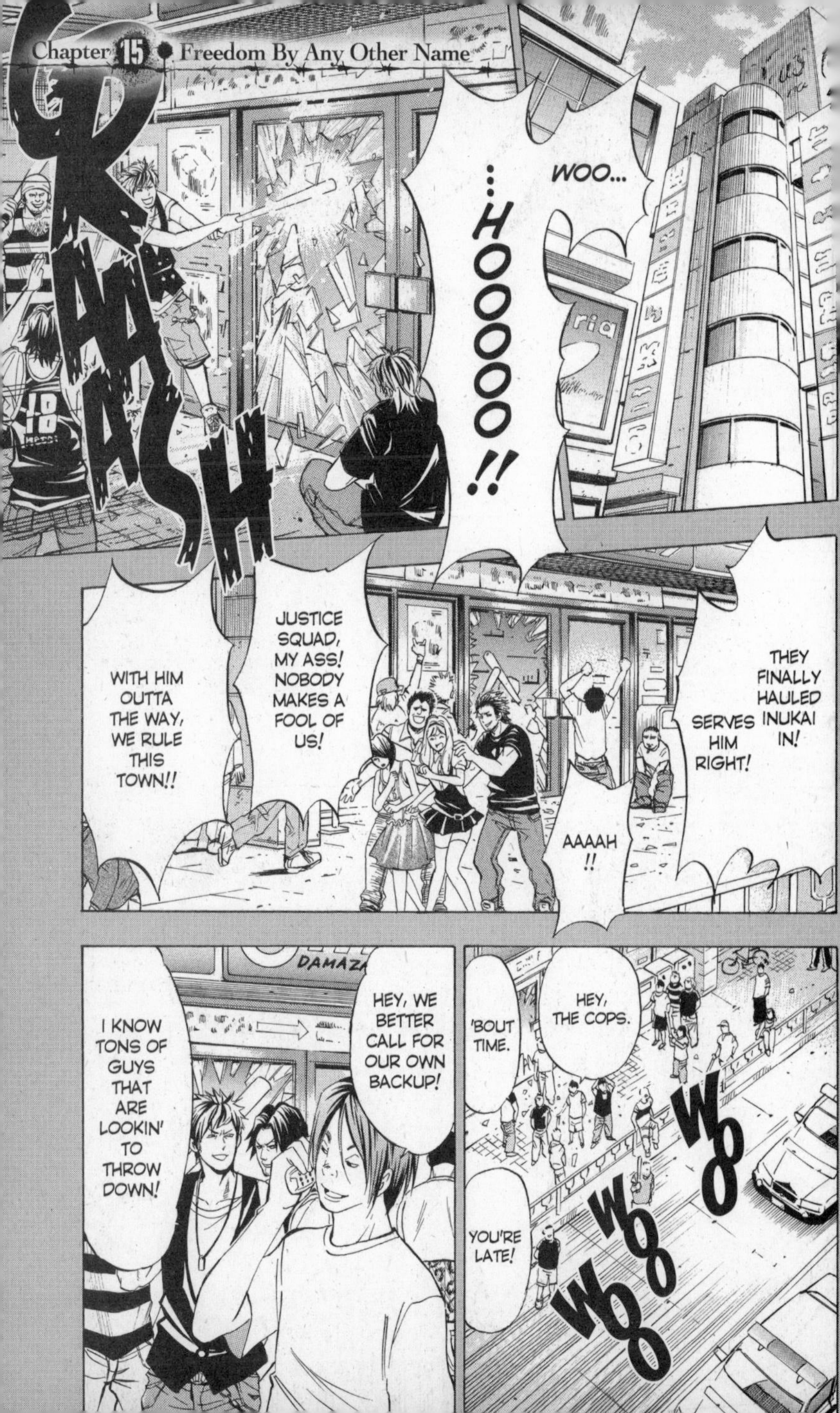
WOO...
...HOOOOOO!!
CRAASH
THEY FINALLY HAULED INUKAI IN!
SERVES HIM RIGHT!
AAAAH!!
JUSTICE SQUAD, MY ASS! NOBODY MAKES A FOOL OF US!
WITH HIM OUTTA THE WAY, WE RULE THIS TOWN!!
HEY, THE COPS.
'BOUT TIME.
YOU'RE LATE!
WOO WOO WOO
DAMAZA
HEY, WE BETTER CALL FOR OUR OWN BACKUP!
I KNOW TONS OF GUYS THAT ARE LOOKIN' TO THROW DOWN!

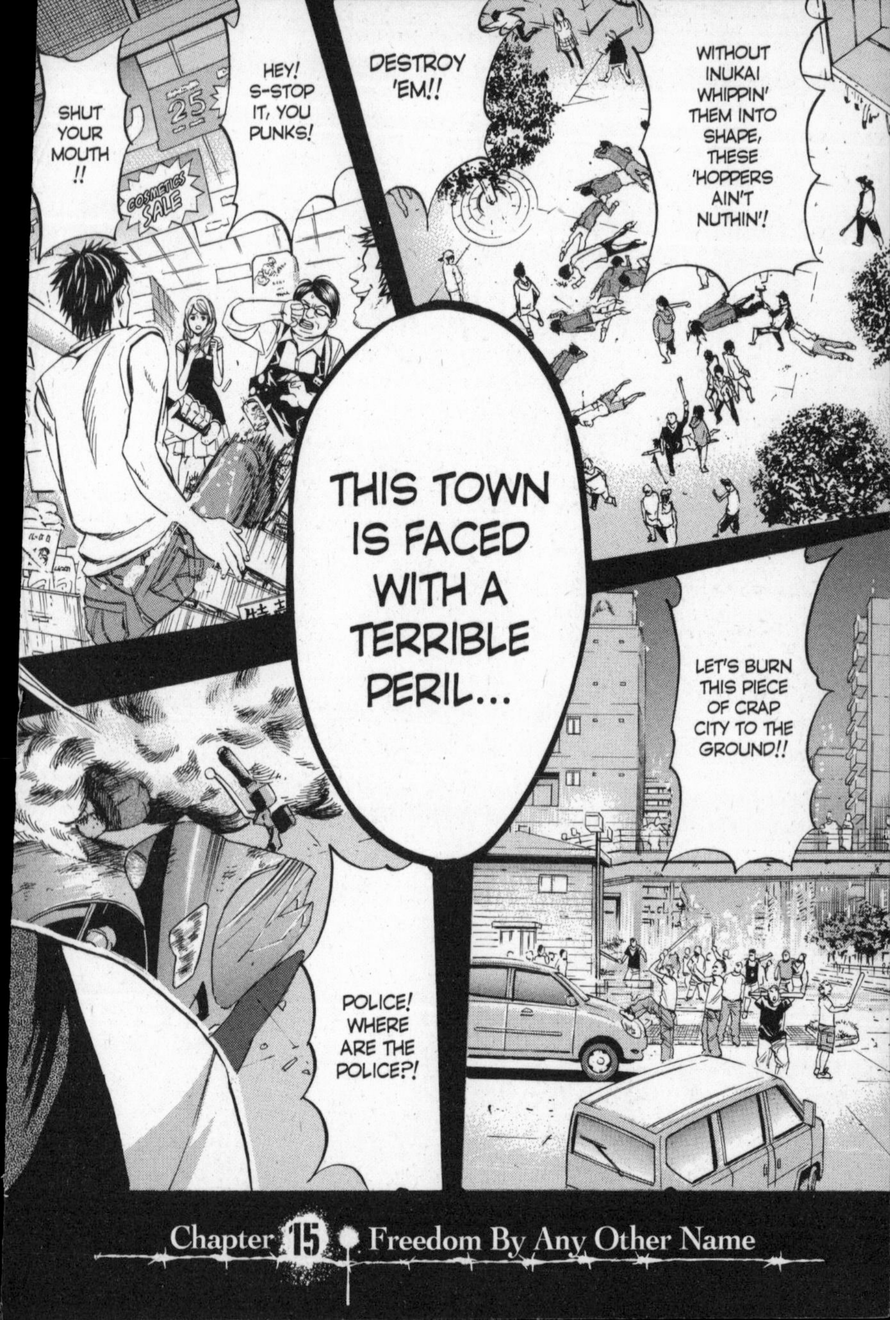
WITHOUT INUKAI WHIPPIN' THEM INTO SHAPE, THESE 'HOPPERS AIN'T NUTHIN'!
DESTROY 'EM!!
HEY! S-STOP IT, YOU PUNKS!
SHUT YOUR MOUTH!!
25
COSMETICS SALE
THIS TOWN IS FACED WITH A TERRIBLE PERIL...
LET'S BURN THIS PIECE OF CRAP CITY TO THE GROUND!!
POLICE! WHERE ARE THE POLICE?!

Chapter 15 Freedom By Any Other Name

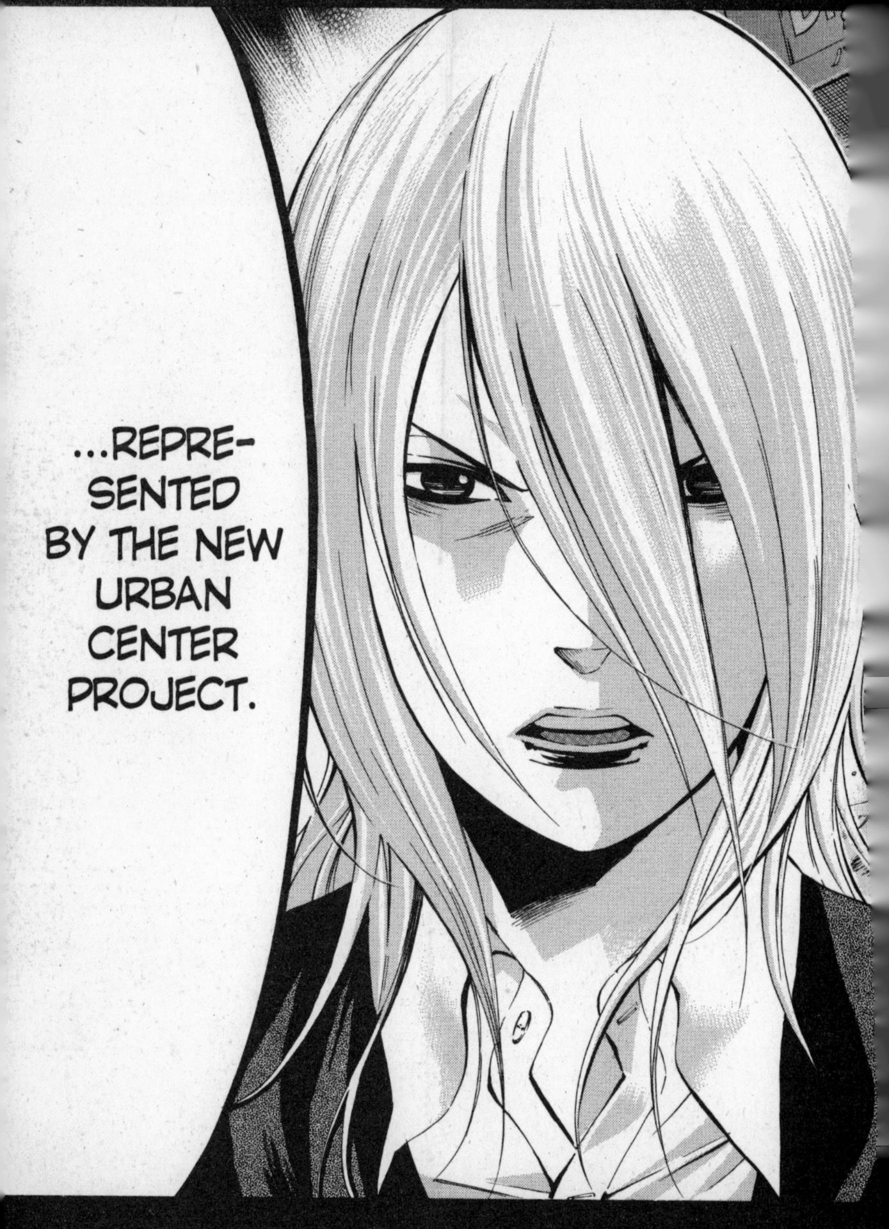
...REPRESENTED BY THE NEW URBAN CENTER PROJECT.

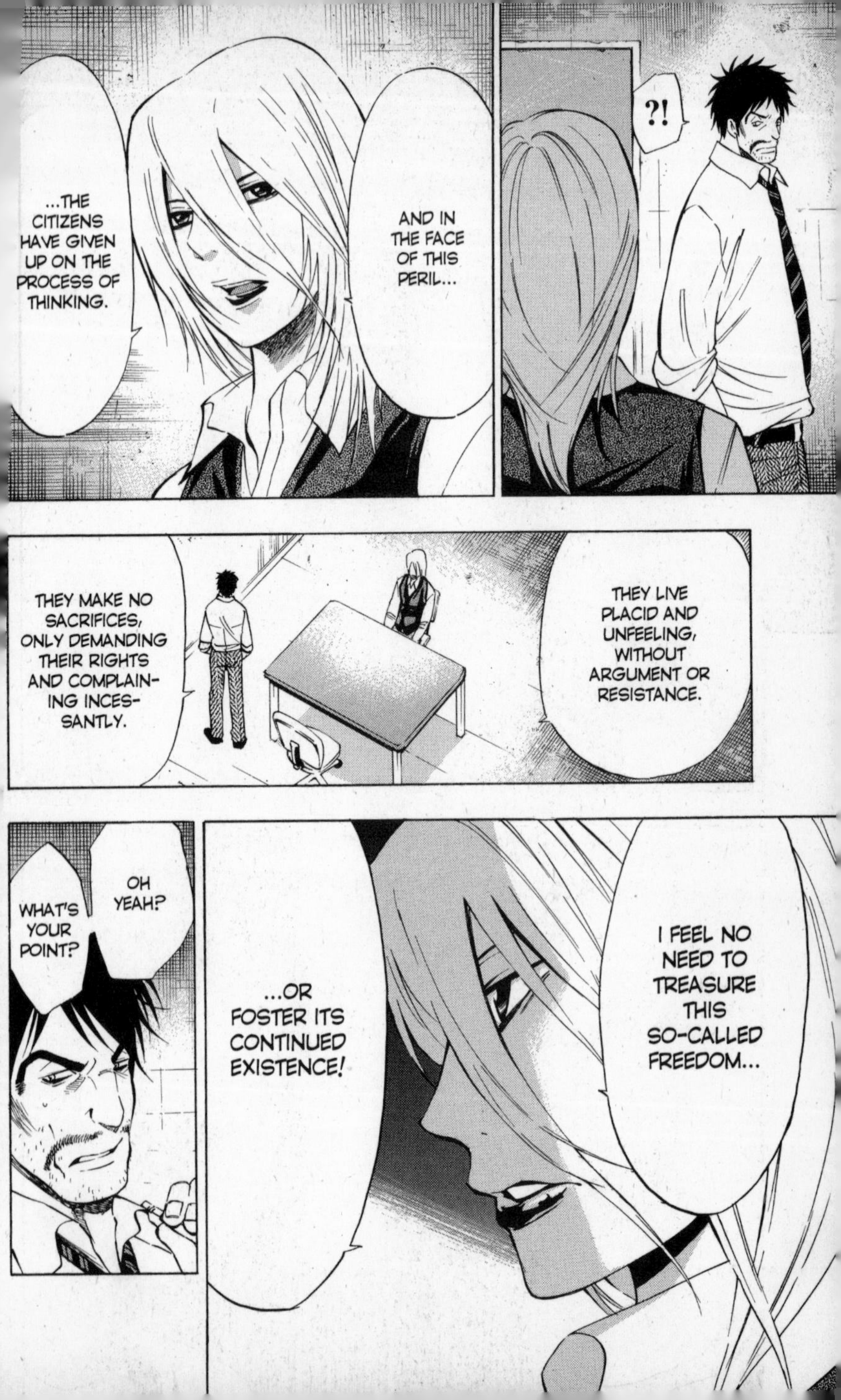
?!
AND IN THE FACE OF THIS PERIL...
...THE CITIZENS HAVE GIVEN UP ON THE PROCESS OF THINKING.
THEY LIVE PLACID AND UNFEELING, WITHOUT ARGUMENT OR RESISTANCE.
THEY MAKE NO SACRIFICES, ONLY DEMANDING THEIR RIGHTS AND COMPLAINING INCESSANTLY.
I FEEL NO NEED TO TREASURE THIS SO-CALLED FREEDOM...
...OR FOSTER ITS CONTINUED EXISTENCE!
OH YEAH?
WHAT'S YOUR POINT?

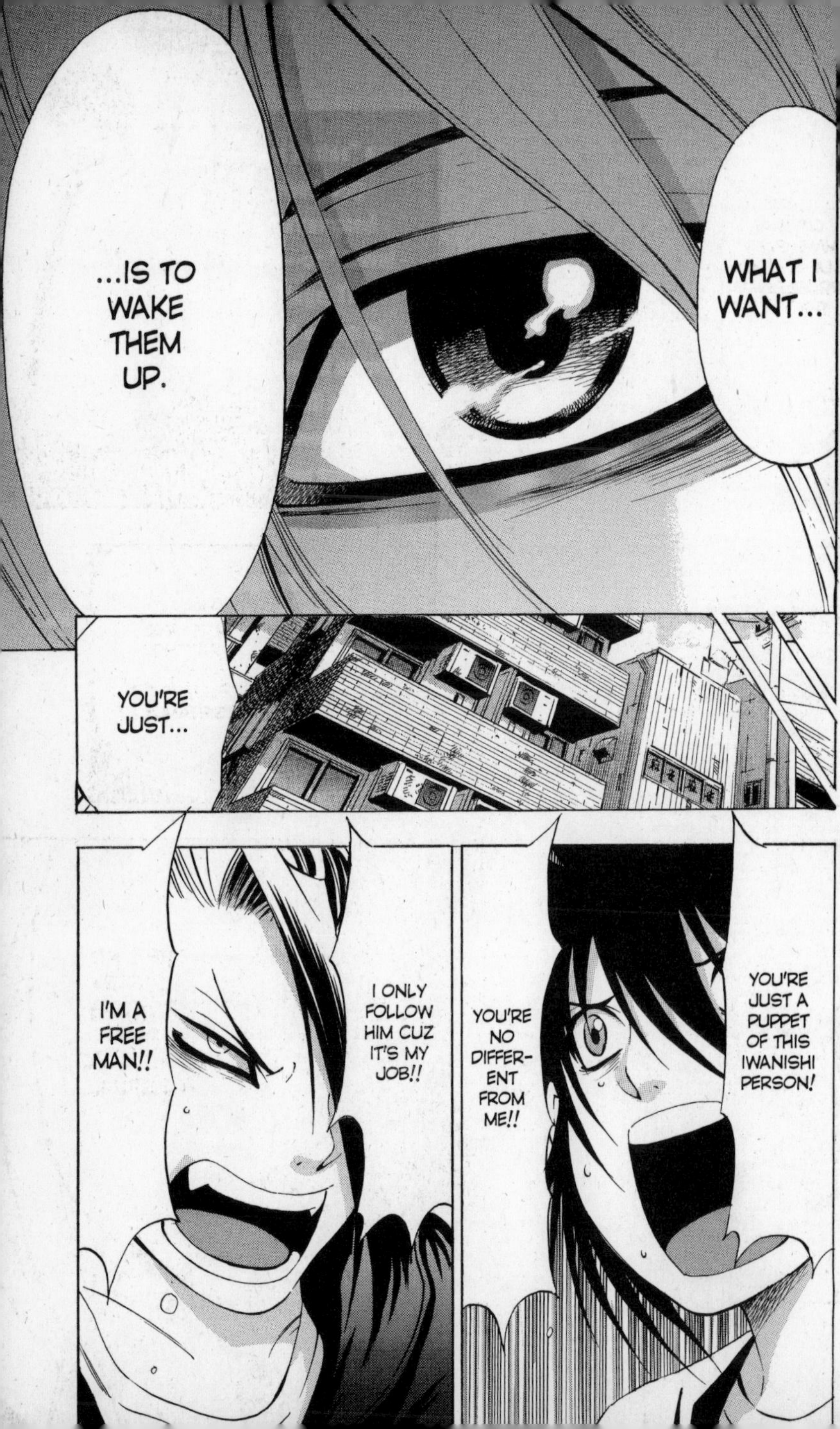
WHAT I WANT...
...IS TO WAKE THEM UP.
YOU'RE JUST...
YOU'RE JUST A PUPPET OF THIS IWANISHI PERSON!
YOU'RE NO DIFFER-ENT FROM ME!!
I ONLY FOLLOW HIM CUZ IT'S MY JOB!!
I'M A FREE MAN!!

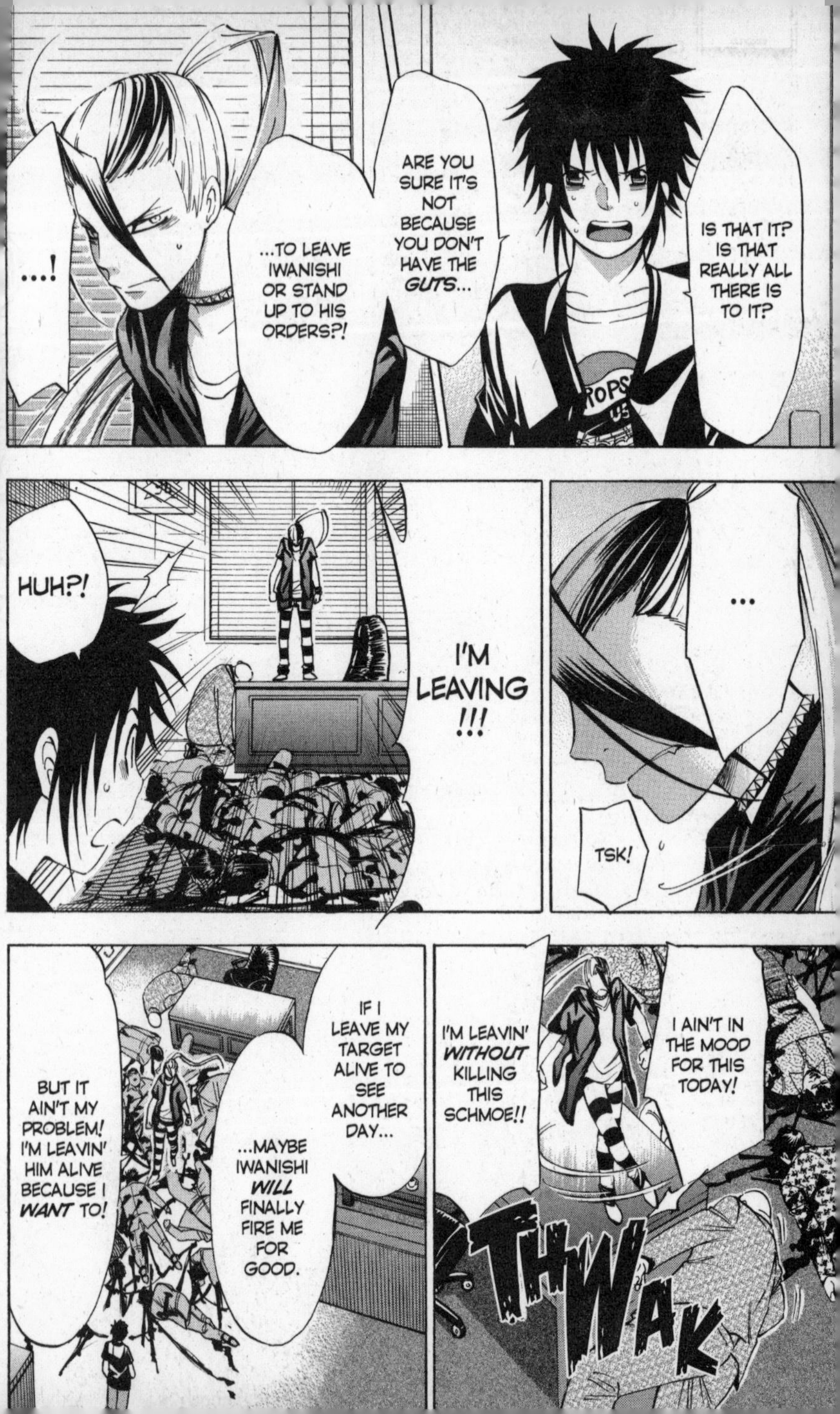
IS THAT IT? IS THAT REALLY ALL THERE IS TO IT?
ARE YOU SURE IT'S NOT BECAUSE YOU DON'T HAVE THE *GUTS*...
...TO LEAVE IWANISHI OR STAND UP TO HIS ORDERS?!
...!
...
TSK!
I'M LEAVING!!!
HUH?!
I AIN'T IN THE MOOD FOR THIS TODAY!
I'M LEAVIN' *WITHOUT* KILLING THIS SCHMOE!!
THWAK
IF I LEAVE MY TARGET ALIVE TO SEE ANOTHER DAY...
...MAYBE IWANISHI *WILL* FINALLY FIRE ME FOR GOOD.
BUT IT AIN'T MY PROBLEM! I'M LEAVIN' HIM ALIVE BECAUSE I *WANT* TO!

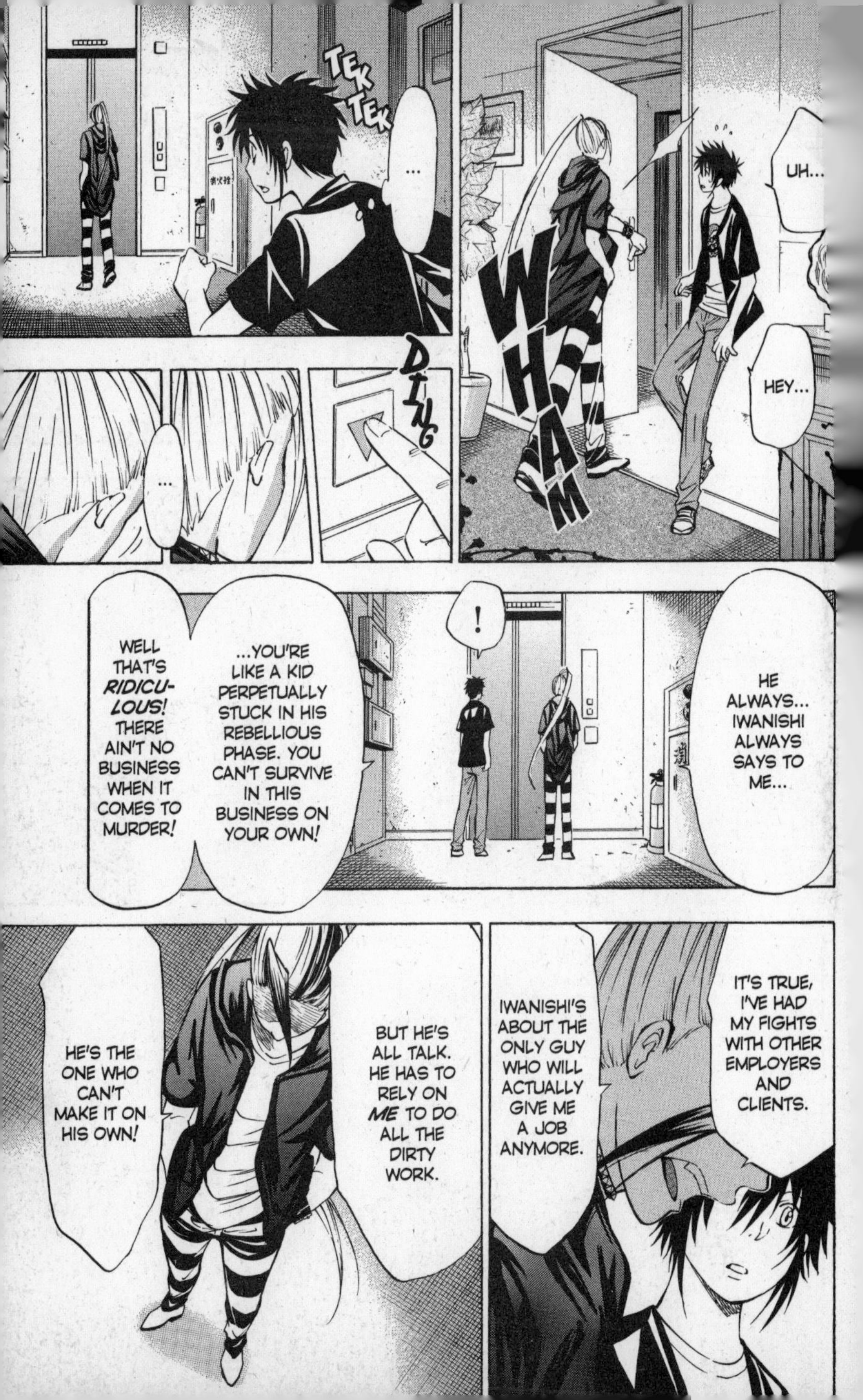
UH...
WHAM
HEY...
TEK TEK
...
DING
...
HE ALWAYS... IWANISHI ALWAYS SAYS TO ME...
!
...YOU'RE LIKE A KID PERPETUALLY STUCK IN HIS REBELLIOUS PHASE. YOU CAN'T SURVIVE IN THIS BUSINESS ON YOUR OWN!
WELL THAT'S *RIDICULOUS!* THERE AIN'T NO BUSINESS WHEN IT COMES TO MURDER!
IT'S TRUE, I'VE HAD MY FIGHTS WITH OTHER EMPLOYERS AND CLIENTS.
IWANISHI'S ABOUT THE ONLY GUY WHO WILL ACTUALLY GIVE ME A JOB ANYMORE.
BUT HE'S ALL TALK. HE HAS TO RELY ON *ME* TO DO ALL THE DIRTY WORK.
HE'S THE ONE WHO CAN'T MAKE IT ON HIS OWN!

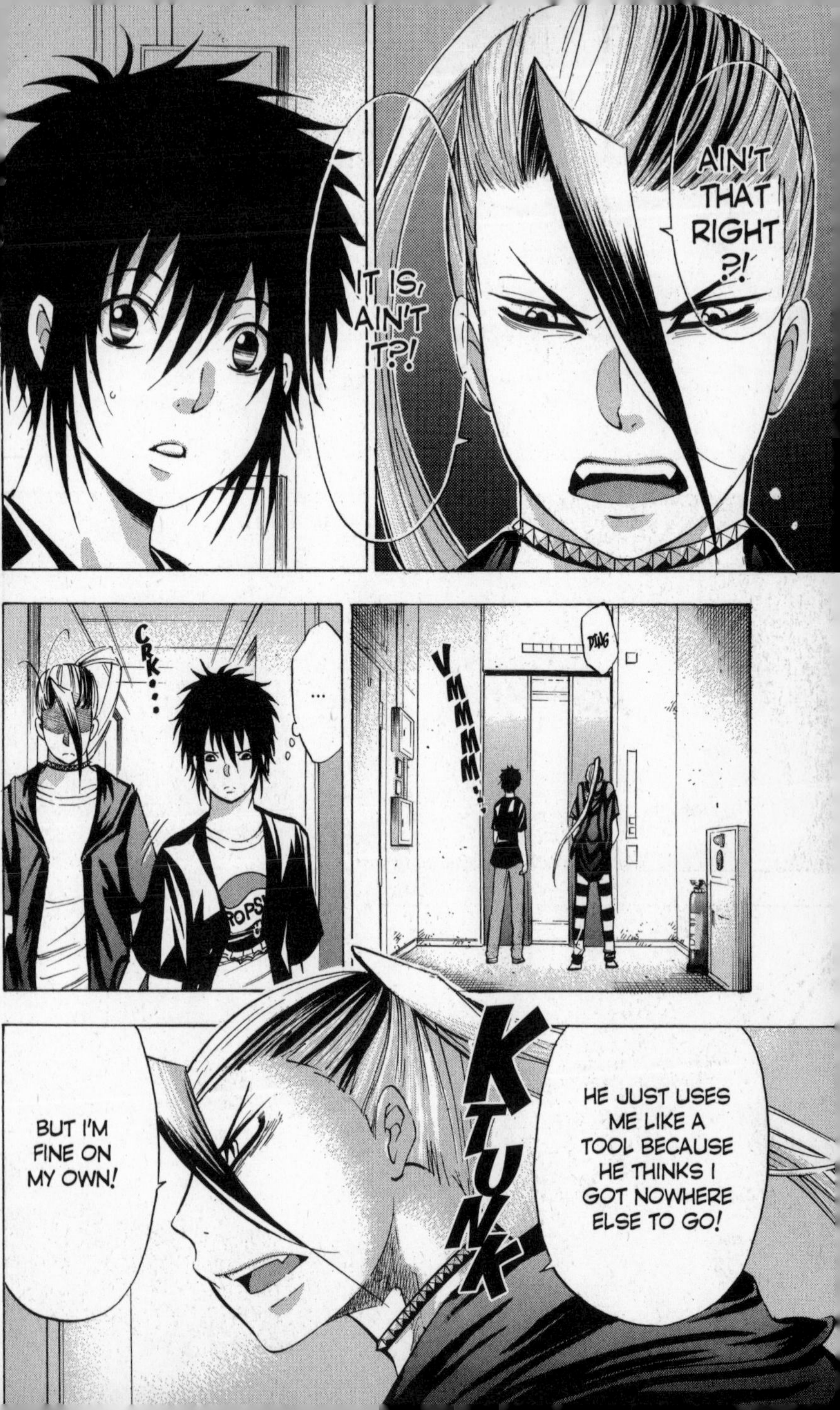
AIN'T THAT RIGHT?!
IT IS, AIN'T IT?!
DING
VMMMM...
...
CRK...
HE JUST USES ME LIKE A TOOL BECAUSE HE THINKS I GOT NOWHERE ELSE TO GO!
KTUNK
BUT I'M FINE ON MY OWN!

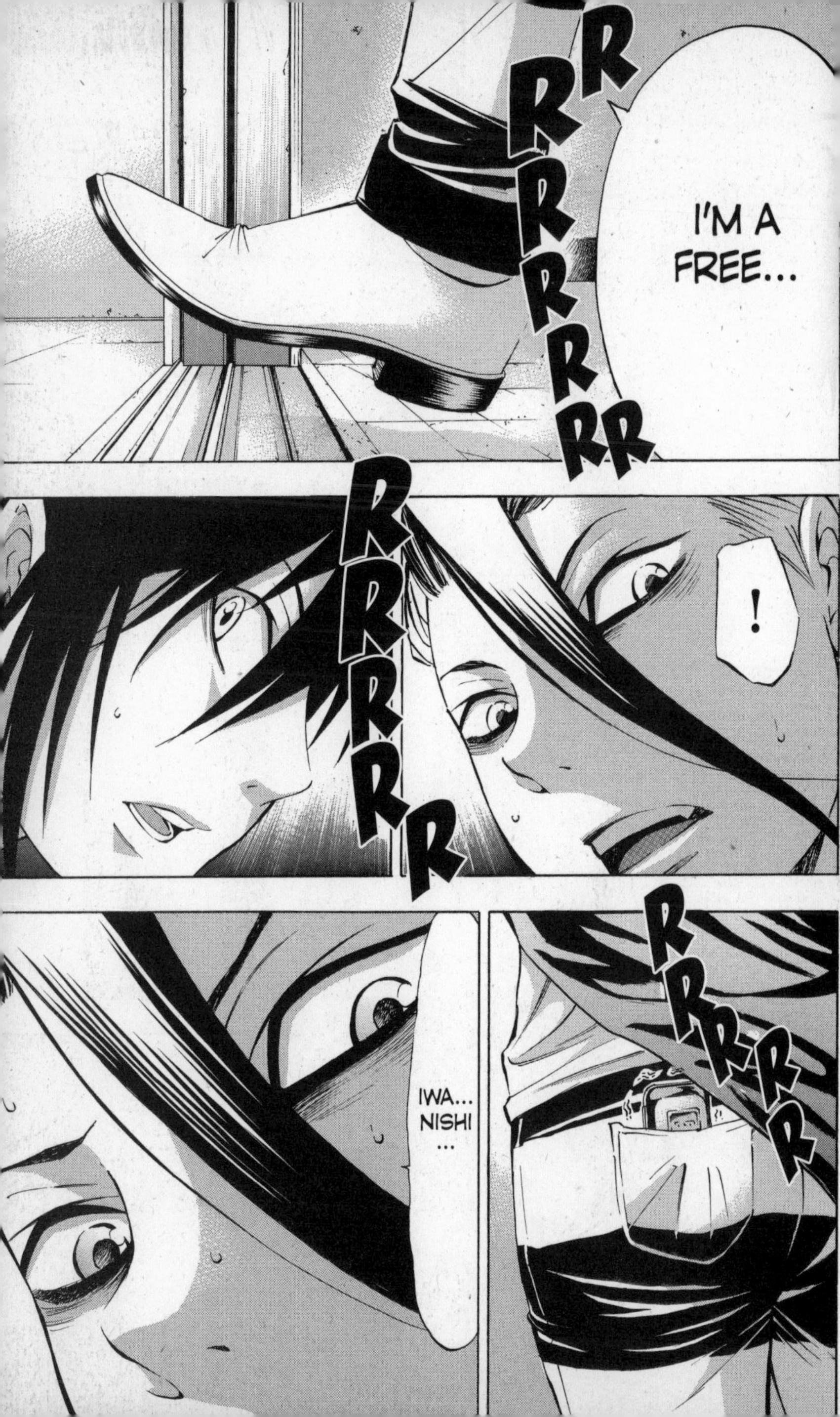
RRRRRRRRR
I'M A FREE...
RRRRRRR
!
RRRRRRR
IWA... NISHI ...

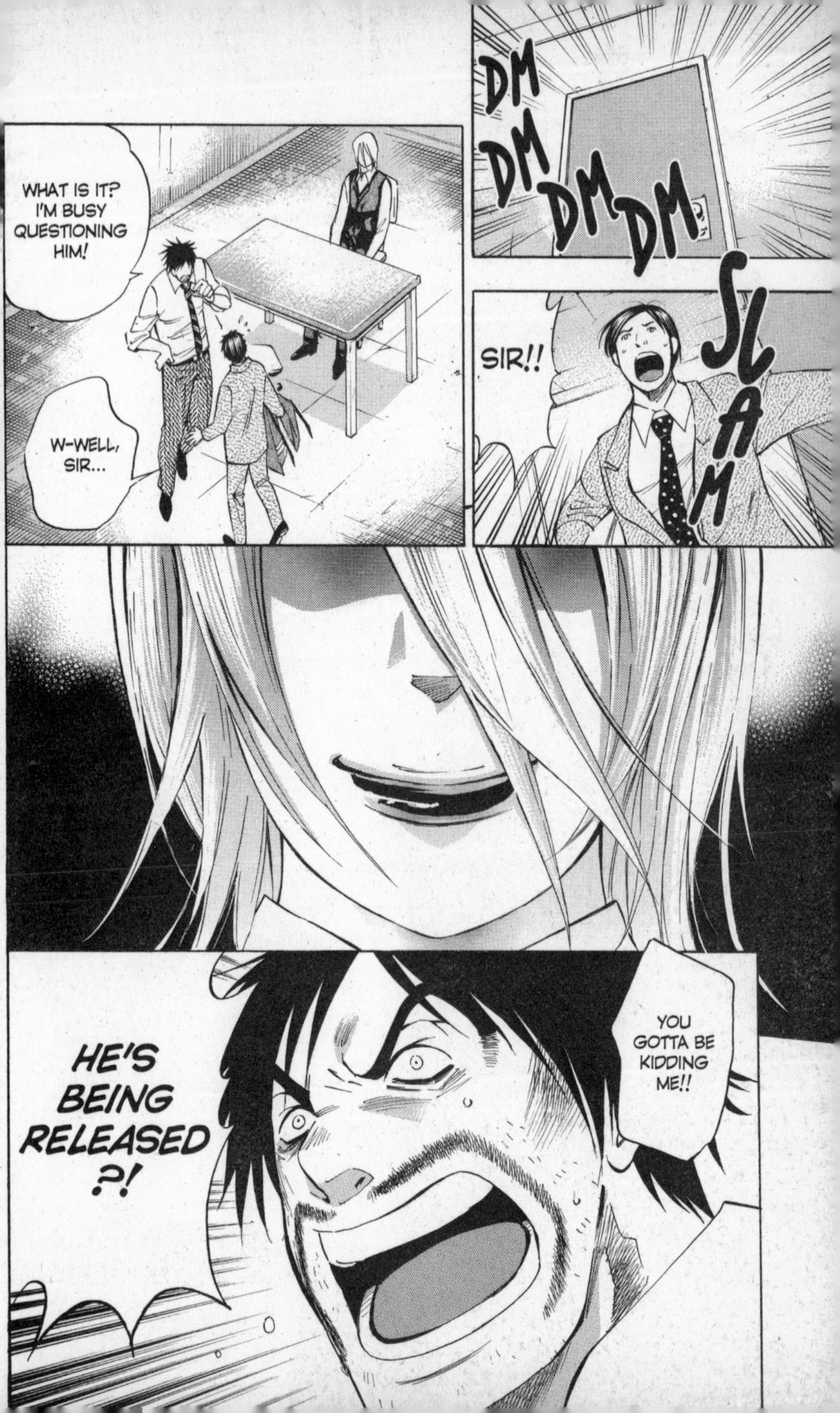
DM DM DM DM
SIR!!
SLAM
WHAT IS IT? I'M BUSY QUESTIONING HIM!
W-WELL, SIR...
YOU GOTTA BE KIDDING ME!!
HE'S BEING RELEASED ?!

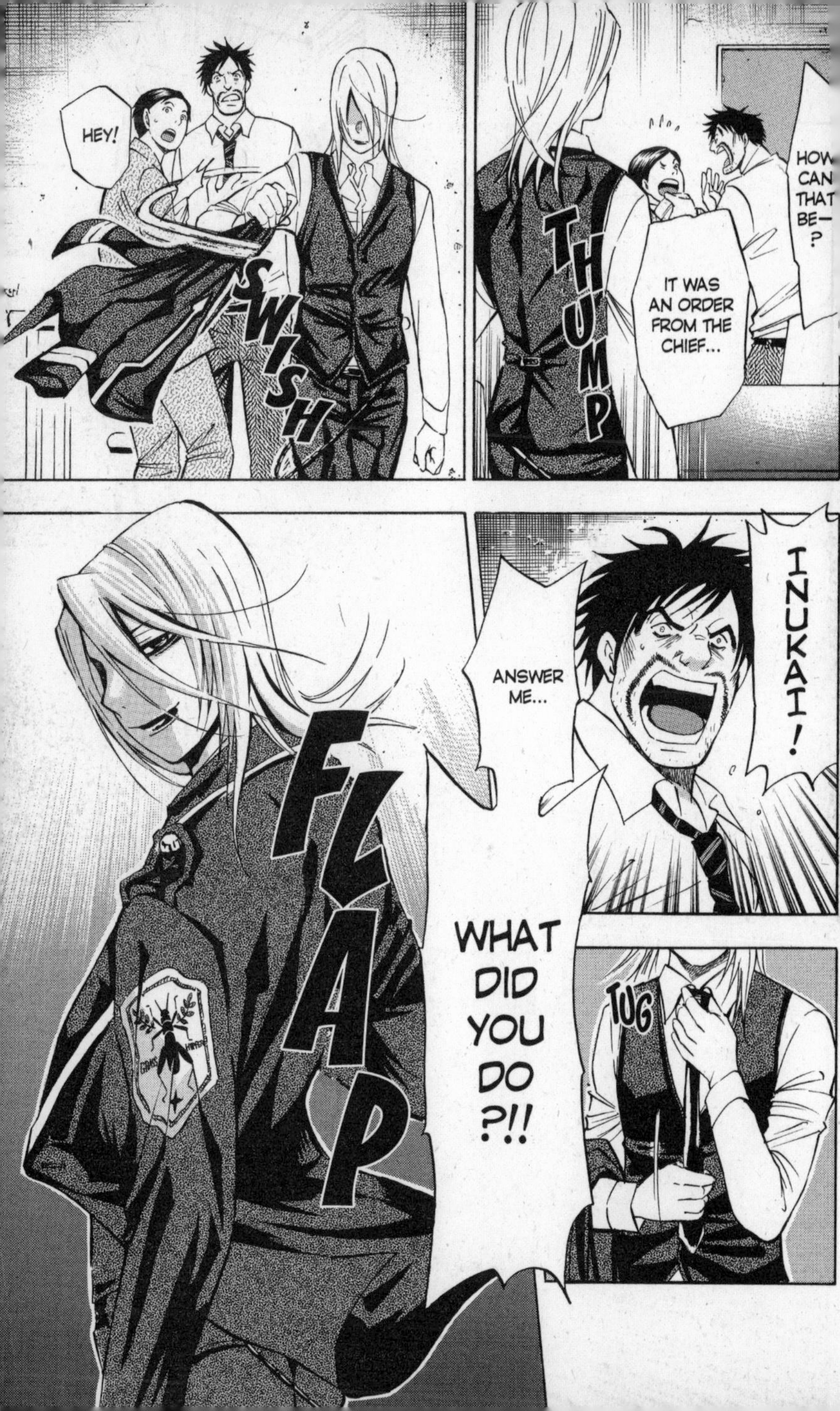
HOW CAN THAT BE—?
IT WAS AN ORDER FROM THE CHIEF...
THUMP
HEY!
SWISH
INUKAI!
ANSWER ME...
WHAT DID YOU DO?!!
TUG
FLAP

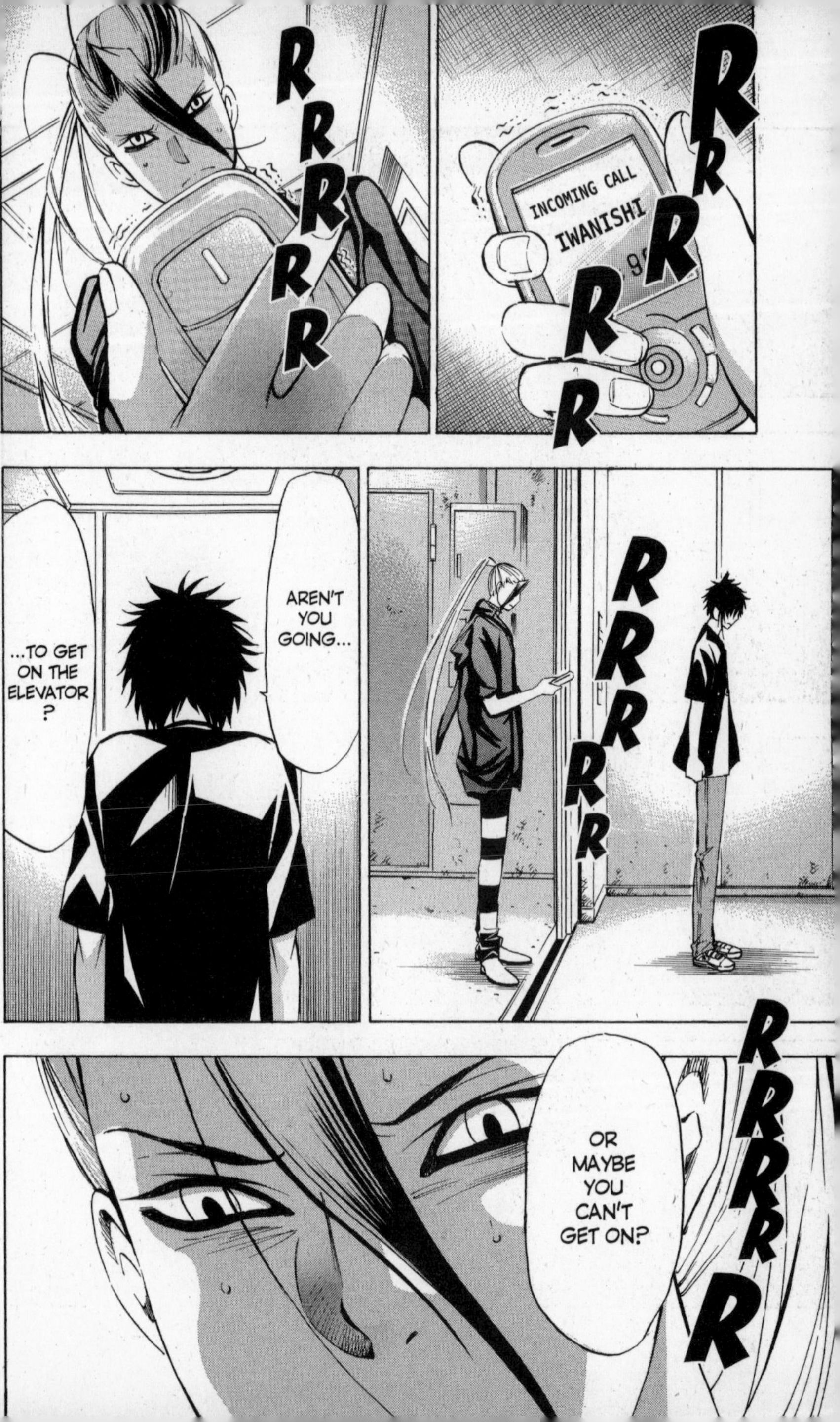
INCOMING CALL
IWANISHI
RRRRRR
RRRRR
RRRRRR
AREN'T YOU GOING...
...TO GET ON THE ELEVATOR?
OR MAYBE YOU CAN'T GET ON?
RRRRRR

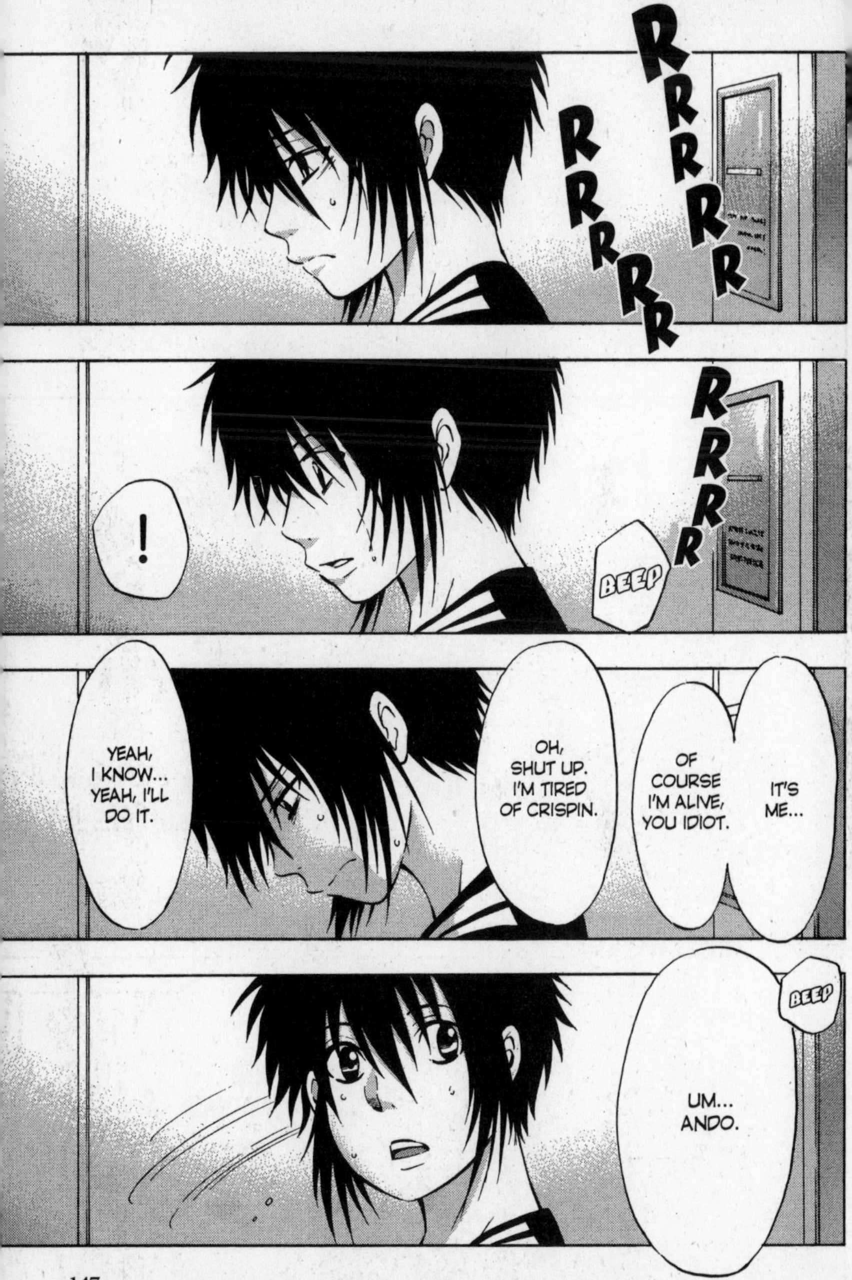
RRRRRRRRRRR
RRRR
BEEP
!
IT'S ME...
OF COURSE I'M ALIVE, YOU IDIOT.
OH, SHUT UP. I'M TIRED OF CRISPIN.
YEAH, I KNOW... YEAH, I'LL DO IT.
BEEP
UM... ANDO.

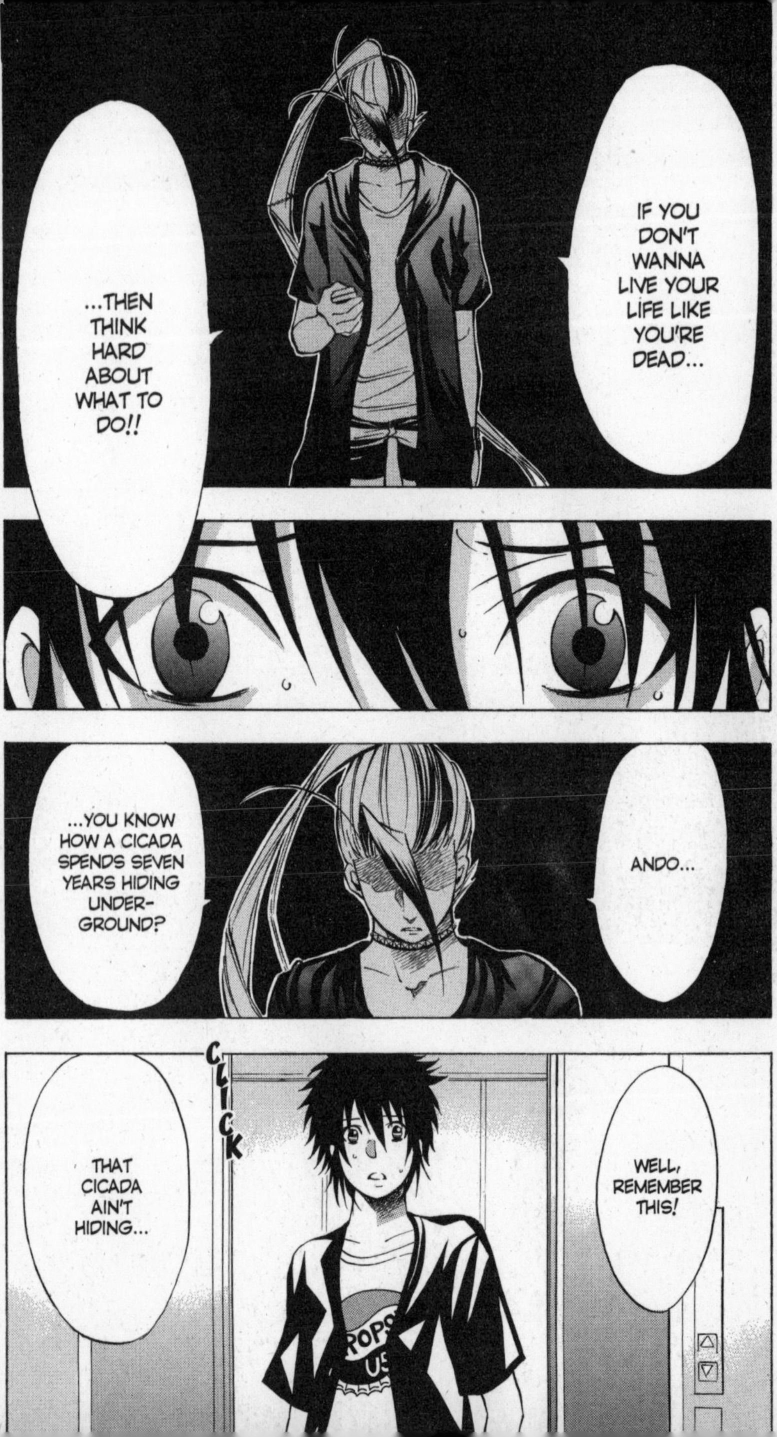
IF YOU DON'T WANNA LIVE YOUR LIFE LIKE YOU'RE DEAD...
...THEN THINK HARD ABOUT WHAT TO DO!!
ANDO...
...YOU KNOW HOW A CICADA SPENDS SEVEN YEARS HIDING UNDER-GROUND?
CLICK
WELL, REMEMBER THIS!
THAT CICADA AIN'T HIDING...

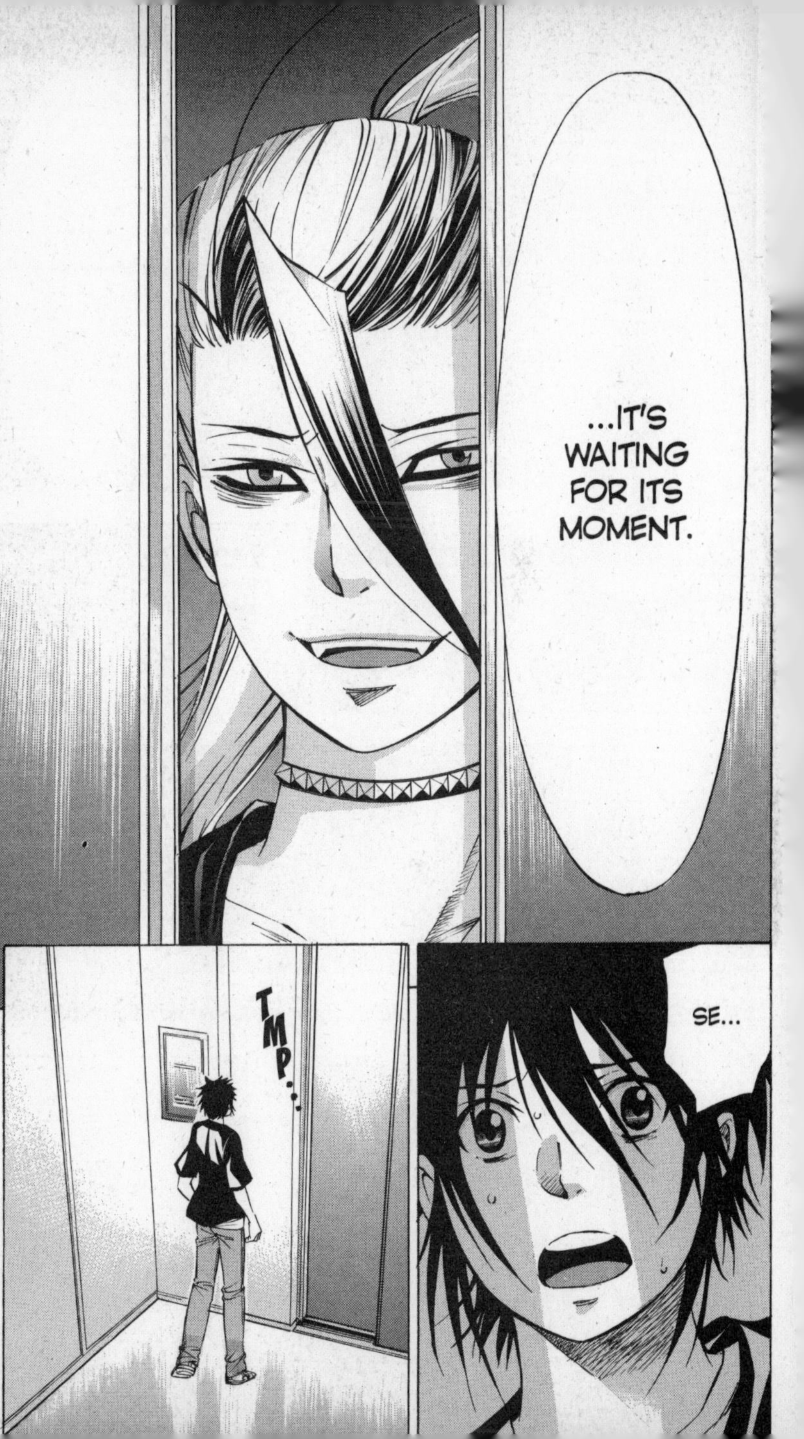
...IT'S WAITING FOR ITS MOMENT.
SE...
TMP...

ARE YOU GUYS PART OF THE GROUP **AGAINST** THE NEW URBAN CENTER PROJECT?!

WE WAS ONLY DOIN' WHAT WE WAS **ORDERED** TO DO! BY THE GUYS FROM THE ANDER-SON GROUP!!

THERE'S ONLY ONE THING FOR YOU TO DO! YOU FIND WHOEVER THIS IS AND BEAT THE CRAP OUTTA HIM!!

FACE-TO-FACE !!!

I...

B-BUT...

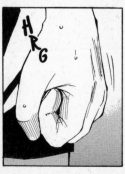

HRG

150

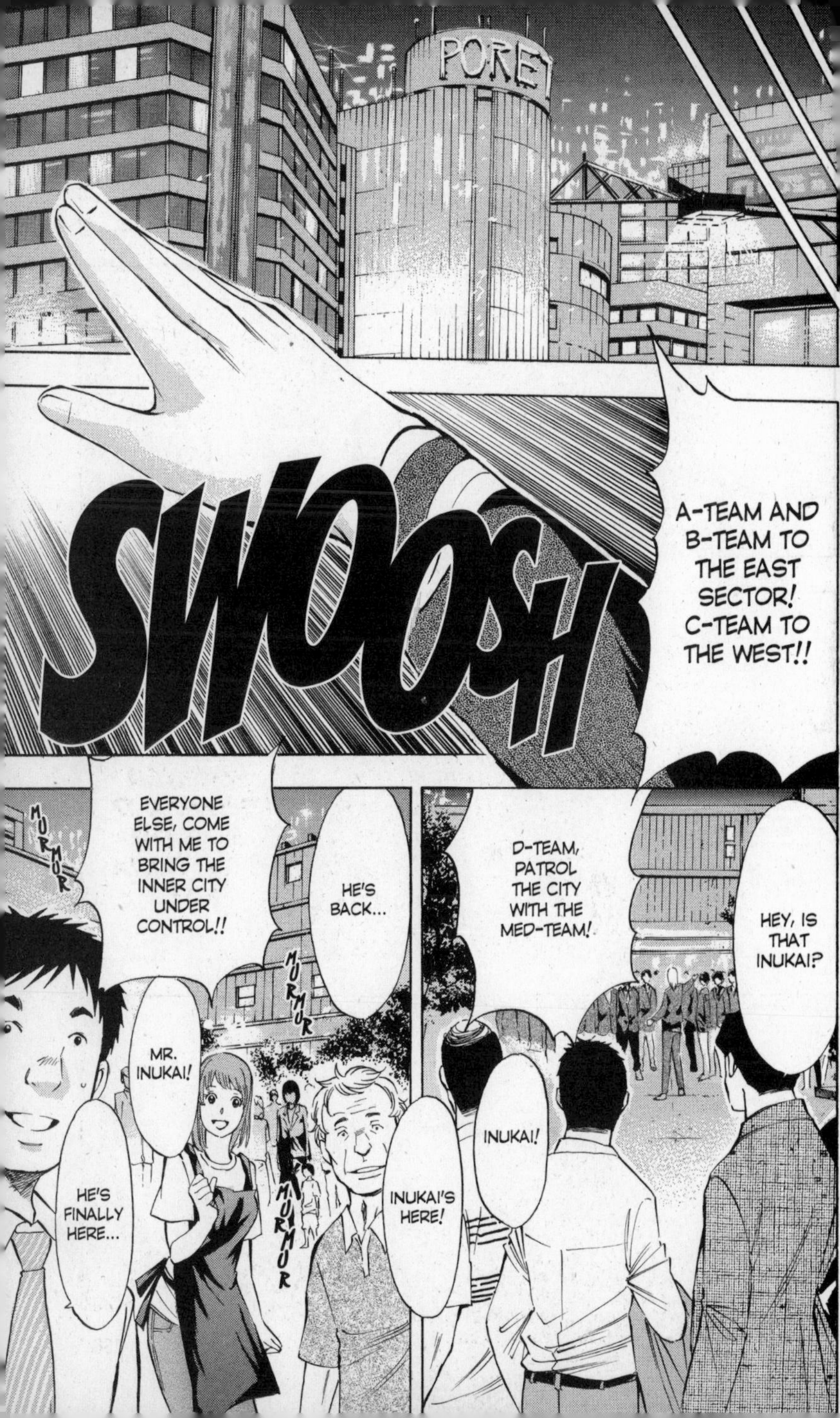
A-TEAM AND B-TEAM TO THE EAST SECTOR! C-TEAM TO THE WEST!!
SWOOSH
D-TEAM, PATROL THE CITY WITH THE MED-TEAM!
HEY, IS THAT INUKAI?
INUKAI!
INUKAI'S HERE!
EVERYONE ELSE, COME WITH ME TO BRING THE INNER CITY UNDER CONTROL!!
HE'S BACK...
MURMUR
MURMUR
MR. INUKAI!
MURMUR
HE'S FINALLY HERE...

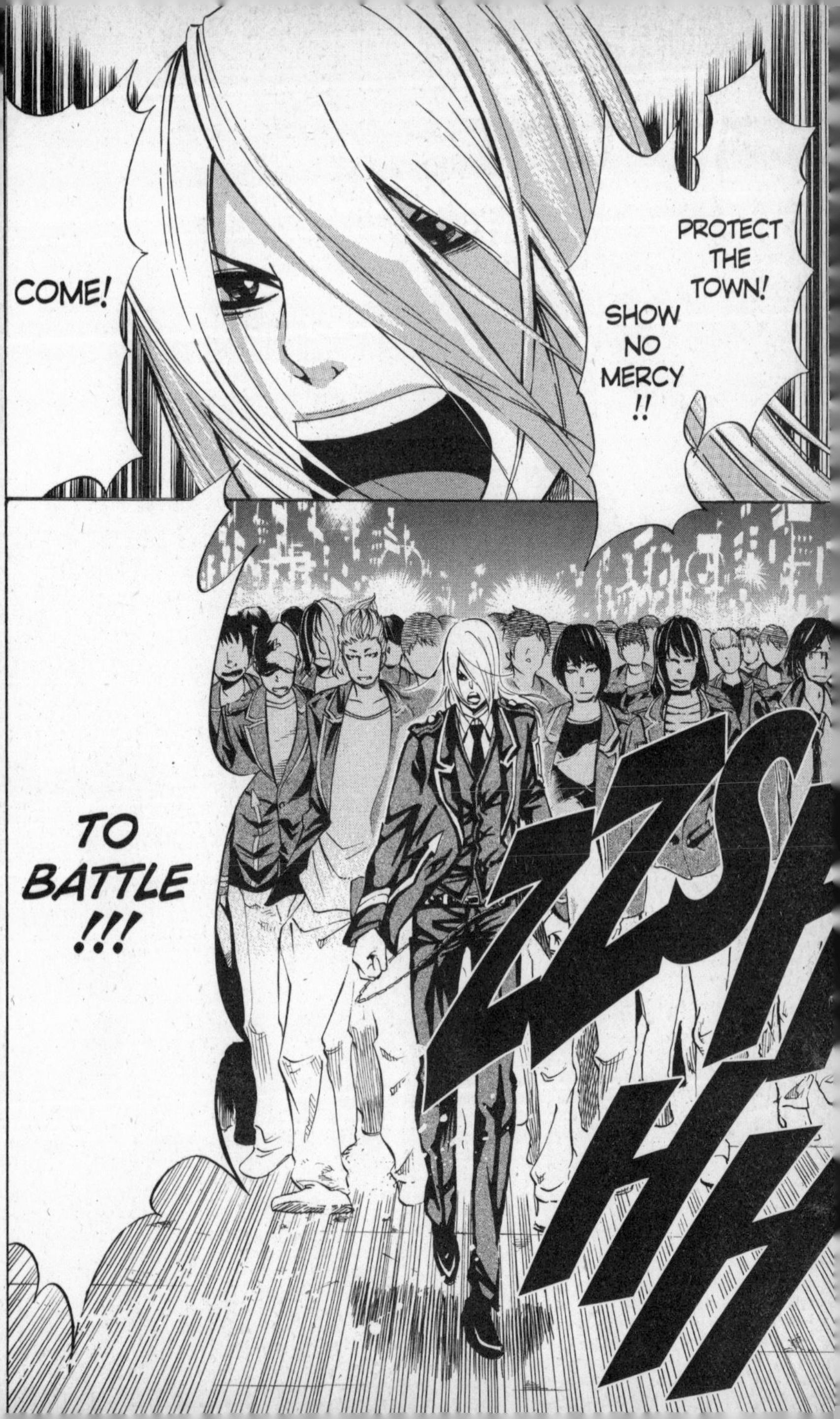
PROTECT THE TOWN!
SHOW NO MERCY!!
COME!
TO BATTLE!!!

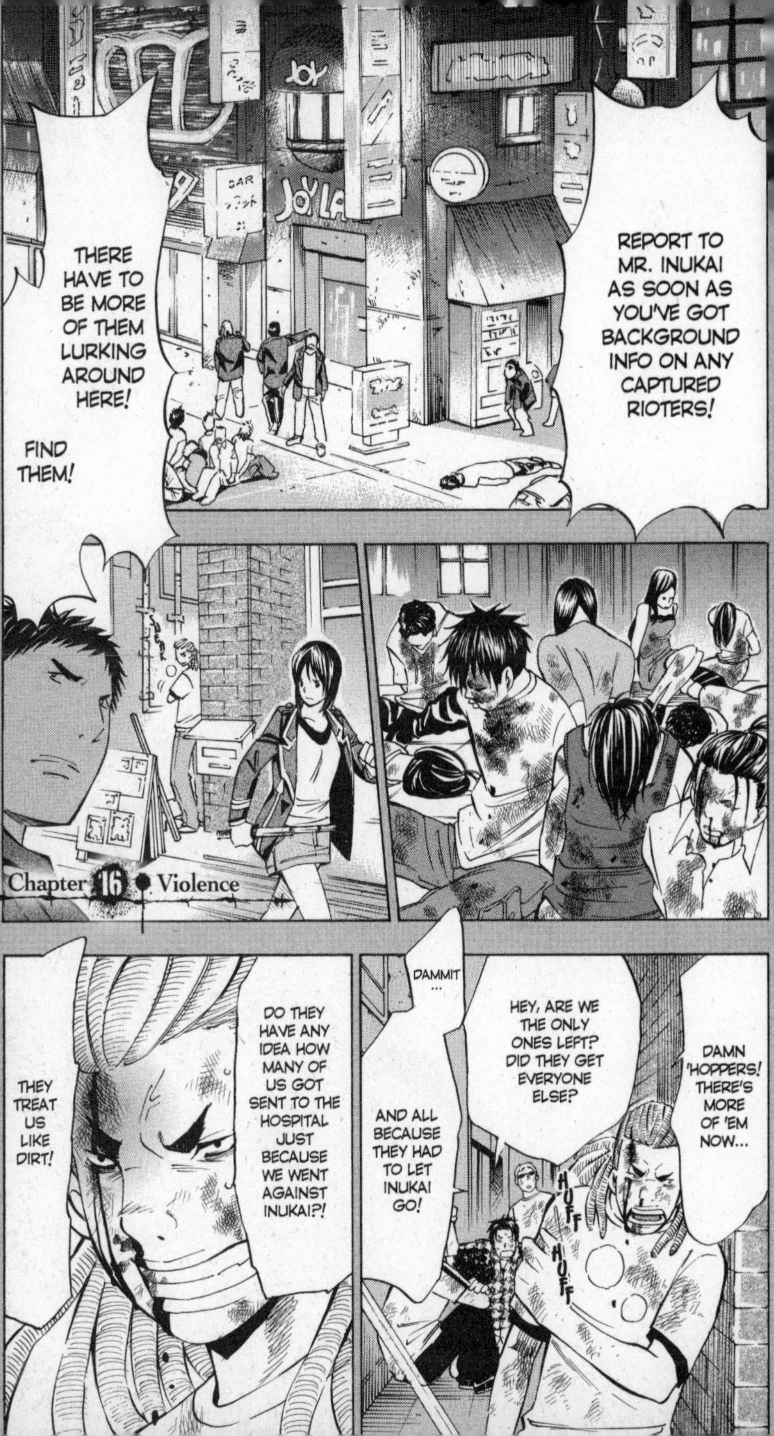
REPORT TO MR. INUKAI AS SOON AS YOU'VE GOT BACKGROUND INFO ON ANY CAPTURED RIOTERS!
THERE HAVE TO BE MORE OF THEM LURKING AROUND HERE!
FIND THEM!
Chapter 16 Violence
DAMN 'HOPPERS! THERE'S MORE OF 'EM NOW...
HEY, ARE WE THE ONLY ONES LEFT? DID THEY GET EVERYONE ELSE?
DAMMIT...
AND ALL BECAUSE THEY HAD TO LET INUKAI GO!
HUFF HUFF
DO THEY HAVE ANY IDEA HOW MANY OF US GOT SENT TO THE HOSPITAL JUST BECAUSE WE WENT AGAINST INUKAI?!
THEY TREAT US LIKE DIRT!

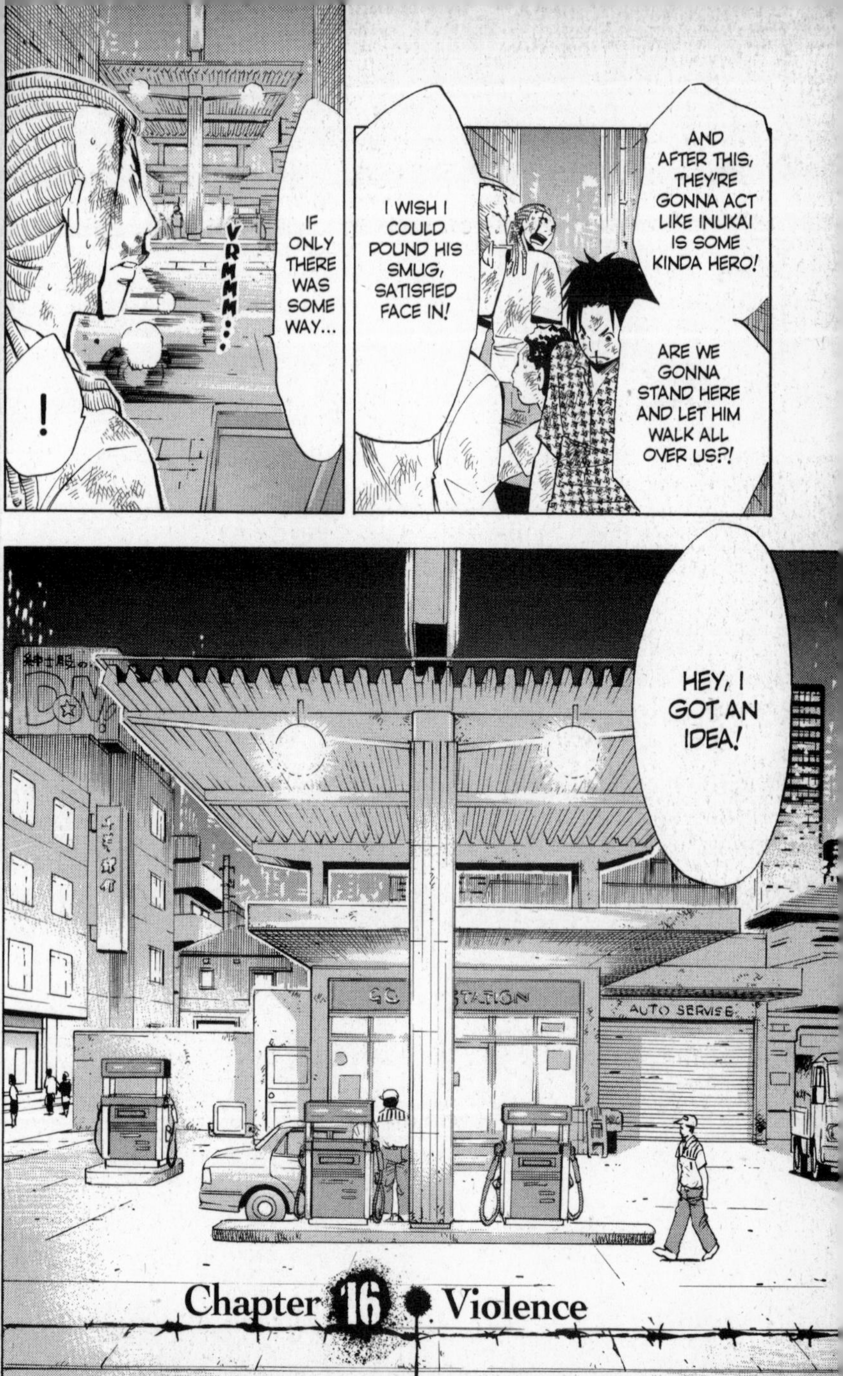
AND AFTER THIS, THEY'RE GONNA ACT LIKE INUKAI IS SOME KINDA HERO!
ARE WE GONNA STAND HERE AND LET HIM WALK ALL OVER US?!
I WISH I COULD POUND HIS SMUG, SATISFIED FACE IN!
IF ONLY THERE WAS SOME WAY...
VRMMM...
!
HEY, I GOT AN IDEA!
AUTO SERVISE
Chapter 16 Violence

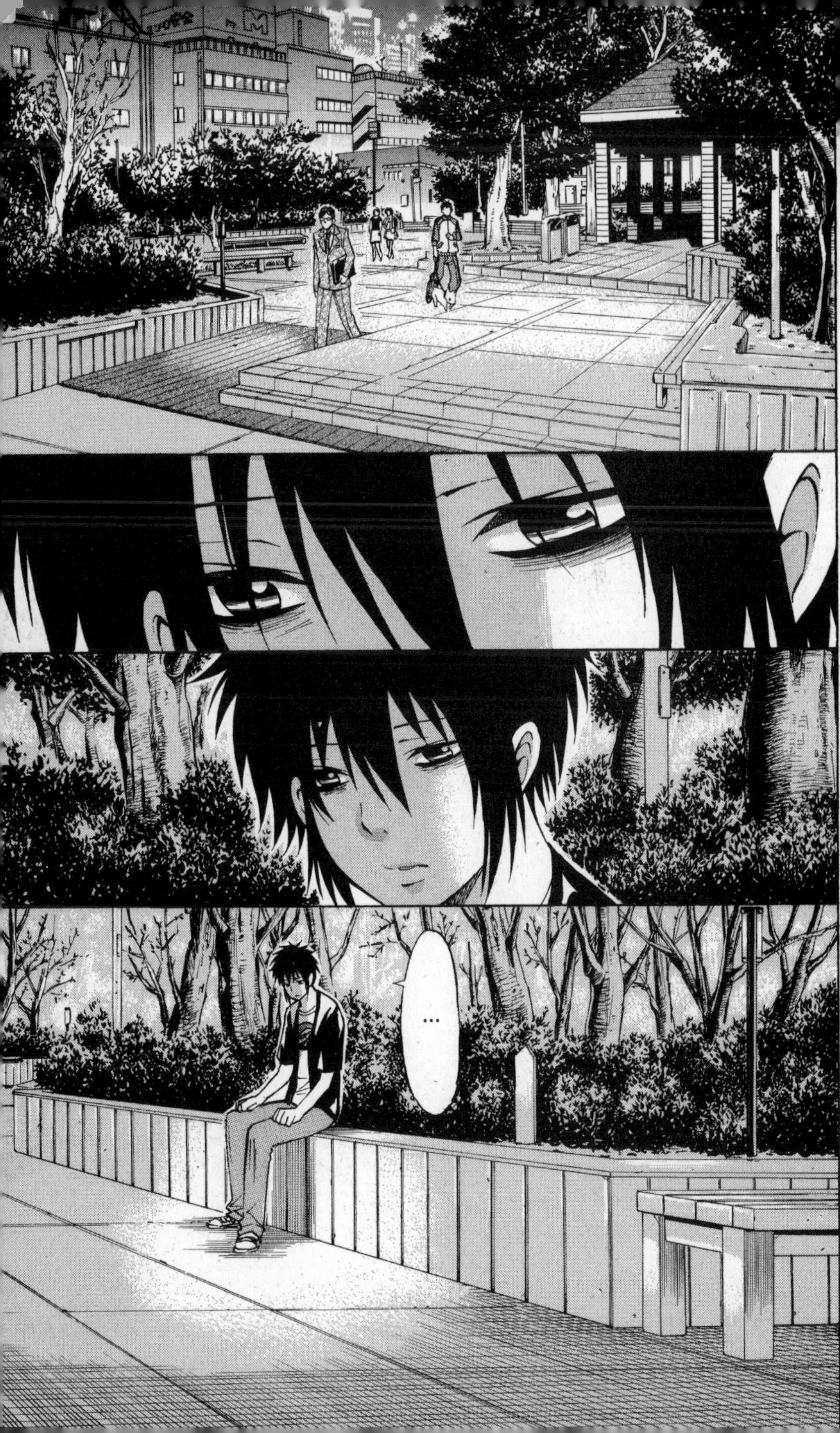
...

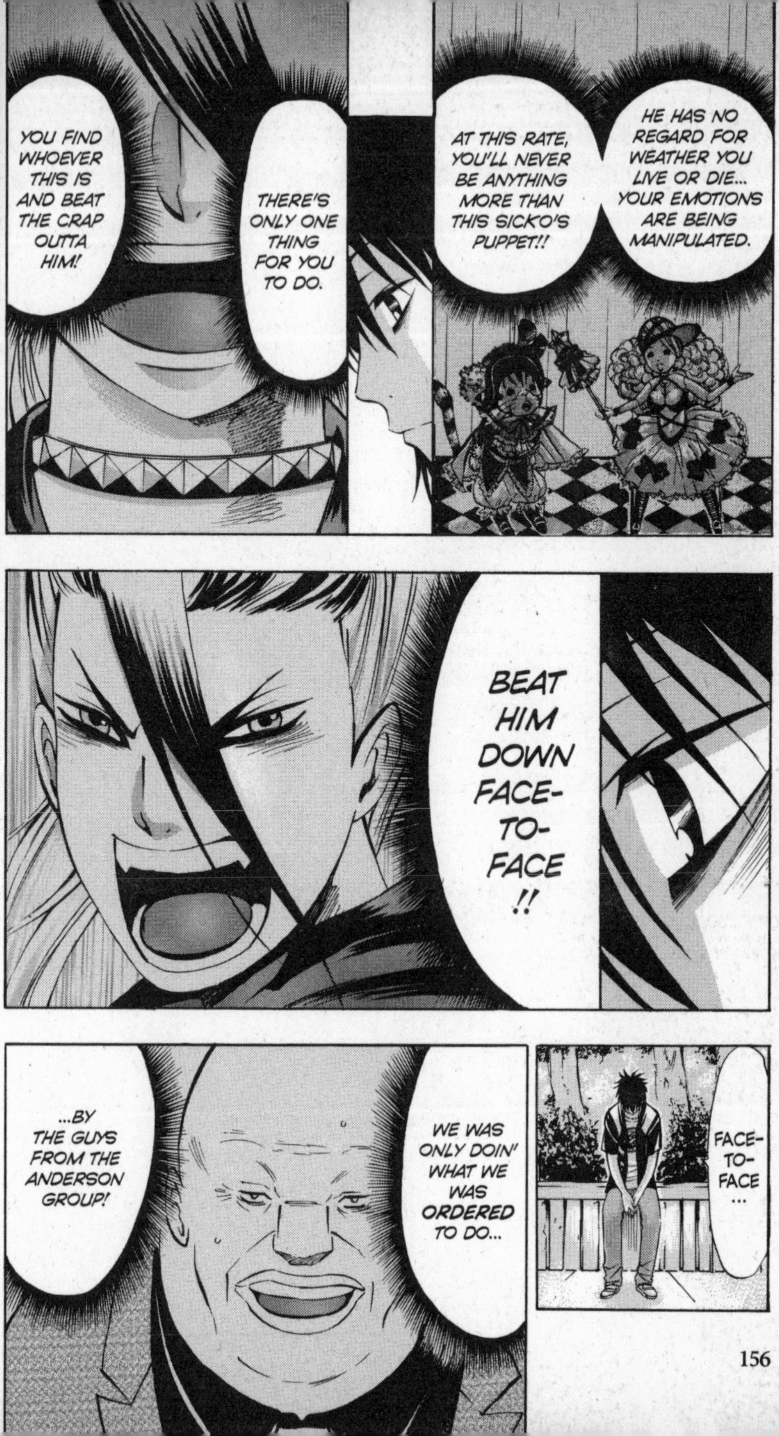
HE HAS NO REGARD FOR WEATHER YOU LIVE OR DIE... YOUR EMOTIONS ARE BEING MANIPULATED.
AT THIS RATE, YOU'LL NEVER BE ANYTHING MORE THAN THIS SICKO'S PUPPET!!
THERE'S ONLY ONE THING FOR YOU TO DO.
YOU FIND WHOEVER THIS IS AND BEAT THE CRAP OUTTA HIM!
BEAT HIM DOWN FACE-TO-FACE!!
FACE-TO-FACE...
WE WAS ONLY DOIN' WHAT WE WAS ORDERED TO DO...
...BY THE GUYS FROM THE ANDERSON GROUP!

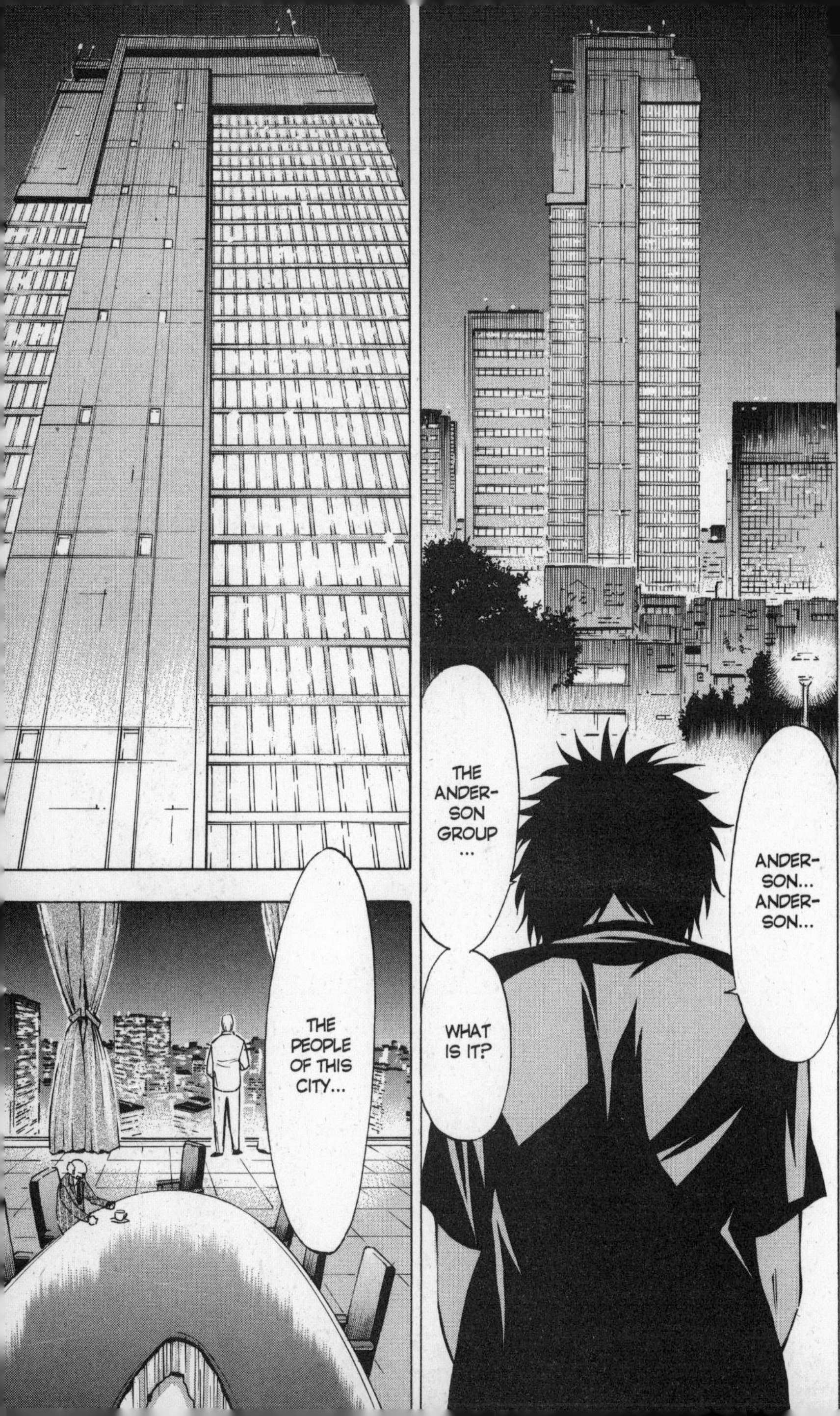
ANDER-SON... ANDER-SON...
THE ANDER-SON GROUP ...
WHAT IS IT?
THE PEOPLE OF THIS CITY...

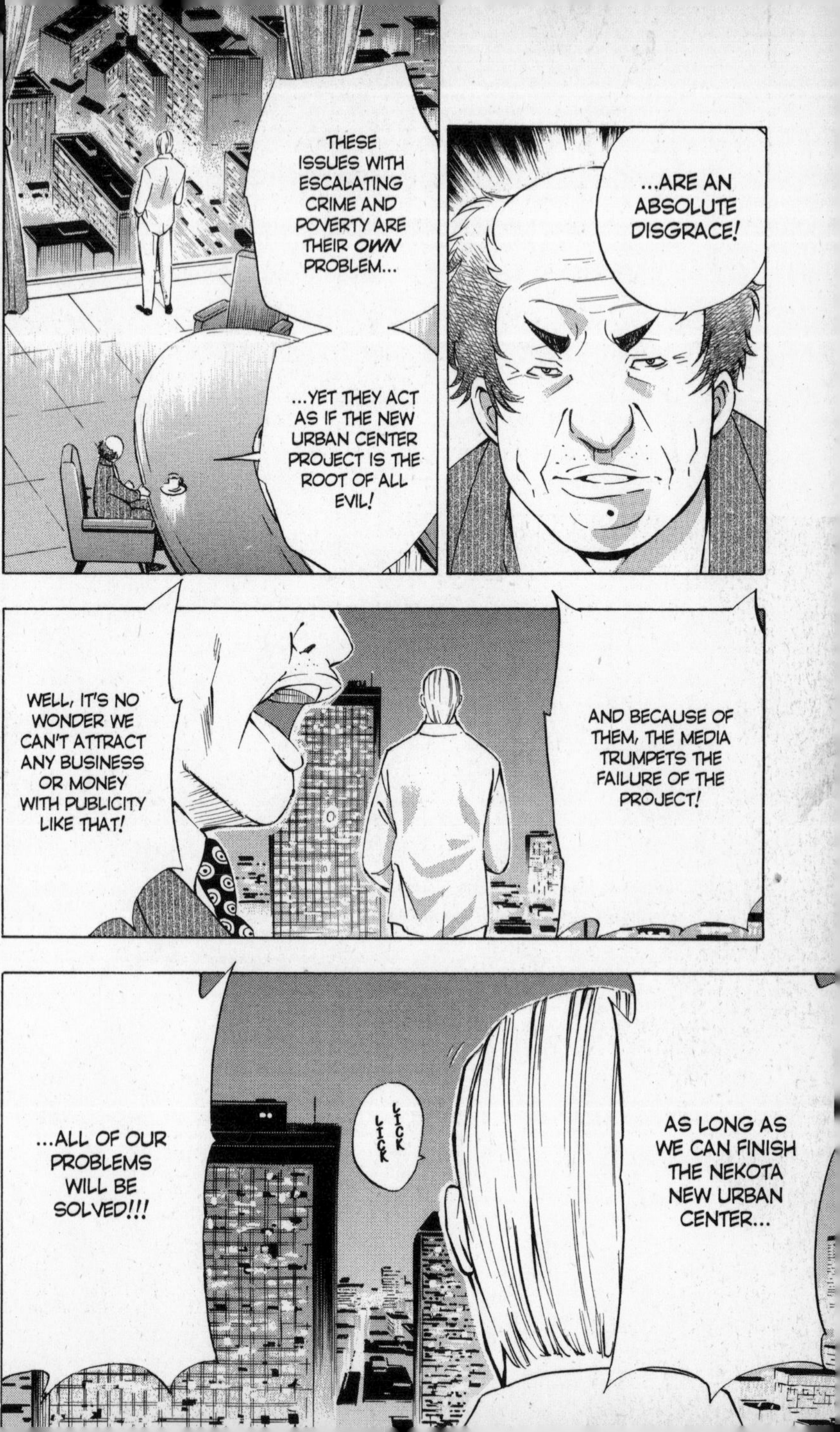
...ARE AN ABSOLUTE DISGRACE!
THESE ISSUES WITH ESCALATING CRIME AND POVERTY ARE THEIR *OWN* PROBLEM...
...YET THEY ACT AS IF THE NEW URBAN CENTER PROJECT IS THE ROOT OF ALL EVIL!
AND BECAUSE OF THEM, THE MEDIA TRUMPETS THE FAILURE OF THE PROJECT!
WELL, IT'S NO WONDER WE CAN'T ATTRACT ANY BUSINESS OR MONEY WITH PUBLICITY LIKE THAT!
AS LONG AS WE CAN FINISH THE NEKOTA NEW URBAN CENTER...
LICK LICK
...ALL OF OUR PROBLEMS WILL BE SOLVED!!!

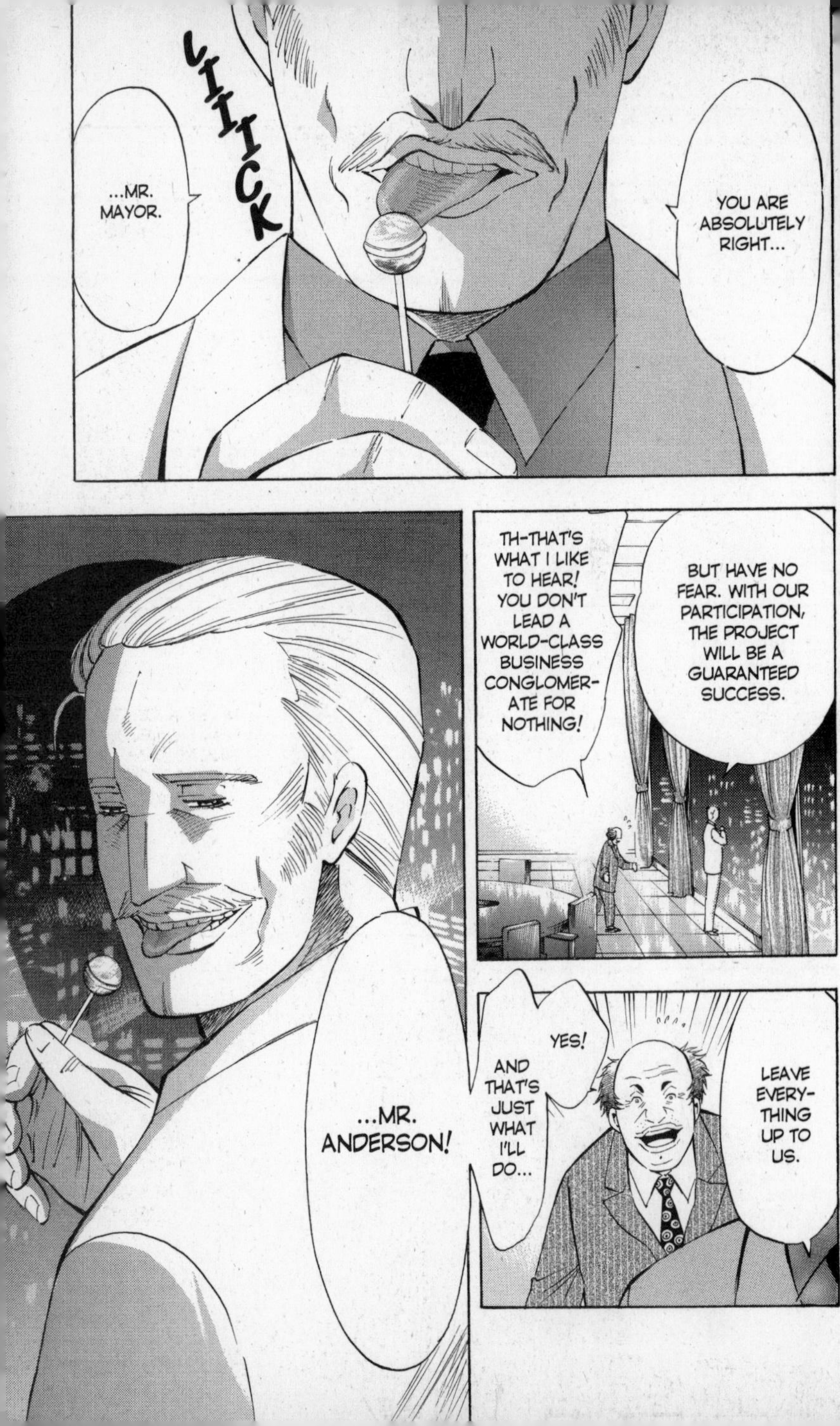
YOU ARE ABSOLUTELY RIGHT...
LIIICK
...MR. MAYOR.
BUT HAVE NO FEAR. WITH OUR PARTICIPATION, THE PROJECT WILL BE A GUARANTEED SUCCESS.
TH-THAT'S WHAT I LIKE TO HEAR! YOU DON'T LEAD A WORLD-CLASS BUSINESS CONGLOMER-ATE FOR NOTHING!
LEAVE EVERY-THING UP TO US.
YES!
AND THAT'S JUST WHAT I'LL DO...
...MR. ANDERSON!

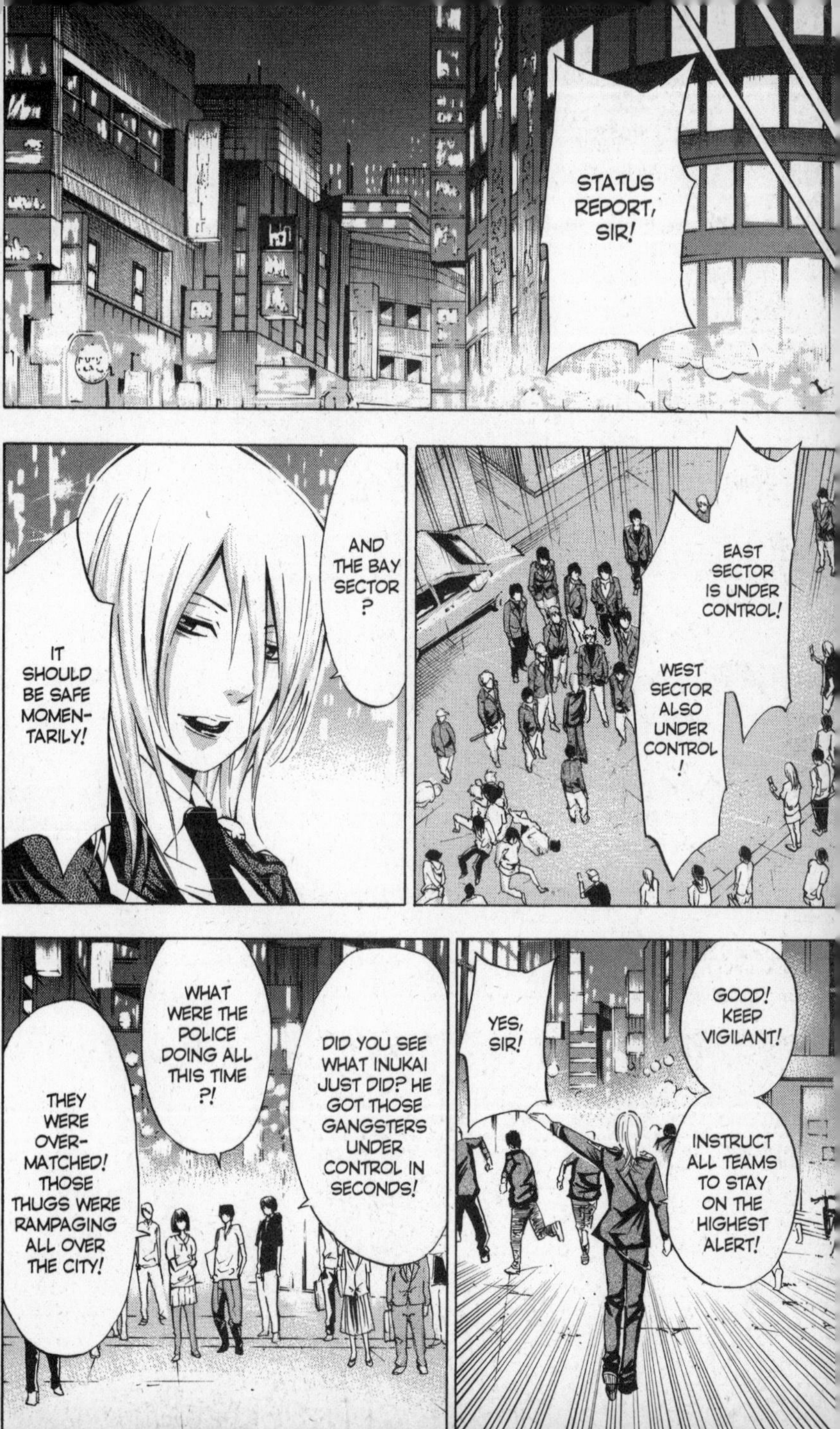
STATUS REPORT, SIR!
EAST SECTOR IS UNDER CONTROL!
WEST SECTOR ALSO UNDER CONTROL!
AND THE BAY SECTOR?
IT SHOULD BE SAFE MOMEN-TARILY!
GOOD! KEEP VIGILANT!
INSTRUCT ALL TEAMS TO STAY ON THE HIGHEST ALERT!
YES, SIR!
DID YOU SEE WHAT INUKAI JUST DID? HE GOT THOSE GANGSTERS UNDER CONTROL IN SECONDS!
WHAT WERE THE POLICE DOING ALL THIS TIME?!
THEY WERE OVER-MATCHED! THOSE THUGS WERE RAMPAGING ALL OVER THE CITY!

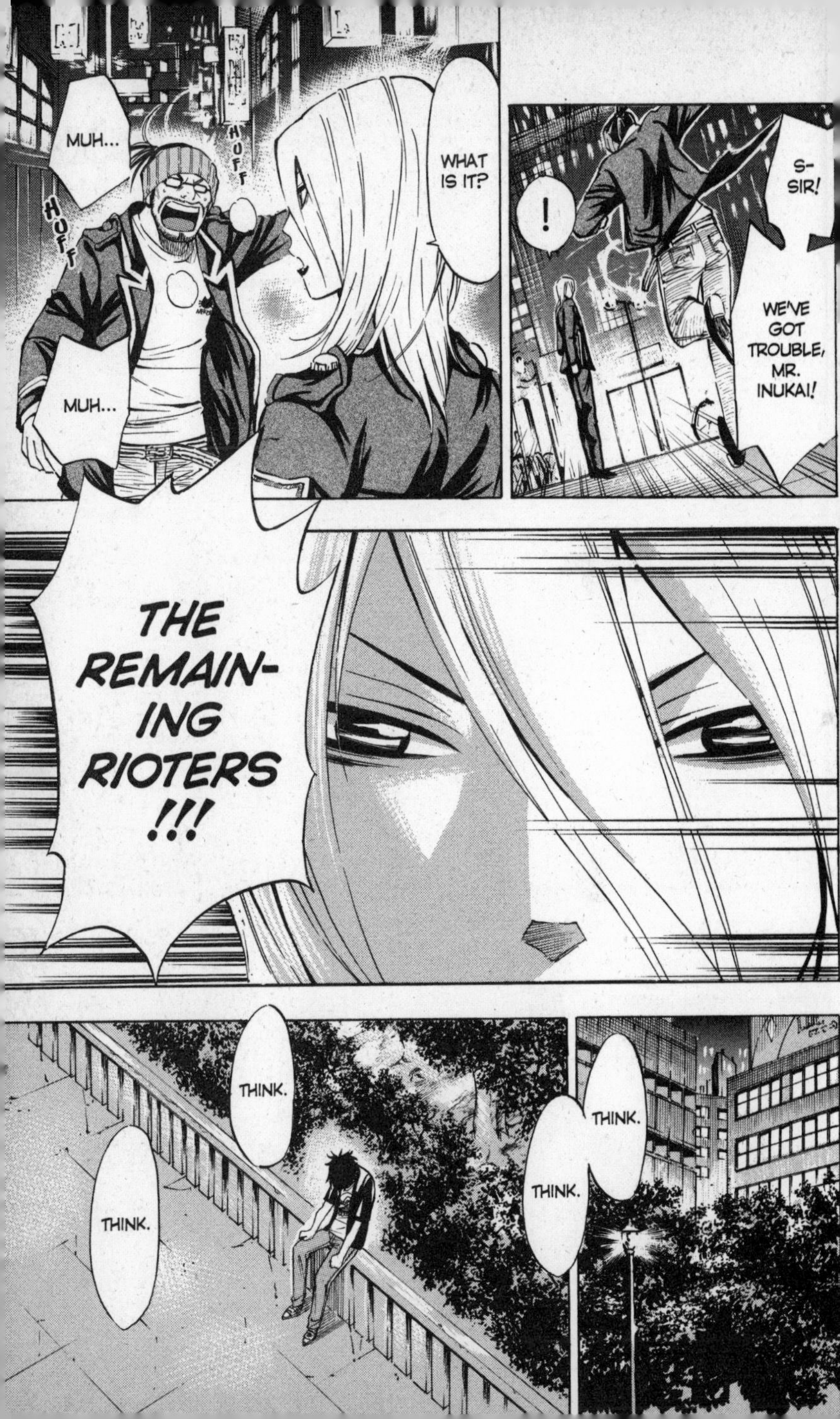
S-SIR!
!
WE'VE GOT TROUBLE, MR. INUKAI!
WHAT IS IT?
HUFF
HUFF
MUH...
MUH...
THE REMAIN-ING RIOTERS!!!
THINK.
THINK.
THINK.
THINK.

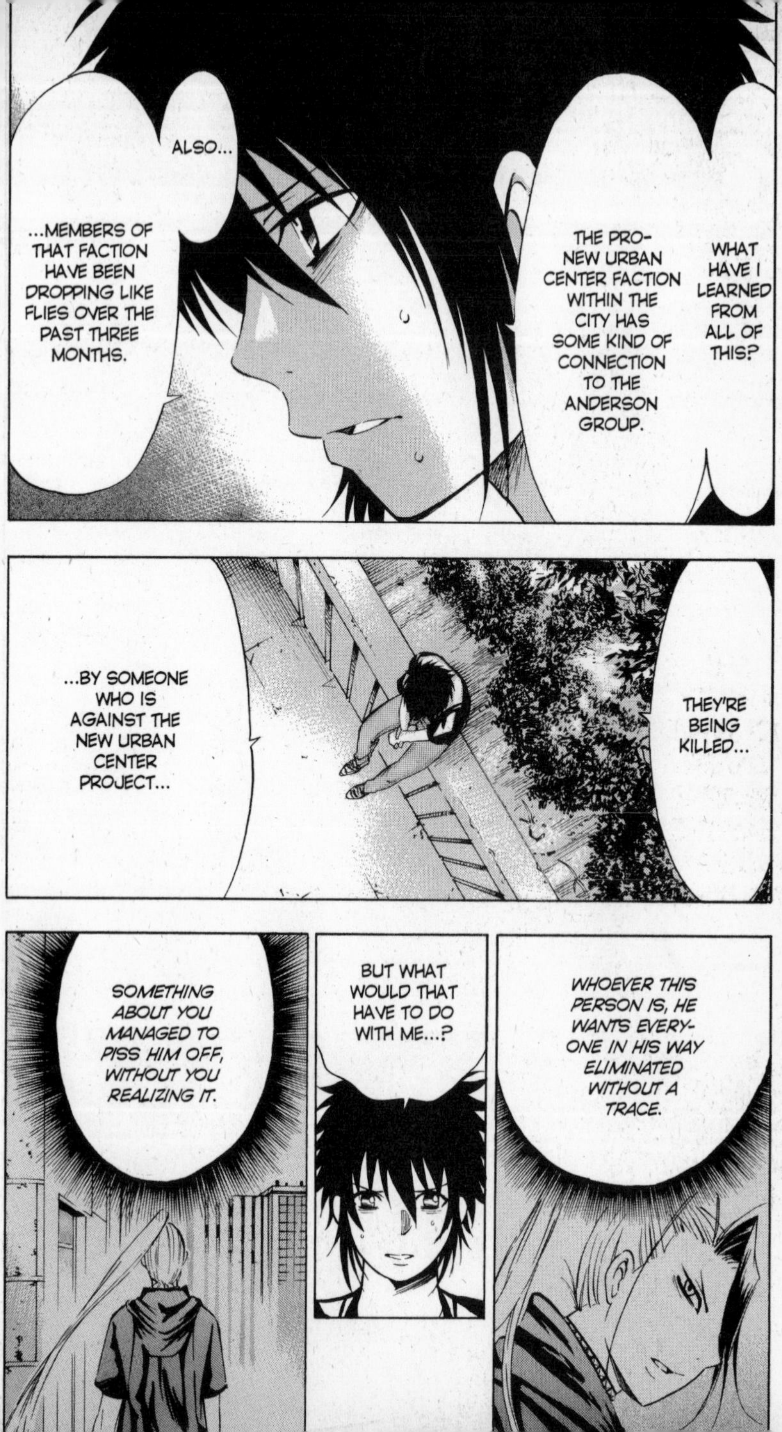
WHAT HAVE I LEARNED FROM ALL OF THIS?
THE PRO-NEW URBAN CENTER FACTION WITHIN THE CITY HAS SOME KIND OF CONNECTION TO THE ANDERSON GROUP.
ALSO...
...MEMBERS OF THAT FACTION HAVE BEEN DROPPING LIKE FLIES OVER THE PAST THREE MONTHS.
THEY'RE BEING KILLED...
...BY SOMEONE WHO IS AGAINST THE NEW URBAN CENTER PROJECT...
WHOEVER THIS PERSON IS, HE WANTS EVERY-ONE IN HIS WAY ELIMINATED WITHOUT A TRACE.
BUT WHAT WOULD THAT HAVE TO DO WITH ME...?
SOMETHING ABOUT YOU MANAGED TO PISS HIM OFF, WITHOUT YOU REALIZING IT.

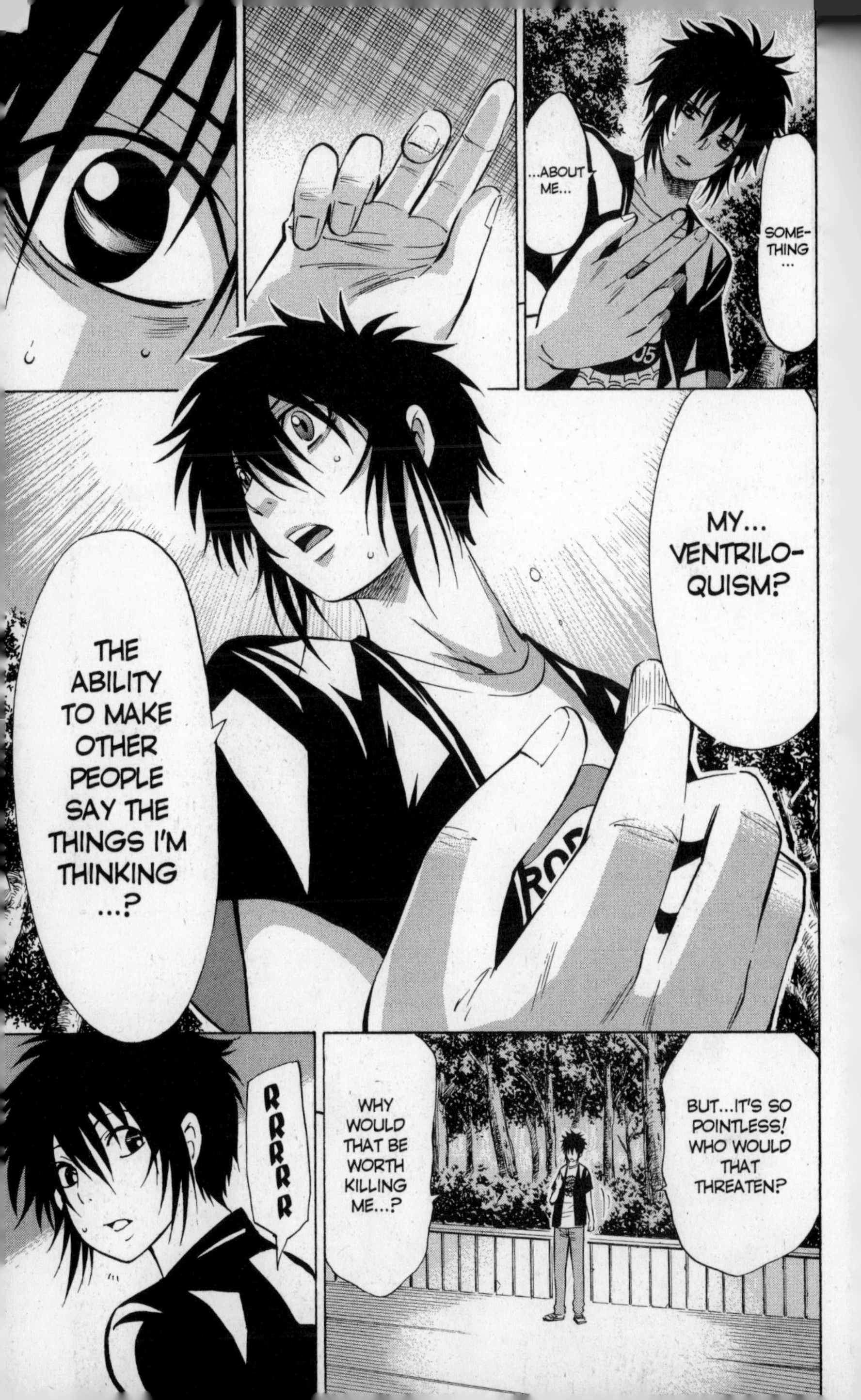
SOME-THING ...
...ABOUT ME...
MY... VENTRILO-QUISM?
THE ABILITY TO MAKE OTHER PEOPLE SAY THE THINGS I'M THINKING ...?
BUT...IT'S SO POINTLESS! WHO WOULD THAT THREATEN?
WHY WOULD THAT BE WORTH KILLING ME...?
RRRRR

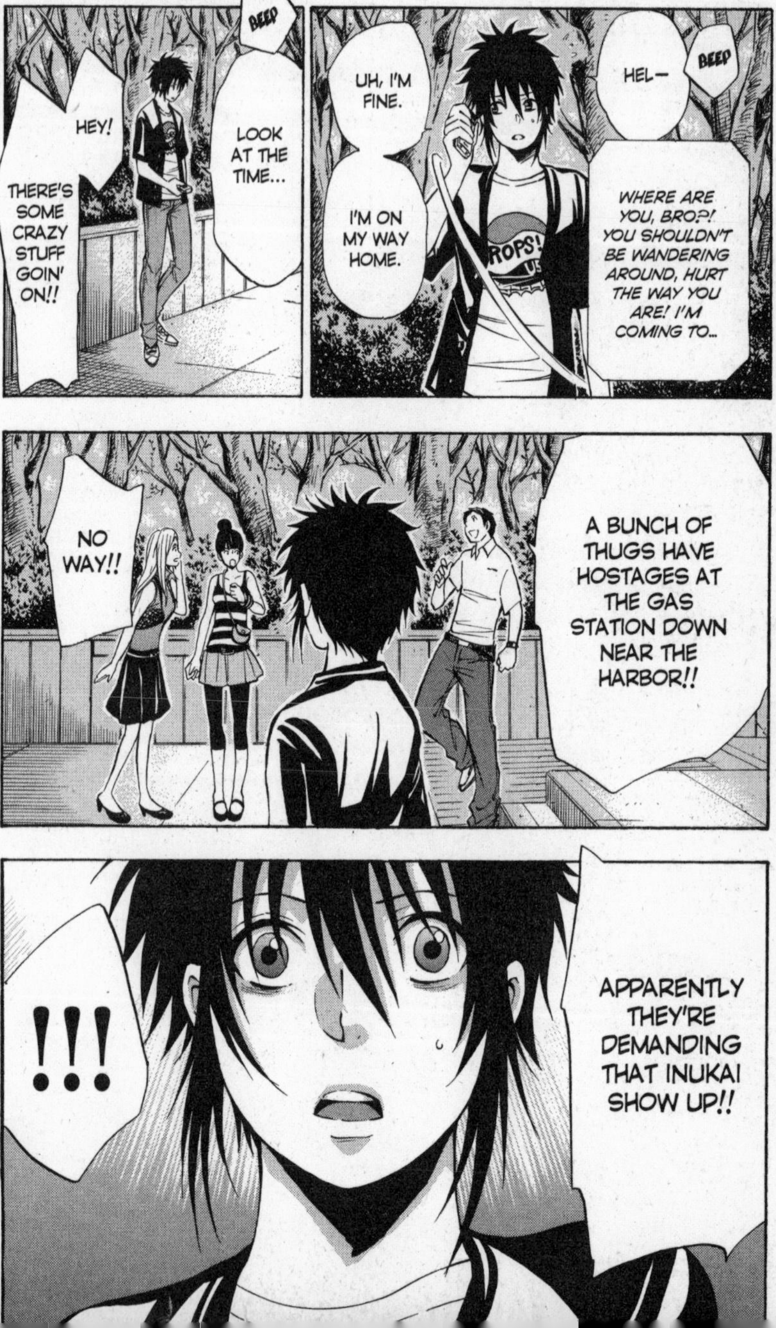
HEL—
BEEP
WHERE ARE YOU, BRO?! YOU SHOULDN'T BE WANDERING AROUND, HURT THE WAY YOU ARE! I'M COMING TO...
UH, I'M FINE.
I'M ON MY WAY HOME.
BEEP
LOOK AT THE TIME...
HEY!
THERE'S SOME CRAZY STUFF GOIN' ON!!
A BUNCH OF THUGS HAVE HOSTAGES AT THE GAS STATION DOWN NEAR THE HARBOR!!
NO WAY!!
APPARENTLY THEY'RE DEMANDING THAT INUKAI SHOW UP!!
!!!

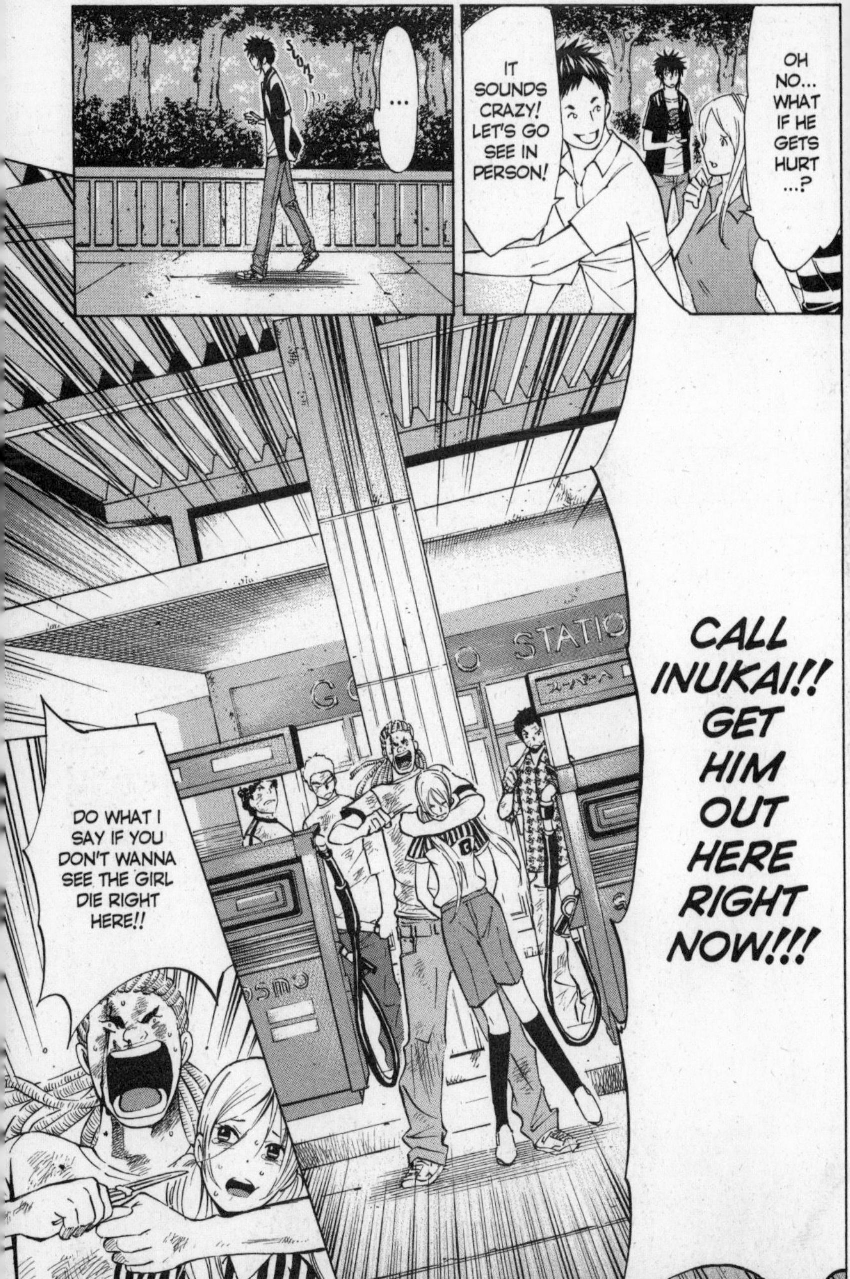
OH NO... WHAT IF HE GETS HURT ...?
IT SOUNDS CRAZY! LET'S GO SEE IN PERSON!
SLUMP
...
CALL INUKAI!! GET HIM OUT HERE RIGHT NOW!!!
DO WHAT I SAY IF YOU DON'T WANNA SEE THE GIRL DIE RIGHT HERE!!

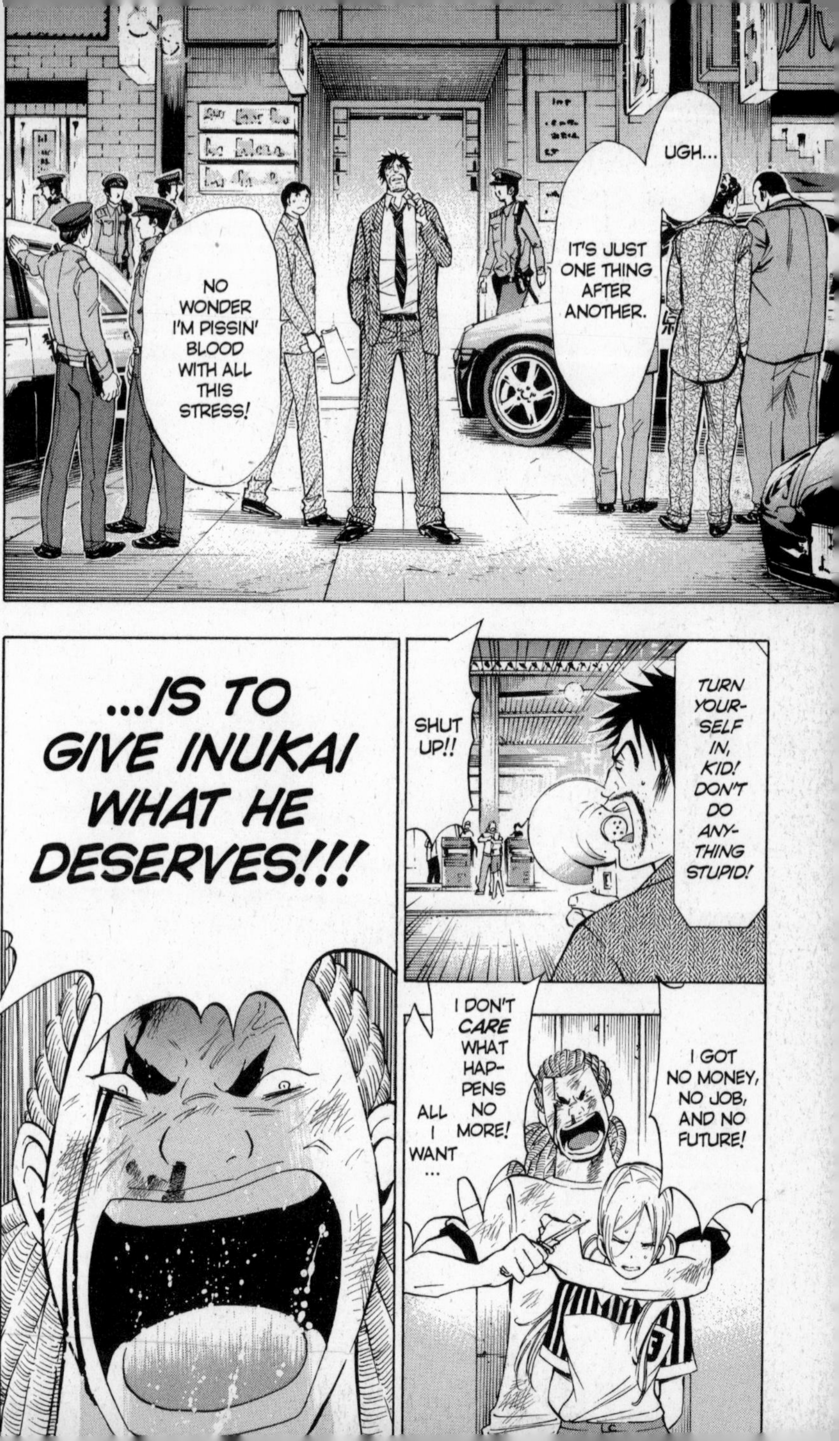
UGH...
IT'S JUST ONE THING AFTER ANOTHER.
NO WONDER I'M PISSIN' BLOOD WITH ALL THIS STRESS!
TURN YOURSELF IN, KID! DON'T DO ANYTHING STUPID!
SHUT UP!!
I GOT NO MONEY, NO JOB, AND NO FUTURE!
I DON'T CARE WHAT HAPPENS NO MORE!
ALL I WANT...
...IS TO GIVE INUKAI WHAT HE DESERVES!!!

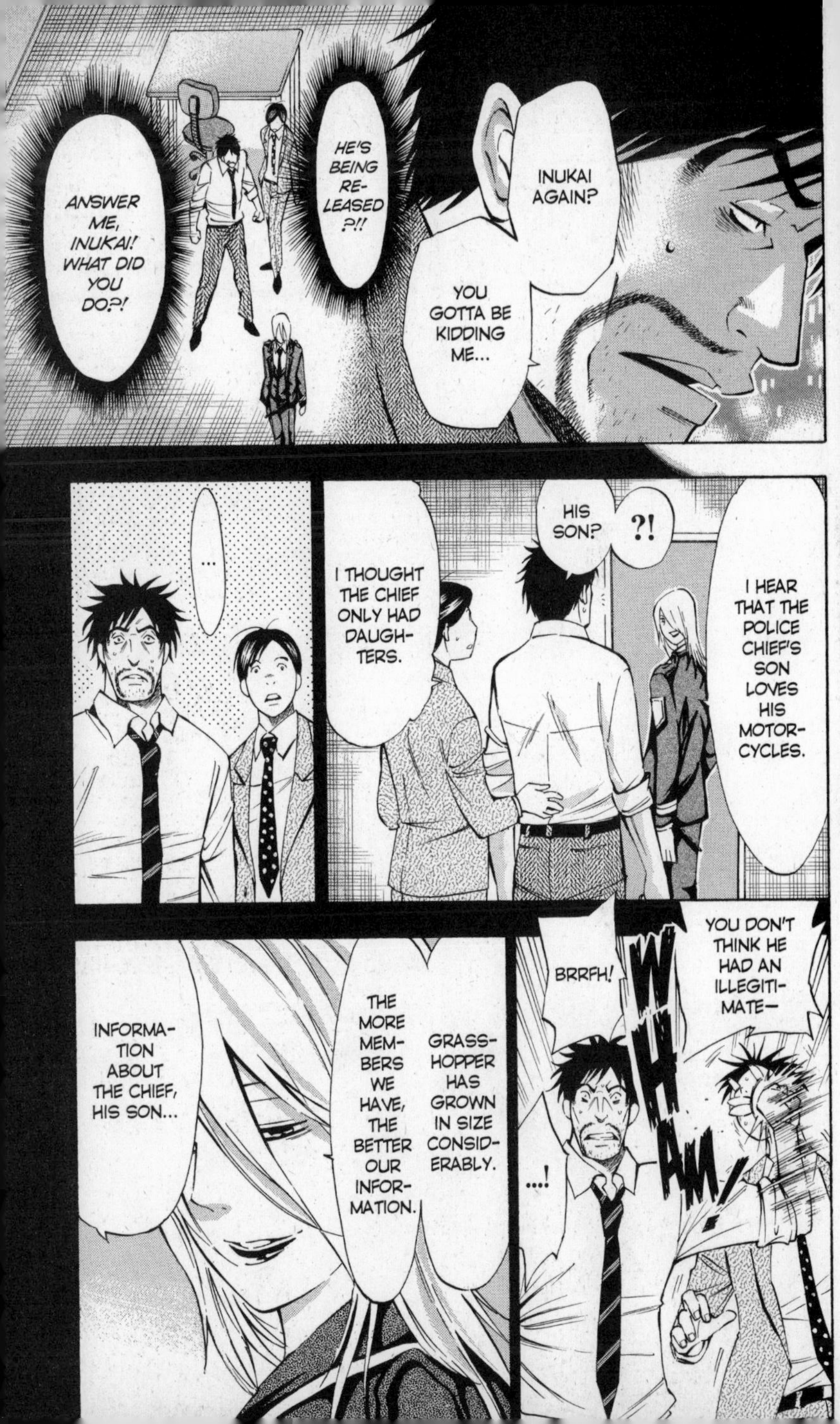
INUKAI AGAIN?
YOU GOTTA BE KIDDING ME...
HE'S BEING RE-LEASED?!!
ANSWER ME, INUKAI! WHAT DID YOU DO?!
I HEAR THAT THE POLICE CHIEF'S SON LOVES HIS MOTOR-CYCLES.
?!
HIS SON?
I THOUGHT THE CHIEF ONLY HAD DAUGH-TERS.
...
YOU DON'T THINK HE HAD AN ILLEGITI-MATE—
WHAM!
BRRFH!
...!
GRASS-HOPPER HAS GROWN IN SIZE CONSID-ERABLY.
THE MORE MEM-BERS WE HAVE, THE BETTER OUR INFOR-MATION.
INFORMA-TION ABOUT THE CHIEF, HIS SON...

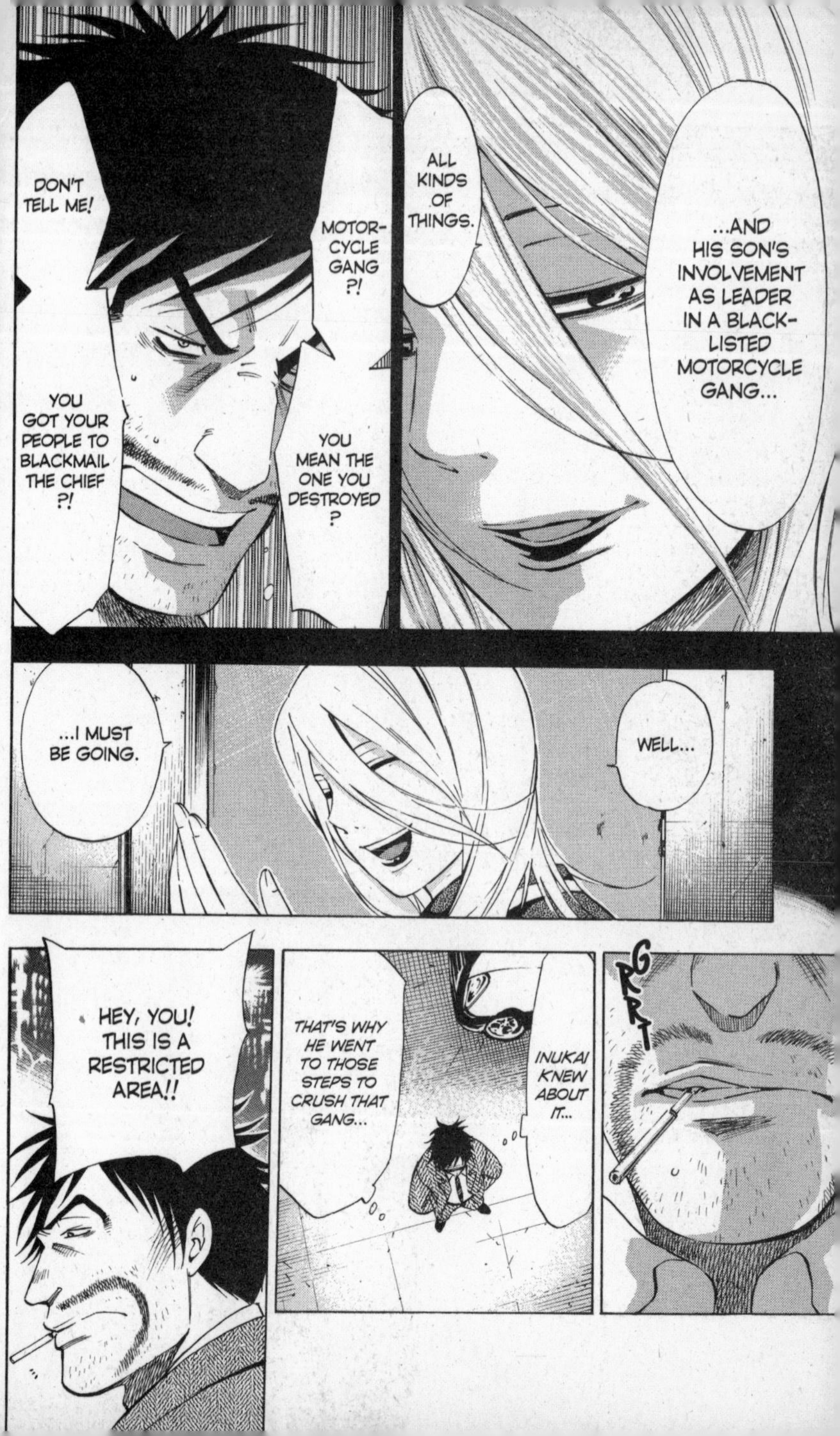
...AND HIS SON'S INVOLVEMENT AS LEADER IN A BLACK-LISTED MOTORCYCLE GANG...
ALL KINDS OF THINGS.
MOTOR-CYCLE GANG ?!
YOU MEAN THE ONE YOU DESTROYED ?
DON'T TELL ME!
YOU GOT YOUR PEOPLE TO BLACKMAIL THE CHIEF ?!
WELL...
...I MUST BE GOING.
GRRRT
INUKAI KNEW ABOUT IT...
THAT'S WHY HE WENT TO THOSE STEPS TO CRUSH THAT GANG...
HEY, YOU! THIS IS A RESTRICTED AREA!!

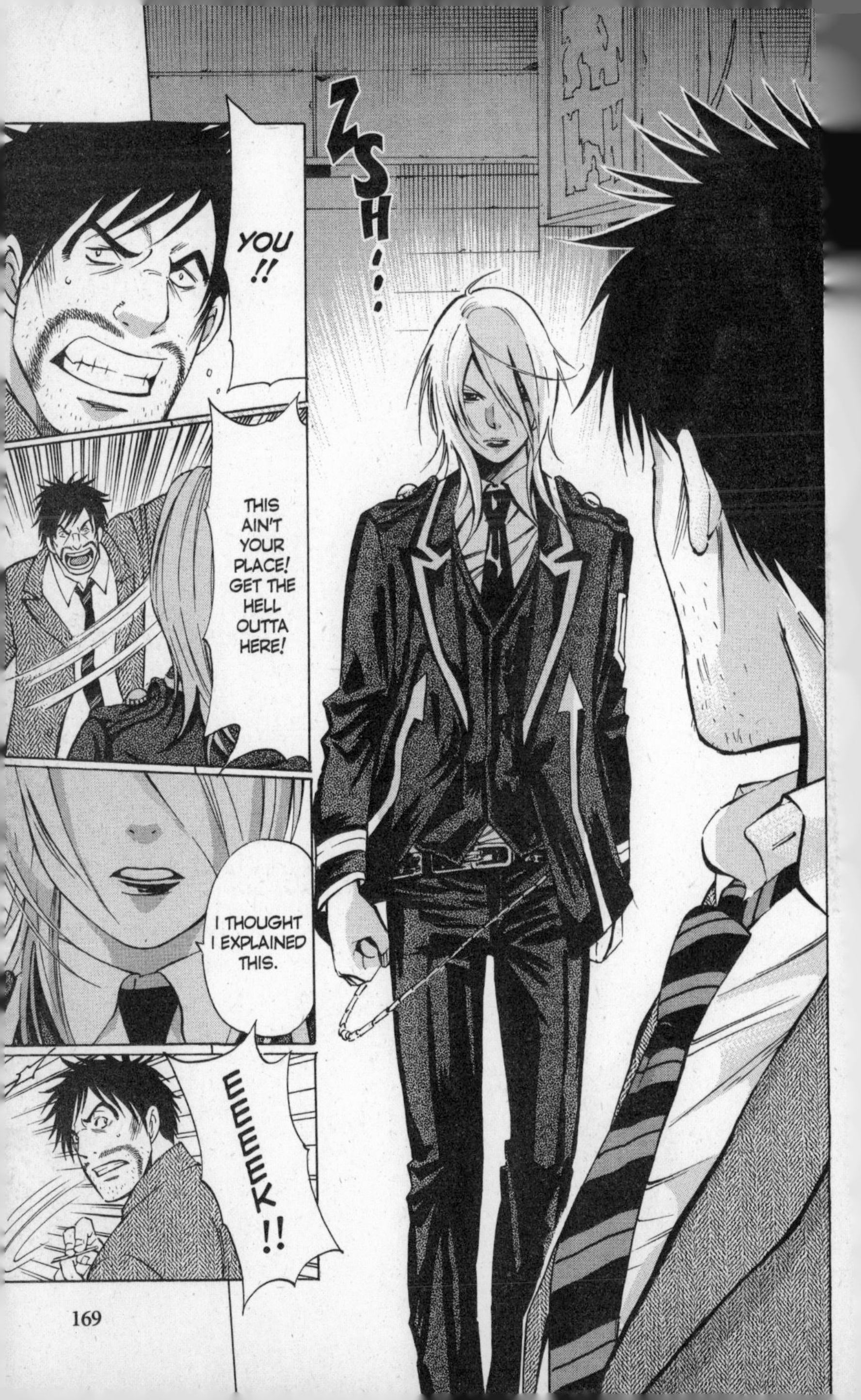
ZSH...
YOU!!
THIS AIN'T YOUR PLACE! GET THE HELL OUTTA HERE!
I THOUGHT I EXPLAINED THIS.
EEEEEK!!

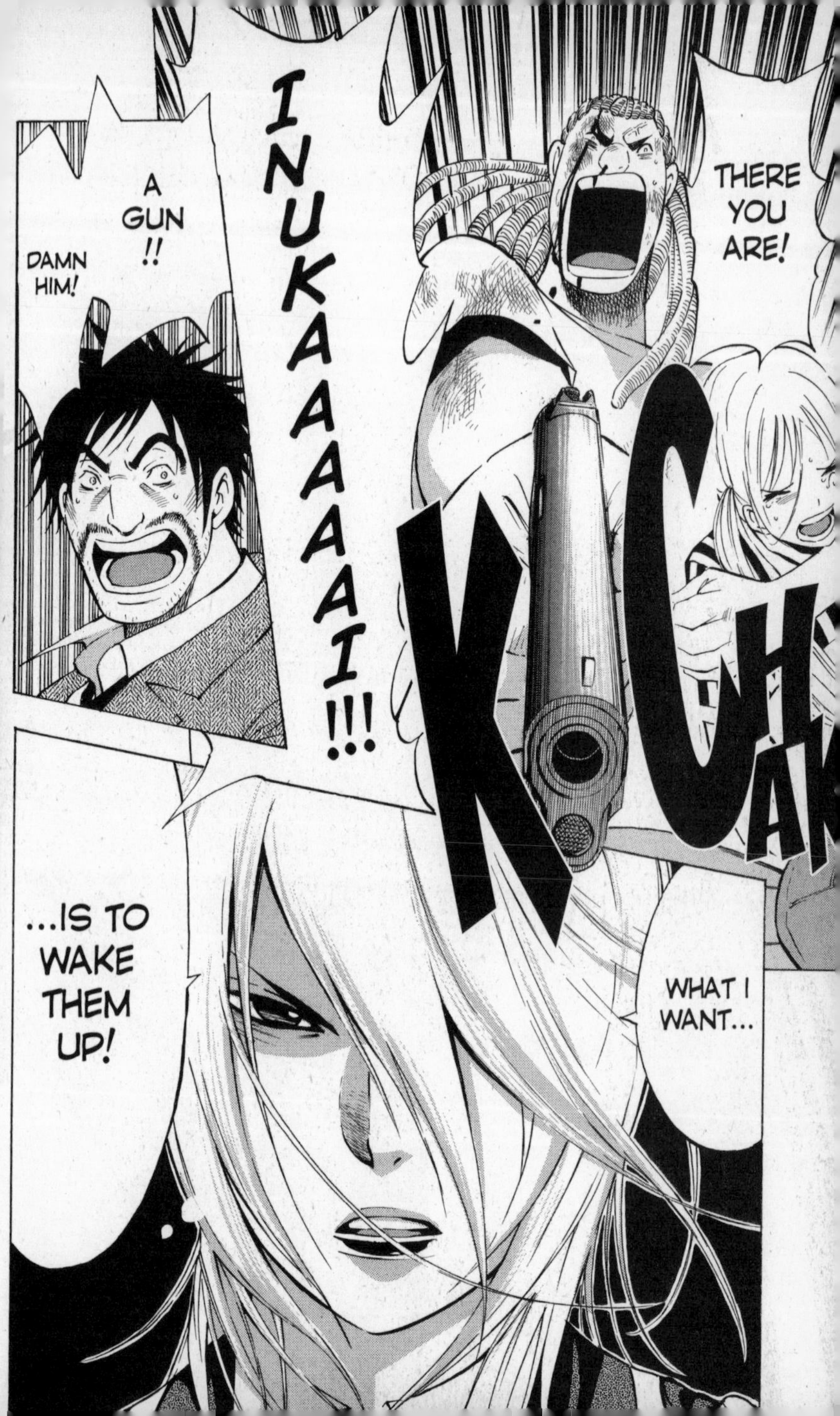
THERE YOU ARE!
INUKAAAAAI!!!
A GUN!!
DAMN HIM!
KCHAK
WHAT I WANT...
...IS TO WAKE THEM UP!

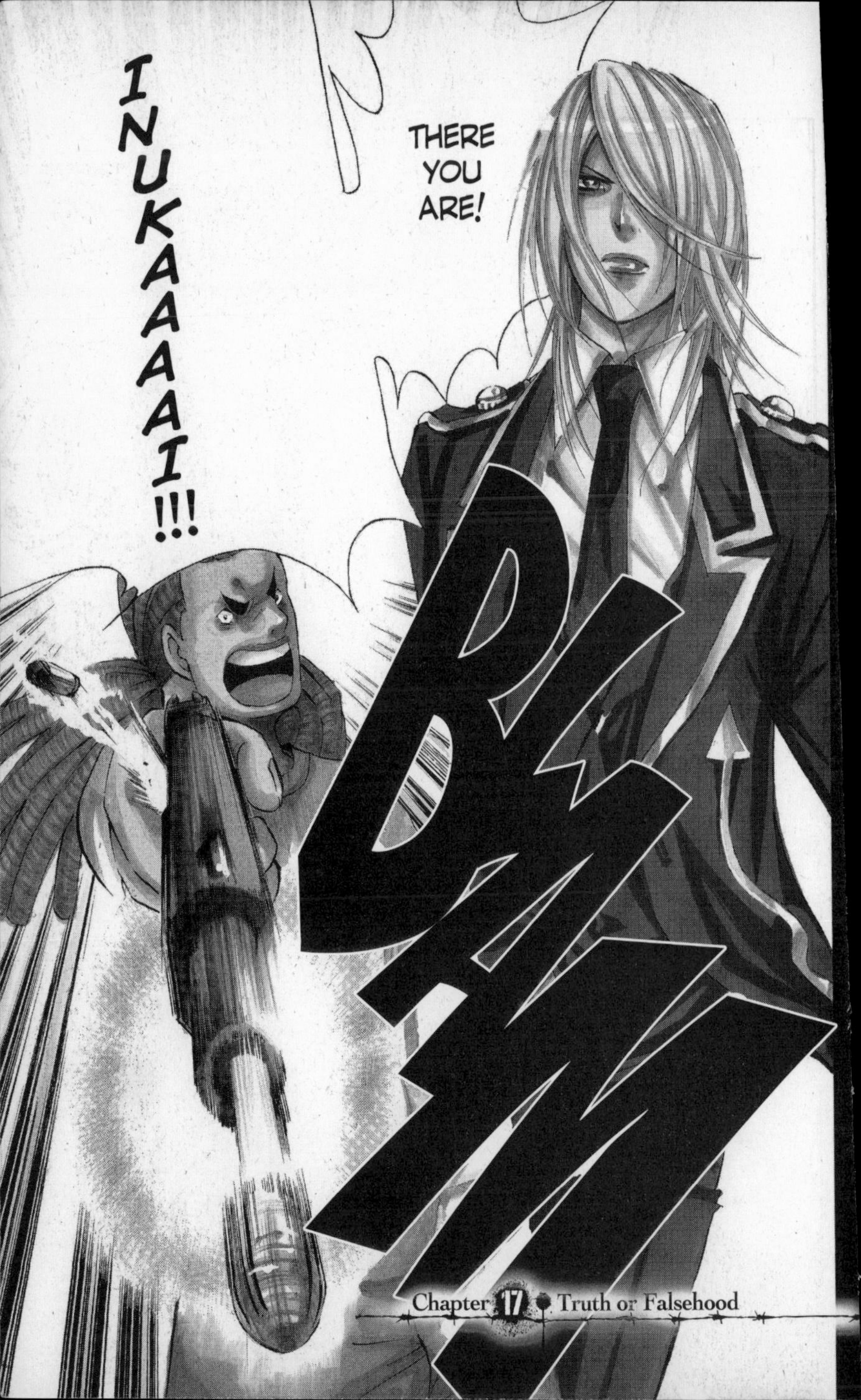
THERE YOU ARE!
INUKAAAAAI!!!
BLAM

Chapter 17 Truth or Falsehood

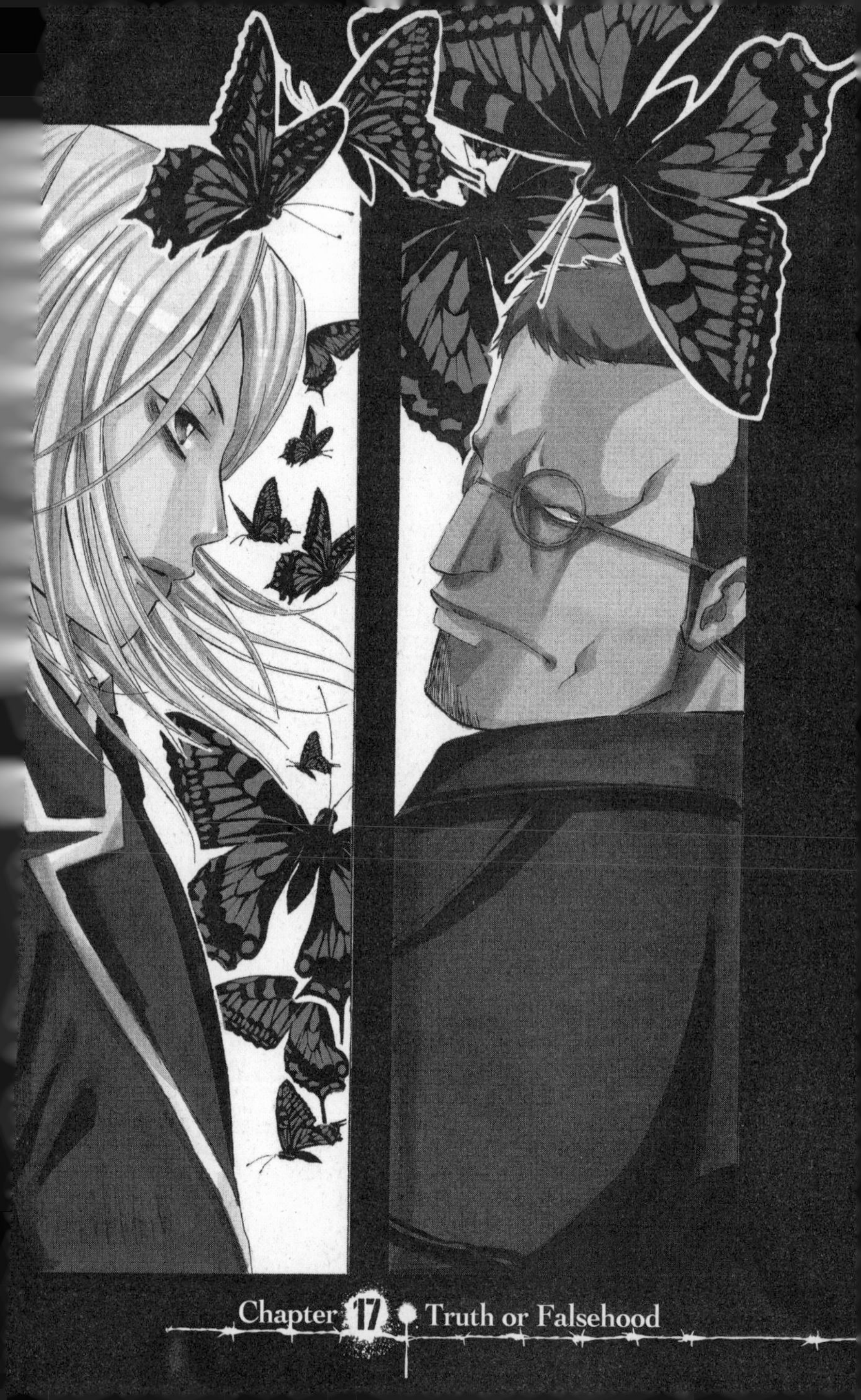

Chapter 17 • Truth or Falsehood

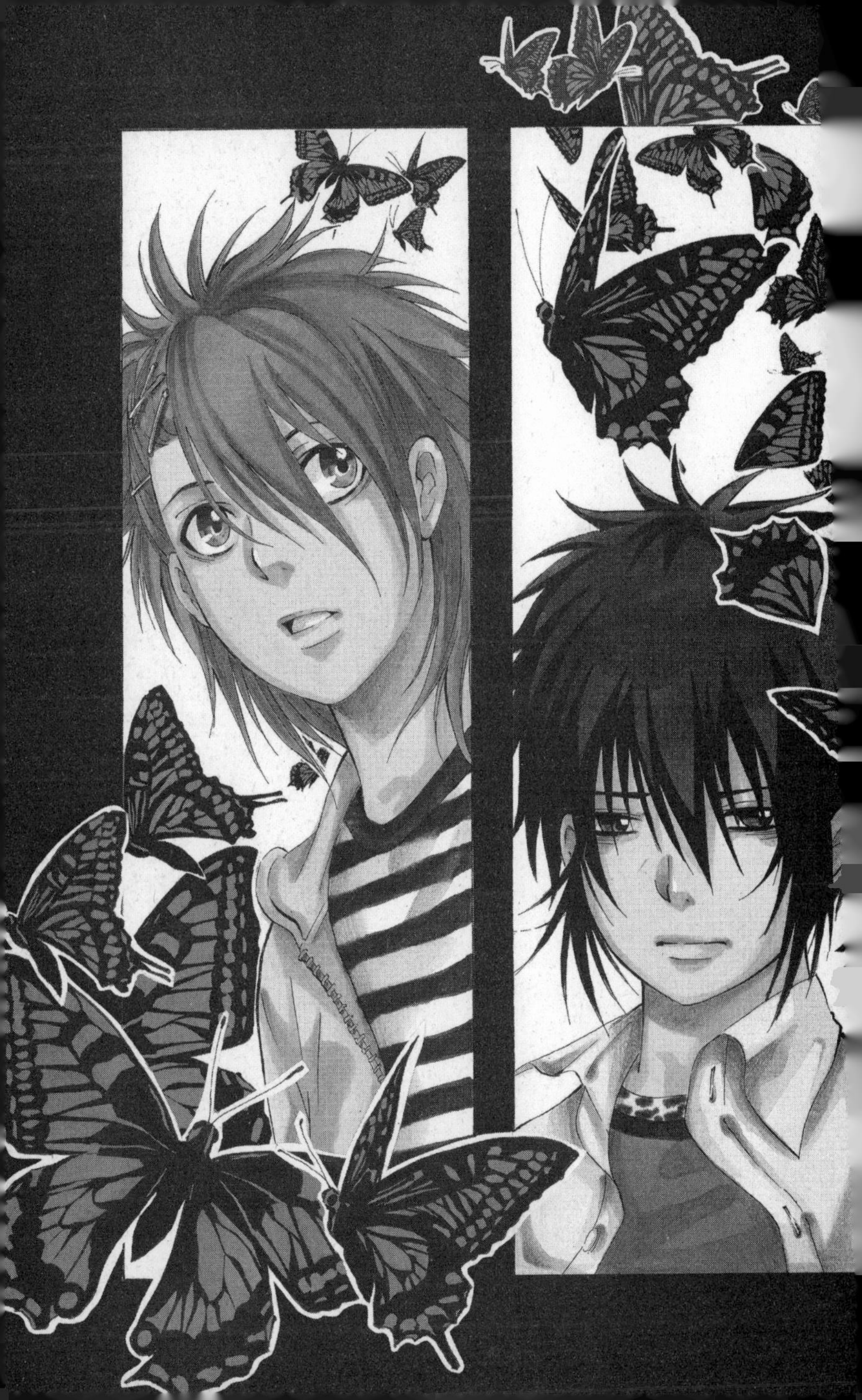

MAOH

JUVENILE REMIX

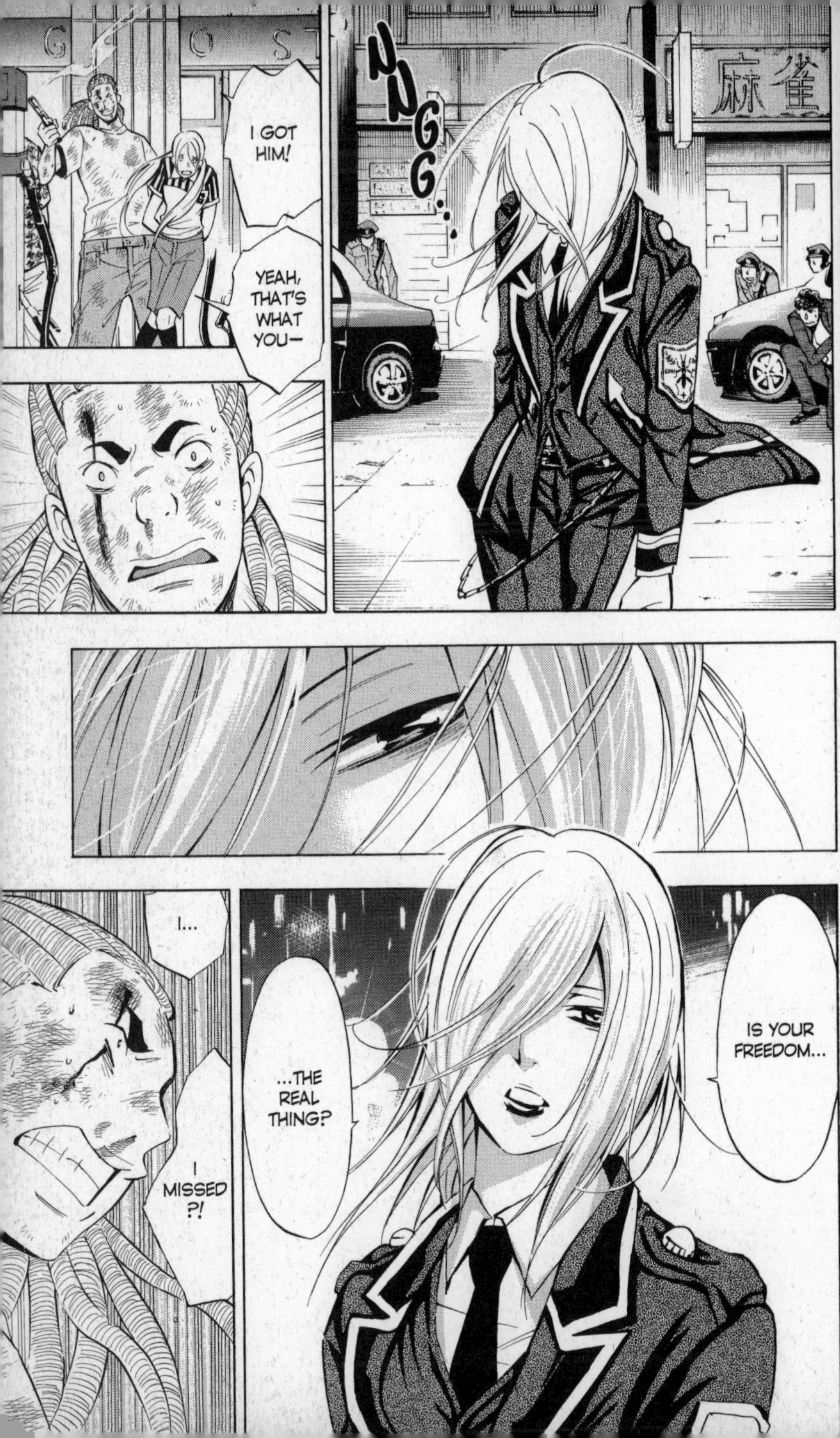
NNGG...
麻雀
I GOT HIM!
YEAH, THAT'S WHAT YOU—
IS YOUR FREEDOM...
...THE REAL THING?
I...
I MISSED?!

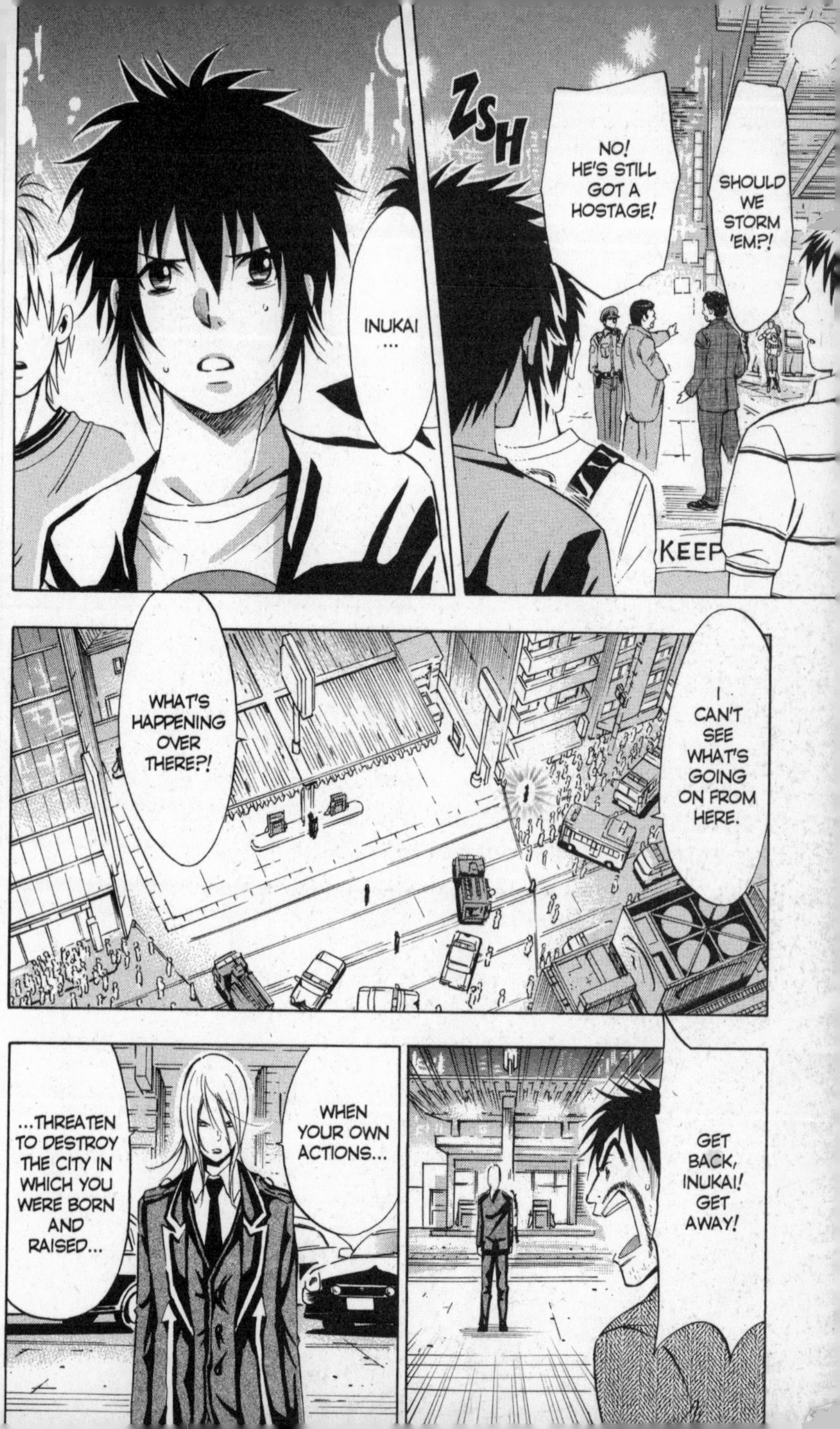
SHOULD WE STORM 'EM?!
NO! HE'S STILL GOT A HOSTAGE!
ZSH
KEEP
INUKAI...
I CAN'T SEE WHAT'S GOING ON FROM HERE.
WHAT'S HAPPENING OVER THERE?!
GET BACK, INUKAI! GET AWAY!
WHEN YOUR OWN ACTIONS...
...THREATEN TO DESTROY THE CITY IN WHICH YOU WERE BORN AND RAISED...

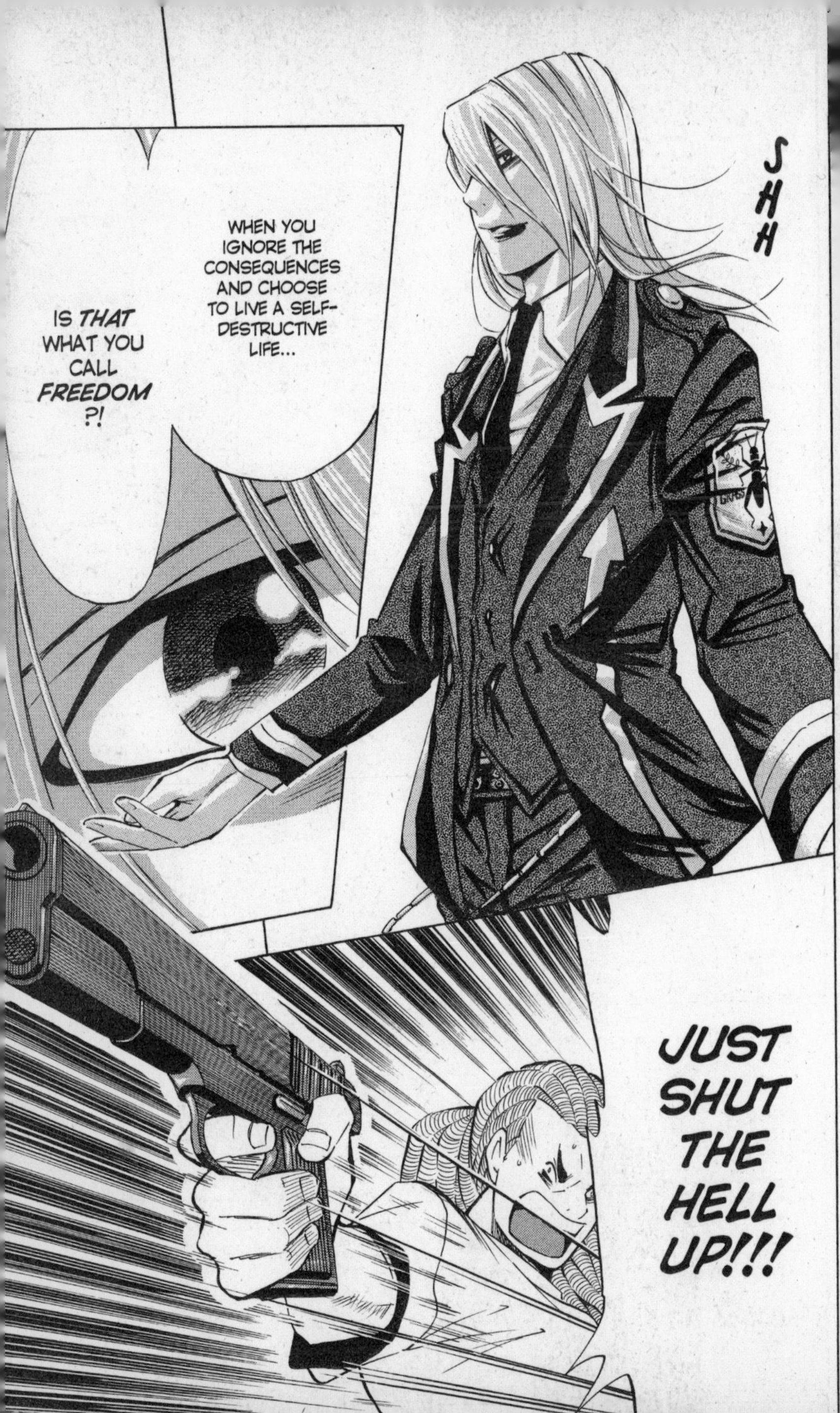
SHH
WHEN YOU IGNORE THE CONSEQUENCES AND CHOOSE TO LIVE A SELF-DESTRUCTIVE LIFE...
IS *THAT* WHAT YOU CALL *FREEDOM* ?!
JUST SHUT THE HELL UP!!!

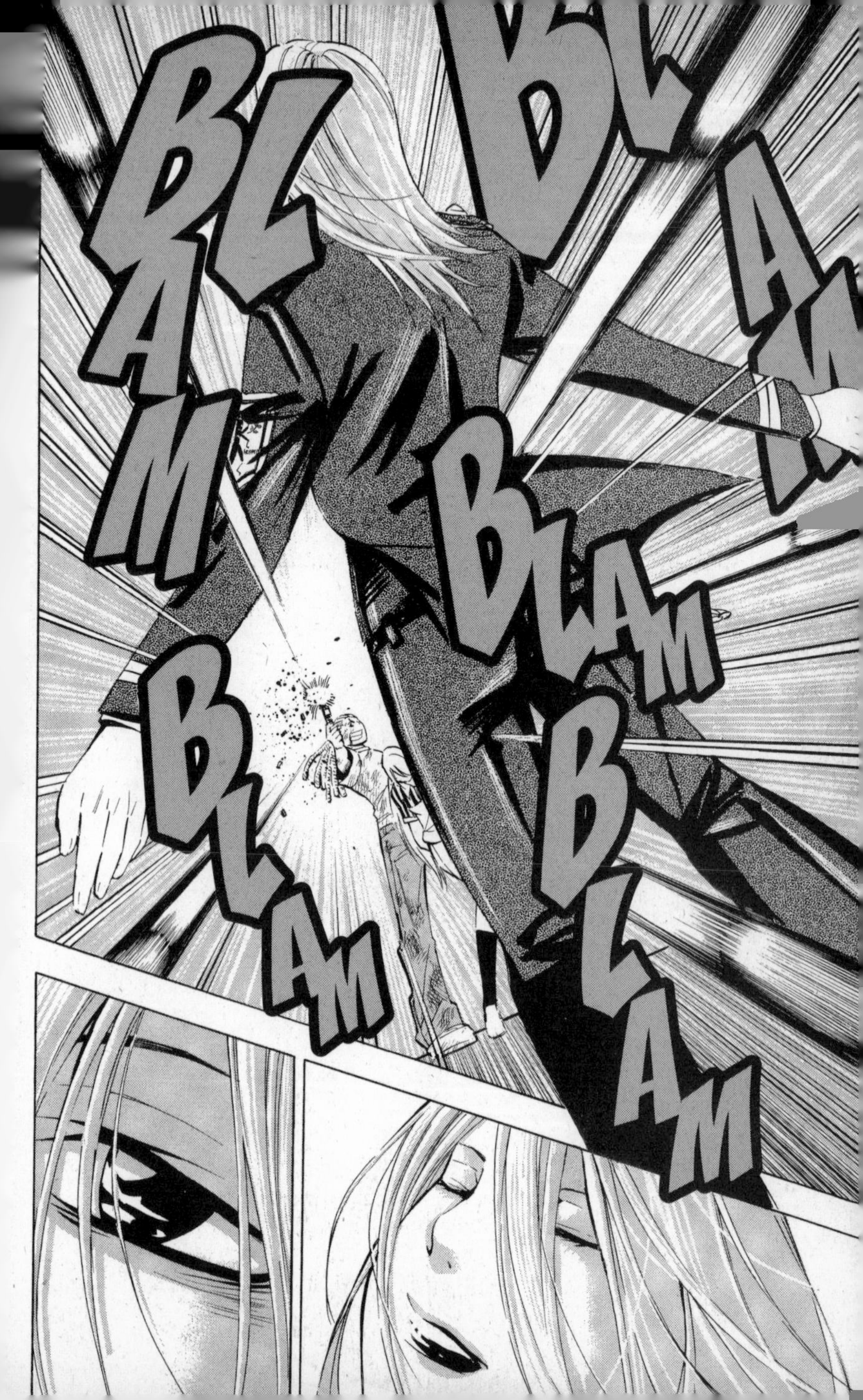
BLAM
BLAM
BLAM
BLAM
BLAM

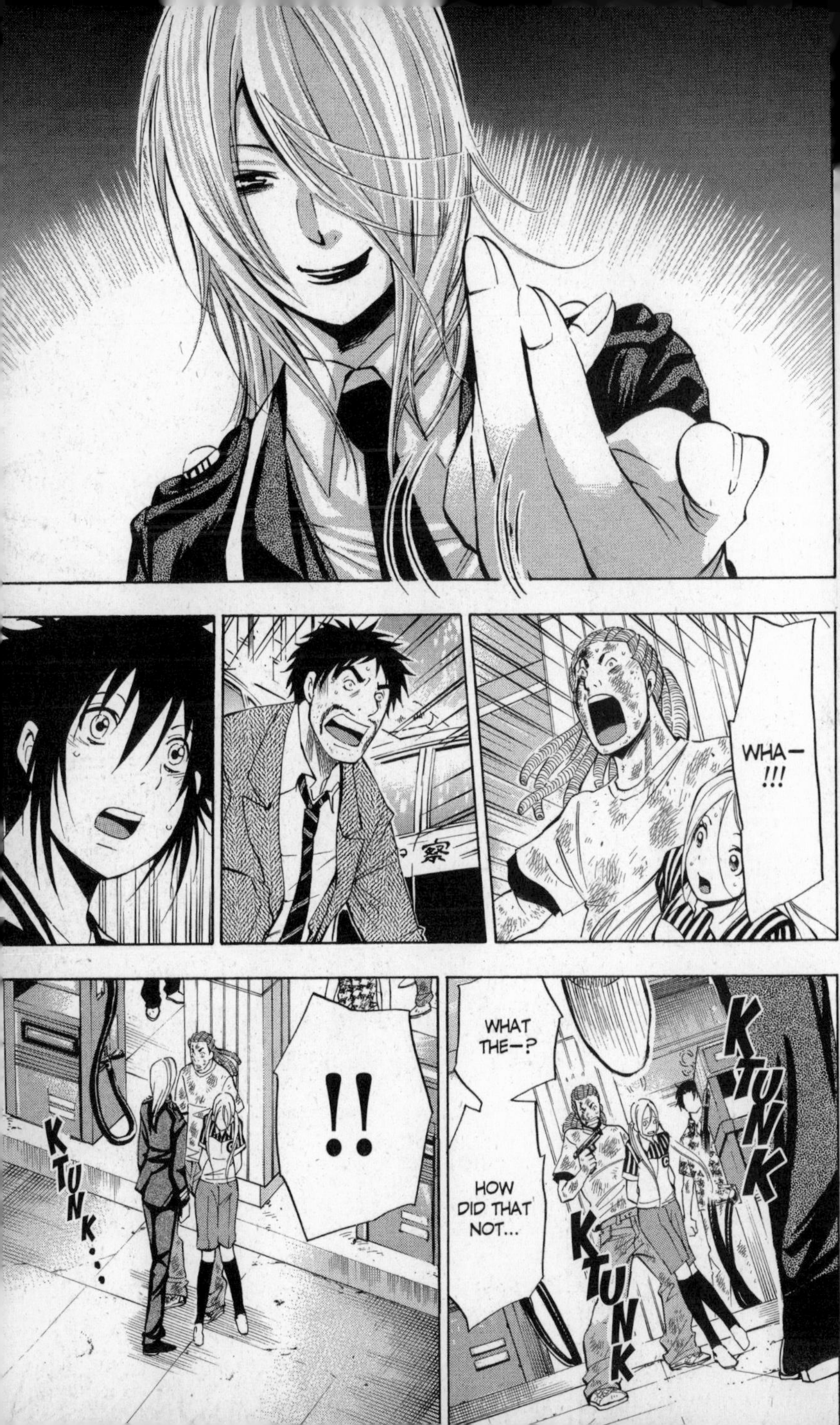
WHA— !!!
WHAT THE—?
HOW DID THAT NOT...
KTUNK
KTUNK
!!
KTUNK...

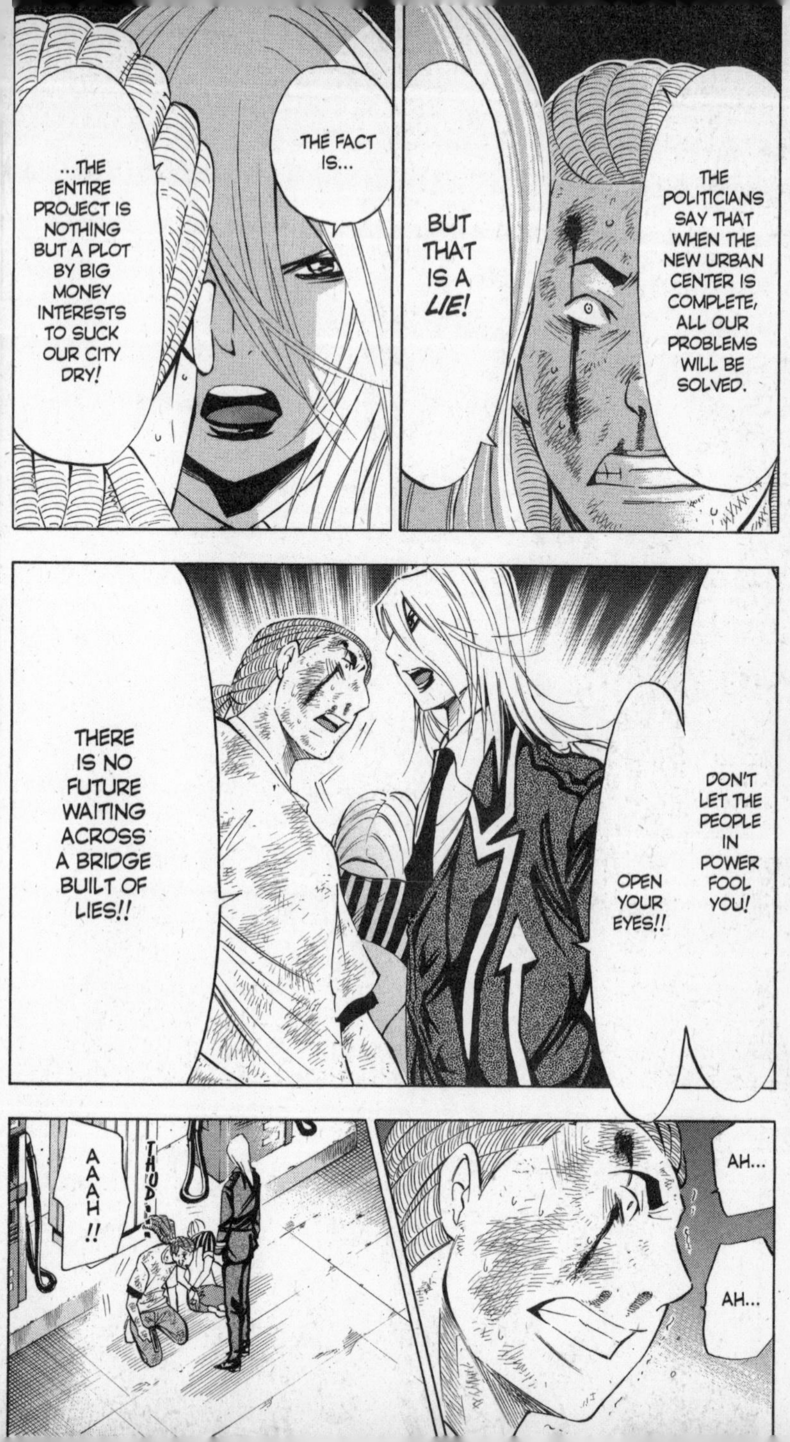
THE POLITICIANS SAY THAT WHEN THE NEW URBAN CENTER IS COMPLETE, ALL OUR PROBLEMS WILL BE SOLVED.
BUT THAT IS A *LIE!*
THE FACT IS...
...THE ENTIRE PROJECT IS NOTHING BUT A PLOT BY BIG MONEY INTERESTS TO SUCK OUR CITY DRY!
DON'T LET THE PEOPLE IN POWER FOOL YOU!
OPEN YOUR EYES!!
THERE IS NO FUTURE WAITING ACROSS A BRIDGE BUILT OF LIES!!
AH...
AH...
AAAH!!
THUD

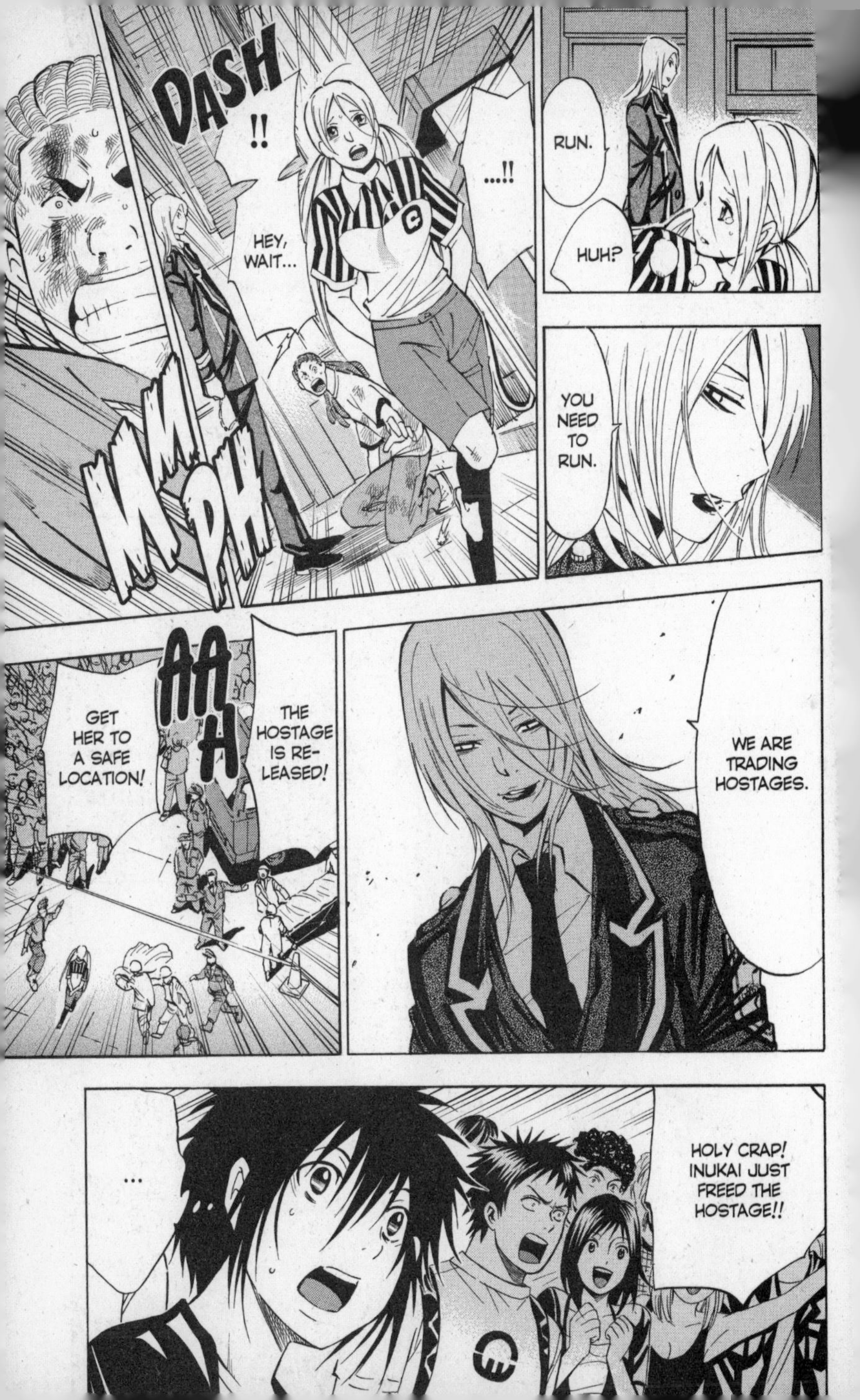

RUN.
HUH?
YOU NEED TO RUN.
...!!
DASH !!
HEY, WAIT...
MMPH
WE ARE TRADING HOSTAGES.
THE HOSTAGE IS RE-LEASED!
AAAH
GET HER TO A SAFE LOCATION!
HOLY CRAP! INUKAI JUST FREED THE HOSTAGE!!
...

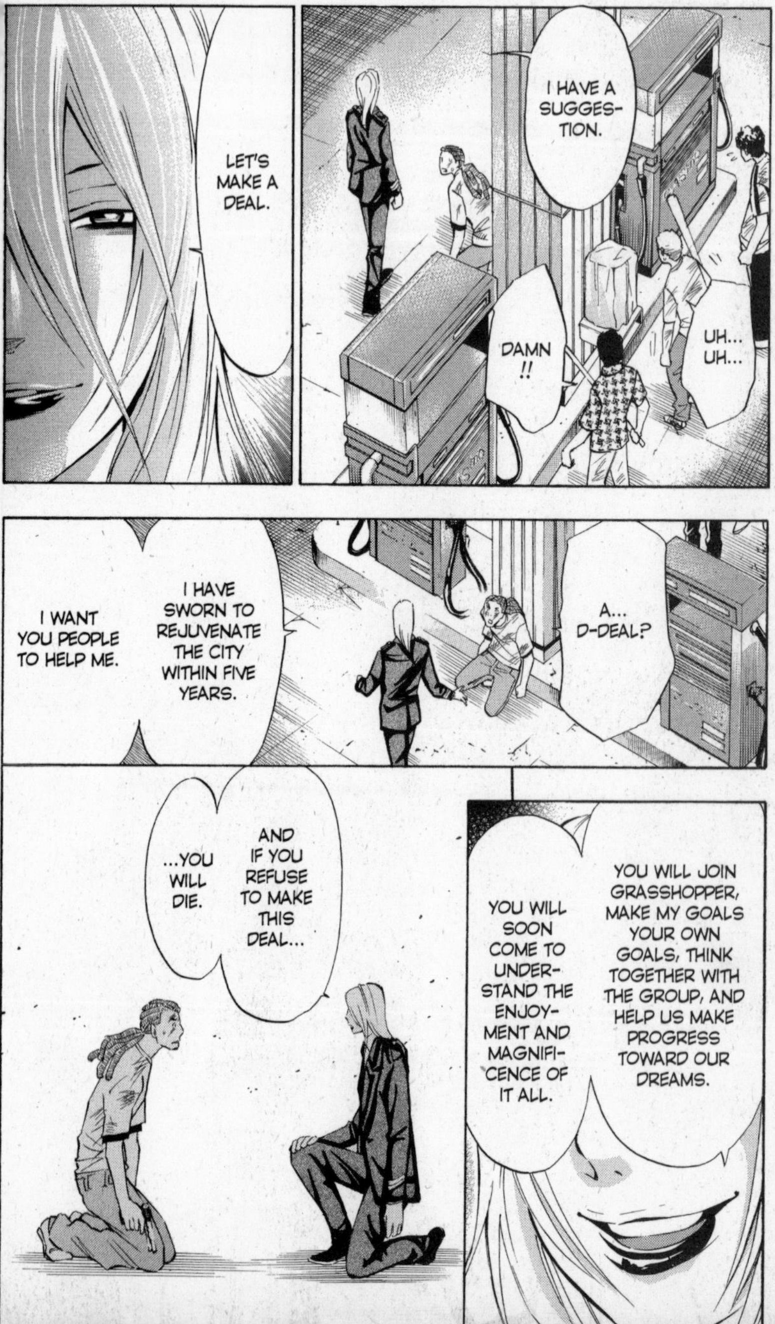
I HAVE A SUGGESTION.
UH... UH...
DAMN !!
LET'S MAKE A DEAL.
A... D-DEAL?
I HAVE SWORN TO REJUVENATE THE CITY WITHIN FIVE YEARS.
I WANT YOU PEOPLE TO HELP ME.
YOU WILL JOIN GRASSHOPPER, MAKE MY GOALS YOUR OWN GOALS, THINK TOGETHER WITH THE GROUP, AND HELP US MAKE PROGRESS TOWARD OUR DREAMS.
YOU WILL SOON COME TO UNDERSTAND THE ENJOYMENT AND MAGNIFICENCE OF IT ALL.
AND IF YOU REFUSE TO MAKE THIS DEAL...
...YOU WILL DIE.

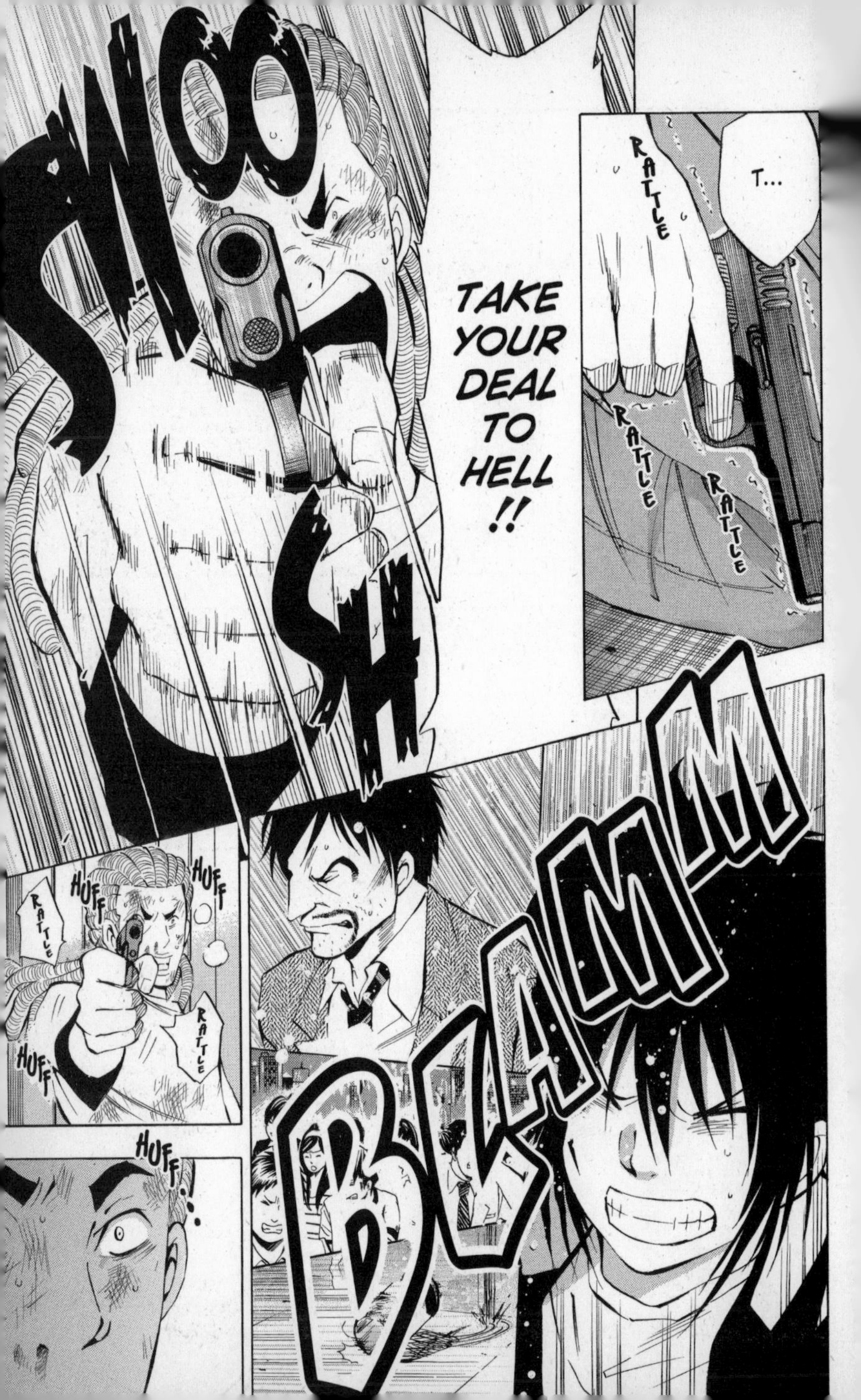
T...
RATTLE
RATTLE
RATTLE
SHWOOSH
TAKE YOUR DEAL TO HELL!!
BLAMM
HUFF
HUFF
RATTLE
RATTLE
HUFF
HUFF!

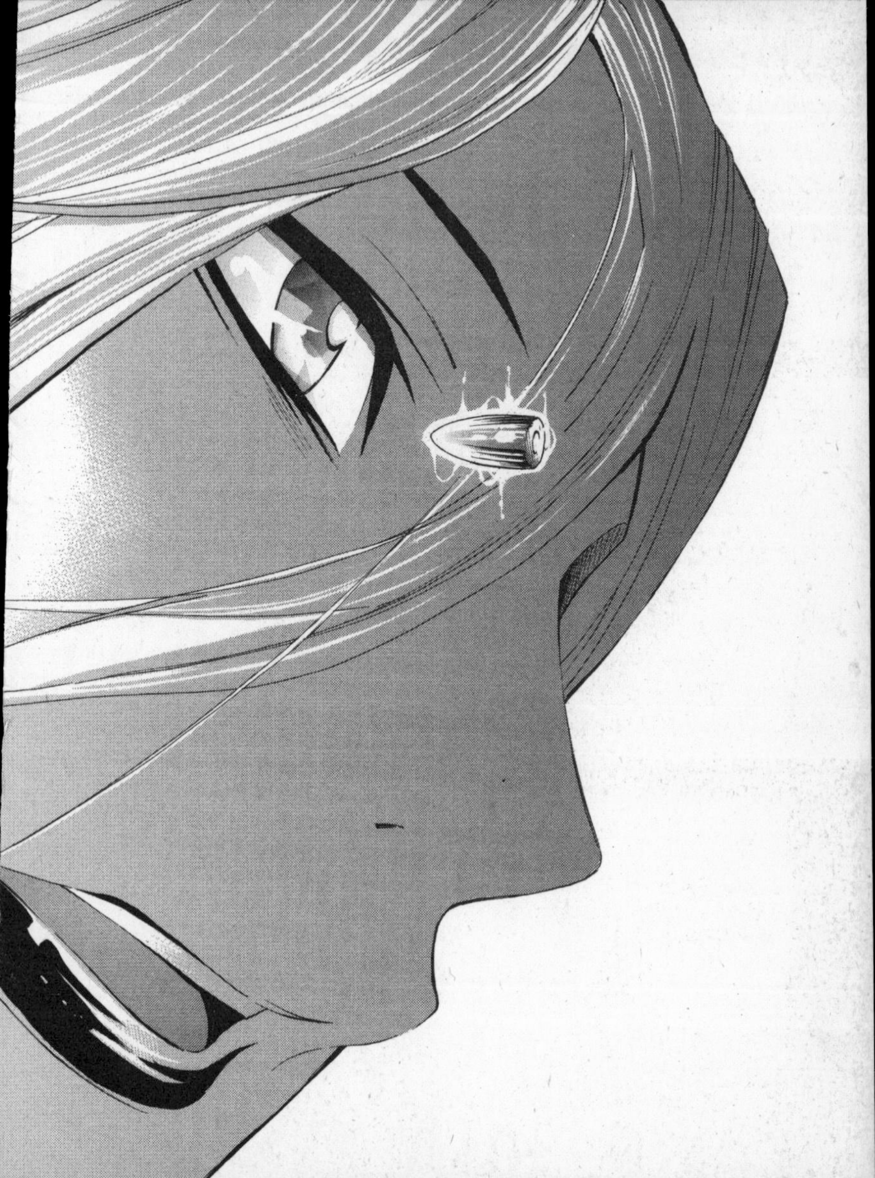

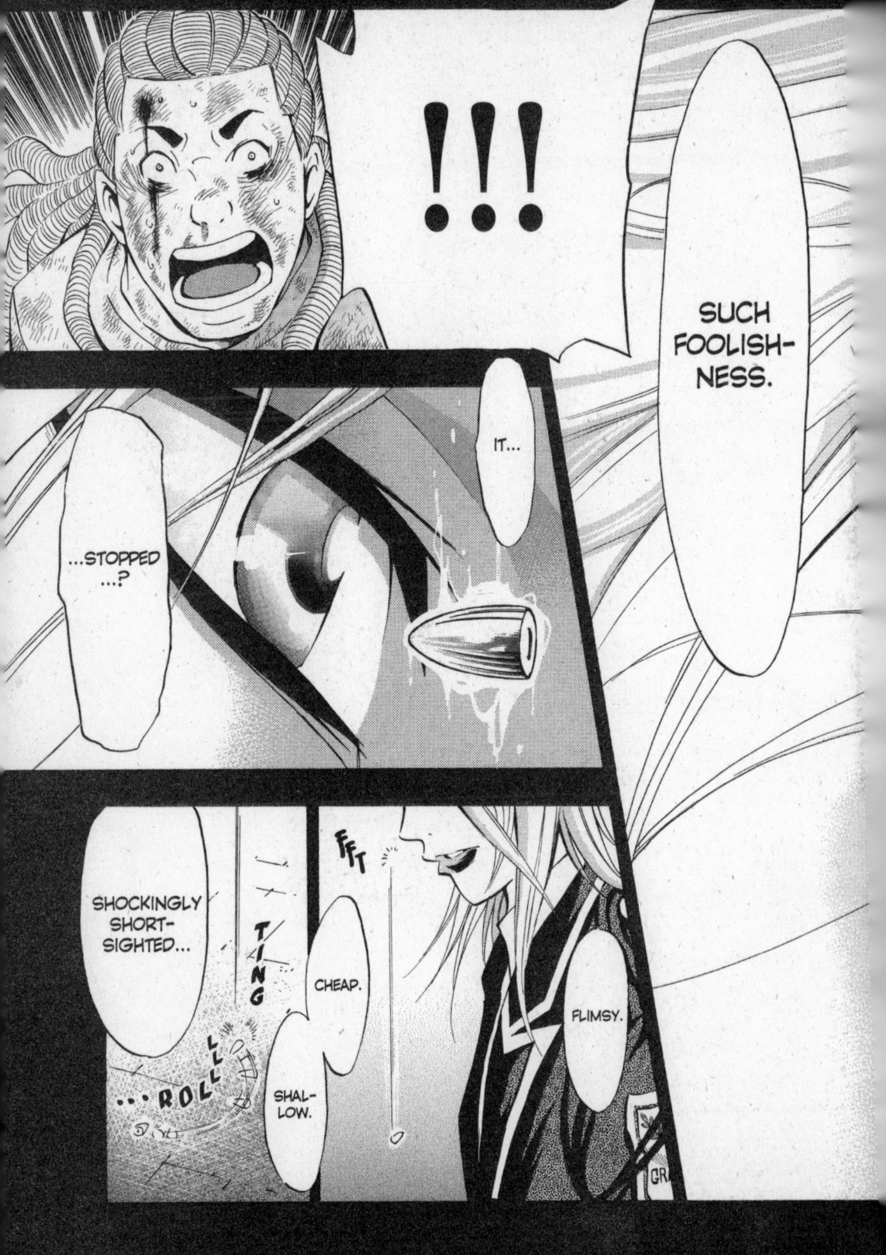
!!!
IT...
...STOPPED ...?
SUCH FOOLISH-NESS.
FFT
FLIMSY.
CHEAP.
TING
SHAL-LOW.
SHOCKINGLY SHORT-SIGHTED...
...ROLLL

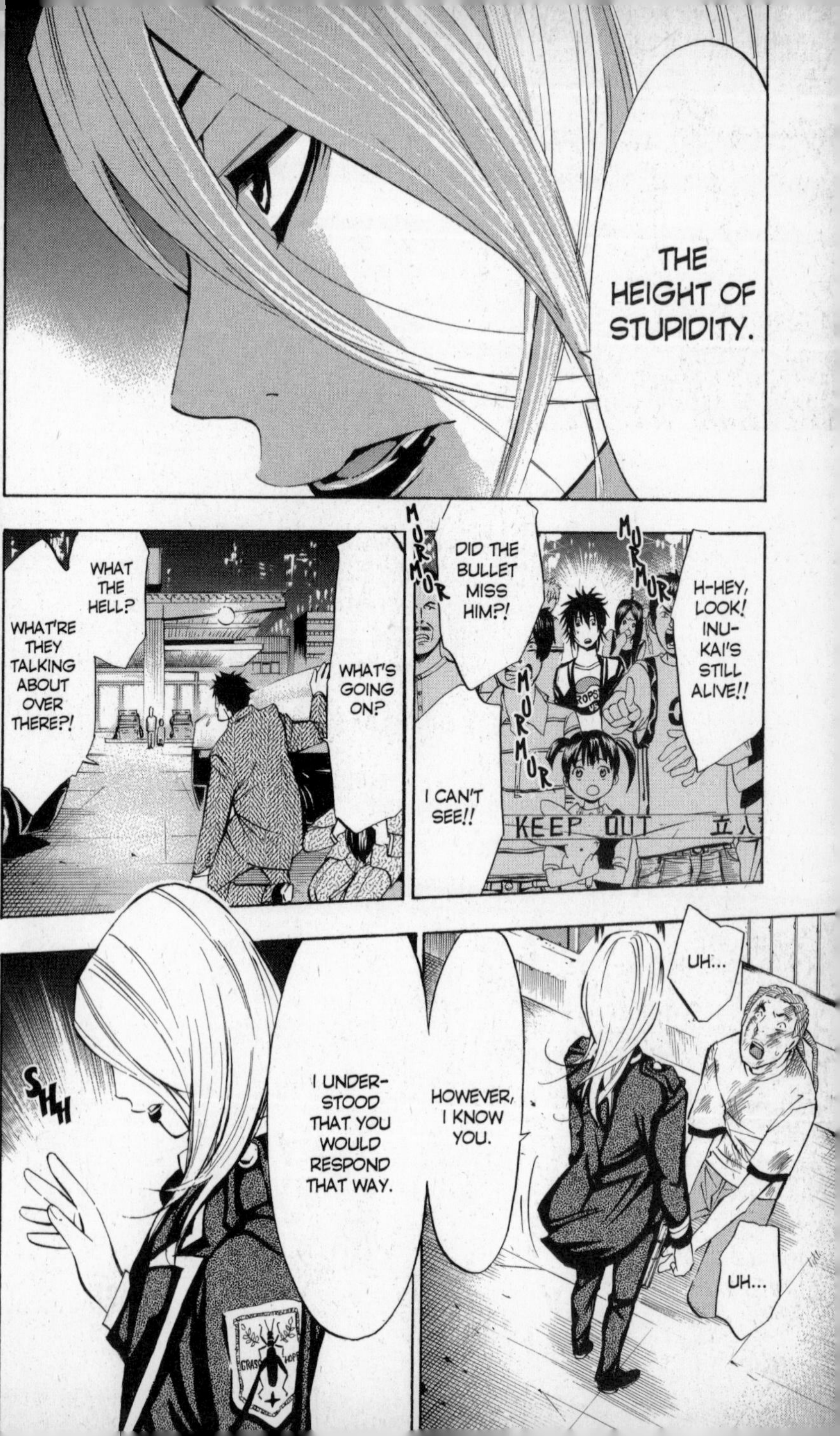
THE HEIGHT OF STUPIDITY.
MURMUR
H-HEY, LOOK! INU-KAI'S STILL ALIVE!!
MURMUR
DID THE BULLET MISS HIM?!
MURMUR
I CAN'T SEE!!
KEEP OUT 立入
WHAT'S GOING ON?
WHAT THE HELL?
WHAT'RE THEY TALKING ABOUT OVER THERE?!
UH...
UH...
I UNDER-STOOD THAT YOU WOULD RESPOND THAT WAY.
HOWEVER, I KNOW YOU.
SHH

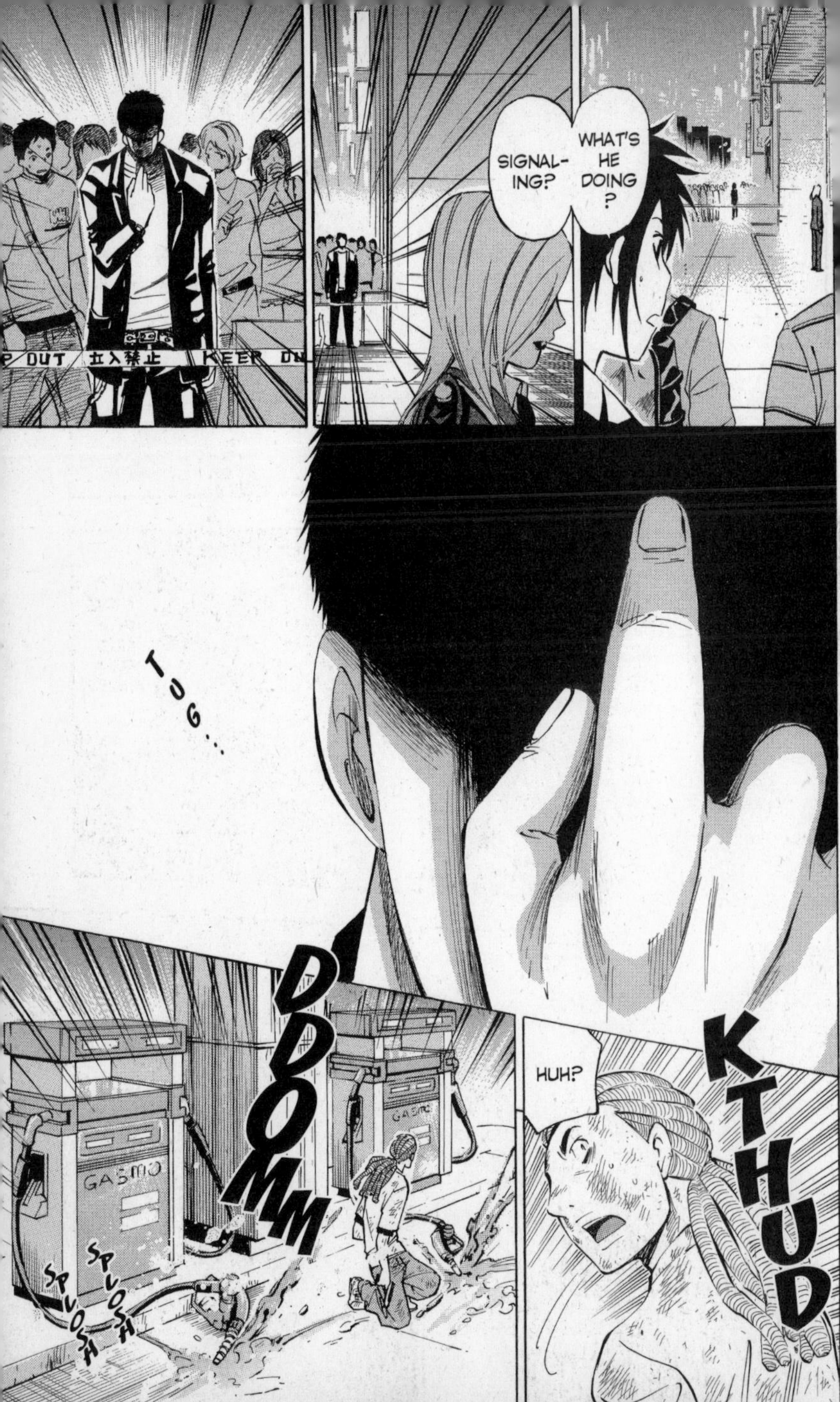
WHAT'S HE DOING?
SIGNALING?
P OUT 立入禁止 KEEP OU
TUG...
HUH?
KTHUD
DDOMMM
SPLOSH
SPLOSH

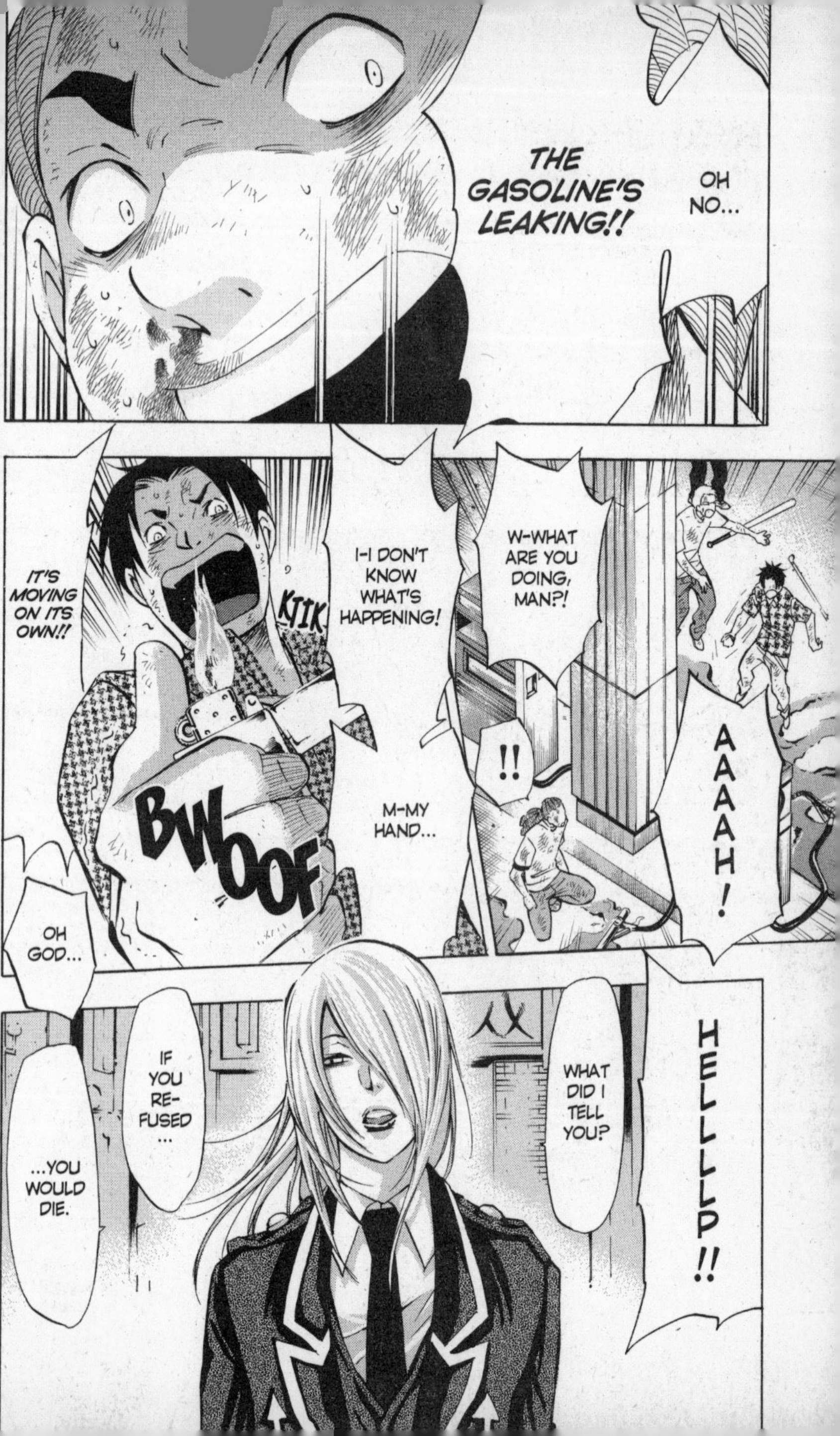
OH NO...
THE GASOLINE'S LEAKING!!
AAAAH!
W-WHAT ARE YOU DOING, MAN?!
!!
I-I DON'T KNOW WHAT'S HAPPENING!
KTIK
IT'S MOVING ON ITS OWN!!
M-MY HAND...
BWOOF
OH GOD...
HELLLLP!!
WHAT DID I TELL YOU?
IF YOU RE-FUSED...
...YOU WOULD DIE.

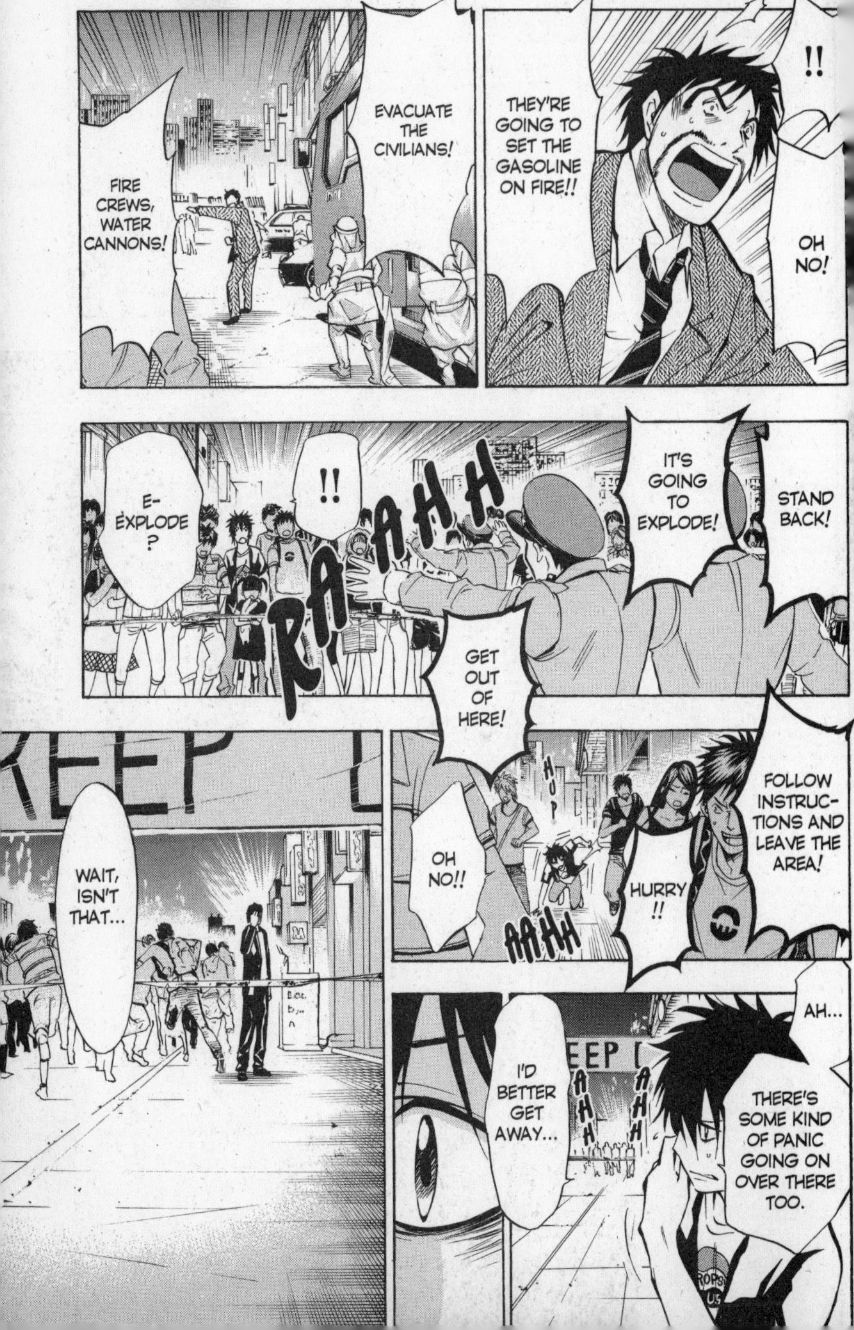
!!
THEY'RE GOING TO SET THE GASOLINE ON FIRE!!
OH NO!
EVACUATE THE CIVILIANS!
FIRE CREWS, WATER CANNONS!
STAND BACK!
IT'S GOING TO EXPLODE!
RAAHH
!!
E-EXPLODE?
GET OUT OF HERE!
FOLLOW INSTRUCTIONS AND LEAVE THE AREA!
HURRY!!
HUP
OH NO!!
AAHH
AH...
THERE'S SOME KIND OF PANIC GOING ON OVER THERE TOO.
AHHH
AHHH
I'D BETTER GET AWAY...
WAIT, ISN'T THAT...

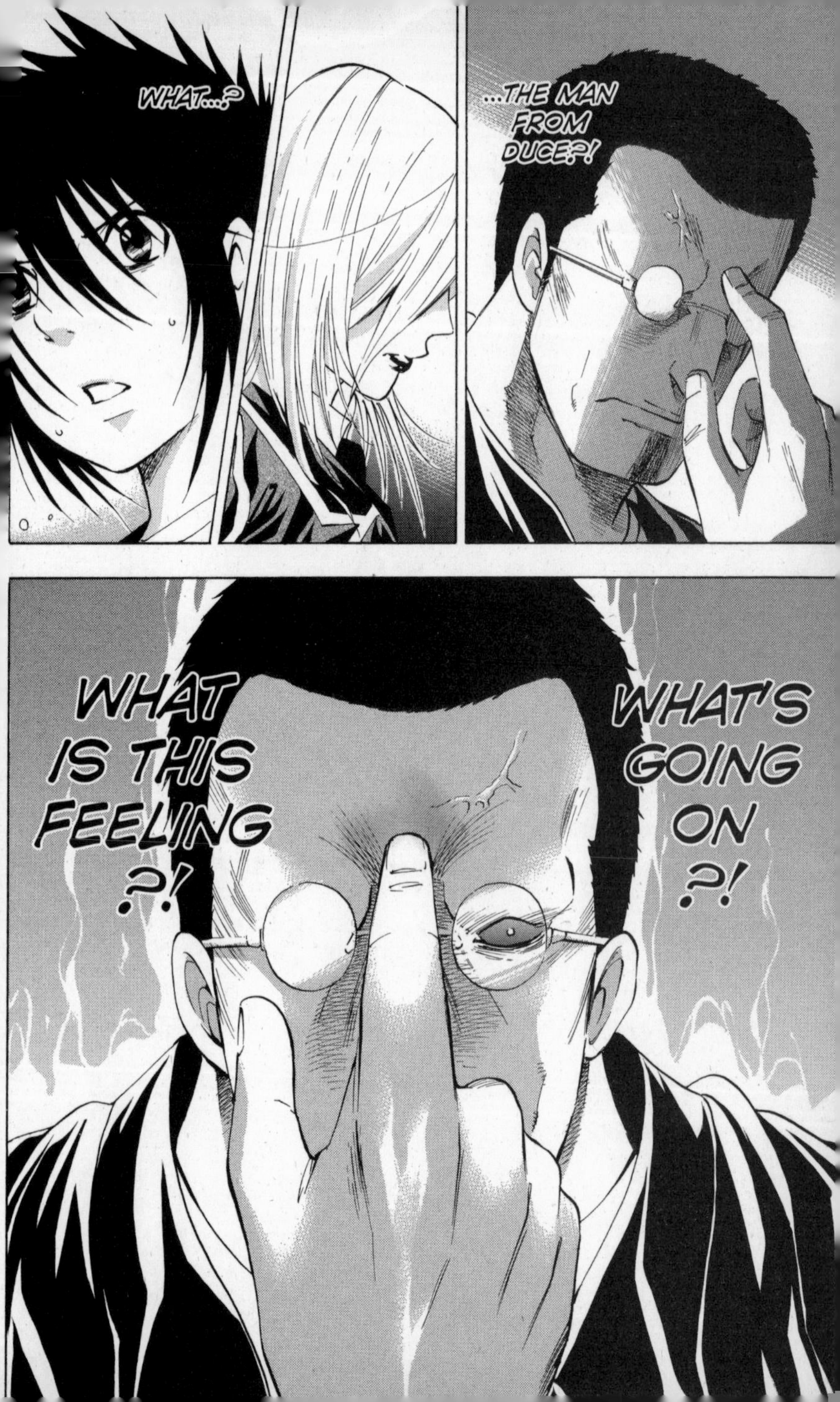
...THE MAN FROM DUCE?!
WHAT...?
WHAT'S GOING ON ?!
WHAT IS THIS FEELING ?!

IT CONTINUES IN Vol.03

And the two finally face off!!!

Forced to make a choice at the gas station, Ando risks it all with his ventriloquism!!

REMIX, COMING SOON!!

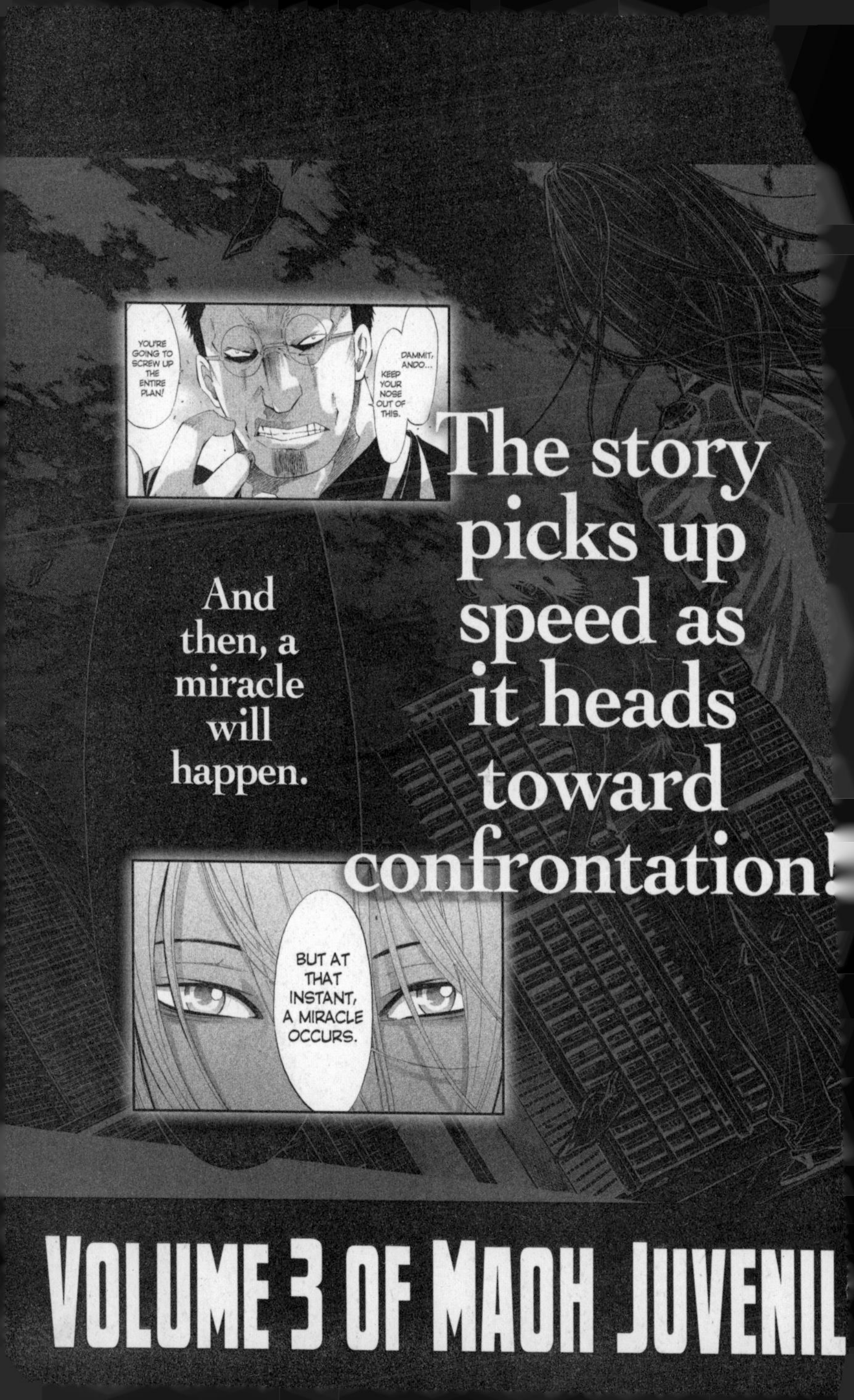
DAMMIT, ANDO... KEEP YOUR NOSE OUT OF THIS.
YOU'RE GOING TO SCREW UP THE ENTIRE PLAN!
The story picks up speed as it heads toward confrontation!
And then, a miracle will happen.
BUT AT THAT INSTANT, A MIRACLE OCCURS.
VOLUME 3 OF MAOH JUVENIL

At Your Indentured Service

ate's parents are bad with money, so they sell his organs to pay their debts.
ate doesn't like this plan, so he comes up with a new one—kidnap and ransom
l from a wealthy family. Solid plan... so how did he end up as her butler?

d out in *Hayate the Combat Butler*—
the manga at store.viz.com!

Hayate
the Combat Butler™

Kenjiro Hata

www.viz.com
store.viz.com

MANGA, ANI-MANGA™ & ART BOOKS!

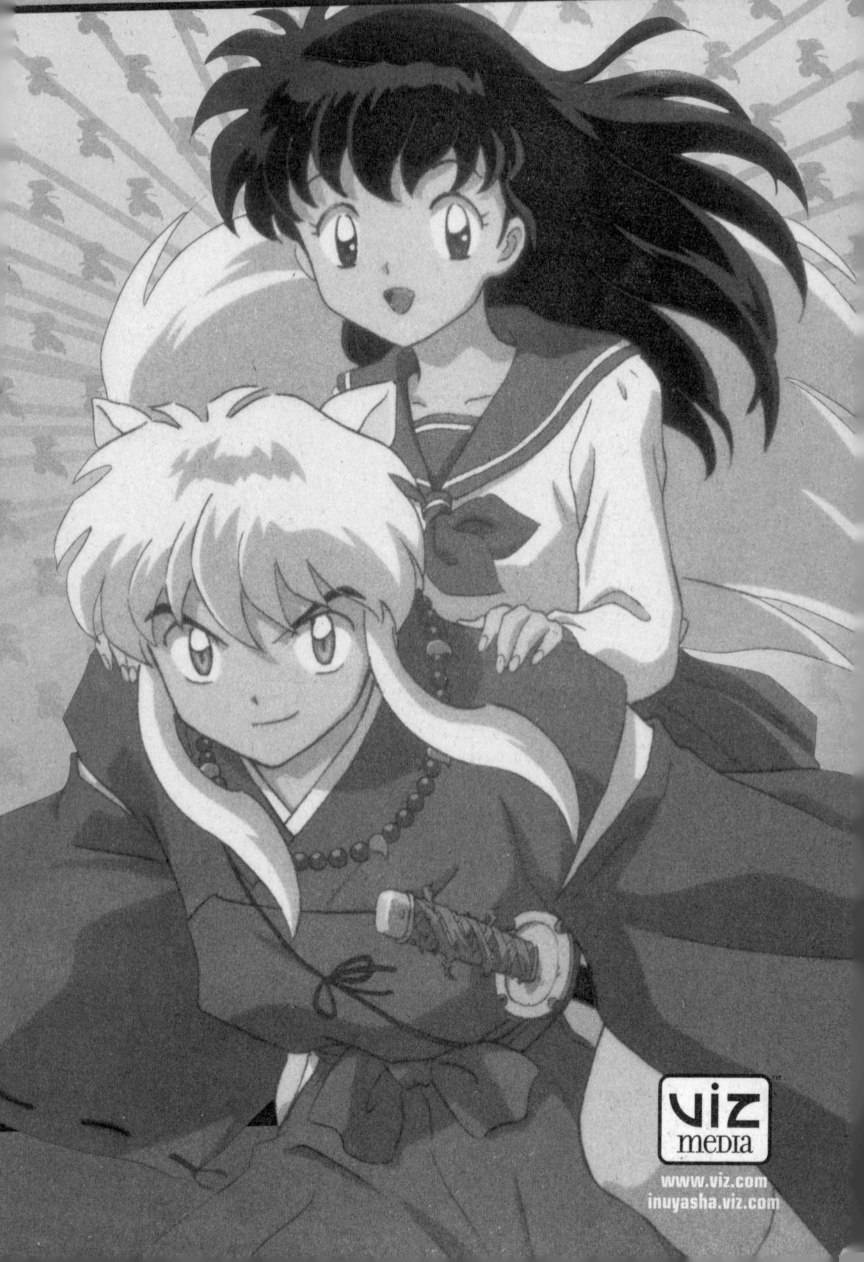
viz media
www.viz.com
inuyasha.viz.com

InuYasha

Read the action from the start with the original manga series

Full color adaptation of the popular TV series

Art book with cel art, paintings, character profiles and more

TV SERIES & MOVIES ON DVD!

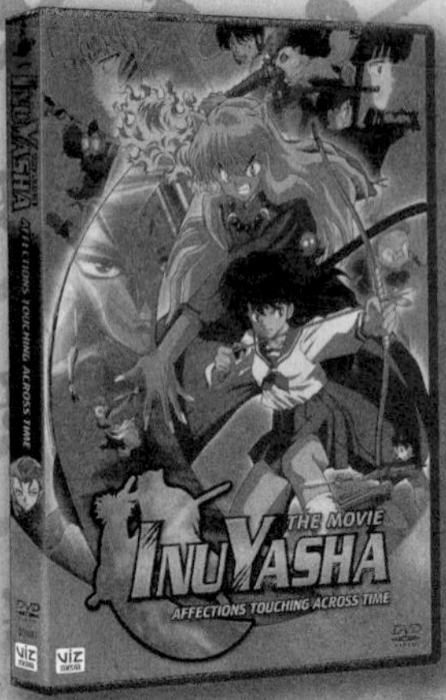
THE MOVIE
INUYASHA
AFFECTIONS TOUCHING ACROSS TIME

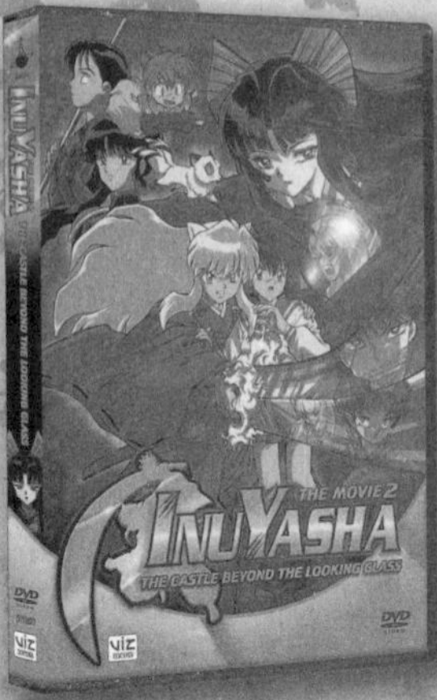
THE MOVIE 2
INUYASHA
THE CASTLE BEYOND THE LOOKING GLASS

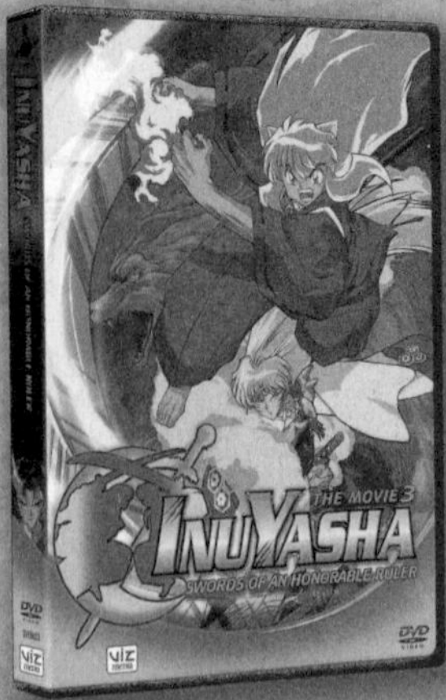
THE MOVIE 3
INUYASHA
SWORDS OF AN HONORABLE RULER

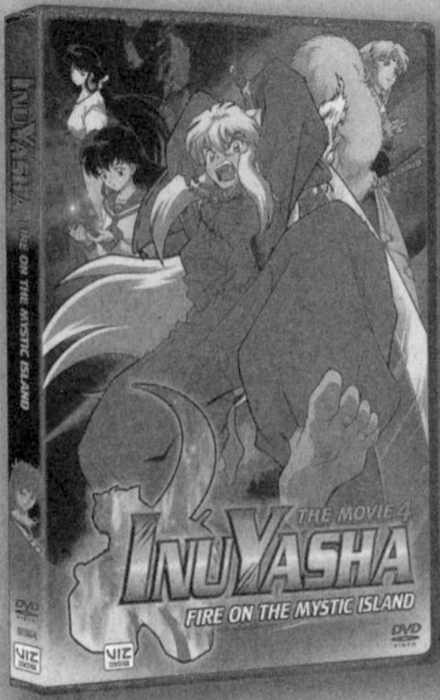
THE MOVIE 4
INUYASHA
FIRE ON THE MYSTIC ISLAND

See more of the action in *Inuyasha* full-length movies

www.viz.com
inuyasha.viz.com

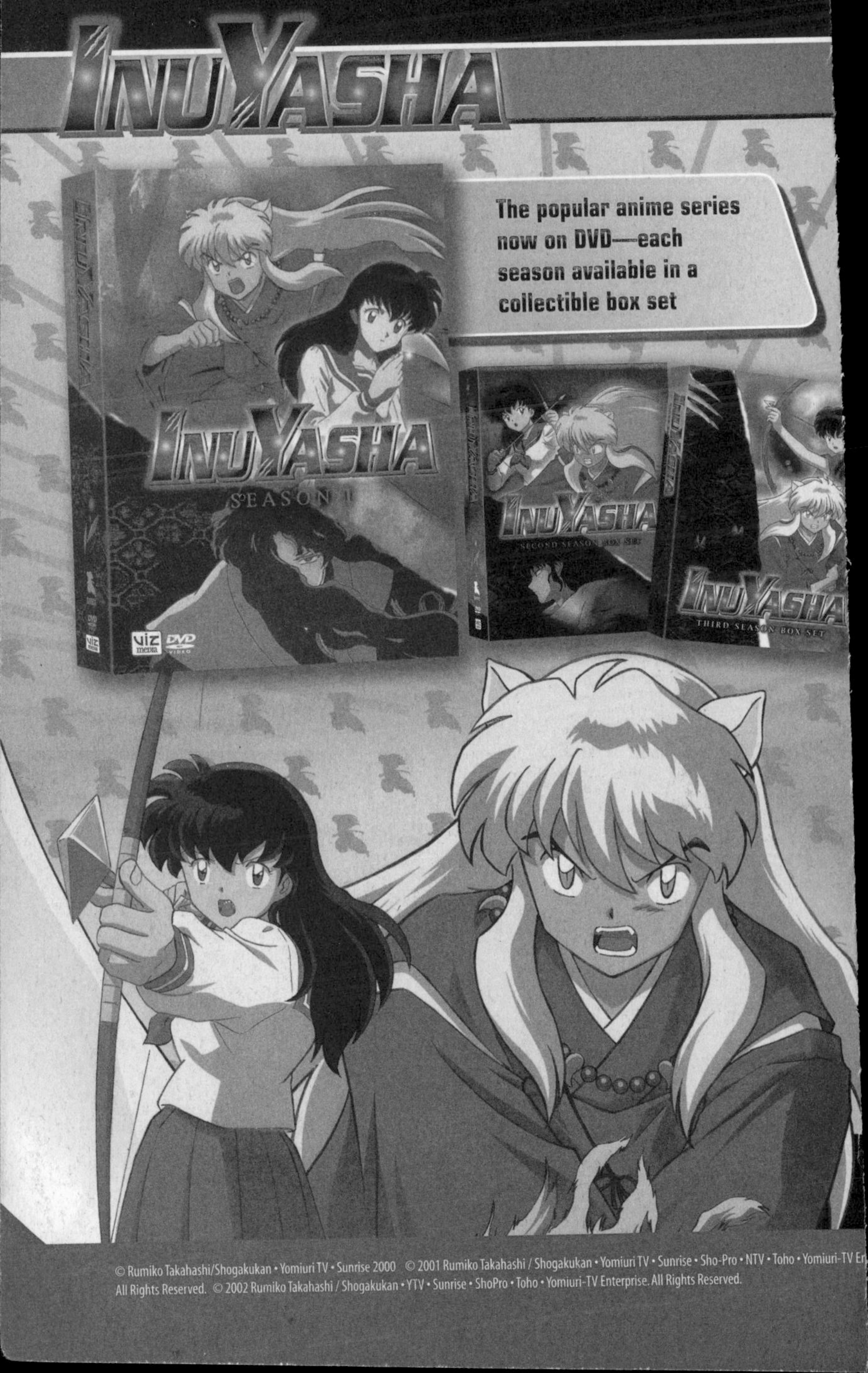
InuYasha
The popular anime series now on DVD—each season available in a collectible box set
InuYasha
Season 1
InuYasha
Second Season Box Set
InuYasha
Third Season Box Set

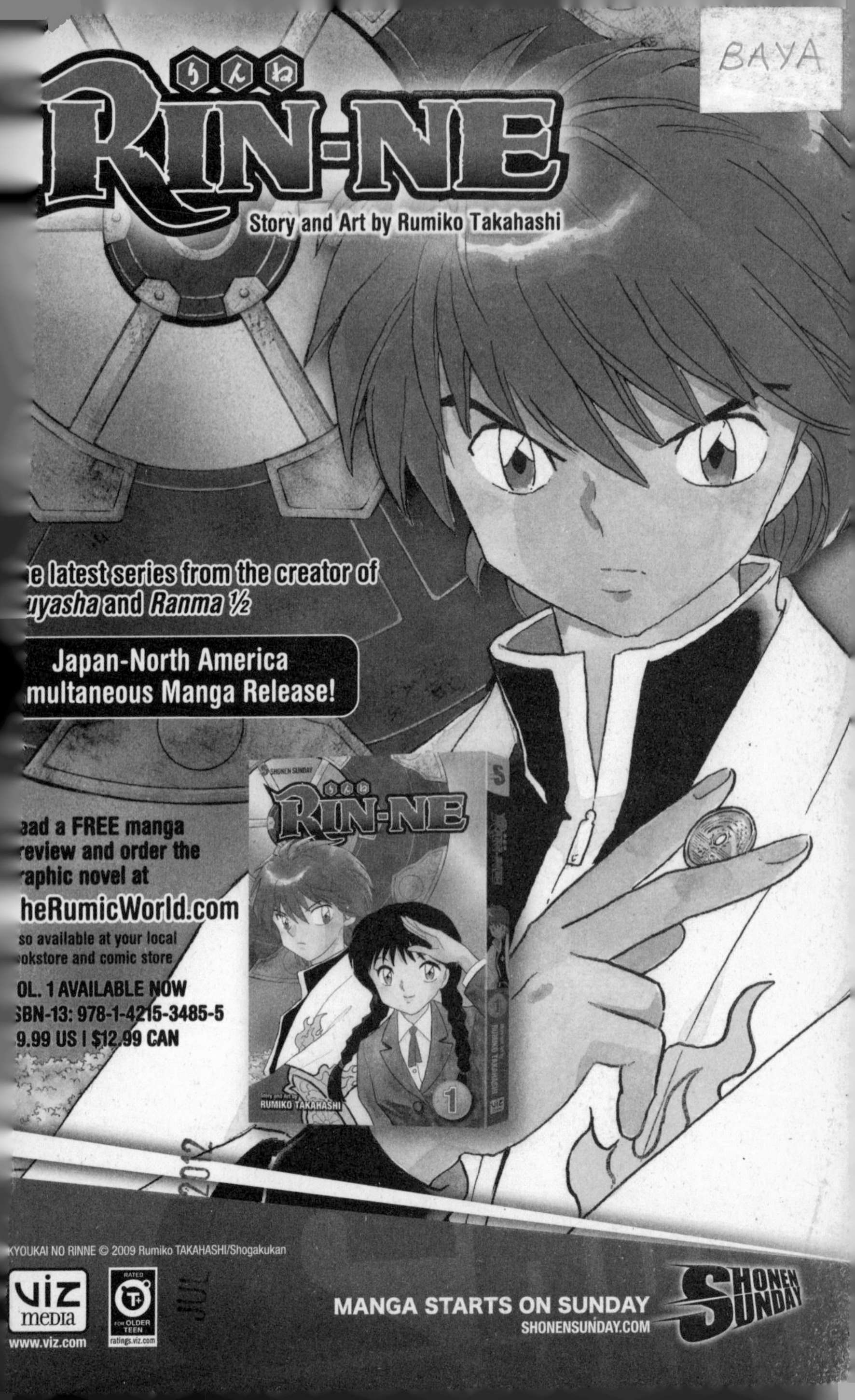

RIN-NE
Story and Art by Rumiko Takahashi
he latest series from the creator of
uyasha and Ranma ½
Japan-North America
multaneous Manga Release!
ead a FREE manga
review and order the
raphic novel at
heRumicWorld.com
so available at your local
okstore and comic store
OL. 1 AVAILABLE NOW
SBN-13: 978-1-4215-3485-5
9.99 US | $12.99 CAN
KYOUKAI NO RINNE © 2009 Rumiko TAKAHASHI/Shogakukan
viz media
www.viz.com
RATED T+ FOR OLDER TEEN
ratings.viz.com
MANGA STARTS ON SUNDAY
SHONENSUNDAY.COM
SHONEN SUNDAY